THE IDLER

20TH ANNIVERSARY SPECIAL

FREE SPIRITS

INTERVIEWS 1993—2013

NO.46 EDITED BY TOM HODGKINSON

IDLER BOOKS

MMXIII

IDLE LTD.

81 WESTBOURNE PARK ROAD LONDON W2 5QH

Idler Books Limited Reg. No. 5897340

A CIP catalogue record for this book is
available from the British Library

I

Editor Tom Hodgkinson
Photography Julia Hember
Typesetting Christian Brett
Proof Reader Nancy Campbell

Photographs reproduced with the permission of Mary Hember who holds
the archive of Julia's photographs. Thank you to Otis Ingrams and the Inklings,
Gaia Lutz, Astrid Bulmer and Alexander Thanki for their excellent typing.

The views expressed by the contributors do not
necessarily reflect those of the editors

The type used is Monotype Bembo Book designed by
Robin Nicholas and complimented with ITC Golden Cockerel Initials
and Ornaments by Phill Grimshaw from original drawings by Mr Gill

Printed by CPI Antony Rowe Ltd., Bumpers Farm,
Chippenham, Wiltshire, SN14 6LH

ISBN: 978-0-9548456-4-3

www.idler.co.uk

THE IDLER

20TH ANNIVERSARY SPECIAL

FREE SPIRITS · INTERVIEWS 1993–2013

NO.46

For Victoria, my free spirit

LIMITED EDTION OF 1000 COPIES
OF WHICH THIS IS
No. 266

Free Spirits:
The Idea of the Idle Life

by Tom Hodgkinson

THE IDLER MAGAZINE WAS BORN AS AN IDEA IN 1991.
I was working at the time as a researcher on the *Sunday Mirror Magazine*, and was pretty miserable there. I was 23 and doubtless horribly big-headed, but the work I was asked to do seemed below my intellectual capacities. I was checking the price of baked beans with Asda, typing in Russell Grant's formulaic astrology column and – on a good day – writing 'amusing' captions for photographs of celebrities at parties. I might also be asked to do what was called a 'cuts job' on a certain celebrity. I would be sent down to the cuttings library and take out a sheaf of A4 sheets with articles attached to them. I would sit down and read through all the old interviews and create a new one, without quite ever admitting that I had been nowhere near the celebrity in question. I also used to get wine in from Asda for reviewing. On one occasion the PR sent me a case of wine to say thank you. This was a treat as I was earning only £150 a week from this job. But when the deputy editor found out about this, he accused me of stealing.

Anyway, that is all for another time. Suffice to say that I kept myself sane by dreaming up and planning the new magazine, *The Idler*, which I was going to edit. The title came from a series of essays by Dr Johnson, which were published as weekly columns in *The Gentleman's Magazine* in 1758 and 1759. This was one of many publications that thrived in the lively Grub Street journalism scene of the day. In it Johnson wrote on such subjects as sleep and sloth.

The Idler would take an 18th-century sensibility and combine it with the radical philosophies of today. So it was that a profile of Dr Johnson in issue one was followed by an interview with the so-called magic mushroom guru Terence McKenna.

Nothing happened until, as luck would have it, following nearly two years at the *Mirror*, I was told I was no longer needed. This was around the same time as the death of Mirror Group owner Robert Maxwell. I walked away from the office in High Holborn with a mixture of humiliation and elation. I was free but I had no job. I went to sign on and got down to working on the *Idler*. I went on a dolies' business course run by the Portobello Trust. It was actually pretty helpful, and one teacher there advised me to get on with the mag by not worrying too much about the finances and just getting something published and out there, even if the print run was low.

Luckily I enlisted the help of my old friend Gavin Pretor-Pinney, and together we produced issue one and printed it with £800 which I had raised in the form of borrowing from family and friends and selling lifetime subscriptions. We had our own magazine. And while the magazine has remained resolutely small, despite the best efforts of various parties to help us – thank you to the *Guardian*, Zone and Ebury Press for taking the *Idler* under their generous wings at certain stages. The print run for issue 46, the one you hold in your hands, and issue one is the same: one thousand copies.

A regular feature throughout has been our 'In Conversation' feature. I used to love the *Playboy* interviews and the *Paris Review* interviews. Instead of the modern habit of attempting a sort of Freudian psychological profile of the interviewee, based on an hour's meeting, these magazines simply presented an edited transcript of the interview. This makes for a very readable piece.

The other point to make about these interviews is that they did not deal with topical issues, and this means that they have dated very little. I tried to avoid discussion of that day's politics or culture, and instead we talked about the big questions: how to live, how to work, love and melancholy.

Above all this is a collection of interviews with outstanding bohemians. Most of the subjects here do not have, and sometimes have never had, what you might call a proper job. Instead they have forged their own path with great courage in a world which would be happier if we stuck with a job in government or corporation.

The interviews also tell a certain kind of history. They remind us of the time when they were composed: the rave years were followed by the Britpop years, which, in my case anyway, were followed by the organic family years. In 1993 John Major was Prime Minister, and we have since gone through Blair, Brown and now the coalition. All of them have been just as bad as each other when it comes to promoting the 'global race' and the ethic of 'hard-working families'. Both concepts are direct descendants of the Calvinist attitude to work and life which came to dominate Northern Europe after the Reformation.

Well, the interview subjects from the *Idler* provide hope to the wild at heart. In different ways, all the individuals collected here have attempted to create their own everyday lives, a process which is sometimes stressful and always difficult. The Idlers don't get paid holidays. We have to scrabble around for every penny. We have to manage our own accounts and tax affairs. Our workload, paradoxically, can be heavy. We live through periods of poverty and uncertainty. We inevitably need to deal with the very 'world' which we have rejected in order to earn money. Our own values are questioned by cynics who accuse us of hypocrisy. Reject the creed of consumerism, for example, and someone will always gleefully point out that they saw you shopping in the supermarket.

But despite the the inevitable privations and difficulties of the idle life, we prefer to cling to responsibility and sweet freedom than enter the workaday world.

Terence McKenna

by Tom Hodgkinson

IDLER I · AUGUST 1993

T HIS IS THE FIRST INTERVIEW OF THE IDLER INTER-
views. I was delighted to have the chance to meet McKenna,
whose book *Food of the Gods* I had loved. He was quite a fashionable figure at the time, having been sampled by The Shamen. I went to
see him at the offices of the record company Mute. Terence Mckenna
died in April 2000. I cringe slightly at my over-written intro, but the
interview still reads pretty well.

*

He's been sampled by the shamen; he believes that magic mushrooms
were the evolutionary missing link between ape and man. He has been
called 'the culture's foremost spokesman for the psychedelic experience'. He is also an idler.

It was with not inconsiderable apprehension that I sat down to my
meeting with Terence McKenna. His reputation as a crackpot – whose
most sane idea is that magic mushrooms are the evolutionary missing
link between ape and man which has puzzled our scientific community
for so long – preceded him. However, *The Idler* is always ready to
approach on equal terms those whose world view has ostracised them
from the mainstream. McKenna turned out, as is so often the case with
the figures castigated by the establishment as misfits only suitable for
ridicule, to be a most charming and stimulating companion. Eloquent
(though sometimes his speeches have the air of rote recitation), witty,
ironic and intense, he threw up such a whirlwind of unfamiliar ideas
that by the end of our two hours together I was quite exhausted.

For those unfamiliar with McKenna and his work, let me add a few comments. He is 46, sports a raggedy beard and speaks in clipped, high-pitched Californian accents. This distinctive voice has been sampled by multimedia dance stars The Shamen. Colin from this group has been influenced greatly by McKenna's thought. McKenna is an anti-rationalist McLuhanite, with a shamanistic impulse, whose favourite philosopher (and this may surprise some people) is Alfred North Whitehead, friend of Bertrand Russell. McKenna is best known for his espousal of the magic mushroom (or, more specifically, the psilocybin this intriguing plant contains). He believes that it is only through experiencing the effects of such drugs that we can begin to approach an understanding of how the world works, and of our place in it. But enough, let's hear what the fuzzy-faced Frisco philosopher has to say. I started my interview by telling McKenna about the philosophy of *The Idler*.

TM You should take a look at Whitehead. He wrote books like *Science in the Modern World*, *Adventures of Ideas*, brilliant essays. As far as his relationship with Bertrand Russell goes, had Russell been a bit more idle it would have gone on much longer, as it was, he had an affair with Evelyn Whitehead, and that tore it. Bertie, what a rake he was.

TH Russell wrote an essay called 'In Praise of Idleness', where he argued that a new machine in a factory should lead not to the redundancy of half the workers, but to a reduction by half of the working day. I wonder why we haven't managed to organise society along those lines.

TM I think the reason we don't organise society in that way can be summed up in the aphorism, idle hands are the devil's tool. In other words, institutions fear idle populations because an idler is a thinker and thinkers are not a welcome addition to most social situations. Thinkers become malcontents, that's almost a substitute word for idle, 'malcontent'. Essentially, we are all kept very busy, and if you do have a moment of leisure time, then you're expected to imbibe the sanitised data stream that the cultural imprimatur has been placed upon [I believe here that TM is referring to watching television]. Under no circumstances are you to actually quietly inspect the contents of your own mind. Freud called introspection 'morbid' – unhealthy, introverted, anti-social, possibly neurotic, potentially pathological.

TH Prague seems to be very popular with idlers at the moment.

TM The place is incredible. I haven't had the feeling I get in Prague since I looked out over Berkeley in 1967 and said, 'This is the place, this is the new Jerusalem, we can do it here.' You can't afford Paris, Berlin, Rome – those places are nightmares for people on limited income, Prague is open, available, it must support 20 or 30 rave clubs, country music bars, all kinds of music. The talent is pouring in there from all over the world, and it's mostly young talent.

TH What have you been thinking about recently?

TM I have a theory, a very radical theory, about what is time and how it works. I see it as a war, a Manichean struggle between habit and novelty. In any given span of time from a millisecond to millions of years, one can say whether habit or novelty is dominating.

It's a very radical theory because it attacks the very core of scientific rationalism, which is based on what's called Probability Theory. Probability Theory assumes that processes are time-independent; in other words, if we are flipping a coin, science assures us that we will not get a greater preponderance of heads over tails if we do it only on Tuesdays at 10 o'clock. That's considered preposterous. But I believe that Probability Theory is in fact a red herring or a wrong turning and that in fact there are moments when the improbable is more probable, and there are moments when the probable is less probable. If it were really true that when you flip a coin the odds of it coming up heads or tails were truly 50/50, then the coin would land on its edge every single time. Well, that's the rarest outcome of a coin toss imaginable. I'm 46 years old, I've never seen it happen.

Science is essentially the area of human concern that tells us what is possible. But what we lack, and have never even articulated the need for, is: how is it, out of the class of the possible, which is vast, certain things are selected for what Whitehead calls the 'formality of actually occurring'? I maintain that you have to picture time differently not as a featureless, Platonically smooth surface, which is how Newton saw time, he called it 'pure duration', but that actually time has a texture at every level. With my computer programme I can look at a few billion years or a few minutes.

TH Are you looking at a cultural movement in time?

TM I'm interested in doing it globally. High novelty moments like the Greek Golden Age, the Renaissance, the 20th century, must be low points on the graph. The graph works somewhat counter-intuitively in that novelty is increasing when the line goes down, and habit is increasing when the line goes up. And then you get turning points, where habit is suddenly overcome by novelty and then you get regression points, where novelty suddenly comes to a halt and traditional pattern, habit, reasserts itself. It was Rupert Sheldrake who suggested that I call it habit. Novelty I think of as something like a density of connection or complexity of a system, and the more complex a system is, the more novel it is. Viewed from that perspective it's pretty clear that the universe is a kind of novelty-conserving engine; it produces novelty, and then it builds yet greater novelty on the previously achieved level of novelty. So for instance, human culture rests on social organisation before writing and language, which rests on primate and mammalian organisation, which rests on complex molecular systems, which are made of atoms, which are made of protons, electrons, neutrons. Every time novelty is achieved, it is then set in concrete and becomes the basis for a further ascent into novelty.

And eventually, I believe fairly soon, novelty will be maximised.

Human history is not something that goes on endlessly into the future: it's something that lasts about 25,000 years and then so much novelty has accumulated that essentially every point in the system becomes co-tangent with every other.

At that point, that's as much novelty as you can have, and that's what I call the transcendental attractor at the end of time. It's the novelty of novelty. It radiates its influence into the past making historical time as we approach the transcendental object more and more novel and complex, and breakthroughs and so on and so forth happen at an ever faster rate. And this has now reached the point at which it is asymptotically accelerating, and I believe some time around 2012 AD novelty will actually reach its maxima.

TH What happens then?

TM That's a good question. We can't see it because it lies below the event horizon of rational apprehendability at this point. It's like being at 1 A.M. and asking what the sun will look like when it rises. We don't know because it's still below the horizon of our intellectual modelling. But long before we get to 2012, we'll have an intimation of what this ingression into novelty, or what Whitehead calls conscrecence. The flying saucer, in fact, is an image of conscrecence that ricochets through time like a scintilla of light thrown from one of those mirrored balls that you see in discos.

TH Is nuclear destruction a possibility?

TM No, I don't think so. I view it as an ontological transformation of the nature of reality, not in a political context at all, but that we're actually involved in a kind of drama of the change of physics. Whitehead talks about what he calls epochs of natural laws, but now we're actually approaching a phase transition. We have an appointment with transformation or extinction. There's no third possibility. Business as usual is off the menu.

Will Self

by Tom Hodgkinson

IDLER 2 · WINTER 1993

IMET WILL SELF IN THE TERRACED HOUSE IN SHEPHERD'S
Bush where he lived at the time, in the summer of 1993. He was on
the wagon but smoked copious amounts of dope.

He gave me a bottle of white wine, which I drank very quickly out
of nerves. I hadn't eaten, so became extremely drunk. I also shared
several joints and a pipe with him. By the end of the interview I could
hardly talk. Will, however, seemed to become more articulate the more
he smoked. He went on to become a great friend to the *Idler*, giving us
advice, encouragement and writing some terrific pieces for no fee
whatsoever.

★

Will Self has a distinguished history of idleness. At 12 he renounced all
sporting activity and involved himself in counter-cultural pursuits.
In his twenties he drew a cartoon strip for the *New Statesman*, 'Slump',
which featured a proto-idler who never got out of bed. It was semi-
autobiographical, as Self himself rarely rose either. Following a flirta-
tion with the world of business as a magazine publisher, he found
himself experiencing success as a novelist, writer of short stories and
journalist. The *Idler* met Self – lanky, loud and louche – in this latest of
his multiple personalities and discussed driving, drugs, small businesses
and the will to dullness.

TH Are you an idler?

WS I'm an incredibly indolent person. I have an enormous natural inability
to do ... virtually anything, actually. For long periods of my life I just
lay in bed and read novels. When people used to ask me what I did, I

would say, 'I lie in bed and read philanthropic novels'. Somewhere round the house is an edition of *A la Recherche du Temps Perdu* which I re-covered entirely so that the spine read 'Lying in bed reading philanthropic novels' because that's all I fucking did, you know. When I did 'Slump' for the *Statesman*, I had that and I had a gig at *City Limits*, the frontispiece cartoon on the letters page. One paid me 35 quid, the other paid me 70, that's 105. I had a free flat. And that was it. It took me a morning to do the cartoons. The rest of the time I did nothing. Between '82 and when I started in a serious suit and tie business in '86, I did very little. That was the nadir of my idleness.

TH Were you confident in your idleness, or did it depress you?

WS I'm reviewing Burroughs' letters at the moment: great literary idler, did fuck all with his life except shoot drugs. And you can see that there was a real purpose to it. He was reacting against the Eisenhower era in the States, and the only proper response was to do nothing. It's less arguable that you can get away with that now, that there's any justification for it. So, I wasn't particularly confident in it. The only sense in which I was confident in my idleness was as a writer. I wrote all the time, although I knew nothing I wrote was fit to publish, so that was my justification for doing nothing. Above and beyond that, no, it used to depress me enormously.

TH Did you feel pressure to do something?

WS Well, I wanted to be a philosopher, which is the idlest occupation in the world. I wanted to be involved in abstract thought, but because of various problems with the authorities I wasn't able to pull that one off. A lifetime of idleness in academia would have really suited me. So I was thrown out, as it were. Other than that, there seemed no possible idle occupations, so writing... although writing isn't exactly idleness. There's an enormous tension between indolence and languor.

TH Dr Johnson said that idlers can be stimulated to activity, as ponderous bodies, forced into velocity, move with a violence proportionate to their own weight.

WS Inertia, yes, fascinating, the property of inertia. I've written three books in three years and I write a lot of journalism, and people seem to think that I'm incredibly hard-working. But in fact I'm incredibly idle. And I'm not one of those boys who would say that and then creep off and study; I am genuinely idle.

TH Do you have any problems with procrastination?

WS No, I'm highly disciplined. I do nothing and then I do something. But it's taken years of investigating idleness in all its forms to be able to achieve this. My discipline is borne out of concerted study of idleness. And of course, drugs are particularly useful if you want to be idle. I mean, you can't get much more idle than that. If you spend a significant proportion of your life in underground car-parks waiting for dealers...

TH Have you ever been in a serious car accident?

WS Yes, several. It's no fun at all. I was in a three-car write off crash on Chelsea Bridge. There's nothing idle about a car crash.

TH But I drove off the motorway and flipped over once. And there is a kind of idle moment when you're walking down from the car to the hard shoulder across a wet field.

WS You call that idle do you? I think the definition's getting a tad elastic there ... yeah.

TH Cars do allow you to enter idleness, when you're driving you can get into those extended...

WS Reveries. Yes that's what it's all about. This cultural taboo against thinking – anti-intellectualism – exists in England because of this protestant work ethic which demands that people shouldn't be idle – ergo they shouldn't think. So driving is a good way to recapture that. It's very close to philosophising, large amounts of motorway driving.

TH That's why people like it so much...

WS Do they though? I don't know anyone who likes it.

TH You don't think the fact of all these people driving long distances on motorways has anything to do with a sublimated desire to get back to idleness?

WS No I don't. I would take a much grimmer view of the generality of mankind. I think they're just getting from A to B, and worrying about which service station to go to. Motorways are more real than anything.

TH Perhaps even more in the US.

WS Americans have a problem with idleness, they're not very good at it, in the same way that their culture is not very ironic. But here ... London is a big city, it's got genuine edge, and it's still boring. We really have cracked it. It's very, very dull. And for a person preoccupied by idleness there's no other place to be.

TH What about the Continental version of idleness, where everyone's outside?

WS Oh, that's terribly Epicurean. We don't like that at all. That sounds too much like fun. Which is inimical to your idler. There are virtually no fun nerves left.

TH There are loads of interesting things going on in youth culture now.

WS No there aren't. They're really boring. I find the rave thing deeply dull. You talk to hardcore ravers, you hear the most asinine panoply of recycled cobblers you've ever heard in your life. Don't you think so?

TH No, not really. Youth culture as a reaction against conventional society may have finished, so you get people who are...

WS There's no avant-garde. There's no inter-generational input from young people into the mainstream culture that is valid or interesting. That's what I mean. And that's for demographic reasons. In my next novel I'm going to write about this particular problem, demography. It's to do with the baby boom, and the way population ages, and that affects the culture in a very critical way. It's why this culture is so dull. Hmm! You've got to take the long view. I take the long view. That's another reason why I'm obsessed with motorways. I hope you realise I'm making this interview intentionally camp and ridiculous, and supercilious, and bogus. Otherwise we might just expire with tedium.

TH What things interest you in an active way?

WS Erm. Virtually nothing, actually. Interest is like a Satanic cult – groups of people abusing you with interest. It's a sinister, horrific thought, a dreadful conspiratorial thought. We'd better keep it to ourselves.

TH So you don't engage with some aspects of modern culture, but you do engage with motorways. Why some things and not others?

WS Give me motorway cafés over MTV any day of the week.

TH Having been an idler, what's your attitude to being high profile?

WS It's very boring isn't it? Enjoyment is not a word that exists in my vocabulary.

TH How have you engaged with that side of your work ... success, basically?

WS Yes, I believe that's what they call it. I do think that the construct that people call the English literary establishment is so full of shit that it's good fun to spoof it.

TH Where does your interest in mental health come from?

WS Well it is interesting isn't it? So we'd better not talk about it.

TH But I'd hate to exclude interest entirely from this...

WS All sorts of sources is the answer. But the most profound was during a big acid phase when I was living in Oxford, and a lot of schizophrenics moved into the house. There was this situation where you were really wiggy and out on the edge, and these people were wiggy and out on the edge, and this seemed like the thing. Do a lot of drugs and hang out with schizophrenics. One used to sit across the breakfast table from me going 'You are the great white spirit, you live in the fifth dimension, you control everything by wires,' and I was 'Yeah, right.' So that was a real catalyst, and I was getting these realisations that people who are mentally ill are really ill, they're really mad. There was an epistemological break, that this wasn't to do with language. All that stuff is so interesting, I don't really want to talk about it, I'll get too excited.

Charles Handy

by Tom Hodgkinson

IDLER 3 · 1994

CHARLES HANDY IS A FRIEND'S GODFATHER, AND SHE recommended I go to see him because his very successful management books had a lot in common with the ideas I was exploring in the *Idler*. Handy foresaw a freelance culture, where the full-time job was replaced by what he called a 'portfolio' life. Twenty years on it is true that the world of work has changed, but the bright future he dreamt of where we all become autonomous self-dependent freewheeling units has not come to pass. Unfortunately the unions and liberal elements still believe that the feckless working classes need to be kept in secure jobs.

Writer, broadcaster, business consultant and thinker, Professor Charles Handy believes that jobs are a form of voluntary slavery and that we should struggle to control our own time.

★

Charles Handy is an expert on work. For twenty years a professor at the London Business School, he is the author of The Age of Unreason, where he set out his ideas for a new attitude to work and time. He organises his own life to include three months of every year doing nothing in Italy, and encourages Radio 4 listeners to be more laid back via his *Thought For The Day* broadcasts. His new book, *The Empty Raincoat*, is published by Hutchinson on 17 February. Here he discusses work, Italy and the idler's paradox.

CH When I started work almost 40 years ago everybody I knew and most of society had what's called a proper job: they worked in an organisation. It never occurred to me or my friends to do anything else. As I reached middle age it became apparent to me that that pattern of work was changing.

TH What were you working as?

CH I started working as an oil executive, and then I became an academic at the London Business School. It became clear that organisations were making very inefficient use of people's time. They were buying time from them and trying to make use of that time for their own purposes. It was pretty inefficient because they bought 40–45 hours a week but didn't actually need the same amount of time from everybody. Then I noticed that the more efficient organisations were buying different chunks of time from different people. A lot of people in their middle age were being eased out of organisations into this part-time pattern. It occurred to me then to start thinking about what happens to the people who no longer have what you might call jobs because they're selling only ten hours a week. In order to make that a more respectable way of life I coined the phrase a 'portfolio life', for people who had bits and pieces of work. It seemed to me that there was more security in a portfolio life than in a proper job.

TH How is that?

CH In a proper job you never know for whom the bell is going to toll on Friday morning. I have many friends who have been called in on Friday morning and been told be out by lunchtime. It's terrifying. Whereas in a portfolio life, where you have seven or eight pieces of work, one or two may go wrong, but you have the rest left. What is interesting is that if you lead a portfolio life you have control over your own time. It has always seemed to me to be slightly bizarre that we should queue up to sell our time to someone else. It's a form of slavery, voluntary slavery. We think it's great, but it's crazy. You've sold 100,000 hours of your life to someone if you have a full-time job for all your life. That's 40 hours a week, 50 weeks a year, for 50 years.

TH People's identities tend to be bound up with their job. At parties, people ask each other 'what do you do?' You can sense the tension at parties of people in their early twenties. If you don't have a conventional career or a job it's a difficult question to answer.

CH You can play the trick the other way round. There was a time when I got so fed up with people asking me what I did – because it wasn't very exciting, I was just an oil executive – that I took to saying 'nothing'. And you should watch the look on people's faces when you say 'nothing', because they don't know whether to be embarrassed because, 'oh gosh you're unemployed', or whether you're very rich and don't need to work. They just didn't know how to respond, it was marvellous. It's quite interesting that in Italy you tend to say 'where do you live', rather than 'what do you do'.

TH The Italians seem to be good at positive idleness.

CH The Italians do work hard but they don't think that work is the most important thing in life. The important thing in life is in a sense living, and that means eating, drinking and having *la bella figura* – putting on a good appearance in the street. A lot of the life is lived in the street. They told me how odd it is in England when you go to any kind of party or meal everybody talks not about the weather but about the traffic – how did you get here, what was it like. In Italy, they said, we wouldn't dream of talking about the traffic, which is terrible, we always talk about food. That fits another part of my philosophy which I call the doughnut philosophy of life. I believe you should look at life as an inside-out doughnut, where the hole is on the outside and the dough is in the middle. There should be a core to your life, to do with earning money, having a house or whatever, but if you let that core fill the whole of the doughnut, you are missing out on a lot. Somebody once said that by the time you die you've only discovered 25% of what you're capable of. It's unprovable but possibly true, and the reason is that people don't experiment enough with life; they let work fill up the doughnut. There's an awful lot of interesting space there, but you have to organise yourself to do it.

TH That's the key thing, what we call the struggle to idleness – trying to gain control of your own life, to allow yourself three months in Tuscany or whatever it is.

CH It's very important you do. People let other people control their lives. You can also look at it in a quite different way. Ten years ago, when I became totally freelance, my wife Liz and I worked out that out of the 365 days of the year we needed 100 days to make serious money – I do that by teaching at various seminars. I also need 100 days a year to write and read, and roughly 50 days a year for my causes and campaigns. That leaves 115 days which we can use for our own pursuits. That's actually very mean to ourselves in a way, because most people have at least that if you add up all the weekends, eight public holidays plus whatever holidays they're entitled to. But by chunking it that way we can spend

90 days sitting doing nothing – except eating, drinking and discovering Italy in Tuscany. I very much approve of the Italian system of education, chaotic thought it may seem, for two particular reasons. One is that philosophy is part of the core curriculum. The second thing is that all the examinations are oral so you have to learn to express yourself. This is why Italians are full of expression, and also why they relate very quickly and easily to people.

TH So are you an idler?

CH If idleness means living, and not just working, then I'm totally in favour of idleness. In fact, I find that I can't work without a proper percentage of idleness. I was telling you at breakfast that writing is very hard work, strangely, though it doesn't look it.

TH Agony sometimes.

CH Oh, it's terrible.

TH You think you've got it licked and then you start writing badly.

CH It's physically exhausting, you are drained. I can only do that for five hours a day.

TH That sounds like a lot.

CH Well it is, to be honest, and that's pushing it. Then the rest of the day I must not do anything, because if I do anything it distracts my mind – my mind only seems capable of concentrated thought for about five hours a day. I have to force myself to be totally idle, to read a novel, not a very difficult novel, to watch television, to walk, to cook – anything to stop my mind working. I think that's essential. I cannot understand these people who work 17-hour days.

TH I have a problem with getting up early because I like staying up late. I get comfortable talking and drinking with friends and don't want to go to bed.

CH Well don't worry, old age cures that. You tend to go to sleep at about midnight even if you're talking with friends. And also you don't seem to sleep so long, you only need five or six hours. I can't actually sleep after about nine o'clock in the morning. On the other hand, when you get older you sleep in the afternoons, whether intentionally or not.

TH I quite often have a nap in the afternoon.

CH Well again, go and live in Italy, it's so sensible. Everything closes at half past twelve and doesn't open again till half past three or four. So you have three hours when you're either eating or sleeping, or both, and it's wonderful once you get used to the rhythm. Then everything stays open till eight o'clock at night. Life happens in the middle of the day and at the end of the day.

TH So civilised. You were saying that it amazes you how few people are trying to take control of their lives.

CH For some reason, most people still want to sell their time to an organisation. I did that once, when I was helping to start the London Business School. I worked terribly hard; I used to leave home at half past seven and I'd come home at nine. My wife said to me after about three years of this: 'I know you're pleased with what you're doing, I just have to tell you you've become the most boring man I've ever met.'

TH One thing that's been worrying me recently is how every office, without exception, seems to be packed to the brim with hideous office politics. I wonder how much this has got to do with the people and how much with the actual structure of the place, the office itself.

CH If you put a lot of rats in a small space, they fight. It's true. If you put a lot of pigs in a small place they scratch each other's tails off. If you put them in a great big field with lots of space around them they're fine, they're relaxed. Shoving everybody together is crazy. I walk through the City and I look up at these little boxes piled sky-high – we actually seem to want to go and spend our days sitting in a little box. It's terrifying. Luckily I think that's going to break down. It's very expensive to organisations to bring people in from their homes in the countryside and put them in these boxes. Interestingly they are there for 168 hours a week, but are only used for maybe 50 or 60 hours a week. It's an extraordinarily bad use of space. It would be much better to let them pay for their space, by working from home, in the car, on the train or in the client's premises, and connecting up with telephones. If you do that then you have more control over your time. Also, it's terribly difficult for women now who want to have a career but also want to raise a family. But it need not be difficult because they can perfectly well do an awful lot of their work without going into the office. They can go into the office two or three times a week. Organisations should say, 'all our meetings are going to take place on Tuesday, Wednesday, Thursday mornings, and everything else is your time, to be used at your discretion'. We're not running factories any more. You don't have to be together all the time, just for bits of time. And so in fact we don't need all these offices. We say we want them for companionship, but you're absolutely right, companionship turns into office politics.

TH It occurs to me that one of the reasons people do this to themselves is laziness. Even though you may moan about your boss, it's kind of comfortable because you're not taking any responsibility for yourself.

CH Well that's right, but it's very important, isn't it, to distinguish between laziness and idleness. Laziness is not taking responsibility for anything, idleness is a deliberate choice to go into neutral. Why do we do it to ourselves? The title of my next book is *The Empty Raincoat*, from a sculpture I saw in Minneapolis of a bronze raincoat which was empty, there was nobody in it. It seems to me that we're all becoming empty raincoats, shadows, silhouettes of ourselves. And we're doing it to ourselves, that's what's so extraordinary, as you say because we're too lazy to take on the responsibility of finding out who we are. Because that's very threatening. People say, what do you do, that's easy to answer – who are you, is a much more difficult question. I end my book with the story of the Rabbi Katya. He prayed to God incessantly. 'God, make me like Moses, that I may lead my people,' he said. Eventually God spoke to him and said, 'Rabbi Katya, when you come to paradise, we will not ask you why you were not Moses, but why you were not Katya.' In other words, the point of life is to be fully yourself, and I think that to be fully yourself you have to take control of your time. To make full use of your time you have to build in a measure of what you call idleness. Do you really want to have written on your tombstone 'he spent a lot of money'? One would like to think that one did more with one's life than spend a lot of money and yet that seems to be the aim of so many of us. We chase our tails earning money and spending it. If what you're preaching in your magazine is that we should have a proper proportion of idleness – not that the whole of life should be idle because if you're in neutral all the time you don't go anywhere – then I'm in favour of positive idleness.

TH This is the paradox that people constantly bring up: 'you say you're an idler', they say, 'but there's a lot of hard work in this magazine'. We say that's the paradox at the heart of the enterprise, that's the idler's paradox.

CH Yes, there is a paradox at the heart of idleness. To be idle you have to be very efficient, you have to work very hard. The secret is to do that very efficiently, so that there's plenty of space left for the rest of your life.

Paul Bowles

by Marcel Theroux

IDLER 3 · JANUARY 1994

N OVELIST AND BROADCASTER MARCEL THEROUX IS ONE
of my oldest friends. Paul Bowles died in November 1999 at
the age of 88.

★

I shuffled from foot to foot in the gloomy hallway, three storeys above
the wet street where a group of children were frolicking and shouting
in Arabic. Telling myself it was too late to let embarrassment get in
the way of effrontery, I gave another blast on the doorbell. I felt like a
literary groupie of the worst kind: persistent, unannounced, and worse
still, I'd never bought any of his books. There was silence behind the
door marked with a brass plate that read 'Mr Paul Bowles' in capitals.
But I knew Bowles was inside, and I was determined to brazen it out.
Finally the door was opened by Bowles's masseur and I went into the
sitting room. Through it in a stuffy little bedroom, lay Mr Bowles
himself.

Paul Bowles, poet, writer, composer, exile, has been living in the
same block of flats in Tangier since 1957. From his modest apartment
he has watched the Beat generation come and go, the city slip out of
international control and the sexual adventurers of the Fifties and
Sixties give way to day trippers from Algericas in shell-suits. Tangier
has gone straight, trading the illicit glamour of its past for a steadier
income as a tourist destination. The literary outlaws have gone too.
Only Bowles, whom they claimed as a patron but who always stood
apart from them remains. Now, by association, he is among the city's
patrons.

'A Frenchman told me, "never allow yourself to become a monument, people piss on them",' said Bowles. He was sitting up in bed in a dressing gown. It was early afternoon but he was laid up after surgery for a blocked artery in his leg.

'People visit almost every day. Some – mostly the French – have the chutzpah to say: "I didn't want to leave Tangier without seeing what you looked like"!'

I disguised my wince as a sympathetic nod. I had got his address from the doorman of a five-star hotel in the old part of the city. He had known not only where Bowles lived, but also that he was ill and best visited in the afternoon.

The bedroom window was blacked out. A portable gas heater directed a naked jet of flame at the single bed. Bowles had been correcting some of his music compositions for publication. The scores lay scattered about the counterpane. The room was hot and stuffy, and smelled strongly of eucalyptus oil.

At 82, Bowles still has a delicate, almost pretty face, and plenty of white hair. He is frail and elegant, like someone's great aunt. His face was rosy, as though he had just had a hot bath.

Throughout our conversation I was struck by his lucid and courtly manner. He chatted aimiably in his soft east coast accent, seemingly unfazed by my intrusion.

'I was here before the Beats ever thought of coming to Tangier,' he said. 'I came here for the first time with Aaron Copland. We didn't stay long that time. He heard the drumming at night – there's still drumming – and he heard the women wailing, and he said: "the natives are on the warpath!"'

'The Beats came twice, in 1957 and 1961. Allen Ginsberg, Peter Orlovsky, Alan Anson, Bill Burroughs, Gregory Corso. The first time they were all working awful hard on the book Naked Lunch, the second time they were just "goofing off", as they put it.

'That first time Burroughs didn't know where he was. He'd finish a sheet of foolscap and drop it on the floor, then he'd walk on it, drop bits of sandwich on it. Ginsberg picked it up and put it in order. Allen lived for the book.'

Bowles is probably well used to recounting Beat generation anecdotes about the gestation of Naked Lunch. The Beats subsequently became literature's pin-up idols, but their interest in the Morocco outside Tangier was minimal. For most visitors the city meant expatriate decadence, or cheap kif, or boys. Bowles, on the other hand, studied the country, learned Maghrebi Arabic, befriended its writers and translated its literature. He even schlepped around the country with a big tape recorder to record folk musicians performing their traditional music.

Bowles's writing shares that fascination with North Africa, and it is often a fascination with the possibilities of the continent that unhinges his characters. In his fiction, those most receptive to Africa's mysteries are usually those most completely destroyed by them. At their most disturbing, Bowles's stories are as exquisite and cruel as the poisoned champagne in Julian Vreden. With terrible clarity, he writes of travellers fatally out of their depth in unfamiliar surroundings. A linguist has his tongue cut out by the Berber tribesmen he has come to study in *A Distant Episode*. In *The Sheltering Sky* one visitor to North Africa gets sick and dies, while his wife goes mad and is raped and enslaved.

Bowles said he didn't enjoy the Bertolucci version of *The Sheltering Sky*, despite a cameo appearance. He felt it shied away from the bleakness of the original, while tampering with the script to inject a more marketable quantity of sex. Like everyone who saw it, he admired the cinematography. And the film wasn't the only frustration of his trip to the première in Paris: he had to get there by plane.

'I hate air travel. Not because I'm afraid of flying. But there are no porters. I used to travel with 20 suitcases. You need books, and I always brought clothes for hot weather and cold weather. What can you bring now? A little canvas thing.'

Bowles was always dandyish. In the Thirties, Gertrude Stein observed that he travelled with enough clothes for six young men. But then perhaps they weren't all his. Even now he was wearing a cravat with his dressing gown. He opened up a silver case and offered me a hand-rolled cigarette. I said I didn't smoke. Bowles put his in a holder.

'I always have tea around four and now it's five fifteen,' he said, lighting up. It was a while before I realised he was talking about the cigarettes. The word 'tea' sounded quaint, like talk of 'wild bop' and 'cut ups'. Soon the privetty smell of his joint was combining with the eucalyptus and the stuffiness of the room to give me a headache.

'I smoke it for the health effect,' he said mischievously. If I had not visited, he would have been tinkering away with his manuscripts until he fell asleep. Sometimes he watches Spanish television on the big Sony in the corner of the room.

'I should get a parabolic antenna,' he mused. 'They have a pornographic channel – channel six. They show everything – fucking scenes.'

Apart from correcting his scores, Bowles stays busy writing and translating. At the moment he is working on a translation of the Guatemalan writer Rodrigo Rey Rosa.

'So you're not an idler?'

'Oh, good heavens no. Whoever said I was?'

By now it was dark outside, though the bedroom remained exactly the same as when I'd arrived. The blacked-out window gave no hint that an unusually damp and foggy Moroccan night was falling. I told Bowles I had better be going and promised to bring him some chocolates on my next visit.

'Everyone's always leaving tomorrow,' he said. As I left, another pair of pilgrims arrived. Two French journalists had come to do an interview. I said goodbye and got his permission to snap a photo.

Mulling over our conversation in a bar later, it all seemed puzzling and inconclusive. Could that courtly old gentleman have written those cruel tales? I drew some comfort from Bowles's biographer who confesses to find the man deeply enigmatic.

At the bar I was introduced to a friend and former protégé of Bowles, the Moroccan writer Mohammed Choukri. Choukri I guessed, was in his late forties. He was a thin man with a rather stylish pencil moustache and wiry grey hair. He was lively and talkative, drinking whisky and scoffing at Bowles for being a nihilist.

'He's a miser!' said Choukri. 'In all the time I've known him he's never even bought me a cup of coffee.'

I thought of Bowles in his dark and overheated little room, his interviewers gone, maybe smoking a cigarette, maybe pouring over the proofs of his music.

'Do you think he's happy?' I asked.

'Happy?' said Choukri. 'You should have asked that question 20 years ago.'

Matt Black

by Tom Hodgkinson

IDLER 4, · 1994

MATT BLACK IS A PIONEER OF ELECTRONIC DANCE music with Coldcut, and has a pretty well developed techno philosophy. However, his predictions in this interview that 'in ten years the guitar will be relegated to the status enjoyed by the harpsichord', and that machines will become more intelligent than humans, now look like naive techno-futurism. But he immediately got the point of the *Idler* and in inspiring fashion, he called on readers to create their own niche in life. You can also find your humble editor here correctly worrying about the capacity for computer networks to spy on their users.

*

Artificial Life, ambient alarm clocks, the crapness of computers, the anti-slack conspiracy, viruses; there's a lot on sampling pioneer and computer visuals experimenter Matt Black's mind.

Matt Black studied Biochemistry at Oxford before immersing himself in dance music culture and releasing, with partner Jonathan, a string of top-selling singles under the name Coldcut. His latest venture is a computer graphics production house called Hex. The following conversation took place in Black's flat with Aphex Twin *Collected Ambient Works Vol.2* and mix-master Morris selections on the stereo.

TH Were you into computers from a young age?

MB Yes. I was into them at school, and I remember even then a kid telling us about a programme called Virus, which his Dad had used to infect the computer of a big company. It seemed that computers were incredibly cool. Also I'm pretty lazy, so computers help there. I'm also into chemistry and genetics, and there are a lot of analogies between DNA – genetic code – and computers. I got into *The Selfish Gene* by Richard Dawkins which shaped the way I see the world. I see everything in terms of competing strategies in the evolutionary sense, whether it's business, economics, biological evolution, culture or changing ideas. That's grown into the field of Artificial Life. I believe that we're the last few generations of humans as we know them – I reckon in maybe 30-50 years we're going to create artificial intelligences and organisms, which may be used to augment us, or which may just replace us. There's never been anything like this before.

TH I don't understand what you mean by artificial life.

MB I believe that technology will, one way or another, allow us to produce artificial lifeforms. Initially they will be unsophisticated, and eventually they might get more sophisticated than us. I believe that we are all cellular automata in the artificial life experiment of God, but we have self-knowledge, consciousness. We'll probably forbid computers from becoming conscious, but they will anyway. Immortality is possible: I could really do with this idea being strapped into some kind of bio-computer support system and being around for the next ten thousand years and flying between planets and stuff. But we're probably the last generation which won't get to be immortal, which is quite sad really. One of the things we want to do at Hex is to automate creativity and be entertained by that ourselves, let the machines get on with it while we chill out.

TH The techno-idler's dream.

MB For the ultimate chill-out attitude, you should read *The Rubaiyat of Omar Khayyam*. He says, there is no God, or if there is he's taking some serious piss, so you might as well curl up in the corner with someone and a bottle of wine and mock that which mocks thee. Just to stick us here on the planet without any guidelines or any proof of what the fuck's going on, and then, to throw us into the fiery pit forever … it's never made sense to me.

But I really must lay on you the doctrine of slack. Slack is the great resource, and the con – the conspiracy – tries to take slack away. Slack is given by Bob Dobbs, the one true living slackmaster who will get you sex. He laid it down: fuck 'em if they can't take a joke, pull the wool over your own eyes, and too much is always better than not enough. Armed with weapons like the Fuck You Boat they are a force to be reckoned with.

TH Are we talking about the Church of the Sub Genius?

MB Yes. It's a massive satirical anti-religion but at the same time it's preaching a message along the lines of 'think for yourself, 'cos no one else is
going to fucking watch out for you, and the world goes to the people
who have the strength of mind to slip between the stupid rules.' In that
way, its message is positive. They've got their own language, virtually,
their own scriptures.

TH So it's a Ken Kesey going-with-the-flow idea.

MB But then they escalate this into a whole funky mythology which they
do very well. They have their own magazine, *The Stark Fist of Removal*.
Whenever you see the face of Bob Dobbs, slack is there. But let's just
contemplate the essential, inevitable, constant struggle between our
efforts to get slack and the demands of the world...

TH And how do you reconcile them?

MB Well it's balance. You don't jump some final hurdle and then chill out
forever. The journey is the reward. You've got to find little islands of
slack, and hopefully the benefits will accrue with more slack. I am a
compulsive sort of person, obsessive about my work, don't know why.
I'm only happy when I'm sat in front of the computer with my stomach tied in a knot. It's unhealthy. The other time I'm happy is when I
sit in the garden, reading.

TH And sleeping.

MB Yeah. It's good to meet an idle crew. I don't need to be ashamed of my
sleeping any more.

TH How do you get ideas?

MB It's easy to have ideas if you use randomness. I've long given up being
analytical, about buying music for example. Because there's just too
much. I used to think I knew a lot about music, then I realised it was
just black music and there were people who knew a lot more than me.
And since I've realised that I do have some areas of knowledge, but
they're oases in a vast desert of ignorance. I will never know or even
hear the vast majority of music, so you have to be content with what
you come across. Anything has the seed of potential. Between the two
chances take the odd. Woo the muse, the odd. Take that sideways step.

TH What about the promise of computers making our lives easier?

MB It hasn't worked yet because they're designed by dweebheads in suits
who have no concept of the needs of real people. A Mac is cooler, a

Mac is for slackers, a PC is for propellerheads. A Mac makes life that little bit easier – but it's still a nightmare. Mac started cool because it was the brainchild of people with individualism and drive but they got taken over by a bunch of suits. That's another thing that's incredibly depressing: when a good project gets successful, it gets bigged up and taken over by massive business, then it always turns to crap. You think you're gonna do the system but the system sucks you in.

TH It happens so much and people are so aware of it, but it still keeps happening. The KLF though have avoided it, by changing all the time. And perhaps that's what you're doing.

MB Not so successfully. The KLF have carved themselves an excellent niche. I would settle for being the KLF some of the time. Although they're not into the graphics and stuff. I like areas that are fun to play with and explore, where everything's fresh. I think it's the money ting that ruins things. But I do believe that technology offers the opportunity to change the marketplace, to make it easier. I think that a lot more people will be information providers than just information consumers, and that there'll be a lot more communication between people. Say you're one of 20 people in the UK who's interested in palaeolithic skulls. For you to be able to correspond on a videophone with 100 other people round the world, is pretty good.

TH You've practically got that on the Internet.

MB You have, yeah, and I hope that the Internet will get bigger and bigger. Maybe what we're going to see now is a massive explosion of ideas. Maybe all this stuff on the Internet will come alive and declare itself to be God.

TH It's the paradox of computer networks that on the one hand they offer a freedom of self-expression, and freedom to communicate with everybody around the world without let or hindrance, but on the other they hold the possibility of total observation by people at the centre, no freedom whatsoever.

MB I hope at worst that it will be a mixture. I think that's probably the most likely outcome because nature is a mixture. The guys at the top aren't that sorted really, they don't have meetings to decide their next plan to continue world domination. It's organism versus organism.

TH There's this phrase that keeps cropping up in relation to the Internet, 'get out there'. I think it's a good phrase for general life – getting out there gives you inspiration.

MB That's right. That's why there's a danger of being too idle. If you're trying to be creative, you need input from other people. Maybe you can get that on the Net. I am quite solitary and introverted, but I would feel sad if all human contact ceased to exist. What we've got at the moment is the media's power to communicate information and images concentrated in the hands of a few broadcasters who broadcast to millions of receivers. There are very few points of dissemination. So we're getting steamed by that, floating in it and trying not to sink.

TH What kind of things are you working on at the moment?

MB Future entertainment. Multi-dimensional products, interactive music video, ambient games. One idea is to have a game that incorporates elements of artificial life. VR multi-user life dance enhancement. But ambient music is where it's at. Everyone's sick of all the club stuff, it's had it. All this rock star bit, that's old. The PR, the photos and shit, do me a favour.

TH Isn't that a bit unsexy? Pop stars are about sex.

MB Well yes, until you see them without their make-up. What you're seeing isn't reality anyway. The pop star bit is on the wane. In ten years the guitar will be relegated to the status enjoyed by the harpsichord and *NME* to *Harpsichord Player Monthly*. For my money, [ambient, festival-like] Megatripolis is about the best club in London, but I like chill-out clubs, like Telepathic Fish. I like to talk to people sometimes. And in normal clubs I don't talk.

I'm trying to rediscover techniques of play, and break down the barriers between work and play, this artificial distinction. I think you can say of today more than any other time that opportunities exist for people who are not content with the normal con of existence to find a niche for themselves where they can build a compromise which works. The idea of going to a nice location with a computer and a modem and doing some kind of computer-based work is becoming more feasible.

TH More people are into the idea of working in the morning and chopping logs in the afternoon. Then you dig up the vegetables, come back, plug in, do a bit of work and then go for a walk by the sea.

MB I'd like to have a foundation which would make very simple contracts with people. Give them a certain amount of money and tools; the ones who come back with stuff, keep going with them, and drop the ones who drop off secure in the knowledge that those computers will go on and be used somewhere. Imagine doing that for a few thousand people

– it could be done. A computer costs $80 to make.

TH A friend of mine was telling me about this guy who has broken down the barrier between sleep and wakefulness: he's always been somewhere halfway in between.

MB I'm a little bit like that. I'm not particularly good at anything. But I'm not afraid to try out doing a few things and I'm quite good at a few things. I'm not a very good computer programmer, I'm not a very good musician but I've got a good ear. I'm crap at the guitar. I'm not a particularly good artist. But I can still do things with computers. I can make connections, and spot resonances. Computers are now beginning to reach the level of complexity of living things, with all their randomness.

TH Are you saying we're going to have therapists for our computers? To go into the computer's childhood to find out the source of the problem?

MB Had its floppy drive invaded by a Syquest. Got hit by a virus bike. One can make endless ridiculous situations based on what will happen when machines think. What I believe is that artificial lifeforms will listen to techno music, maybe 10,000 tracks at a time. I like to think of artificial lifeforms sitting back and listening to acid tracks and saying, yeah man, these early heads really had the right idea ... So really it's up to us all to fucking slack off and defy the conspiracy and carve ourselves a little niche with as much philanthropic feeling and action as we can afford.

Douglas Coupland

by Tom Hodgkinson

IDLER 5 · JULY 1994

OUGLAS COUPLAND'S BOOK 'GENERATION X' WASN'T
long out, and my friend Toby Young, then editor of the
Modern Review, suggested we go to see him, as he was in town.
His prediction that the geek would inherit the earth, and also that the
Internet would come to be dominated by 'wannabe Oscar Wildes wait-
ing to spew their bon mots into the ether' both turned out to be true.

Coupland struck me as extremely nerdy. We chatted in the lounge of
the Portobello Hotel in London, where he was staying (great hotel, by
the way). He was also strangely aggressive, and refused to be taped at
first. At one point in the interview he kicked me under the table. He
later sent us a fax saying it was the best interview he'd ever done. I personally find it irritatingly self-conscious, despite the brilliant insights.

★

Canadian writer Douglas Coupland wrote *Generation X*, *Shampoo
Planet* and has just come out with *Life After God*. The *Idler* caught up
with him in the Portobello Hotel in West London, where we were
joined by man about town Tom Shone. Coupland was nervous about
the tape recorder: we had a chat and then recorded our attempts to
remember what we had said, which set him more at ease. What follows
is a transcription of our conversation about our conversation.

DC We started talking about Hal, and then artificial intelligence, and then
Lego and the construction of entities that breathe.
TS Toilet paper.
DC Toilet paper was right up there, I think. We politely asked Tom 'Two

Squares' Hodgkinson how many squares he used per pass and he said two.

TH It wasn't two per pass, it was two per wipe ...

DC Well, in the industry they use the term 'pass'.

TH So 'pass' means just one wipe.

DC You mean you use one?

TH This is so unfair.

DC So Tom S. and I, first of all, were wondering if, like, maybe all our lives we've been somehow extravagant. And then, because Tom S. was unwilling to participate in this pornography of numbers which he was instigating, he said somewhat democratically and diplomatically that somewhere between Tom H.'s two and a Wall Street ticker tape parade was where we stood. And then we talked about paranoias. We were sitting here in somewhat simian manner looking at our teeth. What do you call that tooth there? I had tartar build-up on it.

TH I recommended Plax.

DC Which I have never tried but must try.

TS And then we recapitulated on it when we were talking about paranoia.

DC Orthonoia.

TS Whereby one is frightened that one's teeth are talking about one behind one's back.

DC Or people are talking about your teeth behind your back.

TH Tom S. was talking about Tina Turner living on his block and I made a comment that was missed ...

DC Yes, you tried to explain a joke of questionable humour in the first place. Three times.

TH But you didn't hear it, so how can you say that?

DC At which point we deduced that point about diminishing humour returns.

TS Proportionately related to the number of repetitions in the gag.

TH You know what we haven't talked about ...

DC No wait, wait, don't introduce a memory! What else – oh, how when you randomly pull out a notion in conversation, sometimes it sticks and elicits a confession. Like: 'I hear you're a kleptomaniac.' 'Who told you?'

TH You accused me of being into body piercing.

DC I said 'Tom tells me you're into body piercing in a big way.' Sometimes that can really work. Then there was Stanley Kubrick and his new movie, which I can't wait to see. It's set in the future with Manhattan rising out of the water, and nanobots.

TS You wanted time to speed up so you could see it.

DC I asked you guys if you were on Prozac and there were nervous giggles. You didn't answer. Then I told you that everyone in Washington and New York is on Prozac right now.

TH You said it was good.

DC Well, there's no stigma. It's like, Americans take you on a house tour and 'Here's the bathroom, what do you think?'

TS Then you came up with a pun on Prozac.

TH Parazac.

DC Which never really went anywhere. But the thing about Prozac was how it was going to change your class system here. Your ruling class, because they know they're going to go mad by the time they're 35, so live decadently before then. And by the time they're 30, they'll be wearing a tutu and sitting on the backstairs with a musket waiting for the masons to show up. And so Prozac means that they'll be buggy-whipping the serfs indefinitely. In the short term this is bad, in the long term good, because they'll breed themselves out of existence, the same people won't be replicating...

TS And you said how popular culture and being middle class are the only two things that glue everything together.

DC Yes, and so why do middle class people hate themselves so much? Who has divided and conquered the middle class to fill them with such self-hatred?

TS We re-stratified it a bit.

DC You guys, being British, know more about class distinctions than I do. Then you guys lapsed into British code for a while, and I felt slightly alienated [laughter] and hurt. But it was OK, I was able to get over it. And there was the way sometimes you can be right in the middle of remembering something and you know as it's happening that you're forgetting it.

TS And I was rather cruel, saying that it was the beginning of the end for you.

DC Yeah, because is this what it's like getting older? When you grow older and you wake up and your day becomes a serial amnesia, a continual process of forgetting. You said, that's already starting with you, and I said, that was pretty cruel.

TS What else? Erm ... amnesia.

TH The low standard of Internet newsgroups.

TS You said you'd had really dull conversations.

DC I've never really found one that's interesting ... all these Oscar Wildes out there are just waiting to spew their bon mots into the ether.

TS You're extemporising a bit here.

DC I know but, it's, NO EXTEMPORISING!, no, all right: but invariably, they're pointless. You got flamed on the Net because of shameless self promotion ... that was later on, but we can circle that back into this. Did you get flamed for being commercial?

TH No, I got flamed for saying, 'Isn't this guy a bit of a nerd?'

DC Well, nerd's not pejorative on the Net. It's an absolute compliment on the West Coast. Even geek is becoming so, too.

TH The cool/nerd distinction is collapsing, or already has.

DC On the West Coast it has. Now we really are deep in, this is interesting. Looking at it from a Desmond Morris standpoint, how can you tell where the power is? You realise that the nerds are the people who are going to have money and power in the future. So, from a Darwinian standpoint, they are the survivors. So the species' survival energy attaches itself to them as winners. I guess ultimately that's what cool is all about, the people most likely to propagate the species. Let's call Desmond, he's British.

TH When do you think nerds started becoming cool?

DC Two and a half, three years ago.

TH Here recently there's been a noticeable scramble towards nerditude.

DC What is the Anglo-nerd?

TH Undergraduate physics boffin, spotty, with glasses, very uncool and unsociable.

DC Oh, you know what we talked about: 'clean enough!' as a fashion statement. How when you first get your wash back from the laundry you have pretensions towards coordination, and then slowly but surely the elements become more random until it finally becomes kind of hip, through sheer randomness?

TS And you said that's pretty much what grunge was.

DC That's just the way people have always dressed there. And there was the beverage equivalent of grunge, the drink we called the Toby Young, which is cranberry juice, Redoxin and tap water. There was the Tom Shone, which was melted Ben and Jerry's chocolate ice cream with eight tablespoons of brandy and half a pint of thick clotted cream. It had to be very cold and you had to have the image of a great big French whisk which would somehow purify this disgusting goo, this redemptionless goo. It's so strange, I have no memory. We were talking about that in the cab last night weren't we?

TS Were we?

DC About how personal memory is always the first to go, and corporate memory is the last. So you'll remember Marlboro long after you've forgotten your family. So is it possible to copy memories like a Macintosh file and restore them somewhere else in the brain? Is the desktop metaphor biologically applicable to the human system?
[Coupland says he has to go to a magazine office on the other side of town]

TH I think it's in E1.

DC Is that how things work here, by postal address?

TH Yes we're in W11 and people will know the character of the area.

DC That's like in Los Angeles. If you say, 'you're really 818', it's pejorative, it means you're from the valley. 310 is now better than 213. And when the area codes were invented in the early Sixties, they had rotary phones and zeros took the longest to dial and ones took the shortest time to dial. So areas of greatest importance got the lowest: New York was 212 and LA had 213. And then you had areas like Nova Scotia which is 702, or Hawaii which is 808.

So we've remembered what we remembered. [Looking at Shone] I think I have Sweater Envy — that's my dream sweater. But I have so little shopping energy.

Richard Linklater

by Tom Hodgkinson

IDLER 6 · SEPTEMBER 1994

AFTER DOUGLAS COUPLAND, A NATURAL CHOICE FOR AN interview was Richard Linklater, who had then come out with the film *Slacker* and also *Dazed and Confused*, and was something of a spokesman for so-called Generation X. *Before Midnight* was just about to be released. I had an hour with him on the phone, where he came across as gentle and serious about his art. What interested me in this one was our discussion of the creative process.

★

Richard Linklater wrote and directed the seminal Gen X movie *Slacker*, and his teen pic *Dazed and Confused* was recently released to rave reviews. We spoke to the laid-back filmmaker at his office in Austin, Texas about his creative processes, upcoming projects, youthful idealism and being cool.

TH In interviews you've often reiterated the point that being a slacker doesn't mean being lazy.

RL Daydreaming is a productive activity. Where do you get your ideas from? If you're working all day, that kills a lot. It's also about visualising your ideal world, both the kind of world you live in and also who you want to hang around with and what you want to spend your time doing, what are your ideal physical circumstances. My ideal world, which I've been thinking about for ten years, is the film world, where I can make films and watch movies and be around creative people.

TH What motivates your work?

RL Every film I've done has been like a kiss-off to a part of my life. I did a film before *Slacker* which was definitely a kiss-off to a certain mindset – wallowing in negativity and being very alienated. *Slacker* was my goodbye to a certain sort of social milieu that I lived in but wasn't really much a part of.

TH So your attitudes evolve?

RL I have very conflicting attitudes towards everything. *Dazed* was about me coming to grips with teenage years, and it took that long to even want to deal with that.

TH After seeing *Dazed and Confused*, half of me thought, well, I still think like a 17-year-old in some ways.

RL Well, you've gotta like both parts – I like the part that still thinks like a 17-year-old, but I'm glad that the other part has gone. It's wonderful in one way, that energy: you don't know your limitations yet, you don't know you won't be a doctor, lawyer, president of the United States. People find out their own limits. I would tell the characters, the world is a blank cheque for you right now. That's kind of a great feeling. But with that openness and possibility there's also a lot of fear. Most people crave to find that little niche: 'Oh good, I can be an accountant.'

TH People grab onto that as a result of fear.

RL Yeah, the most gutsy thing is to reject things you're pretty good at. If a person's good at something, everyone encourages you to do that. And yet maybe it's not what's right. I have friends who have quit law school in their third year. Well, they could have been a lawyer, they could have made a lot of money, but they knew that wasn't spiritually what they should be doing with their time. It took a while for them to find it out because they'd been programmed from childhood. But everyone's going to stoke you if you do something that makes a lot of money.

TH People say get a job, but there are other ways of earning money. Maybe you don't have to get a job. There's a feeling here that you might be poorer for longer, but eventually you earn money doing something you enjoy. Are people thinking along those lines in the States?

RL A small percentage. Nothing really changes. If a few more are, then great. But it would only be people who are predisposed to think like that anyway. You can't tell someone who's very entrenched, and doesn't have the personality or the interest – they're never going to listen. Maybe there are some others on the fence, and if they go that way that's perhaps good. But I dunno. I don't really wish to change anyone. Everyone's on their own.

TH But these attitudes are quite a practical response to the changes in organisation of the work. Those secure jobs aren't really around any more.

RL One thing we've all learned is that the corporate father has no interest in you as an individual. So if people could be aware of that, and stay on their toes, adapt — that's a good thing. Security's not there, but security's not a good thing anyway.

TH What kind of reactions did you get from *Dazed and Confused* in the States?

RL Most people saw it just as comedy. It's a big party film. There was one guy who came up to me, probably 18, and said, 'me and my friends have seen this, like 15 times, but there's a message here, right?' Errr, OK. My biggest compliments were, 'I laughed all the way through, and when it was all over I was depressed.' Oh good. And that's how I felt about that environment: the specifics are kind of fun, the moment-to-moment reality, but the overall atmosphere of it was so oppressed, so limited, that it was kind of depressing.

TH You have Cynthia saying, 'I'm tired of thinking of the present as an insignificant preamble to the future.' I don't think that thought consciously occurred to me as an adolescent, but it does now.

RL I didn't have it that well articulated when I was 17, but I do remember thinking, 'my whole life is anticipation, everything I'm doing in school is to serve some future purpose'. All people would say is, 'what are you going to do when you grow up?' Wait — you mean we're not people right now? You're being moulded to be a little drone worker in the system.

TH What's happened to your slacker friends?

RL My friends have always been creative types. So some are still making music, a lot drift back into academia, get PhDs in philosophy or sociology. Academia is a good refuge. Teach three classes and have the whole summer off. That's a good lifestyle. Plus it's people who want to live in a world of ideas. That's much better. It's outside the capitalist world. But it's always a struggle to try to make a living at what you're doing.

TH What's your creative process?

RL With *Dazed*, I knew five years ago that I had a teenage movie to make. So I think of it for five years, take little notes on note cards — I have a lot of movies I'm always doing this for: scenes, exact memories, ideas, and it slowly comes together in my mind. Then all of a sudden I wake up one day and the circumstances are right. In *Dazed*'s case, *Slacker* had finally come out. So I had time to think, 'next film'. I started buying all the music, finding all the songs I remembered from the period. Then I started writing. As I've planned it all out in advance, the actual writing of description and dialogues comes pretty easy to me. My latest script I wrote really quickly. Same process, note cards, get organised, then boom, wrote it in 11 days.

TH But you can't do that without having had a long period of chewing it over.

RL Superlong gestation period. That's important because by the time I'm actually doing it I've thought about it so much and I'm so much a part of it that I trust my instincts. I don't have to think about things too much. I would feel off-base if I got a script from someone else and was being professional about it. You have to know the film, and sure enough at the end it's what you knew from the beginning. I try to capture that feeling I felt before I even started writing. Yeah.

TH Do ideas come from conversation?

RL Yeah. Every now and then. I might say, I'm going to do a teenage movie some day. A guy will say, Yeah, we had a tree fort we all went to, and teenage lives are so boring you risk your lives to be affected by something. So that idea gets incorporated. But I've never gotten dialogue from overhearing a conversation. I don't even go out that much. The final dialogue is really a product of rehearsal. I'll change a lot to make it real for the character. Some directors who are also writers get so in love with their own words that it hurts their performances.

TH This 'cool' thing is interesting. People in their late twenties, early thirties use the word all the time in conversation.

RL That word has never gone away. You say anything and people are like 'OK, cool.' It's a Beat expression, pre-hippie.

TH Or maybe it comes from Forties black jazz musicians.

RL It wouldn't have lasted if it had just been a white hippie thing.

TH You can bet there was no equivalent a hundred years ago.

RL They might have said 'good deal' instead. I'm doing research now for a film set in the Twenties. I'm listening to tapes of a bank robber character talking, but the word 'cool' is nowhere in his vocabulary.

TH What about your new film, *Before Sunrise* [boy and girl meet in Vienna, spend the whole night talking]? What was the process behind that?

RL Once again, that comes from personal experience. And had a five-year gestation period. I met someone in Philadelphia, and spent the whole night walking around with this woman, talking. There's a very interesting energy at work when you meet someone who you don't know, because you can say things to her and she can say things to you that we wouldn't actually say to people we were in relationships with. Everyone in a way has experienced that. It's like being on a drug or something. In the movie, it hits both the characters at a time when that's exactly what they need.

TH Any other five-year plans?

RL I always wait till a project's over before I commit to anything else, because I never know how I'll feel. You gotta feel for when the time is right. I never look at it as a profession or a career or anything. It's something I feel lucky to be able to do for now. I hope to be able to do it forever but ... Yeah, that's always been the best, I guess. Things change, you've got to be able to roll with it ... actually, I had a thought. You asked earlier what the Slacker crowd were doing. I think unlike other generations before, no one feels like they've given up their youthful idealism. I think that's the best thing, this generation isn't going to be sitting around, wallowing ...

TH ... thinking, 'I've been through that phase, that was a brief interlude away from normality' ...

RL ... yeah, that was youthful idealism and it's been crushed now. It's more of an ongoing process for everyone now. I don't think there'll be any Big Chills coming out of this generation. No one had any illusions to begin with, so no one can sit around feeling disillusioned. That's an accomplishment, because it leads to realistic productive activity.

TH I think that's what I was trying to get at when I was talking about *Dazed and Confused*. It's not just a simple process of nostalgia – the attitudes that are voiced are actually sensible ways to think. Why suddenly relinquish them when you turn 21?

RL For me one of the big things in *Dazed* is when on the football field at the end, one of the characters, Don says: 'I want to look back and say that it was the best I could do when I was stuck in this place.' That could be your metaphor for life. That's probably a more positive attitude than, 'we, as a generation, are going to change the world'. And you do change the world, in your own way.

Gilbert Shelton

by Adam Porter

IDLER 7 · DECEMBER 1995

GILBERT SHELTON IS THE LEGENDARY UNDERGROUND comic artist and writer. Born in Houston, Texas, he currently lives in Paris with his wife after stints in New York (where he lived with Terry Gilliam), Los Angeles and San Francisco. In the Sixties he worked on New York's *Help* magazine, creating his most famous strips, *The Fabulous Furry Freak Brothers* and *Fat Freddy's Cat in 1969*.

★

AP How come you are living in Paris?

GS I've been here for about ten years now. I still feel like a tourist a lot of the time, but I guess I knew there were different ways of doing things to what was, and is, happening in America. I know lots of Americans say it, but you can't avoid the crime. There's only a very small chance of anyone shooting a gun off near me when I'm out at night in Paris. In San Francisco there is a far higher chance. I don't like it. I don't want to be shot or robbed with a gun. The tide of creeping conservatism was something I preferred to avoid as well. The whole way that America wants stupid people in power, and the way they want to remove anyone with any ideas or any education, get rid of the bright people. But then it's going the same way here too.

AP Is America really a stupid nation?

GS You should see how shocked all the European kids are who are on exchanges there. They are always the cleverest kids in the class and they don't expect it. All the American kids learn are these rather odd ideas about 'self assertion' and 'aggressivity'. They learn to tell everyone how great they are without knowing anything. I think the whole nation should go back to school, myself.

AP Do you have any problems getting back into America for the holidays?

GS Because of the dope thing? No, never. I'm still an American citizen. I go back to the States about once a year, but I don't miss much. I guess the thing I miss the most about the States is the food. French food is wildly over-rated. I hate the way, if you are in a reasonably fancy restaurant in France, everyone is so reverential about their food. The way it is so quiet and everyone sits around for five days completing their meal. In America we certainly want to eat faster but we like to do it in a kind of sociable way and of course with big portions. The food in France is a bit pretentious.

AP Is the pot good?

GS Yeah fine. Personally, I've always smoked just as much as I could get away with. There is no doubt that weed does not help you in any way to be creative or spontaneous but if you have thought out what you want to do then that is not a problem. I guess you actually have to have more planning in your life if you smoke weed, otherwise you would never get anything done.

AP How does it affect your work process?

GS Like I say, you have to plan. Alcohol is a better drug for doing things and, well... marijuana is not. I work on average three days a week depending on what we're doing at the time. I'd like to be able to work faster, that's for sure, but that's only so I can spend more time wandering around Paris looking at things. I avoid deadlines like the plague because they stress me out too much. But we keep things ticking over. Believe me, you can always get plenty of things done by taking it easy. I think there should be wild hemp growing in the parks and everyone should be able to pull off a branch or two and take it home with them. It wouldn't be a problem.

AP Do you have cats of your own?

GS Sure. I've always had cats. At the moment I have two called Tache and Gipsy. Tache is a mad shitter because Gipsy is a new addition and only young and Tache, resenting this, has taken to showing how pissed off she is by shitting all over the house. It's a bit of a problem because they aren't too much trouble, apart from the shitting and pissing, and they have this amazing way of being very graceful and also hopelessly clumsy. They can also seem clever but completely dim at the same time. It's what makes them fun, I guess. Fat Freddy's Cat just does everything normal cats do but in a shorter space of time. He also has great appeal to people who aren't quite as into the Freak Brothers, the dopehead side of things. And of course the kids love all the shit jokes.

AP And you invented Fat Freddy's Cat by accident?

GS Not quite. We had a change over from a comic to a tabloid-sized newspaper and in these pre-computer days we had an extra two inches at the bottom of the page to fill. So we ran these four-picture, short cartoons of Fat Freddy's Cat to fill the space and it was a big hit. Kind of an accident I guess.

AP Are cats cleverer than dogs?

GS No way.

AP Are you one of those cartoon buffs?

GS Not really. I don't have a collection or anything like that. I've never been into those superhero comics like Marvel Comics or DC, they were too silly. Sci-fi bores me. No, in the early Sixties I was influenced by Robert Crumb's Zap Comics and a character called Beadle Bailey, a misfit soldier, was an inspiration. I started doing a strip called *Wander Warthog* with the late Tony Bell when I worked on *Help* mag where Terry Gilliam was assistant editor. But I would say that my favourite cartoonist is a British guy called Leo Baxendale. He invented the Bash Street Kids and Lord Snooty. Of course, it isn't as good now, but the original Bash Street Kids were great drawings and great characters. I hear they tried to change it and the public went mad. They tried to make Plug pretty and had to give in.

AP Will they legalise dope in the near future?

GS No. If anything, it's going to get worse. There are powerful interests in keeping it illegal, like the drinks industry. There might be some home-grown stuff that doesn't get you in so much trouble but no, I don't think so.

AP Can you tell us how to grow nice stuff at home?

GS I'm useless on it. You have to make tops (buds) and don't let it go to seed. The tops come about in the Autumn but I've never been able to do it. Sorry. There is a book that tells you how to do it – oh, what is it called – hmmm – sorry, I can't remember its name.

Jeffrey Bernard

by Tom Hodgkinson

IDLER 8 · FEBRUARY 1995

FOR A MAGAZINE WITH BOHEMIAN LEANINGS, IT SEEMED important to interview Soho rake Jeffrey Bernard. I was put in touch with him by his niece, Kate Bernard.

This was easily the most awkward interview I have ever done. Jeffrey Bernard, who died in 1997, was living at the time in a tower block in Soho. I had never met him before, having got the interview through his niece Kate.

My first mistake was to forget which flat he lived in. I called him from a phone box and he shouted 'FOURTEEN!' at me, as if I was the greatest imbecile ever to cross his path.

The flat was tiny. I entered it using a key attached by a piece of string to the letterbox. I found Bernard – scowl at the ready – sitting on the sofa, his one remaining leg stylishly clad in Levi 501s.

It struck me as sad that the window opposite him was positioned too high for him to enjoy the view over London from where he was sitting. He could see only clouds.

He made no attempt to make me feel at ease. As usual, I had not prepared any questions, relying on the conversation to produce its own momentum.

This led to long and agonising pauses.

A couple of hours later, however, he softened somewhat, and became chatty. I made him a cup of tea.

It was like he didn't want me to leave.

★

Jeffrey Bernard, one of the country's best-known journalist had a leg amputated a year ago. We visited him in his 14th floor Soho flat and talked about working, life without booze and how cosy things used to be.

TH Do you enjoy doing nothing?

JB I enjoy doing nothing. There's no virtue in work for its own sake. It's a myth that was invented by people like D.H. Lawrence ... back to the earth. As if there was something romantic and glamorous about hard work like being a coal miner in *Sons and Lovers*. If there was something romantic about it the Duke of Westminster would be digging his own fucking garden, wouldn't he?

TH That nobility of labour thing is a ruse by the people with money to make people happy doing a shitty job.

JB Well, yeah, shitty jobs are alleged to have dignity. There's nothing undignified about lying about all day and being waited on by servants, sipping bloody champagne.

TH Do you find it easy to work?

JB I'm fed up with working. Now I find it very difficult. I do as little as possible.

TH Have you been driven to do things in the past?

JB Well yes, a lot. Driven by a shortage of money, by nothing else. Not bloody ... what, you mean a muse or something? Good God, no. Has to be done for bread and butter. Being a journalist is a shitty job. It's a building up and then a breaking down of anxiety and tension. It's only pleasant when you finish it.

TH When you're writing are you like Dr Johnson and trying to get it out of the way as quickly as possible?

JB Yeah. I dictate most stuff nowadays, since I've had this leg off. I've made up book reviews on the phone pretending that I'd already written them. I made them up off the top of my head as I've been talking to the copytakers at the newspapers. Very risky business because – oh, I was going to say ten times – it's fifty times harder than it sounds.

TH But you had read the book?

JB Oh Christ yeah.

TH Do you ever feel guilty doing nothing?

JB I don't think I've ever felt particularly guilty about it. Although I have to admit I have despised a couple of people simply because they have never had a job in their lives. Which I think is a bit wet of them. I just

Jeffery Bernard at home in Soho. [Julia Hember]

don't trust people who have never really been up against it. [Long pause] You have to ask me questions, I've got nothing to say.

TH What do you mean by up against it?

JB Skint, hungry, cold.

TH Why don't you trust them?

JB There's a half of life that they haven't seen. Like the other side of the moon. Incomplete.

TH I wanted to ask you about when you stopped drinking. How has that been? Why did you stop?

JB I stopped because I was ill. I mean really ill. I had a haemorrhage last time. Like Peter Cook. He was up here a few weeks ago. Yeah.

TH What's it like not drinking?

JB Awful. Boring. Miserable. Lonely. It's like being half-dead.

TH What does drinking give people?

JB A cerebral kick, a lift. Confidence. The ability to chat up crumpet. Oh,
    to me not drinking is like being dead, almost. I sit here taking endless
    journeys down memory lane. It gets boring.

TH Have you ever been interested in other drugs apart from drink?

JB I've tried them. I'm not interested really. I've never tried heroin. I've
    got my drug which is alcohol, it's the one that suits me. I took a lot of
    amphetamines in the Fifties, which I hate now, because it's another way
    of talking rubbish. Marijuana I actually don't like, I don't like smoking
    pot. Physically I find it unpleasant. It makes me cough. It doesn't do
    much for me. I did like LSD, I must admit. It made me feel very cheer-
    ful, happy. I took some and I went to the Groucho Club and I sat in the
    reception hall. And everyone who came in apparently said to the staff
    and barmen, 'what's the matter with Jeff? He's smiling. Can't stop smil-
    ing.' Usually I look bad tempered, when I'm not feeling it. But on this
    occasion I really was grinning from ear to ear. It felt really good. But I
    don't want any more habits, you know. All these things interfere with
    the smooth running of day-to-day existence. I think cuntstruck is a
    boring drug too.

TH What?

JB Cuntstruck.

TH What's that?

JB How old are you? Cuntstruck means obsessed with cunt.

TH Oh I see. Why is it a boring drug?

JB It interferes with life, that's part of it.

TH Drinking doesn't get in the way of everyday life, does it?

JB Unless you can control it, it does. I mean it doesn't with me now. Most
    alcoholics dramatise themselves. They think it's romantic and macho.
    They end up not being able to cope. I pay the bloody bills on time. I eat
    three meals a day. That's the difference. I know what I'm doing and
    what I'm about. With some drunks it's like having Alzheimer's in the
    gut – they don't know what the hell's going on at all. I don't want to be
    like that.

TH Have you ever been close to that before?

JB Once. I'm not a drunk anyway. I drink … these words are all wrong. I
    mean, do I appear to be a nutcase to you?

TH No. Who called you a drunk, though?

JB You did, about three minutes ago.

TH I didn't call you a drunk, I was just talking about drinking.

[long pause]

TH So, what sort of things do you think about here?

JB I think about the past a lot. I'm not doing anything, am I, now? I'm
disabled. I don't go out so much, since that came off. It's eleven
months. My home help sometimes takes me to the Groucho. I go there
a lot because it's the nearest. Now that pubs don't exist any more.

TH What do you mean?

JB They're awful. All pubs are terrible places now. I mean you wouldn't
have known a decent pub at your age, I shouldn't think. They didn't
have fucking music. They didn't have cigarette machines. They didn't
sell the chemical beer. They were for proper drinkers, not for fucking
yobs, hooligans. I want to go into a pub and meet interesting people,
not to look at a lot of people sitting on the floor drinking out of tins. I
can't stand it. Mostly people in your age group. Ruin pubs.

TH So do you feel nostalgic?

JB For company, yeah. I feel nostalgic for Soho, for what it was. There
were a lot of genuinely interesting people in it. Genuine bohemians.
Now it's full of advertising agency creeps. Suits. Bloody Essex Man
and Soho man – there's very little difference nowadays. But it was like
bloody Disneyland.

TH Because of the fun?

JB I talked to people. It's not name dropping, but not many people can
say, like me, that they spent the day with the likes of Francis Bacon or
that boring drunk Dylan Thomas. You don't forget things like that.
Because they were outstanding insofar as they stood out. Simple. I've
met some extraordinary people round here over the years.

TH Would you say that's the essence of life, for you?

JB Yeah. Being with people. Eating and drinking and talking with people
that you like. And sometimes fucking them.

TH What do you like reading?

JB I don't read as much anymore. I find it hard work now, my attention
span is not as good as it used to be. I read mostly journalism nowadays.

TH How has journalism changed?

JB I don't think writing's got any better, despite Fleet Street trying to
insist on more undergraduates in the business. Having been to university doesn't help anyone. Reading English has got fuck all to do with
writing. A lot of girls annoy me who go to university... one girl told
me she was going to Oxford because it was something to do between

leaving school and getting married. And I've got to pay for that being an income tax payer. I said to her, why can't you read bloody *Pride and Prejudice* in the fucking kitchen? Why have you got to go to Oxford? No answer. The only reason I would have liked to have gone to university is because I like cricket. Not a very good reason to want to go, but as good as any, I suppose.

TH The student lifestyle is quite attractive though, loafing around, reading ...

JB If you've got money ...

TH But even if you haven't got money ...

JB But you've got to have money for comfort, which obviously doesn't matter as much when you're young, but even so. I always like to bloody eat well and be warm. Have a drink when I want it. Which of course hasn't been the case, but I couldn't go through all that shit again. Being on the breadline. I've done some terrible bloody jobs.

TH What depresses us is the party conversation, 'what do you do?' Everyone has to have some sort of job that they can quickly describe as if that somehow sums them up for the other person.

JB Yeah. That's boring. It was never like that. It's got quite a lot to do with the Conservative party, I think. Mrs Thatcher. I think work should be secondary. I mean life isn't just about working, Christ. I suppose this is one of the nice things about being a freelance writer. You just come and go. What is quite nice is being quite well known, because people are different to you. Which is true, I'm afraid. It may not meet with one's approval, but nevertheless, it's a fact. They're nicer to you, generally. I wonder how I'd be treated in the Groucho if I was a dishwasher.

TH I suppose what you've done with your work is make the work out of your life. That has to be the best way.

JB I've just written about myself, that's all. That's all I know anything about.

TH Things you write about in your column, would you write it without having talked about it with people?

JB Oh Christ yes all the time. I don't talk to people about what I think about, necessarily. I think mostly pretty gloomy thoughts. I think that life is an absolute bastard. I think it's awful. But I don't go around saying so. I don't like much about today, at all.

TH Why not?

JB It's not cosy any more.

TH Not cosy? Too big and sprawling?

JB Yeah.

TH But don't people make their own cosiness?

JB When did anyone walking up Berwick Street at this moment last sit down by a log fire with a good book and a nice glass of something to drink? As opposed to going to watch Arsenal on a Saturday, fucking beat someone up then get pissed on lager, go home and listen to pop music till three o'clock this morning while you're smoking pot? No. I hate it, hate life today. I wouldn't like to be your age. Do you know Tom, the word is cosy. People as I've said were skint and life was hard, as it is now, but there was something more cosy about it.

TH Were people supporting each other?

JB Yes. You would have been asked to supper tonight by friends, at his or her flat with three or four other people. You don't have to go out and have your eardrums smashed in some fucking pub by muzak or something. I suppose families don't count for anything now ... although I loathed mine. I don't know whether they've ever counted for much. All the bloody hate and anger generated down.

TH I'm not sure you're right about young people. If you're talking about cosiness and people looking after each other, it seems to me that's around more perhaps, than it was ten years ago.

JB Oh good.

TH People do seem to be relaxing.

JB I don't remember ever being full of dislike and hatred for people, like some kids I've come across now. One of the things that goes with getting older is that one becomes more conservative – and I emphasise that when I use the word conservative I do not mean politically. I'd rather cut off the other leg than vote fucking Tory. I suppose I am conservative. I don't know what's going to become of people. I mean the great miracle of inventing the computer was that it was going to give the people more leisure. What are they going to do with it? Beat each other up or ...

TH Not if you can somehow build it into the culture ...

JB Well they won't will they? I mean what will the culture be?

TH I mean it isn't just beating each other up, there's all sorts of other things people do.

JB ... watching Philip Gascoigne playing football.

TH But you know there's ...

JB Paul Gascoigne.

TH There's quite a lot of non-beating-up type activity going on now...
    there's lots of groups of people who enjoy doing things together,
    like putting on parties, doing little magazines, printing T-shirts. And
    having their own cosy little families.

JB I wish I knew where I could get a T-shirt without something stupid
    fucking written on it.

TH Well do you want an Idler T-shirt? They have a snail on the front.

JB No, I've got a phobia about slugs and snails.

TH Oh.

JB Slimy. Like our beloved Chancellor of the Exchequer... what's his
    fucking name... Clarke... no, Portillo... all fucking monsters of all
    time. Oh, it's disgusting. [calls out to a cook who has just come in]
    Augustine did you buy lottery tickets today?

AUG No, I haven't bought one today.

JB I was just wondering.

AUG Do you want to pick a number?

JB 27 is a lucky number

TH So you're not into the lottery.

JB Fucking 14 million to one against? It's hard enough racing and I really
    know what I'm talking about when it comes to racing. 14 million to
    one. And you've got to be a special person to win. You've got to be
    either a housewife from Scunthorpe or a panel beater from Warrington
    as far as I can make out. Not a freelance journalist from Soho, Christ,
    that's asking too much.

Nicholas Saunders

by Tom Hodgkinson

IDLER 9 · MAY 1995

IN THE LATE NINETIES NEAL'S YARD FOUNDER NICHOLAS Saunders became a fan of the drug Ecstasy and wrote a book which explored its various benefits. Naturally this made him an interesting figure to those of us involved with rave culture. Saunders died in a car crash in 1998 at the age of 60.

*

Nicholas Saunders made his name in 1970 with his subculture guide-book *Alternative London*. In the Sixties, he abandoned a career as a mechanical engineer to go on the hippie trail to India. In the Seventies, he founded the Neal's Yard group of wholesale food shops. Two years ago, he self-published *E for Ecstasy*, a book that took a calm look at both the benefits and potential dangers of E. As well as running a desktop publishing studio in Neal's Yard, he now lectures across the country and is operating a testing programme for Es.

TH What is your own experience with Ecstasy?

NS I first took Ecstasy seven years ago and I was really knocked out by the experience. It made me realise that I'd not only been depressed for several years, but exactly why. It allowed me to let go and move on. It was so helpful. But then, having heard how people could drop dead unexpectedly, I started researching it. I was amazed by how little knowledge there was around. Even now there's a lot of folklore con-nected with it: people think there are different kinds of E – speedy Es, or whatever. Or that they're cut with heroin. The thing is, it's not just a happy pill. It allows people to let go. And letting go in some moods or situations may bring up unpleasant experiences. I'm very keen on this testing programme I'm running. In Holland, the government finances a testing laboratory and indirectly funds several drug agencies which collect samples, test them and then publish the results. So anyone who bothers to find out can tell what they're taking. Over here, the government has the opposite tactic. Although the police test Es, they won't publish the results. When they are published, they go into this very glossy magazine, printed on thick paper and in full colour, called *Drugs Arena*. But not even the ordinary police are allowed to see a copy. It's a restricted document for the Drugs Squad. It's mad. I suspect the government thinks the more tabloid scare stories the better. Whereas I think the more real information the better. So what I've been doing is arranging for tests. We ask people who take Es regularly if they could buy an extra one. We send those to a laboratory and put the results on the Internet.

TH What have you found?

NS Our results actually show a higher proportion of bad Es than the police seizure results. Which may be because the people collecting the samples are reluctant to send on ones which they know are good. In each batch, we have found ones which contained ketamine, which is nothing like E and could have quite an unpleasant and shocking effect if you're expecting MDMA [the active ingredient in Ecstasy]. On the other hand, about half have been MDMA. Fairly low quality, but not as bad as a couple of years ago. We also did some tests on herbal Es that people are selling as a safe substitute, and found that the active ingredient is a herb called ephedra. Now ephedra is actually highly dangerous: it increases the heart rate and causes loss of fluids, which is ironic.

TH Do you think that one of the attractions of rave culture is that in a world where it's actually quite difficult to get time on your own, space on your own, and time to think, spending five hours dancing is a way of forcing a space for your head?

NS It can be a form of meditation. I took Zen Monk to a party, and he had used E for meditation, in a very serious way. He was curious to see what it would be like for dancing – he couldn't imagine it at all. Eventually I persuaded him to come along to this party. He watched people dancing. First of all he couldn't stand the music, then after a bit he suddenly said: 'This is meditation. These people are completely in the moment. They've cut out the internal dialogue.'

TH Living in the present.

NS Yes. There's a Rabbi I interviewed who said that major religions have lost the ability to provide a mystical experience, and young people's best chance of finding a mystical experience is through taking drugs like LSD and Ecstasy while dancing. He actually thought it might cause a religious revival, that people might move from them onto non-drug ways to find experiences of that sort. He also said that priests should take drugs like this themselves so they could first of all see the validity of it, and secondly be on the same wavelength as the people they're trying to seduce into their churches.

TH Can you describe the atmosphere now, as compared to the Sixties?

NS The Sixties was a very inspiring time. There were a lot of people like myself who, having experienced LSD, had the knowledge that there was a lot more to life than what we had been brought up to believe. It gave us a whole new perspective, a notion that we were at the dawn of a new and better and more high-minded age. But what happened in the Sixties has faltered. This is because LSD gives you an altered experience, where you see things in a completely different, and in some ways, more convincing and real way, but it is an experience you can't bring back to normal life. It's too different. What has happened now with Ecstasy is very interesting. There's a vast number of users – far more than ever took LSD in the Sixties, and among a much wider range of people. And I think E is having a bigger impact on the way they relate, on their values, on the sort of relationships they want to make. Because although the experience you have on Ecstasy is timid compared to LSD, it is in the same realm of consciousness, and so you learn. You can remember exactly what you thought and felt, and you can bring those realisations and ways of behaving into everyday life.

TH How did you come to write for *Alternative London*?

NS I didn't want to spend my life doing something that other people would do if I didn't do it. Since I'd spent a lot of time searching around and seeing what was going on, a lot of people were calling me and asking me about mystical movements or whatever. So I thought I'd make it into a book. I was at first unable to find a publisher or even a printer, because it was seen as too dodgy. Eventually I got it printed by a company that was set up to print telephone directories but had lost their contract and were desperate for any work. I eventually got 250,000 printed and it sold out very quickly.

TH What then?

NS I did a couple more books and then spent a year living in Christiania, a community in Copenhagen. I was so impressed. All these people in England were *talking* about their alternative ways to do things – how to make windmills out of old oil cans, how to recycle things – but it was all theory. In Christiania they weren't writing about it, it was just happening. I actually think that the arrangement in Christiania is closest to a living situation where people feel good. It's not hierarchical, it's about 1,000 people. That's enough so that after about a month or so everybody there is familiar. If you're doing a job there like working in a shop or sweeping the street, people appreciate you for your efforts. There's not this feeling of doing work which disappears off. That size of community is just right. If you have a terrible row with the little group of people you move around in, you can stay in Christiania and get away from them. Or if you split up with your lover, likewise. You may not be able to avoid her completely, but you're more likely to stay friends, to be close people, without being on top of each other all the time.

Even so, after a year there, I saw the falsity of it all. People were talking about it as if they had discovered a visible, alternative way of living which the rest of the world should follow, but actually they were living off the scraps of a very rich country. They didn't even pay for their electricity. A lot were on the dole but didn't contribute anything to the Danish economy. There were a few industries, but they didn't pay VAT. Basically they lived off the benefits of a rich society without supplying anything to it.

TH Have you always had an entrepreneurial bent?

NS I do seem to have a nose for it, but I just do things I really believe in. The *Alternative London* book was make or break. It was a very emotional thing. I spent all the money I could muster on getting this thing done, which was pretty neurotic looking back on it. I would do anything necessary. So it's not just an entrepreneurial bent, it's a question of committing yourself to what you really want to do and putting everything into it. But I do certainly enjoy all sides of the business. I did enjoy publishing my own book because I like to have control.

TH It's difficult for people to get going on their own these days. People use dole and housing benefit as a base, but unfortunately that's illegal. One of our main problems is that we're making our entrepreneurs and visionaries into criminals and outlaws.

NS   But that may not be a bad thing. I'm familiar with Denmark where the government is very generous with grants and subsidies to get people going. But it actually, I think, has an extraordinarily negative effect because people won't lift a fucking finger unless they get a grant first. And of course they only give grants to things that are approved, and the people who approve things, obviously, are rather older and more established and unlikely to approve something really outrageous. Whereas if people are doing it in a semi-criminal way, they may come out with more original and lively things.

TH   Do you find the mood positive among Ecstasy-taking teenagers and people in their twenties?

NS   I think there are two groups. There is one group, unfortunately larger, which is not very positive. For them, the experience of taking Ecstasy makes ordinary life seem boring in comparison. The other group feel they actually learn from the experience and don't need to take it so often. They fit it in with their life. It's a question of maturity in a way. A lot of teenagers who are perhaps not particularly sophisticated know they can have a wonderful time dancing on Ecstasy but they can't see how that relates to the rest of their world, they just live for the next weekend. They get run down and get in a bit of a mess – not very positive at all. But it's very difficult to make a judgment because most of those are teenagers, when things are changing very fast anyway.

TH   A lot of people in their mid-to-late twenties and early thirties seem to be unwilling to give up their hedonistic impulses.

NS   I met someone who started taking E five years ago at university. He said that the only friends of his who have stopped are those on teacher training courses, because they couldn't face seeing the kids, the ones they teach, out at night when they're off their heads.

TH   These E people are moving into positions of power in the media, too.

NS   I'm sure the media will change. My book came out two years ago, and I'm sure the main media people thought it was just a passing fad, like punk, here today and gone tomorrow. But if they hadn't experienced it, they couldn't know that it was quite an amazing and nice experience that was going to stay. I'm quite convinced that it's here to stay. Actually, I think there's going to be a development into other drugs, those which are less toxic than MDMA but will have similar effects.

Damien Hirst

by Tom Hodgkinson

IDLER IO · JULY 1995

THIS INTERVIEW TOOK PLACE DURING A PERIOD IN MY life during which I was quite dazzled by the Soho life, the drinking dens like The Colony Room and the Groucho Club, which at the time were filled with various hacks, artists, filmmakers and so on. Damien was at the centre of all this, drinking, smoking and being rowdy.

While out one night at the Groucho Club, Damien Hirst came over to our table and started talking about dogs. Recently back from a long stay in Berlin, he was throwing himself into Soho life with unparalleled gusto.

To my amazement he had heard of, seen and enjoyed the *Idler*. I spent the next few weeks trying to track him down in order to get an interview.

I finally found myself walking down to the Chelsea mews flat he was then renting with his girlfriend Maia one Saturday lunchtime. He peeled a fifty pound note off a pile on the sitting room table, and we walked down the pub over the road, where we drank all afternoon.

I was so skint at the time that I had to borrow a tenner at the end of the interview to get to my next destination.

Hirst is probably one of the most inspiring people I've met. He pours ideas at you, he's infected by a deep love of life and is completely fearless. He makes you feel good.

He also went on to give us a limited edition of 25 signed cigarette butts, which we gave away to readers.

★

We met the artist Damien Hirst and discussed smoking and drinking, working and living.

TH Someone told me that a few years ago, you had a period of six months or so before you started working, when you were just drinking and not working?

DH It's not actually like that. In fact, the first piece of art I ever sold, I paid someone else to make the next one, so I could actually keep going out drinking. I sold a medicine cabinet for £500, and I was making spot paintings as well. And then I paid somebody £200 to make three spot paintings for me, and sold those. The idea of the spot paintings were that they're an endless series, so the idea of painting spots for the rest of my life, after I'd done five, was completely tedious. I could visualise the whole thing, so it then becomes a bind physically to get in there and paint it, when somebody else could do it just the same. I numbered all the colours and I numbered all the spaces and drew the spots out and said this is where they go. A lot of people thought I wasn't doing anything because I was spending a lot of time socialising and going out, but I've always managed to get work actually done.

TH Quite a lot of writers have a year or so in their young life when they're not actually doing much, but when their ideas are developed. Everything that follows after that is a variation on those original ideas.

DH It's not like that for me. Whenever you look back, you can always pull something out of it, no matter what you're doing. There's always something you missed or something you didn't notice or somehow you got wrong ... I don't really have a beginning. Obviously ideas are formulated early on, we're human beings, we go like that. One thing leads to another with my work. Like *The Acquired Inability To Escape*, I made those sculptures and became, like, Damien Hirst. So then I made new sculptures and cut them in half. So in a way I don't go back to the beginning, I go back to the last lot.

TH So it's one idea that's constantly mutating and growing tentacles.

DH Because it's visual art, a lot of it comes from childhood experience but then a lot comes from the visual language – in advertising and stuff like that – which is around us. Commercials are so contemporary and up to date that when you're involved in that visual world, you can't really go backwards. Oxo commercials from the war wouldn't really make very good artworks ... or maybe they would. As an artist you've just got to look everywhere.

TH The *Idler* theory of creativity is that you need these little patches of just wandering around and staring out of the window and going out with your friends and stuff.

DH But I think you can do that on the move. Whenever I go to another city to do an art exhibition, the only way to get through it is to get drunk, because it's so similar to the last one. Every time I go somewhere, I've got to meet these collectors and these people who want to meet me and ask the same questions … and you get drunk and you hang out. That idea of an artist is being an alcoholic, suffering, no-money bum … it's because of that.

TH What do you mean?

DH A lot of people think all artists should hang out together and really love each other and all that, but if you sit down with an artist and they go, 'oh, my work's about the way society's congenitally deformed', I just want to go, oh fuck off, get the beers in. Artists are like everybody else. I think as an artist you have to reinvent yourself every day. Which I think is what you do anyway as a person, which is why people fall out, split up, get together, get into new bands or new ideas. It's like a turning over.

TH Keep moving.

DH Yeah, but it gets quite complicated because I guess it all boils down to an urge to live forever. The goal in life is to be solid, whereas the way that life works is totally fluid, so you can never actually achieve that goal.

TH How do you mean solid?

DH How you can't say one thing one day and something else the next day, it's not acceptable. And you say, OK, I changed my fucking mind. But everybody changes their minds. The idea of solidity is somebody who always says the right thing at the right time and knows what they're doing and is concrete: 'This is what I think and you can rely on that forever.' It's like, a sexy girl in a magazine is always going to be that sexy. A death thing comes into it. Immortality is really desirable, I guess. In terms of images, anyway. It's a contradiction between images and desire. I was having sex with 14-year-old girls when I was 14. But if I was to do it now, it would be really bad. But then you still find them sexy, so does that mean you're a pervert? So if you're having sex with a 14-year-old girl when you're 14 you're always going to find them sexy but you're not 14 any more. You've got to change.

TH   What about the process of getting ideas?

DH   I get them everywhere. I'm always on the lookout for anything ... all the time. It's so easy to do that. And everybody does it. You walk around the streets and see a Benson & Hedges commercial and it's got an anagram in it and you try and work it out. It's that kind of looking. Sometimes when you're drunk you can see better. I have titles floating around in my head; I have sculptures floating around in my head. It's like a collage. Or if someone says something. The title of my film is *Julie and Jane*. I overheard someone say 'Julia and Jay' – who I work with in my gallery – and I thought they'd said 'Julia and Jane'. And I thought maybe that would work as a title.

TH   It's a question of grabbing hold of those things and realising that they're interesting. Everybody experiences that process of things occurring to them, but what artists do I suppose is actually act on them.

DH   What I really like is minimum effort for maximum effect. Like with Picasso's *Bull's Head* ... a bike seat and handlebars making up the bull's head. Such a brilliant thing because it takes that tiny amount of effort to create. To connect a bull and a bicycle makes no sense at all. But it doesn't matter, because visually it's so strong that you think of an everyday object in a weird way.

SMOKING

DH   I think an ashtray is the most fantastically real thing. I went to some posh person's house and they had this tiny fucking little ashtray, it was about two inches by one inch. And they had a beautiful house. It's like they're trying to reduce that horror to such a point. You could only fit about three cigarette butts in it, then they'd empty it. It's almost like that dot on the television, it never fucking disappears. If you have a party then you've got to have an ashtray, but you get it so small ... to isolate the horror.

TH   It should be celebrated. That [pointing at grotty pub ashtray] is a really honest ashtray.

DH   Yeah exactly. You could have it full like that [imagining huge mound of butts]. In an artwork you're always looking for artistic decisions, so an ashtray is perfect. An ashtray has got life and death. It's like a graveyard, if you want to get metaphorical about it. But I quite like the idea of all these people's mouths and dirty habits all combined into one place. I'm making a sculpture for my show in New York called *Party Time* which is an eight foot ashtray, made to the scale of a normal ashtray, blown up in white fibreglass. It's filled with bin liners full of normal-size cigarette butts, absolutely packed. So it'll smell like smoke. But it's the opposite of that thing at the party: such a simple idea ... if you're going to do that, then I'm going to do this. It's not like Claes Oldenberg where you create huge-size cigarette butts. If you enlarge the ashtray and leave the butts the same size and call it *Party Time*, there's something positive about it. There's a great book I read called *Cigarettes Are Sublime*. You realise how smoking's never talked about. It's probably the most powerful thing of the 20th century. There's no country in the world where smoking is allowed where they don't smoke. Even where it isn't allowed they still find a way to smoke. People are killing themselves. I think suicide is the most perfect thing you can do in life. The whole thing is you don't know when you're going to die. It makes everything not make sense, there's this unknown factor. Whereas if you suddenly go, OK, I choose to die now, you take the matter into your own hands. So smoking is the perfect way to commit suicide without actually dying. I smoke because it's bad, it's really simple.

MULTIPLE PERSONALITY DISORDER

DH I had this idea for a video where you have two people talking, and one says, hey, how you doing? And the other says, great, and the first one says, yeah but how do you really feel? Oh, not so bad. Yeah, but how do you really feel? Oh, fucking shit. It was going to go from great to shit to great again.

TH We were getting annoyed the other day about people who go, yeah, great! fabulous! when you ask them how they are on the phone. Because they can't be.

DH But like I said before, there's a lot of people in your head and it depends who you're asking. I was sat talking to a girlfriend once and she was so depressed, she was going, 'I can't do anything with my life, I'm shit.' It went on for three hours this conversation. I was trying to cheer her up. I'd got into this situation where we'd pierced through the layers and got through to this deep depression underneath. I was going, cheer yourself up, pull yourself out of it, and I'd been going out with her for three years. And the phone rings and it's an old friend of hers from Italy. And

she says, 'Hi! How are you? Haven't seen you for ages! Let's go out!'
And I'd just spent three hours trying to cheer her up, and the phone
rings and some stranger can just do it like that. You can go through the
layers but on the top layer that's the only relationship they had. So if
someone cries now in front of me I just go, fuck off, and kick them.
Not quite. I liked that thing in the *Idler* about dreaming being like
virtual reality.

FLOWING

TH   We try to be open and go with the flow.

DH   I think that's what I do as an artist. I've just had a baby and I'm looking
at things for babies. I thought of doing a sculpture called *Lambi Loves
Snoodle* with a pram with a skull in it. And then those walkie-talkies
you get from Mothercare. So the pram is like communicating with the
skull, so they're looking after each other. But I probably won't do it.
But do you know what I mean? If that stuff comes out then you have
to be open to it. The worst thing I can do is make a Damien Hirst. I
don't believe in talent.

TH   What's idleness for you?

DH   It's about minimum effort, maximum effect. And it's about people who
work and play in a way in which you can't separate one from the other.
It's like when a car is idling. You have the possibility of going somewhere, but you're not going anywhere. But that doesn't mean you're
not doing anything. The energy's there. I could very easily make shit-
loads of money. I know exactly how to do it. But I know if I did it, it's
a slow decline into nothing. Whereas if I constantly make an effort to
be more than that, to compromise without compromise ... that means
you really give someone what they want, to give someone else what
they want, and get what you want. So in a way, it's a compromise, but
you get so much of what you want that you're not really compromis-
ing.

HOW TO LIVE

TH   We're interested in the question of 'how to live', and in people who
arrange their lives so that they have somewhere to go to in the country.
It always sounds very posh and aristocratic when you talk about it,
but ...

DH   I've done it the other way round though. Most people live in the city and go to the country at the weekend, and that's posh and aristocratic, but actually to live in the country and come to London when you can't take it any more is different. But whenever I look at the question of how to live, the answer's always staring me in the face. I'm already doing it. I go, so that's how you do it! The answer to how to live, is just live. And I go, oh fuck I've been doing that all along. And I ask myself, what do I want? Well, I want to get up in the morning and not have too many problems. I want to walk around a bit, think a bit, I want to slow down, so if I fucking live in Devon, it's three hours from London ... if my home's in London I can never relax. I can't open the window and have a fag without thinking, oh shit, my neighbours have seen me with a baby and now they've seen me having a fag ... there's always some-body else to think about. And also in Devon there's nine pubs between where I live and the sea, in a quarter of a mile. I'm gonna get a big horse. And I'm gonna go to the pub on my horse and park it outside and drink, and the horse is gonna know its way home. So the owner can just lie over it, slap it on its arse, and say 'take me home'.

TH Much better than a car.

DH It's fantastic ... But the answer to how to live is to stop thinking about it. And just to live. But you're doing that anyway. However you intel-lectualise it, you still just live.

Keith Allen

by Tom Hodgkinson

IDLER 11 · SEPTEMBER 1995

AMIEN HIRST HAD SUGGESTED WE INTERVIEW KEITH
Allen. This was at the time when Damien, Keith and Alex
James had recently made friends and were hanging around
together, making videos and drinking. It was the Cool Britannia era.
Keith was wilder and crazier than Damien, but again, inspiring and
fearless. At various points in the evening, he took off all his clothes, lay
on the snooker table, and put his tongue in my mouth. On the evening
we did the interview, we also met Alex James, who went on to be a
contributor to the mag.

*

We arrive in Soho at seven: Gavin the art director, Michele the
photographer and me, Tom the editor. Keith Allen is drinking with
Damien Hirst and Alex from Blur. They have all been working
together on the video for Blur's single 'Country House', and are pretty
excited about it. We get in taxis and go down to the Carlton Snooker
Club in Shepherd's Bush, a huge and fantastically appointed hall, with
rows of tables, elaborate cornicing and little phones to order drinks
from. Snooker tables are huge. Going for corner pockets, I can hardly
see the other end. It's embarrassing. Everyone orders pints bar Alex,
who is on his one day a week of not drinking. After a couple of games,
Damien goes, 'just get the fucking interview done, Keith, I can't stand
the tension.' So we go up to the terrace.

TH How was Glastonbury for you?
KA Glastonbury? Glastonbury? It was my eighteenth. Oh yes, I've a rela-

tionship with Glastonbury. It's changed commercially in the last four or five years. There was a time in the late Eighties when to see a burger was unheard of. You could always get meat there, you could always get meat. But to see sausages and chips and those pictures of meals. That was the change.

TH Didn't you think it was extra brilliant this year?

KA I think they always are. A lot of it's drugs.

TH But there's something else about it, you come back and it's like ...

KA Why can't life be like that?

TH You think, I've turned into a hippie.

KA But that's fucking bullshit, we met Michael Stipe the other night. Somebody said something about Glastonbury and Stipe said, oh that hippie festival. I said, you're fucking daydreaming. He said, oh yeah, really, some people said they had a rave tent last year. Now just hang on a minute here ... in '88 when Hawkwind were playing with the travellers, they had laser shows and raves then. The people doing Glastonbury were the people doing Shoom. I was really offended by him saying it was a hippie thing. In '82 and '83, I was being touted as the punk comic. I was at Glastonbury, I used to sell beer there in the back of the van. A pound a can, and a free snort of amyl every purchase, that was my game. I was always kind about it, I didn't make loads of money. I remember all these fucking twats from the *NME* and *Melody Maker* would be walking round in their little suits and raincoats, going round for the hippie angle, and it really confused them when they met me. I was going, this is fantastic, don't you get it? When the whole rave culture started, the people who were clubbers and football fans got into Glastonbury ... and it was through the drugs really. It's interesting that you can still find a little niche there that doesn't offend you *vis-à-vis* commercialisation, because it's so big, there's something for everybody, and that's what I love about it.

TH You come back from it, and you think that really is the way to live.

KA Bollocks, don't fall for that. That's a load of cack, it's just shit. What you're talking about, is being that relaxed, that's the way to live. Well I'm that relaxed all the year round, you understand? You can't live like that, don't be so ridiculous, you wouldn't be able to drive your fucking car, the traffic lights wouldn't work.

TH It's that way of thinking.

KA Well it is for me. It's a logical progression. It's everything that Billy

Butlin was trying to sell the world after the Second World War. Go and have a good buzz. But when you leave, don't forget it. Don't put it in a compartment, and say, 'oh that's my weekender holiday.' I can get all those drugs here, but I can't camp. I can't fall out and stumble across people at three in the morning.

TH It's like learning from taking E.

KA Yeah, transfer the knowledge. Once you've experienced E, you can meet people who are on it, when you're not, and because you've experienced it, you know what they're going through, immediately you're ten points more relaxed than you would be if you didn't know what was going on.

TH So how do you carry that relaxed feeling over into everyday activities?

KA It's ever since I came into the big world and had to get my fucking knickers washed and buy cornflakes. I realised very early on that you can do anything you like, anything as long as you have some kind of integrity about yourself.

TH Isn't it something to do with controlling your time? That's why people like holidays. Because for 50 weeks of the year, most people haven't got control.

KA I don't like holidays. But I think that's fairly patronising POV... for the lumpen proletariat, yeah, you're dead right, because they're always going to be forelock tugging, cap-doffing shit-cunts anyway. Well, forget them, although I suppose they're the larger mass of society, and I suppose you're trying to affect them... and it's working by the way. I can take massive amounts of drugs when I want to, I do what I like, I will never ever be a victim. I do it 365 days a year. Holidays mean nothing to me because I think I'm on holiday all the time. The weird thing is, I'm not the best actor in the country. I'm not the best comedian, I'm not the best writer, I'm not the best director. Having said that, I'm not a jobbing actor, comedian or writer, but I still make a fucking living. And that has got something to do with not being a victim.

TH Have you always been like that?

KA Listen man, I enjoy my life. Having said that, there are a lot of people who enjoy themselves but feel guilty. It's about how you structure time. It's a bit like Kafka; you could say he was a victim, but having read his stuff, you think, actually he wasn't. When I was 25 I'd done fucking loads of things. By the age of 21, I'd been expelled twice, been to public school, comprehensive, I'd run away from home to France. When I was 15, I was a ligger for Geno Washington and the Ram Jam Band, Jimmy Jones and the Vagabonds. The police came to pick me up twice and they put me in Stanford House, just down the road here, in need of care and protection, cunts. Did a bit of thieving, went to Borstal. When I was 17, I was earning £180 a week cash, in my hand, touting for fishing boats in Tenby. I was brilliant at it, I could fill up a boat. The cry was POLLOCKS! I said, Pollocks madam, you naughty girl. I'd done my 'O' levels, got educated in Borstal, in terms of meeting people and having conversations, I'd never had a conversation before. Went to college, took a couple of 'A' levels, met my guru, who was my English teacher. Made all the mistakes in the world, came to London, fucked around. In the interim, I'd been a coal miner, butcher's assistant, apprentice lathe operator, lithographic printer. I'd done it. I never ever – even when I was inside – felt like a criminal. Some of the guys in there, they hadn't done as bad things as me, but they were already feeling like criminals, feeling naughty. I never once felt like a criminal. Once you know that, you turn it into something for your own good. I was the first ever Borstal trainee to be taken on by Community Service Volunteers. I ran a children's home at St Hilda's in Bethnal Green. I took all of them out thieving from building sites. We stole paving stones, sacks of cement, to build the playground. Anyway, I had a lot of information. Went to drama college, fuck that, which was top shit. I only went 'cos there were loads of women. But I ended up playing football, I was an apprentice pro for Southampton. I spent two years playing football. Loved it. Fucked loads of women, bought a Morris Minor, summer job with my old man on the water board, another 50 quid a week. Came up to London, squatted Eaton Square, squatted it for two years … two ballrooms, everything. People would say, what are you doing? Fuck off, I'm just having the best time of my life. Became stage manager at the ICA Theatre, when fringe theatre was big. Saw every fucking fringe company go through our theatre. Suddenly I've seen everything, and of course it's all information, I'm taking what I want. Got sacked, met two guys who worked at the ICA, both doctors, one of genetics, one of biology, they left Aston University and became master printers. I started to silkscreen, did all the Clash posters, Buzzcocks, The Police, for Miles Copeland.

I've got so much information, it's painful. So I'm buzzing on this, I'm going into the West End, pissing myself up. I'm doing everything except acting. But I know what acting is. There were two things I learnt early. One was, find out what you want to do. Do it. Then find out if you can or can't do it. If you can't do it, stop. Do something else. Really doesn't matter. I knew that what defines you as an actor is never what you're doing either in front of the camera or on stage ... it's what you're doing when you're not on stage and not in front of the camera ... that's the stuff. That's what makes you good.

TH How do you convince other people?

KA Fuck other people. Who cares? You've either got it or you haven't. I'm terribly sorry. A lot of people have got it, and then they fuck up big time. I worked with Harvey Keitel. What a cunt, what a wanker, what a buffoon of the highest order. Oh a buffoon. Of the highest order. Went for dinner with him, shared a cab back with him. Monosyllabic twat... but not because he is a monosyllabic twat, it's because the pressure of what he does makes him a monosyllabic twat. That is death, you're killing yourself. Good communicator, still doing it – CAN'T COMMUNICATE. Can't be a human being. Michael Stipe is still a person. That's their battle in the fame game – how do I sell myself now? But the key is, never sell yourself, EVER. Just give. Just fucking give. And that's the way it is, you understand? And I know, that's why I get away with what I get away with. Because I haven't got an ounce, a fucking nano-ounce of protective layer about me.

TH That sounds quite spiritual.

KA It is. But you've got to play the game. How you define your life is the level of compromise you're prepared to entertain in the 24 hours of a day. You gotta compromise, don't be ridiculous. But just give.

TH So you've never had any desire to accumulate huge amounts of money?

KA Don't be so ridiculous. It's funny – the Child Support Agency, the tax people, come to me all the time, and they're astonished, but it's true: I have no house, I have no car, I have no material goods, I have nothing, nothing at all. I love it.

TH That's quite an achievement.

KA Fuckin' is, I've worked hard at it. I have nothing, it's fantastic, all I've got is some clothes. It's true. Ha ha ha. They try and bankrupt me, and I go, TAKE IT. What do you want, my shoes? And they've been through all my fucking history. But I still pay for my kids – all that's taken care of. I'm in debt permanently. And I love it. And I'm not being a smart motherfucker who's just saying, I'm going to die in debt, you cunts. It's just that my outgoings are so massive – it's mostly about children. But I've never ever needed money, I don't want money. If I got loads of it I wouldn't know what to do with it.

TH One of the challenges is how to keep your dignity...

KA I've never lost mine. But Blur will come up against it, they're a great act. They're an important act. They've got ideas. They've got a pump action shotgun of music. This album will be the first step. The next album, I bet you, will be one of the greats of all time. I'm not like that. I am a cult figure, but I'm also big enough to be a star. But a lot of my work is underground. I'm responsible for a lot of things that people have heard, but they don't know it's me. That's my game. I can do what the fuck I like. And I love it. But I've worked at it. I haven't just arrived here. I don't do television, I won't do commercials. But I still eat, I still drink, I still get respect, and I still give.

TH It takes courage.

KA Well, you call it courage. I just say fuck you. I've been on the dole. I've walked the streets. When I was married and had no money and had nothing, do you know what we'd do? We'd find out where the parties were at the weekend. I had a Pakistani mate in Westbourne Grove. We'd go round the parties and fucking farm out the beers when they'd run out. We made money like that. Well, we lived. But you're still having a laugh. Career to me is anathema, but I know it. I did NOTHING till I was 28, NOTHING. But I had a fucking great life. I loved every second of it. And I love every second of it now. At the moment I take six kids camping at the weekend. I love it. I won't be tied down, is what I'm saying. Years ago, I used to say, if the world was full of bank clerks then I'd be a bank robber; if the world was full of bank robbers, I'd be a fucking bank clerk. Heh heh. And that's a fact. Ha ha. Let's get back to the snooker.

I hang around drinking pints on the edge while the others play snooker. We order a bottle of champagne. Everyone's smoking like mad. Michele is taking pictures. Finally we do the cover shot. Keith refuses to do anything except take off all his clothes, lie down on the snooker table, cover his crotch with snooker balls while saying 'Come on Damien, put the ball right up my arse' and grinning satanically at the camera. We settle up the bill. Michele and Gavin go home.

I join the others to go back into town. We get a cab. I'm amazingly thirsty, so I ask the cab to stop so I can get some water. Keith abuses me for my wimpiness and the other two join in, which I think is pretty unfair, me being the only non-celebrity in the cab. Back in Soho, I am given a tequila and a sea breeze. Keith takes down his shorts about three times. He snogs Damien, then Alex, then me. We go to Browns, a sort of celebrity nightclub. It is cold and pretty empty. Alex leaves; Keith and Damien have gone into the loo. What are they doing in there? It's three o'clock. I decide to scarper.

Bruce Robinson

by Tom Hodgkinson

IDLER 12 · NOVEMBER 1995

BRUCE ROBINSON IS ONE OF OUR HEROES, HAVING WRITTEN
and directed one of the most quoted films of all time, the incom-
parable *Withnail and I*.

I got the train up to the Welsh border, where he had recently bought
a sprawling farmhouse, having quit Hollywood after nearly a decade of
agony working with studios.

He had sounded posh and distinguished on the phone, so on the
station platform I approached a posh and distinguished-looking gent
with short grey hair. He wasn't Bruce.

Bruce was in the car park, leaning against his Land Rover, wearing
shades, long hair and Levis. He looked like a Rolling Stone.

To my disappointment, he was on the wagon. He had asked if I'd like
to stay the night, so I had anticipated sinking a few bottles of red with
him. We did the interview in two parts, one that afternoon, and one
the following morning.

Another original mind, great thinker and great talker.

★

The writer of *Withnail and I* and *The Killing Fields* now lives with his
family in rural Herefordshire, where we discussed speeding up and
slowing down ...

TH [gazing through the window at idyllic pastures] It must be fantastic
waking up here.

BR It's fantastic waking up in an environment that hasn't changed in so
long ... but really it's you, what you bring with it. I get quite tired of
cows. Sometimes you need that pile of sick on the pavement down the

Earl's Court Road just to get you into focus.

TH There's a kind of romance about London as well.

BR Yeah, there is. Cities are best when there's no one in them. At four or five in the morning they have a real magic to them. I remember coming back from Los Angeles and the first thing I wanted to do, partly because of the jet lag, was get in the car and drive around London as the light was coming up. It's a phenomenal place because you own the town. Everything is yours and then you see the newspaper sellers and get on with the day. I guess you're into the magic of it now in the same way that I was into it 20 years ago.

TH New things round the corner all the time.

BR But it's the cost of it now. I used to go to a restaurant on the Brompton Road when I was on National Assistance, which was about eleven quid a week. Every Sunday you could go there and have lunch with full anaesthetic: a couple of bottles of red, and a plateful, and you'd get out of there for four quid.

TH When you had no money and were living on the dole, what sort of techniques did you have for living?

BR It was very difficult, but it was much much cheaper. We used to drink Guinness in the morning and wine after lunch ... though lunch itself didn't exist. We accumulated an enormous amount of Guinness bottles. So when we had two to three hundred Guinness bottles there would be a convoy of people taking them back to the off-licence for the deposit. Wine was about eleven and six a bottle or something. But it was extremely difficult.

TH Were you paying rent?

BR Well, ostensibly we were paying rent but the guy who owned the place we were living in was a friend and we never gave him any money ... we probably still owe him about six hundred quid. The thing you do when you haven't got any money is cut out luxuries. If it was a question of fags or eating we would always go for the fags.

TH It's funny how your priorities end up with clothes and eating way down. You have beans on toast which is 40p, to save money. But you'll easily go to the pub and have five pints, or go and buy a bottle of wine and not think anything of it. At lunch you'll think, 'Mmmm, I don't know if I want to spend two pounds on that sandwich, I'll have that cheaper one at one twenty.'

BR Well that's right. One twenty, it's sort of a horrible currency. When a sandwich was one and six it seemed more amenable, more acceptable. We had a café round the corner in Camden Town. It was an Italian one owned by a woman called Gina, a real old fat Italian mamma. She used to feed us if we didn't have any money. And then when we did have money we'd go in there and pretend we didn't. She was really sweet ... you couldn't get a steak out of her, but you could get an egg. I look back on those days in dread. Sometimes I have nightmares about going back to that flat. It got so bad by the end, when everyone had moved out and all the furniture was gone and I was there. I literally had one light bulb. I guarded it like a Russian prisoner of war. At night I'd take the light bulb up and put it in the bedroom, and in the day I'd go down and put it in the kitchen and – because the gas was still on at this point – get the oven open, sit there in your overcoat and get warm. But it's OK because it is the classic thing of aspiring and going on to something else. And in a sense that's what *Withnail* was. Being able to look at it and see how ridiculous it was. All that stuff with the bags on the feet in the countryside was all true. The worst thing that could happen was a burst bag ... so we got six to eight bags per foot all burst, but which would slow down the intake of water.

TH It's that priorities thing ... you'd get given some money for Wellington boots but it'd all get spent on booze.

BR That's exactly how it would happen. Occasionally I'd go down and hit my parents. Scrape up the dough to get me the train fare down there and sort of lay on the couch ... with hunger ... and try and get some money. My grandmother, who I adored, used to give me a few quid. In those *Withnail* days my friend Vivian had parents who lived on the Isle of Islay, and all the people who worked in the whisky distilleries were forbidden to drink the stuff on site. So apparently there was a massive upsurge in spin drier sales and what these buggers were doing was getting the whisky filters – with 160 proof in them – and taking them home, sticking them in the spin-drier and sucking the whisky out – they called it Yon White Stuff and it was like fucking aviation fuel. Every time Viv came back from Islay, he would have a crate of Yon White Stuff which we'd murder ourselves with. It was like the scene in *Withnail* where he drinks the lighter fuel ... that actually happened. The events in *Withnail and I* that take take place over about two weeks actually happened over four or five years. Various things I used, other things I made up and I integrated, squeezed, concertina-ed all this into

Bruce Robinson at home in Hertfordshire. [Julia Hember]

one story. But the lighter fuel scene actually did happen. We always used to have those terrible, awful fucking English Sundays that extended for 11 months, because it's always winter and always cold when you've got no money, you're always shivering, living off the vitamins in cigarettes. I remember one Sunday we didn't have the money to go to the flicks and Vivian was under the sink with the Guinness bottles after the dregs ... some of the bottles you'd pour out a fag end trying to get enough together to have a drink. Freaking out, in a terrible mood, he picks up a newspaper – he read *The Sun* and I read the *Guardian* – he hated my paper and I hated his. He started ranting about the *Guardian*, 'The *Guardian*, what do they fucking *guard*? What do they *guard*?' all of that, stamping around this flat with his Guinness dregs and – it was very acrimonious, nasty afternoon – his eyes finally alight on the Ronson. And he grabs the Ronson and tears off the top, 'RAUGHH, glug, glug, glug!' He had a three or four day hangover, went blind in one eye and I often wonder – because it's an incredible carcinogen, kerosene – whether that was the thing that kicked off his cancer of the throat. He drank a can of lighter fuel and was in a most terrible state.

TH What must it do to your bowels?

BR Well the thing is, there's a big difference between methyl and ethyl alcohol, isn't there. Methyl alcohol is actually inconsumptable – human beings can't drink it. You get a terrible crisis affecting your central nervous system. It was around this time that the whole thing was collapsing. I knew very clearly in the sane, the government side of my mind, that I had to stop doing this and get away from this environment. Because at this point I used to write quite a lot, and that's what I wanted, even though I was in this totally destructive environment.

I've always had this epithet 'art is the opposite of death', and I still think about that whenever I feel really black about anything. I get in front of my typewriter. The function of writing is the opposite of being dead. You're living. This is the thing that always motivates me, because I hate the process of writing. I find it hard and hateful to do. But at the end of the day, if I write a couple of good lines, or I write a page that I think is good work, I feel justified in being alive. I feel I've got the right to be, in a shoddy way, pleased ... I don't want to say, happy.

The nightmare for me is that over the years I've developed an obsessive way of writing. You know the way computers and typewriters justify the right-hand margin? I justify the right hand margin, but I do it by hand. So if I've got a word like 'fundamental' that spills one letter at the end of the line, I have to think of a different word so the margins all end straight. It's crazy. I have to type it ten or twenty times. Say the flower I really want to use is a chrysanthemum, and it's important to the plot it's a chrysanthemum, sometimes I'll have to go back and turn it into a dahlia. Curiously, *Withnail and I* doesn't follow any of the rules I use now. It's a rambling fucking thing. I wrote it as a novel before I wrote it as a screenplay, and I was sitting there, writing with great joy as an amateur – it's like a poker player who wins, you've never played poker before and you clear the fucking table, and I had that with *Withnail*. It was coming with ease and great joy and I'd be laughing my fucking head off as I'd be typing. I could hardly see the page because I was crying with laughter. So I figured, if it makes me laugh it's going to make other people laugh.

But Viv hated me writing. He was a strange fucker. He could have been a writer – he used to talk like a writer – but he never wrote. He could have been an actor – he used to talk like an actor, look like an actor, but he never acted. He could never get a fucking job because he was always arseholed. He was too smart: an intellectual, erudite man. He'd go to an audition to play a priest, read up all this cackle of theo-logical bollocks and then say, 'It's very strange you should be consider-ing me for this part because before I became an actor I was considering the priesthood.' And they knew it was nonsense, so he'd never get a job.

He wanted – what's that Bob Dylan line? 'They want you to be down in the hole they're in' – he wanted us to be in our hole forever, and I'm sure he'd like us to be 50 year old guys sitting there in the hole still.

TH   But there's comfort in that: having an ego and ambition but never try-ing so you're never going to fail.

BR   Yeah, you've precisely put your finger on where Vivian was at. He was such a dilettante, very lazy guy but very funny and I had some of the best days of my life with this bastard. He could have been a really good writer if he'd ever written, but he never wrote, so maybe he wasn't a writer because the first function of trying to be a writer is trying to write. You've got to sit there week after month after year to learn how to do it. It's not something you pick up from some book or ridiculous course. The only teacher for a writer, is the writer and that's how you learn to write, by writing. You learn what will work and what won't work, your own tricks of the trade. One of my rules of writing is never to tear up the stuff you hate, because if you pull it out of the machine, say 'God, that is shit!' and throw it in the fucking litter bin and at the end of the day you've got three bottles of wine, 60 fag ends and loads of bits of torn up, stained paper and a bit of snot and quite a lot of phlegm that's coughed up and thrown in there. Then you're on your hands and knees at ten at night going through trying to find the bit to

sellotape it together again because maybe it works better than what
you've got. So I always crumple … that's a kind of daft rule, but nevertheless one I use. Don't tear it, crumple it. You can get all the balls out,
flatten them and find your good bit. But that ain't worth writing a
book about.

TH But the *Withnail* stuff was not funny at the time.

BR No, it's deadly serious. When we were tramping around in those fucking bags up some fell in Ullswater, there was nothing funny about it –
it was fucking horrible. Awful. The comedy comes out of it post the
event, taking an artistic view of it. For example, the drunken landlord
in the pub in the Lake District was based on a publican from a dump
called The Spreadeagle in Camden Town. He used to get completely
wasted and very acerbic, and say, 'Isn't it time you two cunts left?'

TH What steps did you take to escape that old life?

BR Well, it's like the end of the film which is symbolic of the end of the
decade with the haircut: 'They're selling hippie wigs in Woolworth's
man.' That's exactly what happened. I got a job in a play called
Journey's End, in Theatre 69 in Manchester. I came back one day with
that very haircut. I was moving on, I was moving out. I still have nightmares about having my hair cut, because in the late Sixties it was something that fucked with your head. Everything was about long hair,
Granny Takes A Trip and all of that. And when I came back and went
for Sunday lunch with my friends in a restaurant I would be stared at
like a Martian because I was the only guy with short hair. Because the
rest of my clothes were like everyone else's they'd all think I'd been in
jail.

The reason I used alcohol for many years as a writer is that it makes
you drink-drive a typewriter, it allows you to do 80 miles an hour in a
30-mile-an-hour limit. You sit in front of the typewriter and the first
thing you have to deal with is the government of the mind, the super-
ego, sitting up there on top of your head saying: 'Who are you kid-
ding, they're going to find you out on this one. You're not going to get
away with it – you can't fucking write …' So I drink and that cop voice
shuts up and the ego and the id are working and now I'm doing 60 in a
30-mile-an-hour limit. I don't care.

TH It's a kind of focus narrower.

BR But it also diminishes your working day because it sends in quite heavy
bills: you've got to go to sleep now, you've got to have your headache

now. But I don't use it any more, and because of that I don't think my writing's as good as it was 15, 20 years ago. [Sophie and Lily (Bruce's daughter) come in. They are discussing buying a cage for Lily's snake]

SR Garter snakes grow really big and the woman in the pet shop in Hereford says you need a cage three times bigger than your snake.

BR It'll have to be nine feet long then – it'll have to have a room of its own. I've seen anacondas curled up in a cage in the zoo. If she gets one of those, we'll have to have a tube 70 feet long.

[We drive to Hereford station]

TH How do you organise your work?

BR When I'm writing I normally get up at six, lay the breakfast for the kids, get the Alpen and the cornflakes out, and then I like to start writing about seven o'clock. Drink maybe 20 cups of coffee by noon. My wife brings me in a bun, and I work till about four in the afternoon. And that's sort of it. Very obsessive. Sometimes I go for a walk. And I do that five days a week.

TH Is it an act of will or do you just want to do that?

BR Writing is an extremely disciplined thing: there's no boss there. If I wanted to I could stay in bed till noon, go to bed at five. I can do what I like providing I turn in the goods – otherwise I don't get paid. If there was a way of waking up one morning with 120 neatly typed pages next to the bed I'd take that route. But that isn't the way it works. I write ten pages to get one. So I've written well over a thousand sheets to get that 120. It's hard to do.

Dexter Brierley

by Gavin Pretor-Pinney

IDLER 13 · JANUARY 1996

GAVIN SUGGESTED THAT FOR OUR CHILDHOOD ISSUE, we really ought to interview a child. So he did.

★

Dexter is four. The *Idler* went to discover his views about money, the workplace and kids' icons.

GPP   Have you decided what you want to be when you grow up?

DB   A fireman.

GPP   And what will you do as a fireman?

DB   Put out fires.

GPP   And what will you wear?

DB   Suit.

GPP   And how will you get to the fire?

DB   In a fire engine.

GPP   Have you got no school today?

DB   I did go to school today, but I stayed inside. You can go out in the garden, but some people that feel ill can stay inside.

GPP   Do you ever stay at home when you feel ill?

DB   No, not really. [Pause] I've got a fireman video.

GPP   Do you watch *Postman Pat*?

DB   No. I hate Postman Pat. I never watch him.

GPP   Last time I was here you said you were gong to live in a flat with your friend Jack ...

DB   I am but we're going to live in separate flats. Jack's going to a different flat. I should tell Jack that. I'm going to live with all the firemen. At night-time I'm going to eat my tea and fall straight asleep.

GPP So at the end of the day you'll be tired.

DB I'm already tired.

GPP If you were a girl and wanted to be a fireman, do you think they'd let you?

DB No. [Pause] The BBC came over to record someone in the bath.

GPP Do you like being in the bath?

DB No. Because I always have to have hairwashes and I hate it. It always gets in my eyes.

GPP Do you like using the telephone?

DB Yes. Oh. I've got to show you something. It's a backpack for my holiday.

GPP Do you prefer being here or being on holiday?

DB Being on holiday. [Pause] If you climb up the stairs you can see my bedroom. All the way to the top of the house. It's a long way.
[Go up to his room]

GPP What do you use your desk for?

DB Work. At home.

GPP Do you like working at home?

DB Yeah.
[Sits down at desk; picks up mobile phone]

DB Hello Bengy. Bubbye Bengy. I've got to get something from my desk.

GPP What does your daddy do?

DB He always shoots film, every single morning. And he always comes back so so so so late. In the night-time.

GPP Do you think he works too hard?

DB Yeah. He has always worked every day.

GPP Does he need to work so hard?

DB Yes. Because he needs to do lots of filming and lots of work. And always when he's at work I always feel tired. We should watch this video.

GPP What's Elvis doing up there?

DB He tells me the time, Monster Elvis. He tells me to wake up at 8.15. My mum and dad were lying in bed until very late ... I woke them up.

GPP Do you find it easy to wake up or do you sometimes want to sleep?

DB Yes. Sometimes I want to sleep all day.

GPP What are those [metal objets d'art]?

DB That's Mummy's, she worked at her art. You always give them to people. Chop chop chop chop it off. We always give them to people.

GPP How does Mummy make these?

DB Well, she makes them out of metal. I don't want her to just give them away. I want her to keep them. She's not going to give these away. We should watch this video today.

GPP What other videos have you got?

DB I don't know. I always play this in the morning. Jump-ee jump-ee jumpy jumpy jump. Jump-ee jump-ee jumpy jumpy jump.

GPP Now that trampoline at the end of your bed is useful, isn't it?

DB Yeah. We're going to move it into the hall. My mum thinks it's silly to have it here. So when I wake up in the morning I go out into the hall and say: jump jump jumpy jump jump waaargh!

GPP To wake them up?

DB Yeah.

GPP How long could you go on doing that for?

DB I could do it … jump jump jump jump jaargh.

GPP What's Elvis' job?

DB I go baaargh.

GPP Is he dancing?

DB Yeah.

GPP Is he a real person?

DB No. Shelley gave it to me.

GPP Is that your Auntie?

DB You know Shelley, you've met her before.

GPP Oh yes, I do.

GPP Dexter, is this you in this picture?

DB [Laughing] Yeah.

GPP What are you wearing?

DB A dress. It's silly.

GPP Why?

DB I hate wearing dresses. [Pointing to a poster] That's Batman and Robin.

GPP What do Batman and Robin do?

DB They always go, run run run, fight fight fight fight. Because there are always baddies that are chasing them.

GPP What would happen if there was no Batman and Robin?

DB There wouldn't be fighting. Da da da da da da.

GPP But if Batman and Robin have to stay in bed …

DB They don't ever go to bed, they just stay up the whole night long.

GPP Don't Batman and Robin ever get a break?

DB No they don't. That's the baddie's ship. Batman has a ship, but that's not it.

GPP Do they get paid?

DB No. They never buy anything.

GPP Where do they get their boats and things?

DB I think it would be cosy and warm in Batman's coat. Every people in my class when they play always play Spiderman. They play SPIDER MAN JUMPING SPIDERMAN JUMPING WARRRGH WAR RRRGH WARRRGH WARRRRGH.

GPP [Pointing to a furry toy] Who's that?

DB Monkey. He says, shall we go down to my mum and dad's bed. Yes. I go with monkey. He says, daw daw dawdy dawdy. It means I WANT TO GO OUT OF BED, I WANT TO GO OUT OF BED.

GPP Do your friends like going to bed?

DB Yes. Thom-as the Tank, Tho-mas the Tank. Mar-my. Mar-my. MAR-MY!

GPP Who's this purple friend?

DB That's the baby teddy, and that's the daddy teddy.

GPP Where's the mummy?

DB They don't have a mummy.

GPP Did the mummy leave?

DB The mummy died. She went out in the road where the water was, and then she swallowed all the water all at once, and she died.

GPP After she died, where did she go?

DB [long pause] The doctor. [Voice of 'Snowy' his hand-held puppet] 'I want to live in the same flat, not separate flats.' I'll find you a flat. Come with me.

GPP When you get a flat, will your friends move in?

DB Yes. My flat will be in the fire station. Tommy, do you want to live in the fireman's flat with me, with the firemen? He said, yes please. OK.

GPP Who's going to do the tidying up in your flat?

DB Me. Wah wah wah wah wah. Dee dee. [More crazy singing and shouting]

GPP Shall we go and watch your daddy's video? You'll have to put your top back on. Do you think you could live all by yourself? Do all your shopping and stuff?

DB Yes.

GPP How would you get your money to do your shopping?

DB I would work in my dad's office, and I would just get money, buy money, and I'd get loads and loads of money to pay things with. [We go downstairs to the television room]

GPP Are remote controls good?

DB Yes.

GPP Why?

DB Because they turn it on.

Freed of our impertinent enquiries, Dexter finally settles down to watch his video. It is called *Mean Machines*, and one certain emergency service vehicle is featured heavily. We'll leave it up to you to guess which.

Bruce Reynolds

by Tom Hodgkinson

IDLER 14 · MARCH 1996

URING THE LATE NINETIES WE USED TO HOLD PARTIES at a venue and arts centre in Clerkenwell known as The Tardis. It was a meeting place for a wide range of free spirits, and it was here that I met Bruce Reynolds, whose artist son Nick, harmonica player in Alabama 3, had a studio there. Bruce Reynolds died in 2013. He was 81.

★

Escape! Adventure! Limitless cash! Bruce Reynolds, the Great Train Robber, now 65, had it all. But his quest for freedom led to frequent and lengthy spells inside. Was it worth it? Maybe ...

TH Were you ever interested in conventional jobs?

BR I started off with a regular job, I was a messenger boy at Northcliffe House, where the *Daily Mail* was, at aged 14 and a half. Then I got a job in the accounts department, and it was basically filing invoices. There must have been 100 people working in there, in long lines and all graded. You start working as a junior and get moved up. I used to look up and see the old boy who was head of the department. He was about 50 and I thought, I don't want to be like that. I was doing a lot of cycling at that time and I thought, that's what I want to do. So I left the job I was doing and got a job at a cycle firm. They had an independent team. I was more or less a bike bum. Me and a couple of other guys, we lived on nothing, we used to run up and down on the coast. And then I met what you might call my nemesis in the shape of a wide boy, then I got educated. I didn't know any criminals as such. And the life of the young outlaw appealed to me tremendously. Till I got nicked.

TH How long were you locked up for, the first time?

BR I got three years, but you could be out in nine months theoretically, if they thought you was the right material. As an outlaw, I thought, 'I've got to escape'. We had compasses, iron rations, which was chocolate stolen from the kitchen, and three of us escaped. I was the only one that got away. I left the other two out 'cos they wouldn't swim the river. I was home for about three or four days before I got nicked then I went to what was familiarly known as the Hate Factory. It was very, very tough. You could only talk to other prisoners on a Saturday afternoon. You had three library books which you couldn't change with the guy next door. And of course there was no radios then, it was 1949. The whole thing was supposedly to teach people a lesson, but what it actually did was make people harder. What do people care about society if society's never cared about them? I mean it's total nonsense, all it ever did was brutalise. As soon as I got back to borstal I was away again. Then they put me in a closed borstal. I escaped again. Escape! it's magic, romantic. And the only thing you can do on the run is a bit of crime. At the time that was basically smashing shop windows, nothing particularly skilful, but I didn't know any different. I was in London, staying in various people's places, and we got nicked on burglary charges – putting in a whole front window. I did go back into the army once and of course I ran away again and then when I got nicked, they said three years imprisonment, which was a very heavy sentence then. I went to Wandsworth. What you get of course, is you going from prep school to university. From smashing shop windows, I was talking to people who had blown safes.

TH Did you get a reputation at that point?

BR No, not really. The way you actually get on in the criminal world is to make a reputation for yourself and basically I had more bottle than anyone else. I got nicked for shoplifting and while I was away I got a contact and he said: 'I'll have you go into safe-blowing.' So when I came home I had this in mind. My closest friend at the time had moved up the criminal circle and I realised that there was a circle within the circle. I thought, that's where I gotta get.

TH Were you making money at this point?

BR Not really, no, but that's when – this is 1954 – I got introduced into the country house business which is called 'climbing'. That means you went round a house, found a ladder and opened the window. I was game for anything. If someone said they had a safe to blow I said yeah, but because you were a jewel thief your self-image was a little bit different from smashing a window. I was mixing with an older crowd at that time, who dressed well, had nice cars and I had some excellent mentors in this respect. Everything was new: I got my first car, it was a Triumph TR2 and then an Aston Martin, and I was having suits made in Savile Row.

TH   How much money were you making at that time?

BR   At my peak, which was just before I got nicked, I had three cars, including a Zodiac convertible, and I was paying about six quid a week for a flat in Streatham, which was quite a bit of money.

TH   When you were going in and out of prison, was there ever a moment when you thought, I'm going to get out of this?

BR   No. By this time I was committed to it and knew that this was where my destiny lay. I'd met enough people to see that you could make a business out of it, and that a lot of these people didn't have any brains at all. You put a little bit of skill and little bit of research and a little bit of expertise.

TH   Did you have regular hang-outs?

BR   We had one pub, the Star in Belgravia, which at that time was a bit of a hangout but all sorts of people came there. Once your reputation started then you start getting invites to things and people think oh, good worker, and also the great thing was, everyone wants to be with someone who's lucky, who is successful and if they see you're successful they think it's going to rub off on them.

TH   If you were running away from the police and you got caught, would the police beat you up?

BR   Oh yeah, badly. You bash a policeman up, they're going to bash you up. I mean that will always be the case. I had a very hard time during that three and a half years locked up. The girl I was with had an alliance with a friend of mine, who subsequently killed himself as a result of what was going on. She disappeared to America or Canada and I haven't seen her since. And this is when I had this plot to try and get some time back and had a gun brought into the prison.

TH   What do you mean 'try to get some time back?'

BR   Well, the old king of the underworld, Billy Hill, whilst he was serving his sentence, he got a pal of his to attack a screw and then Bill rescued the screw from his pal and he got six months off. So I knew that had been done a couple of times, I thought they won't wear that, but if I have a gun brought in, and make out I was disclosing an escape plot ... anyway, it went wrong, because the weekend I did it, the governor was off-duty, so when he came back Monday, the deputy governor had got all the kudos for discovering this plot. He didn't like that, the governor, so he suggested it could be a plot. To prove it wasn't a plot, I had to get someone to stab me. They moved me to Durham prison, which made me tougher, a lot more bitter. So I thought when I get home, there'd be no more messing about. Of course in that period, things had changed, the criminal climate had changed and I realised that the old ways was out.

TH What's it like, the contrast going from expensive cars and champagne to being in prison?

BR You never get used to it. When you're first nicked, you literally want to cry. Because it's all gone, you've lost everything, the women generally, and just a bare cell.

TH Can you get over-confident? If you have a string of successes?

BR You think 'I can't go wrong' and that was bullshit, you get drawn into it don't you? You think 'I can do that, I can do anything'. And that's how you get nicked. So that's what really started the confrontational aspect and then I realised that we had to organise; in other words we had to have other people with us. Initially we weren't too successful, I think we were waiting about for something and we waited too long.

TH So you're out in 1960?

BR I'm out in 1960 and I'm fully active. I had money. I went straight over to the south of France.

TH What about the money? Did people keep it for you?

BR I had bank accounts. They never used to look in the bank accounts like they do now. When I got out in 1960 I had £20,000. When I came home, I went round to see a friend, and he'd just found a piece of work that was as easy as anything. Someone was selling a house, they had an au pair girl in the house. They were away, she was there but the house was also up for sale so it's just a case of ringing up as someone who wants to look at the house. She opened the door, showed us around. I opened a cupboard and said 'What's in there?' She said, 'Nothing.' I said, 'Well there is now', and pushed her in and shut the door. There was a safe upstairs. We got £20,000. It was so easy.

TH In between doing jobs, what was your lifestyle?

BR Basically, living as expensively as I could. All the restaurants at the
time. You've always got The Caprice, not so much The Ivy; all the big
hotels. We all used to like to go to the south of France, you'd have two
or three months in the south of France.

TH A holiday?

BR Yeah but we always used to justify it as research or planning. And of
course I loved that. Cary Grant, it's just like *To Catch a Thief*.

TH Did you feel the Great Train Robbery was really going to be the big
one?

BR Yeah I did. It was my Sistine Chapel. And really everything went right.
The only problem was the fact that Mills got whacked, Mills the driver.
Everyone was under orders that he mustn't be touched because we
needed him to drive the train, even though we did have our own driver
with us.

TH How did he get whacked?

BR Well, I wasn't there. I was further up the track, identifying the train.
The train stopped. The signalman stepped down to phone the signal
box, leaving the driver in the cab. So all it needed was someone to say
'What's going on mate?' and get up on the cab and just get hold of him.
But this guy anticipated a move and instead of him getting hold of him
physically, he whacked the guy. People are nervous. He reacted. No
one could really blame him and at the time Mills was perfectly all right.
He drove the train so it wasn't that bad and there was no other gratu-
itous violence. The whole operation went well and we had approxi-
mately 30 minutes to unload. We had a trouble-free drive back to the
farmhouse. I went to bed and Buster woke me up a couple of hours
later and he said, 'It's two and a half million, mate.' I said, 'How do you
feel about that?' He said, 'Oh I think that'll do nicely.' I said, 'Yeah,
that'll do me.'

TH Did you feel at that point that you could do anything you wanted?

BR Oh yeah. What we'd done was a challenge really. The highest authority was the country, and we'd challenged the country. But none of us
envisaged the wrath that was going to fall down upon us.

TH Was it because the establishment had been humiliated?

BR Yeah, there's all of that plus you've got to remember the government
then was suffering under the Profumo scandal and they was really in a
fucking state of fucking disarray. But it's 1963, it's the first televised

crime. By this time television had just about become universal in most
homes and of course they could follow it day by day: 'Oh, another
one's been nicked.'

TH So what did you do with the money?

BR This was a big problem because it was a vast amount of money.
Everybody you knew was liable to be searched. Eventually I got a
friend of mine to buy the lease of a mews house down in South
Kensington and I moved and stayed in there until the passport came
through safely, about six months.

TH What was it like to have pulled off this amazing thing, to have all that
cash somewhere, but not be able to go out?

BR I had some freedom as I had two guys helping me. I used to give them
my shopping list at Harrods. I had a weekly order at Christophers –
used to be in Jermyn St – and I'd have a dozen bottles of champagne
and a dozen bottles of what he'd recommended, plus a little barrel of
bitter. I blew up to about 16 stone. A friend had the rest of the money,
he was putting it through to Switzerland. Which was a standard proce-
dure, you pay 10% I think. So I was imprisoned in luxury in this mews
place. My friend had flown from Elstree to Ostend to test out an escape
route. There was no customs, no passport control. I'd had an introduction to someone who supposedly knew the president of Mexico.
Mexico was the place to go.

TH You were planning to get out and stay out?

BR Oh yeah, we had the money. So Mexico. We landed at Ostend and he
said 'You go through that gateway there.' I walked through the gateway. There's no officialdom whatsoever and another one of my guys
stepped out from behind this Mercedes that he'd hired and he had a
white trench mac on. The Man From Interpol – that's who he was
playing that day. We drove into Brussels, spent the night there, flew to
Toronto, spent the night there and the next day, Mexico. I'd already
worked out I was going to stay in The Hilton because that was central.
I walked in there and had a couple of days looking around, just famil-
iarising myself with the place. I liked it. Soon I just walked into this
tailor's and the guy said 'Yes I speak English, I am English.' He'd been
born in Manchester of Syrian Jew parentage, he was multi-lingual so
we got talking and I made a friend. He introduced me to all the right
people – all the politicos, because they used to use his store and as such
I was virtually above the law even if things had gone wrong. I had a

lovely name – Keith Clement Miller. I had six Cadillacs in Mexico City.

TH How did you get the money to Mexico?

BR It was in Switzerland so all you needed to do was telephone through and get it in a bank in Mexico. And when you're abroad you're more accepted because culturally they accept people who speak like I speak. When you're travelling abroad, they don't know the class thing. If you're staying in the Metropole Hotel, same as them, you must be the same as them. We left Canada and I thought there's only one thing left to do – go back to the South of France. A good excuse. And we get a place there and work out what the next move is going to be.

TH Didn't you still have enough money to retire?

BR Not then. If I'd decided to retire when I got to Mexico, yeah, for sure. I suppose I thought to myself that the money would always be there. I was just living for the moment as much as I could and I'd always had a supreme confidence that something would turn up. I came back to this country and I didn't have very much money. We had unlimited champagne before, now we were eking out a bottle of vodka.

TH Where was the money?

BR We'd spent it in about three years. Then I did have a bit of luck. We had another big score and got 50 grand. My plan was to go to New Zealand. I knew Ronnie Biggs was in Australia and there was another group of fellas that was on the run and they was in Australia so I didn't want to go there. But I was out on something, came home, got nicked the next morning. '68. When I was nicked in Torquay I had about three grand – that's what I was down to.

TH Literally three grand in the bank, that was it?

BR Hardly even that. So, Butler, who was in charge of the case, he said we'll do you and I said, 'Well, it was all those years ago, you can't.' He said: 'Bruce, we got your fingerprints on all the labels, all the equipment, that was down at the farm.' I did buy all the equipment. Naturally I burnt all the receipts. How they got duplicates, I don't know. Not only that, he also said, 'Your wife's nicked, your dad's nicked, your stepmother's nicked' – and a great woman friend of mine who had been looking after my son – 'she's nicked. And Terry your best pal. They're all nicked for aiding and abetting and passport offences.' That's the deal he presented me with: plead not guilty and they'd all be nicked. I gave him the look; he gave me the look. I got 25 years.

TH That must have been the longest stretch you'd had. Were you able to adjust to it?

BR Of course. I went straight into maximum security. Who's in there? Charlie Richardson doing 25 years, four or five others doing life. So you're all in it together, I didn't feel that much different. In a way we're fucking different from other prisoners. We're doing in effect, longer than life sentences. Really and truly, I don't think anybody thought they were going to do that sort of time. It was outrageous, it'd never been done before. It was a crime with a minimum of violence. OK it was a lot of money but murderers were doing ten years for really violent murders so it was definitely a political thing handed down to teach them a lesson.

TH So what year did you come out?

BR In 1978 and you are totally institutionalised after ten years in prison. Your whole life's been laid out for you. You don't have to worry about food and things like that. It's all done for you. You're pampered really. If you've got a position, which I had in the nick hierarchy, you get things done for you. I never wanted for anything really. I wasn't into drugs. I started smoking cigarettes while I was away. That's one bad habit. I wasn't interested in booze. I finished off at Maidstone, which is a good prison. I had a year in the library there and a year as a gym orderly when I used to run ten miles a day, play badminton and then swim. Fucking marvellous life. All my aggro with my wife had gone so I didn't have any women worries. As we used to say, we had the best looking girls in the world. I'd swap my Mayfair with his Fiesta and that was it. Everyone had photoboards and put up pictures of their wives or girlfriends. Frank my mate used to say 'She's nice isn't she?' and 'Do you want to see my photographs of my wife?' and we'd swap them for the night. It's what we called wife swapping – only a joke. I got into smoking dope there which was a revelation. It was an absolutely marvellous time. Those two years were the happiest years of my life.

TH Really.

BR Because I had no contact really with the world. I used to have visits. A pal of mine used to fetch me up a girl so I'd be groped on visits just to make sure you were still alive. Other times, my son Nick used to come and see me, that was a different type of visit, but in the main I couldn't wait for the visit to be over to get back to my pals when we'd sit down and smoke a bit of dope in the evening. The governor of the prison

used to come round and push the doors: 'Oh it's a bit smokey in here.'
He was very liberal. When I came out I was alienated from the people
that had been my friends before because I had ten years living with
different buddies to the buddies they lived with. With my oldest and
best friend – at one particular time I would have died cheerfully for
him and he for me – it was totally different. I had nothing in common
with him. I felt really lonely. I used to walk the street at night. I used
to think, 'How can I get back in prison without making it look as if
I've volunteered myself to go back?'

TH   So you felt freer in prison?

BR   One of my friends was in the textile business and another one was part-
ners with him. That was it: I was going to go straight into the business
but within two months of my coming home, whether or not I was the
grit in the oyster I don't know, but they started to row very badly and
the partnership split up. So that lost me my safe position in the textile
business. Then I didn't know what to do. I was 46 at the time, what can
I do? Drive a car. I never saw myself as a mini-cab driver. Some people
that I'd been away with came up and said 'We've got a bit of work. Are
you interested?' It involved a major train shipment of money to
London Airport and it was half a million each. So I said, yeah. Looking
back on it there was no hesitation. I thought 'That's it, cause half a
million could set me up and if I get nicked I don't give a fuck anyway.'

Alex Chilton

by Kira Jolliffe

IDLER 15 · MAY 1996

KIRA JOLLIFFE, WHO WENT ON TO LAUNCH 'CHEAP DATE' magazine, produced this excellent interview with pop maverick Alex Chilton of Big Star. Chilton died of a heart attack in 2012. He was 59.

★

At 16, Alex Chilton achieved teenybop stardom with Sixties group the Box Tops, and later Big Star. At 20 he walked away from it all, swapping fame and fortune for obscurity, and becoming one of music's most influential cult figures. Any regrets? asks Kira Jolliffe.

KJ Do you think you're jaded?

AC Maybe in some ways. I mean, I don't look at myself that way. I know a lot of people do. I think of myself as being one of the most positive, born-yesterday sorts of people that there is, but a lot of people don't seem to think that.

KJ How do you space your time?

AC I'm lazy. That's not necessarily a good thing, I just love to be lazy. Just the business of living takes up a considerable amount of time. My year is basically spent making enough money for six months to have the next six months off. I don't feel an urge to work incredibly hard. Every six months or so I look at my situation and decide what needs to be done from there. That's about as far in advance as I think. It's the greatest existence I can have. I don't know how long it'll last, maybe I'll be back washing dishes. Having a publicist or any engine of people working around me – I'm really not interested in that.

KJ How do you regard work?

AC Everybody's got to have something productive that they do. I don't know why, but that's what I think.

KJ Are you satisfied with your work so far?

AC I wouldn't say that, I just enjoy the life I live. I wouldn't say I'm satisfied with anything I've done or anything, but I do enjoy myself.

KJ Do you think you could have achieved more?

AC Perhaps, but what would I have achieved it for? I can't think of any reason to achieve anything.

KJ You had teenybop-style fame at 16 with the Box Tops. Do you think that being so young allowed you to absorb fame better so that it hasn't mattered to you as much since?

AC Maybe. I've got nothing against a couple of million dollars coming my way tomorrow, but then again, I don't want to be some kind of megastar who can't walk down the street. I'd rather make loads of money and not be recognised anywhere.

KJ Do you ever think in a businesslike way of how to achieve that?

AC No, I don't. Being businesslike is just too much, there's no point in that.

KJ When did you realise that you didn't want too much fame?

AC A long time ago. Do you think people really want to be stars?

KJ Definitely, but maybe they don't know what it is.

AC A lot of people want to be admired, but when they become a star, all of a sudden, it's not all admiration. People who get into it don't know what they're getting into.

KJ Why are you less well known in Britain than anywhere else?

AC The music business is so strange in Britain. I've made four, five or six albums in the last ten years and they really haven't been available for the most part, and neither is my latest one. Britain is a hard place for anyone from outside to break into. If you don't have an English record company, then you're not going to sell any records in Britain, and I've never had an English record company. Other countries are not so protective in their record markets as Britain is. I think that the British think I'm some really obscure record artist just because I'm really obscure in Britain.

KJ Do you feel strongly political?

AC Well, I'm a left-winger I guess, but I don't know. Everybody sees people every day of whom they say, 'Jesus this person needs to loosen up', or 'that person needs to get it together'. I see people that I certainly have a lot of thoughts about what they're doing.

KJ Could you generalise about those people?

AC Politically I think a lot of people have been brainwashed to believe all of this free market economics stuff. That's a sort of general criticism about the population at large. They've been so propagandised by 50 years of Cold War.

KJ Are you at all religious?

AC No, I mind religions very much. That's another large criticism I have of the world. Religion, forget it. Organised or even disorganised. It creates problems everywhere because people get some kind of moral thing going on that if people are not conforming to their moral thing then they don't deserve to live. Religion is a strong promoter of that sort of thing. Man, we're sure getting heavily philosophical here.

KJ Were you brought up to live religiously?

AC No, philosophically but not religiously. Ooh, somebody just brought a big bottle of wine into my space.

KJ So it sounds like you're not into AA or anything?

AC No. I was a heavy drinker for about ten years.

KJ Was giving up drinking difficult?

AC No, not in the least. Quitting drinking was easy. It wasn't like I was quitting something that I really loved. It's sort of a habit that people get into. Once again there's all this propaganda around to make people think that drinking is fun. In one way it is, but in ten other ways it's really not. And drinking too much is not going to be a pleasurable experience for anyone who does it. It's like any other drug. If you do too much, it kind of takes over, and you're not you any more, you're the drug that you're on and, I don't know, there's endless bad things to say about drinking, but you know, if somebody enjoys doing it, let them. It was in the early Eighties that I quit drinking, I caught a cold or something one time and it was sort of severe probably because I'd been drinking so much. It took me maybe two weeks to get well, and at the end I remarked to myself that it had been ten years since I'd been two weeks without drinking. I just thought, well it's been two weeks, might as well make it a month.

KJ You see the same self-delusion with pot-heads who think it's not affecting them, and they only realise after they've stopped.

AC Well, yeah, I think pot's okay. I agree with what you say, but when you put it on a scale next to drinking, on a scale of badness, I think pot is minuscule by comparison. Maybe some people do get extra lazy and sometimes the pressure of daily affairs is a little too stressful for them. They would however still have obstacles in their way even without the pot. Pot just makes them more afraid of them.

KJ   What did you do after you quit drinking?

AC   Moved to New Orleans. Maybe a year or so I didn't really play music, I had several odd jobs around town like washing dishes. I'd been getting by in various ways and music kind of slipped away.

KJ   Is music your *raison d'être*?

AC   No, not really, it's just what I do.

KJ   Why did you get into music in the first place?

AC   Dad was a jazz player, it wasn't something he made a living doing but he played. There was always a jazz band playing round at our house and at the age of eight I would often go to sleep to the sound of them playing. It was kind of cool. I'd been hanging out with old jazz musicians all my life, and then The Beatles came along. I got very caught up in it. I was 13 years old and I loved it. It made me buy a guitar and try to learn how to play. I got active about being interested in music.

KJ   Where are you living now?

AC   New Orleans. Just bought an old place there. As I get the notion to do it up ... It takes effort to do that, and once it's done, then a lot of good things can flow from that ... having a little fortress all of one's own. I've spent time just finding a place to live and settle down. I was unsettled ... spending six months in Tennessee and six months in New Orleans, dreaming about spending half my year in Peru.

KJ   What are you up to these days?

AC   Nothing much, really, I don't have any plans or any projects.

John Michell

by Tom Hodgkinson

IDLER 16 · JULY 1996

MYSTIC, PHILOSOPHER, SOCRATIC QUESTIONER OF received opinion, John Michell, who died in 2009, was a kind and cheering man. You would walk away from a meeting with him feeling energised and positive.

★

John Michell is a writer and thinker who has explored the worlds of UFOs, corn circles and most recently, the questions surrounding the authorship of Shakespeare. He explained the universe to us while sitting at the table in his West London flat.

TH What led to your obsessions?

JM I think there was a big rift between authority and what was actually happening with the UFO thing in the Fifties. It showed people, really for the first time, that the world is not entirely explained. When people heard the government's, the authorities' reactions of denial, a lot of people knew for themselves that things weren't so much in control as they'd been bought up to think. And the further you go the more you find that the whole world is one big mystery, and everything in it, and in almost every subject the orthodoxy is either arbitrary or completely wrong. No one knows any more now than they did in the beginning about the UFO thing, except that it continues folklore themes. It's as if that other world, which we thought we'd banished in the Age of Reason, found its way back in the UFO framework.

TH Is one of the attractions of the UFO that it offers a synthesis of science and religion?

John Mitchell in his Powis Square flat. [Julia Hember]

JM It leads to broadening one's outlook and the inclusion of mystery in
    one's view of the world. Again, as with so many of these subjects, crop
    circles for example, it's not so much the thing itself, as what it leads to.
    Does it lead people to take a wider interest in the world generally? The
    effect of all these things is beneficial, but I imagine they're all part of an
    inevitable process. When you get extreme rationalism, the opposite
    breaks in.

TH Do you think that this extreme rationalism has got worse or better?

JM It's certainly untenable now, isn't it? You see orthodoxy in all kinds of
    fields challenged in way which would've been inconceivable 30 years
    ago. Institutions have largely lost confidence in themselves, and one
    sees more and more clearly that the first principle in world order is
    confusion. Once you get beyond evil conspiracies, you see confusion.

TH So the paternal structures were noticeably stronger in the Fifties?

JM Oh yes, the line was being held quite well through the Fifties. Then it notably crumbled in the Sixties with new music, new drugs and so on. It takes a long time for changes to make themselves visible in say the education system, because people have vested interests in keeping the thing going as it was before.

TH People who challenge orthodoxies often seem to challenge the idea that it's good to work hard and have a steady job.

JM It is good to work hard and have a steady job, if you can stand it, and people who do it are very good people. But I feel they are in need of something better. People say, oh everyone's so greedy nowadays, but it's what you're meant to be, isn't it? I think society can demand a lot of people before there's a spontaneous reaction or refusal. People will keep going under all kinds of evil tyrannies. But luckily they don't last very long. Human nature always outlives every system imposed upon it.

TH So you don't think things are getting worse?

JM In some ways things are getting worse. But then I think everything is more or less as it has to be, that one process follows another, rather like the processes of alchemy – separation, split, break down, coming together – one situation inevitably leads to the next one. I've now become very accepting, it's all in the hands of the gods, and perhaps the less we interfere, the better, or at least it's better to be rather careful before one interferes with one's wonderful notions, revolutionary ideas and alternative systems. If one insists on them, one becomes obsessed and in danger of frustrating God's will, as it were. In the Sixties and Seventies, when people seemed to be much more politically alert and optimistic, then a lot of effort was wasted in street political activity and protest. I suppose it all has to be, but personally I rather kept out of it, because it didn't seem to be effective. It seemed to me that this effort could be better spent elsewhere. The most radical change has to be a completely different basis for looking at the world, a different image of the world altogether. Until the whole system of values is changed and a more natural and balanced view is established, local actions won't make any difference. Then I was doing much what I do now, which is talking and writing. I had a campaign for traditional measures, the Stand Up For the Foot campaign, largely on the grounds that our measures are ancient cosmological measures which relate human beings and their functions to our surroundings and the whole universe. Also a sort of literary campaign against Darwinian evolution. When you write about that, that gets the biggest response, usually a very angry one. The whole evolutionist idea is towards movement and progress, so it has supported the scientific belief in progress, the colonial belief in progress, and indeed the racial belief in progress: there was indeed an established religious belief that the rational white man would take over the world, and the others would lose out in the evolutionary arms race.

TH   Science has that idea of going towards a final point, where everything will be finally explained.

JM   There's a touch of Marxism in that, of moving towards the perfectly rational, atheistic state. Marx called for the clearing of whole continents for rational agriculture. What kind of agricultural boom can arise out of that? That's the attitude of mind which created the problem.

TH   Did your questioning of evolution come from an objection to the state of mind that believing in evolution led to?

JM   Indeed, yes. I don't think it works on a biological level – there's simply no good evidence for it – but when it becomes a paradigm, a metaphor for the state of the world generally, it becomes destructive. Destructive of clear thinking, as everything is projected into the future. The man who said, 'be here now' had the right slogan.

TH   That's one of the things about lazing around and doing nothing. The ideas of 'work' and 'working towards something' are pretty entwined in each other. So people who are working are working towards the point where they can buy their own house, or earn x amount of money – after that point everything will be fine. Always deferring. But staring out of the window, a completely useless activity in those sorts of terms, that does mean you're living in the moment.

JM   It's like Krishnamurti said, it's better to do nothing than to do something.

TH   That's good. We'll put it in our Idler book.

JM   As Plato said, things are better taken care of than you can possibly imagine. An Indian told me that you've got to live in paradise now, ha ha. That is the only practical way of living, to live in God's paradise.

TH   What one detects now is people stepping outside the political process, no longer believing that it can change things …

JM   … to the fury of all the political parties, and the incredible propaganda and abuse which the travellers had – it borders upon the Nazi treatment of the travellers and minorities. It's less excusable, even, because we've got their example. Propaganda is easier now, because the mass media is so powerful and easily manipulated, and turned to hate. When you read these horror reports of Ecstasy deaths you find they drunk 20 special brews beforehand, or something like that. The government shouldn't really concern itself with drugs because it only creates problems. That seems to be historically demonstrated: whenever you get clampdowns you get a problem. Before drugs were illegal, opium and cannabis were freely available and no one really thought much about it. The laws have created the drug hysteria which is entirely motivated by emotion and political advantage-taking, point-scoring. I think all drugs have their uses, as long as they're used creatively. It's when they're used idly – or purely sensually, for raving and so on, that they can waste the spirit. Speed has a bad reputation, but a lot of writers and painters and others have worked with it, and benefited from it, and taken the consequences – of tiredness, loss of spirit and such.

TH I've noticed you use the word spirit quite a lot. What does it mean to you, and its relation to 'spiritual'?

JM There's spirit, as in the word 'spirited', and spirit is morally neutral, it can take different forms. It's energy and activity, we talk of people being good-spirited, their interests seem to be engaged, and they speak in lively voices, rather than an apologetic mumble. So whatever wakes you up. What I'm really interested in is the kind of science you get, for example, when you study the dimensions of the Great Pyramid, or Stonehenge, or any relic of the ancient science. And indeed the constitution of ancient societies. I'm interested in a real human-centred constant view of the world, as opposed to empirical science with its fantasies of black holes and so on.

TH In your book *Who Wrote Shakespeare?* you seemed to be saying that what's interesting is that all these different things exist at once; not arguing that one is more true than another.

JM It always fascinates me that from the same data, rather limited data in the case of Shakespeare, that people of much the same education and background can arrive at completely different beliefs and then hold onto them with the force of religious faith, and quite unworried by the fact that other people who have studied the subject have come up with quite different ideas. They get a little hurt sometimes, and angry, thinking that people are being mischievous or stupid by not seeing it their way. It's so easy to follow a belief and then become slightly dependent on it.

TH How have you avoided that?

JM By assuming that there's nothing firm to believe in, except for exis-tence itself. All theories are just products of the mind. The ones that exclude least last longest.

TH You know there's this neo-Luddite movement in the States?

JM Yes, Kirkpatrick Sale, the computer smasher. Great man.

TH But the original Luddites weren't so much against technology per se, but the way it was being used by the capitalist mill owners.

JM Yes, but the two are related, aren't they? It degraded work. When I was at school, they explained how stupid and ignorant the Luddites were, how they couldn't see that they were going to get good employment from this stuff. I couldn't argue against it at the time, but I wasn't con-vinced by it. But now my sympathies are with good Ned Ludd. People in offices stare at screens, but before they used to be discussing things. They might have looked idle, as if they were wasting time, but in fact this was a creative process. Now there's no communication, nobody knows what's going on, and when a computer goes down they're left helpless – can't stick two bits of paper together.

TH In some workplaces, people don't like it if they think that someone else is enjoying themselves or is having a better time.

JM I think the level of cheerfulness is abnormally low – the accepted state of mind is artificially low. People getting on well and being happy and cheerful seems to attract suspicion. And then the convention now, much encouraged by television I suppose, is to look for causes for self-pity. The more self-pity you can get up, the more pleased with your-self you should be. The more grievances they can have the better they're doing. But it just doesn't, as a matter of fact, get you anywhere – in fact it stops you from doing anything. You see that a lot in psychi-atry, I think, people are encouraged to harbour their own grievances and problems instead of not worrying about them. In near-death expe-riences, what seems to be common to them all, is that when the people come back they say: stop worrying, there's nothing to worry about. Stop taking it all seriously. The only practical way of living is as an ide-alist. Because everything else is setting one's sights too low. There's no shame in falling short of a high ideal but it's ridiculous to be content with … oh, I'm talking at random now, so I'll shut up, I think!

John Cooper Clarke

by Tom Hodgkinson

IDLER 17 · NOVEMBER 1996

JOHN COOPER CLARKE IS ONE OF THE FUNNIEST PEOPLE on the earth. Just being near him makes you laugh. When organising this interview, he said his condition was that we would drink Vodka Martinis at the Groucho Club. And we did manage to arrange that. We got very drunk and were thrown out at about one in the morning.

★

From his early days as a pep pill swallowing mod, John Cooper Clarke, Manchester's legendary poet, performer, writer and comedian, has always looked good and lived well. He took the train down to London from Colchester, where he now lives with his wife and daughter for an afternoon of chat and Vodka Martinis.

VODKA MARTINI ONE: Pictures are taken at the Café Royal.
VODKA MARTINI TWO: 5pm. Soho drinking club. Studying the Vodka Martinis before us.
JCC The closer to ether a drink is, the better. One stage further and that would be a gas.
TH So ... what's your relationship with idleness?
JCC Me and idleness go way back. I've had a few jobs, but if you want to be a writer, you're better off getting a job that doesn't require that you do anything. There used to be a lot of these jobs around. The best one I had was as a firewatcher on Plymouth docks. I had to be there, but once I was there, there was nothing to do. It's ideal because you're not surrounded by distractions of your own choice. You're doing the Graham

John Cooper Clarke at the Café Royal. [Julia Hember]

Greene thing ... you're going in at nine and coming back at five and that's a long time to write. Some of it's good, some of it's shite. It's a lot easier to write under those circumstances than it is when you're a completely free man. You can always find something better to do than writing when you're at home.

TH We're interested in people who stick to their own path ...

JCC ... and create that idle world, which is quite a job in itself. I wish I had a modus operandi for that, but sadly it's an intuitive thing, instinctive. Idleness is the poet's friend, but enforced idleness. A job that you have to go to, but not necessarily do anything.

TH What other sort of jobs have you had?

JCC My first job was as an apprentice motor mechanic, just after I left school in the mid-Sixties. Things get pathologized today, don't they, but this was pre-patholigization. Everyone in our class had an amphetamine habit, but we didn't see it like that. All our mums had a prescription for amphetamines. They were called pep pills. They were an aid to modern life, they were a labour-saving device. They weren't looked upon as drugs. It was no big deal. When I got this job, I thought I'd better knock it on the head. I gave up the pep pills. Then I got peripheral hallucinations. I'd see a hedgehog running along the skirting board, then I'd do a double take and it wasn't there at all. Little animals running up and down your shirt sleeves. So little things were pathologized, I didn't equate the two.

TH So what did you think it was?

JCC I thought I was going mad. I went to the doctor's. I'd only been working six weeks at the time. I said, 'I can't cope, doctor, y'know. What's wrong with me?' I told him the symptoms: little animals running up and down my shirt sleeves; peripheral hallucinations of small furry or spikey creatures running along the skirting board, but upon further inspection they weren't there at all. The doctor immediately says, 'Oh, you've been taking too many pep pills.' It shows you how attitudes have changed. It was a question of quantity: not, you shouldn't take amphetamines, but, you've been taking too many. Anyway, he said, 'You'd better take a couple of weeks off', and he gave me some downers. He wrote me out a sick note and I wish I'd framed it. He handed me the sick note and there it was, 'amphetamine psychosis'. I gave it to the foreman, Mr Jeffries. He looked at it and said, 'amphetamine psychosis, eh. My wife had that. She were right poorly with it'. [Laughter]

TH That suggests there was much less moralising about that sort of thing.

JCC It was just a question of quantity. Don't get on a 12 step programme. People ask me how I stay thin. It's a strict regime. It's a combination of supervised fad diets and amphetamines. I took them all through the Sixties, but if you'd told me I was a drug addict, I'd have laughed in your face. I think it's the most harmless drug isn't it? It's a high achiever's drug. Jean-Paul Sartre ... you wouldn't have any of that stuff. The whole of the Second World War was run on amphetamines. The RAF, American air force alike. Without amphetamines we'd have been under the jackboot. We'd all have been on methadone ... Hitler invented methadone. The opiate supply routes were cut off, and they had to invent an opiate substitute like, rapid style.

TH What else did you get up to in the Sixties?

JCC I was a mod ... it's the only youth cult I've ever actually been a wholehearted member of. The great thing about mod was that it was a very snobbish movement. We went to a club in Manchester called the Twisted Wheel ... it was the mod club of the country. We used to get people from all over. It was the first place I heard soul music. You never heard any guitar music there; it was all Stax, Motown, Memphis Horns, Booker T and the MGs. Guitar solos not allowed. Strict dress codes, no guitars. At the Twisted Wheel, by 1965, you didn't actually call yourself a mod any more. People in Burnley called themselves mods, people with targets on their parkas. We called ourselves 'stylists', and shoplifting was the big national sport of the stylists. You'd go to John Michael and pinch things: £80 sunglasses. It was a full-time job. Food wasn't high on the agenda, there was no hip food. You blew your wad on cloth, not even records.

TH   And when did you get into writing and performing?

JCC In the mid-Seventies. I was trying to get a career going as a nightclub performer. I wasn't particularly interested in progressive rock, and so for a while my social life suffered. Everybody lost it in the Seventies, except Frank Sinatra and Jack Lemmon. They were the two guys who looked OK, even in the Seventies. Everybody lost it. All that denim. Awful bands like Barclay James Harvest. I already wrote poetry, and I thought maybe this could be put in a nightclub context and be funny. There was a thriving club circuit. I did manage to get a residency at this club called Mr Smith's. They'd have Shirley Bassey, Matt Munro ... top acts. I got £30 for a 20-minute set: that was an engineer's wage. Then I met Howard Devoto and Pete Shelley. And punk didn't look that outrageous to me. I slotted in. I was wearing three-button suits with narrow skinny trousers, skinny tie and Perry Como haircut. At the time it came across as quite unusual, because then middle management were wearing mustard-coloured flares. Howard said, you should do some of these punk rock gigs, John. I'd heard the term but equated it more with the American side of things. He said, come to the Free Trade Hall and play with the Sex Pistols. I did a couple of support slots for the Buzzcocks, and it got me out of Manchester, and then around the world. So, great, thanks Howard, thanks Pete. It was right place, right time, I looked right, my face fitted.

TH   You were never attracted by the hippy stuff?

JCC Oh yeah, my first wife was the last of the flower children. She took acid every day of her life. I was on nodding acquaintance with it, I just didn't like the clothes, but y'know, the free love, the drugs ... OK, I'll go along with it that far. But, you know, everyone judges by appearances. It's a pity that people didn't judge by appearances in 1936 Germany, then they'd have known Hitler was a cunt ... ha ha.

TH It was important for Baudelaire and that lot.

JCC People are going to want to know, if someone looks good, what do they do. It's important.

TH In a way, the aristocratic ideal – not in the class sense – seems to be available to more people nowadays.

JCC Yes, the aristocratic disdain for work. It's the one legacy they've left that's really worth something. But the aristocracy aren't like that now. They're always at great pains to point out the good works that they do. Which I think is a mistake, I think they should be more unapologetic about it.

VODKA MARTINI THREE

JCC People age better now than they used to. Marianne Faithfull looks fabulous. Some people can just do it.

TH It gives the lie to the idea that people who have had a druggy or wild lifestyle age badly. If you become bitter and vain or bored, that might be more ageing.

JCC [Possibly mishearing 'bored' as 'bald'] Baldness used to be the kiss of death as far as pulling was concerned. It was time to buy the mustard cardigan and the gardening supplies. You go bald now and it's not the end of the world. It's all down to role models. There are people who look like that who are cool people. It's a lot easier now than it used to be. That's why Frank at 80 is the fanny-magnet he always was. You know what I mean? Your bird runs off with someone like Frank, don't lose too much sleep over it. What a guy. That's the thing, the world of men and the world of women. My parents, God rest their souls, are a case in point. If they were to be evaluated today, you would say that I come from a dysfunctional family. But nothing could be further from the truth. My dad went out drinking every day of his life. Weekends, afternoons as well – I'm a working class guy but my dad was well paid, an engineer. But we were never without nothing. People like me, guys of my age, really don't have any quibbles. We've had the best of every-thing. Welfare state, good education. I went to a secondary modern, but by today's standards, it's like going to Oxford or Cambridge. It was rammed down our throats. You will be educated. You don't like

Shakespeare now, *you will*. Thanks, guys. I'm glad you did it. I'll never
be able to repay the debt. Council house. I had TB when I was five – I
wouldn't be alive if it weren't for the welfare state. That's why I'll
always vote Labour. For that alone. Thank you Mr Atlee. And thanks
to all those guys who fought Hitler.

TH Do you have quibbles about that way things are now?

JCC No, how can I? I'm not having a bad time. It's up to the young people
to complain about how things are now. But then there was the world
of men, and the world of women. The issue of divorce never came into
it. Not just us – we were a Catholic-Jewish family. They were both
perfectly happy. My mum met my dad 'cause she was a barmaid. My
mum never had a drink, only at Christmas and then under duress. I
never saw my dad drunk, and that says it all. There's a guy who goes
out seven days a week, and I've never seen him drunk. Before my first
job, I was a bookie's runner. When other kids had paper rounds, I was
a bookie's runner. I was the richest 12-year-old in the neighbourhood.
I used to go the kids' matinée with a box of Black Magic.

TH So you've always been quite a sophisticate?

JCC Kind of. I'd get money for taking the bets, and then if someone comes
up good, they've got to give you a treat. I was on more money at 12-
years-old than when I left school. I had to take a drop in my living
standards when I started working. So I was going in pubs when I was
12. It was the mysterious world of men. These guys playing cards. I
always dug that. They were all real good dressers. Tasty geezers, do you
know what I mean?

TH One of our concerns at the *Idler* is how to live well; that's more important than fame and fortune.

JCC My best mate, Rick Goldstraw, lives like an aristocrat in the true sense
of the word. And the man is penniless.

TH How does he do it?

JCC Well, that's what makes him an artist. He's got to speak for himself, but
he's one of the great unsung heroes. Every hundred years you get
someone who is a true aesthete and who is a heterosexual. And that's
Rick Goldstraw. He's a Renaissance guy. He can paint, he can write
poetry, he can write songs. He's a rock'n'roll hero but he's just too
good for the world. The population at large is never ready for this type
of person in their own lifetime. He is role model number one to me.
The way he dresses, he's the tastiest cunt I could name. He ran a club in

Manchester, the Russell Club in Hulme, a very rough West Indian club. It started off as a bus drivers' social club. Eric put on some of their best acts, Link Wray, David Johanssen band, the Only Ones, Johnny Thunders. He met all these people and he got on with them seamlessly. He didn't have a name, but he got on with them. He knew where they were coming from. Secondary modern, Catholic education, Manchester guy. He's a truly tasty geezer. I've known him since the hippy years. He's never worked, he always looks good. That guy taught me how to be idle. But he'll never be famous because he's not a career person. I sometimes like to think I'm not a career person, and I'm not, but compared to him I'm a hot shot. His only brush with fame was playing with The Fall for a while, and then with the Blue Orchids. They played behind Nico for a while.

TH   I suppose if you're idle to your bones, then you wouldn't be interested in having money and being famous.

JCC When you're a poet you have this frisson, that you're entitled to idleness. Because that's what you do for a living. But you've got to have one foot in the ordinary life. You've got to brush up against authority ... you know, I'm not really allowed in this place. I love this place [the Groucho Club] ... but I haven't really achieved enough to be able to walk in here and go, 'hi, everybody!' But that's good for a poet, you've got to have that outsider status. If you're inside, what do you write about? How everybody's your mate and life couldn't be better ... who wants to read about that shit? It's like, I'm 45 and I still don't get no respect. I always thought you got to 45, and then people respected you 'cos you're 45. I don't get it, because I don't really look for it, so I still get treated like a juvenile delinquent. No one's ever used the term 'venerable' about me. The Rick Goldstraws of this world, they will never have their due in their lifetime. He's just too tasty. Too cool. He had a great image. He looked like Johnny Thunders ten years before Johnny Thunders. Did you meet Johnny ever? He must be one of the *Idler*'s role models. I spend a lot of time looking in the mirror; I think about clothes all the time. I always have. I wake up in the morning and the first thing I think about is what I'm going to wear. It's never left me, that. That keeps me in bed. I don't want to put something on and then have to change. I'll work it out now, and that's the look of the day. It never goes away, that. You think about what you've gotta do. I could wear this, but that means I've got to check it up every so often in the toilet. This outfit I've got on now, it's smart but it's easily maintained. I've got a wardrobe full of suits but they're all the same. I reckon by the time you're 45 you know what you want to look like. They're all three-button jackets. I'm pretty conservative. One thing I've got on my side is being thin: if you're thin you can kind of wear anything. You know Kramer in Seinfeld – he always looks great. He wears a lot of those zip tops. The zip jackets are always made of gabardine – have you noticed that? – and gabardine hangs off your shoulders. Which polyester will never do. Materials is the thing. Jerry Lewis is another good sartorial role model. The look I like is that natural shoulder. The main thing to bear in mind is that the hips should be narrower than the shoulders. So if you are a thin guy, you should wear as natural a shoulder as you can get away with. And Kramer has obviously read a few tips. Have you read *An Englishman's Suit* by Sir Hardy Amies? That's indispensable. He's the guy who took Savile Row on to the High Street. He's the guy. Even Frank took to the Anglophile image. Put that at the top of the list – *An Englishman's Suit*.

Vodka Martini four: Chris Evans, a JCC fan, appears and is overjoyed to bump into his hero. 'Buy this man a drink!' he shouts.
Vodka Martini Five: JCC realises he isn't going to make it back to Colchester in time for tea. Drinks are spilled; politics talked.
Vodka Martini Six: JCC realises that not only has he missed his tea, but also he is not going to make it back to Colchester that night at all.
Vodka Martini Seven: We are encouraged to go home. Pay the bill. Gasp.
Cab Home: We dance around in my front room to The Beatles.
Following Morning: Find JCC asleep on my compact two-seater sofa. He is still wearing his shades. Wake him.

JCC [Having extricated his lanky frame from an unappealing looking sleeping arrangement] That is the smallest sofa in the world.
TH Why didn't you take the cushions off it and put them on the floor and sleep there?
JCC [Pause for thought] That's why you went to grammar school and I went to the secondary modern ...

Suggs

by Tom Hodgkinson

IDLER 18 · 1997

THIS INTERVIEW TOOK PLACE IN A PUB IN KENSINGTON.
Suggs is immensely likeable and charming.

★

In the pub at teatime with Suggs, and he's been drinking since lunch.
Pop's greatest boozer, loafer and nutty professor shares his philosophy,
such as it is, for the edification of *Idler* readers.

TH Have you always had a boozy lifestyle?
 S There's never been anyone more idle than me in the history of the
human race. The only reason why I became famous was so I didn't have
to work; I really tried hard at that. I remember it was halfway through
a sociology lesson. I was arguing with the teacher, because she said men
and women are equal. I said, well, not if they're putting the shot. I was
sent out of the class for being ideologically incorrect. It was while I
was wandering around that afternoon that I realised I wasn't cut out for
the real world, I was never going to get on. It's all that agreeing you
have to do. It's like chaos theory; all the bits that don't fit in are pushed
to one side, but in fact they're the interesting, important bits. The
Victorian thing was to quantify everything and subjugate nature.
They did, amazingly, but there were still those bits of grass poking up
between the paving stones, and the fact that they were whacking themselves with table tennis bats on their penises at night ... It's like calcu-
lus, the 0.23222 at the end, which doesn't quite fit, so they go, fuck
that; we'll chop it off. I was that 0.23222 ...
TH Being in a band is a good way of doing it, because that kind of behav-

iour is excused.

s   There's nothing more peculiar than a punctual pop star. Apparently Liam Gallagher is very punctual, that sets the whole thing wonky. Punctually having fights ... My mum's a drinker – I don't think it's as romantic as it's made out to be, and I hate the idea of advocating being a lazy boozer ... but there is a philosophy in it. Because there is a certain amount of work involved. Enabling yourself to be in the pub all afternoon means you've got to have some money; and no responsibilities. That's a contradiction in itself – money and no responsibilities. You're either a Lord, or you're on the dole, but if you're on the dole, you can't afford to sit in the pub all day. The undercurrent of society, the black market, drug-dealing and all that: that really is the fundament of everyday life. It's not on the records.

TH   At the same time, as the government renews its efforts to crack down on the evil pushers poisoning our children, John Major gets up on stage and says Britain is swinging again, our pop culture rules the airwaves ... taking the credit for things that start underground and thrive *despite* government policies.

s   Absolutely right. Most music forms at their core are to do with some sort of drug. R&B was booze, bourbon, maybe a bit of speed; jazz was heroin. With Ecstasy, there's a lot of misinformation. I had a dalliance with that stuff, but the trouble is it burns your brains out. A whole week's enjoyment in six hours, someone's gonna pay. I lost me marbles a bit. Burnt out, no thought processes left. You're just left with paranoia and neuroses, the ones that happen naturally, that don't need any encouragement. You're just left with the hollow bit underneath. Good fun, though, good fun.

TH   People always go back to drinking in the end, don't they?

s   Really it's simple, isn't it? You go in the pub, you have a pint of beer, you feel better. You don't have to hang around on street corners with weird blokes talking strange languages and buying things where you don't even know what you're taking. There's a pub right there – get a pint of beer and feel better. When you see old blokes in pubs who don't say very much – well, there isn't that much to say, actually. Another pint please. Who's going to win at 4.30 at Haydock? Life should be simplified as much as possible. That's what I found out. You go back to the simple pleasures. It's not even a philosophy. It would be too pretentious to imagine that I had a philosophy.

TH Sounds like Tao.

s Yes: it is, as it is. You do feel happy when you go in the pub. If you find yourself drinking before midday too often, then stop, 'cos that's a problem. It's that sledgehammer mentality – sledgehammer to crack a walnut. No one can be bothered will all the subtlety and detail – cigarettes are drugs, aspirin are drugs. Same with booze – but not every night of the week. It's the same with my idleness: one, two, three days I can stay in bed till midday, and then my wife starts going completely mad, as we have kids. And then you get up and say wa-hay! She says, that's enough, and it is enough. If you get over a few bumpy bits, your mind does say go home at eleven, and you really want to go home. And Sunday comes and you don't want to go out on the piss again, so you put your feet up. And you know it's going to be the same conversation again, so at least leave it a few days. The thing about pubs is, for instance, if pubs sold green gas that came out the pipes, we'd all be standing round breathing green gas. It would be peculiar wouldn't it, all these people coming from their enormously comfortable homes, to sit in all these horribly smelly smoky places. But because it's so ingrained, you take it for granted. Some are getting fancy with their food, but on the whole, they have the worst food, and all the curtains are shut.

TH The ones that are open are annoying, because when I was a kid you would wonder what was going on in there. Now the kids can see how sad pubs actually are.

s The Churchill Arms round here, which has a load of old geezers who sit there every day. Camden Town has gone peculiar, they picked the worst pub in the world to popularise. Now it's packed with French students. It's The Spreadeagle. 500 people go there to have a quiet drink. There's fucking bouncers outside The Spreadeagle now on Fridays. I've been pushed further and further out, now I'm at the Edinburgh Castle which is the last pub before you get to Regents Park. But you can sit down there, you can play pool and it's not packed. The Dublin Castle I used to like, but it's like a homage to Madness in there, so it's hard to have a quiet drink.

TH So you've gone through different stages of fame ...

s The little fame I've had is perfect, because more often than not, I'll get into a conversation with someone who's all right. I lived in the same street for most of it. At the height of Madness it was a bit mad, then I had five or six years of anonymity. The height of Madness was the most unpleasant in terms of fame, not being able to go out, people outside the front door. I need some failure on anything I do, to offset the success. Don't be too cool, or you've fucked it. That's just right for me. But you're got to aim up there, and you might get halfway. But you might get there, if you're not careful! But the whole thing can eat you up, always comparing yourself to your contemporaries and young bands. Reviews. Today, who gives a fuck, but at the time you're mortally wounded. There's also a feeling that you want to do what you do the best you possibly can, which I've always avoided as well. Apparently there's a lot of satisfaction in that. The only thing I do with any real commitment is write lyrics and perform.

TH Madness lyrics are quite outstanding compared to most bands.

s   There's got to be some love there, Madness's strongest feature was self-deprecation, a legacy I've tried to hold on to. Because that is what saves you from the lunacy of it all.

TH What about working with a group of people versus working on your own?

s   It's very different. Lonelier, eh, strangely enough. I don't miss the rows and all the intensity, the meeting about the meeting about the meeting, and all that. It was very lucky though, Madness, it just happened, there was no planning. The difference is that when you're on your own you have to plan a bit more. [Suggs goes to the loo. Returns.] I tell you what would make a great radio series – recording sounds of men in the urinal. There's always that whistling [whistles], big fart [big fart noise], big sigh – weary of the world, that semi-orgasmic 'wooargh'.

TH It was interesting that you chose to cover John Lennon's 'I'm Only Sleeping'.

s   I'm sure he was being ironic, but at the same time there was that attitude. Paul McCartney had a real work ethic. John Lennon would turn up late, write his songs at the last minute. To write a song about sleeping, especially in England in the Sixties, must have been disgusting, work of the devil. He wrote another one 'Watching The Wheels Go Round'. That was the same, it was about how he'd been out of the music business, and people kept saying to him, why don't you do something?

TH Did you have that?

s   I had a bit of that. But I'm a singer, I sing in the bath, I sing in the park,

I'm not not singing just because I'm not singing to a huge audience. When Madness ended, there was no great plan, it just ended one drizzly afternoon on the Caledonian Road. Mike the keyboard player had gone, there were four of us left, and I thought this isn't it anymore. I walked home and for about two years didn't know what we were going to do. The money was trickling in. There's a reasonable income. The Finsbury Park things are very reasonable – they keep us going for six months or so, idling. In the meantime you've got all that time. We're wondering whether to do another record. Obviously, we're not round each other's houses every day, as we were when we were 17. Also, what endeared people to Madness was that it wasn't planned. The videos *were* fun, we weren't just trying to have fun. With seven extroverts, something was bound to happen.

The Real Kramer

by Louis Theroux

IDLER 20 · WINTER 1997

LOUIS THEROUX SENT THIS STORY IN FROM NEW YORK. Kramer is a real idler hero, and so it was a pleasure to feature the character who inspired him. And Louis did a fantastic job.

★

The scene is the health club of a luxury apartment complex on Manhattan's West Side. I am about to experience a jacuzzi in the company of Kenny Kramer, the real-life model for *Seinfeld*'s Cosmo Kramer. The gymnasium is fabulously appointed. Two jacuzzis the size of paddling pools. A pool so big I can't see all the way to the other side.

Kenny and I have just emerged from the locker room dressed in our swimming trunks.

'Okay, we have to get our hair wet so they think we've had a shower. I generally fake this. Dancing in! Dancing out!'

This last part Kenny sings as he passes momentarily under a shower head.

Some background on Kenny: in the Eighties he did stand-up comedy and lived next door to Larry David, *Seinfeld*'s co-creator. (David is himself the real-life model for George.) When David was coming up with characters for the show, he proposed basing Jerry's 'wacky neighbour' on his own real-life wacky neighbour. Naturally enough, Kenny was keen to play himself in the series, even though he had no acting experience. The part went to Michael Richards instead. But a short five or so years later, Kenny figured out a way to cash in. He started up Kramer's Reality Tour, a bus trip round some of the New York landmarks the show has made famous, hosted by Kenny.

If it sound like a scam, it really isn't. Kenny's bona fides are beyond doubt. Larry David has plundered their shared history for plotlines and used bits of Kenny's character, so it only seems fair that Kenny should do the same. Item: the episode about George's Chinese remedy for baldness is based in fact. And Kenny still has a video of Larry David's pre-treatment bald head, taped as a point of comparison to see if the remedy was working. Like Cosmo, Kenny has had numerous get-rich-quick schemes. Though he never actually proposed a coffee table book about coffee tables, he did used to flog electronic disco jewellery *and* record jingles in his apartment.

K [Luxuriating in hot bubbling water.] This event takes place once a day, minimum. Sometimes twice. Sometimes I'll start the day with a jacuzzi and top it off with another one at night. In between, I go for a little swim, a little running and perhaps we'll take a little steam and sauna. But real men sweat together naked. That's what real men do.

I am bobbing about a little bit aimlessly, trying not to get my tape recorder wet. I love jacuzzis in theory but I'm never sure what to do when I'm in one. Also, I prune very easily.

LT Do you like the show, Kenny?

K Oh yeah! I love it!

LT Have you seen all 163 episodes?

K Every single one – more than once! Do you have a jet on your back? [His tone is becoming slightly professorial.] Now each jacuzzi has several jets. So if you check around and notice each jet – like this [pointing at a jet indistinguishable from any of the others] is one of my favourite jets right here.
[We relocate to the second jacuzzi.]

LT What are we feeling?

K We're feeling about 104 degrees right no. Okay, let's take a minute or two because this is really what it's supposed to be. Mmmm!

LT Aaargh! Man! It's like *too* hot, though.

K No, not when your body gets used to it.

LT How much of the other Kramer is you?

K Well, you know, the character is based on me, so it's got my gold game, my hobbies, the sex without dating ...

LT What do you mean?

K   I don't believe that you have to like *date* – that you have to go to a place and have an event and then have a drink and then have a dinner and then do this and then do that, you know? Let's just hang out, take a hot tub, we'll smoke a joint, and then we'll fuck.

LT Has that ever worked? In theory – that's an ideal, but has it ever actually happened?

K   Yeah. That's the basis of most of my relationships. I sleep with my friends.

LT Who's your favourite character?

K   George has probably got the most of the depth and depravity of the human condition.

LT You've got to like Kramer best.

K   I like Michael's portrayal of me. I wanted to play Kramer originally and lucky for them that they chose him over me because the show would have gone right in the shithole had I been Kramer. I never would've thought to walk into a room stupid like that. I walk into a room like a normal person.

LT The philosophy of the *Idler* is basically, you know, being about idling. Would you think of yourself as an idler?

K   Well, they say hard work never killed anybody, but why take a chance?

LT That's good.

Bez

by Tom Hodgkinson

IDLER 21 · MARCH 1998

THIS PIECE WAS HEADLINED 'BEZ: MAN OF LETTERS'. We were playing with the idea of one of the letters being E, for Ecstasy, as Bez was known for being druggy, but was now writing a book. In retrospect this was a really laboured joke that doesn't work. And our intro is a tad pretentious: to describe Bez as 'the Id of an entire generation' perhaps overstates the case. However, it was great to meet Bez, real name Mark Berry. He's a very affable person. Now touring again with the Happy Mondays, he did get into a lot of financial trouble at one point, and was saved by winning *Big Brother*.

★

These days, Bez is a man of letters, more letters than just E. But during the early Nineties, he was the distillation of our sweaty summer dreams, the Id of an entire generation. With his easy-rolling style and first anti-authoritarian beliefs, he remains an icon of the decade. So the *Idler* took him to our spiritual home, Dr Johnson's house off Fleet Street, for a chat about his philosophy on God, life, work and drugs.

Mark Berry is one of those fortunate or gifted people who can make a living out of simply being who they are. As 'percussion' man in the Happy Mondays, he had the important role of dancing around on stage and taking huge quantities of drugs. He was the court jester, the wise fool who tells the truth to the court. Bez is still working on musical projects, with Joe Strummer and Pablo Cook, among others. But he is also living the life of a gentleman of leisure. He lives with his girlfriend Deborah and their two children in a small village near Manchester. It is here that Bez indulges his new incarnation as a philosopher and writer.

He and Debs are working on *Freaky Dancin'*, Bez's book about his childhood and the Happy Mondays, to be published by Macmillan in September. As Bez is now a man of letters, following lunch at The Ivy, we took him to Dr Johnson's house. We then repaired to the pub, where Bez started talking about his attitude to drinking, drugs and work.

BEZ   I only take drugs and drink when I'm working. That's true, man. I just use them. It just happened me work was about getting off me head. So drugs stopped being a leisure activity, and became a tool of me trade.

TH   Is it still fun?

BEZ   All depends. I've took that much drugs in my time, it's become a bit of a bore. I prefer to save it for the moment I need them.

TH   Were you a wild teenager?

BEZ   Some people might say that, but I was just being me. I just done what I done. I was lucky enough to turn what everyone sees as a problem into me working tool. I've gone through life following me nose, so to speak, and seeing where it takes me. And it just so happened that it took me there. But if it weren't for drugs I probably wouldn't be here now sat talking to you. Very Dr Johnson isn't it? But I ain't saying it would work for everybody. But there are other people for whom drugs are their work. Depends what circles you're in.

TH   How did you get into bands?

BEZ   It was a dare. I got told I was a soft cunt, and couldn't do it. And no way am I a soft cunt, so I went out and done it.

TH   You must have been pretty determined.

BEZ   Well, I was into music before I was into drugs, y'know, and music and drugs go together. When you listen to a record straight, and then you have a spliff or what and listen to it again, you could be listening to a different tune. I get a heightened sensitivity, and go off into my own self when I listen to a tune stoned. When I'm straight, it ain't got the same effect.

TH   Was it more than luck that allowed you to make a career out of it?

BEZ   I believe it was my destiny, I think every man's got his own fuckin' destiny. I had no control over it whatsoever. It just like happened.

TH   Do you think drugs helped?

BEZ   I wouldn't sell drugs to anybody. It's like fucking trying to sell everybody the idea that it's all right to get pissed up and drink seven pints every night, which it isn't. But human nature has always been looking for a way to escape, and whether its alcohol or drugs, or whatever your fuckin' tickle is, you do it. You can trace it right back through time and history, and it's always happened. At the end of the day, human beings have always liked to get off their heads.

TH I guess you are quite lucky, but you must have had a lot of confidence in the first place, to do what you do.

BEZ I decided long ago that I wasn't going to conform. I was anti-everything: anti-school, anti-establishment, anti the lot. I had this inbuilt hatred of being a conformist. But maybe I am a conformist, maybe I conformed in my own way... so maybe I'm not that fucking clever!

TH You've also got a family, which you've managed at the same time. Sean Ryder, for example, seems to be in his own world so much that he hasn't paid much attention to things like that.

BEZ Everyone's different. He's doing the right thing in his own mind, and I wouldn't question that. But we all know what we do wrong and what we do right. If you're not comfortable with what you're doing, or with who you are, you're going to end up like a right fucking schizo. My life wasn't planned. It just happened that way. I try to keep things going. It's the only way I know to make an honest living. I know two ways of making a living – being a personality, or being a fuckin'...

TH Criminal?

BEZ Well, I don't think of it as criminality. I think of it as surviving. People survive in different ways. No matter where I go now, everyone points their finger at me and goes 'there's Bez'. I can't escape.

TH Does that make you feel weird?

BEZ No, because I was well-known before. In my own little way, that is. I've always made sure people knew who I was. I think it comes naturally.

TH But lots of people who get involved in the music industry can't really handle it in the end.

BEZ I can understand that. Oasis and that, people slag them off, but I'd never slag them, 'cos I understand. They come from nothing and they've developed into what they are now. They've never had a day off to really reflect on it all, and that's just as important as doing what you're doing. To take a step back. I used to swear to God it hadn't changed me, but now I realise I'm lying when I say that, because I know it *has* changed me. I tried denying it for ages, saying I'm still the same old Bez and all that carry on. It does change you. The best thing that happened to me was the Mondays splitting up and having that time to know that I had changed.

TH Was the split a shock?

BEZ No. We was an explosive element. We'd never been stable. It was always going to end in an unstable way, because of who we were. So it wasn't no surprise to me. It started with an explosion and it ended with one. The beginning of the universe and the end of it, do you know what I mean?

TH That chaos can be very creative, can't it?

BEZ The best things come from chaos. The French Revolution – total chaos, but out of it came order. I chose my lifestyle from early on. I thought school was shite. I could have done all right if I'd wanted to. Maybe it was because my old fella was a bizzie [policeman], but I hated being told what to do, I'd go and do the opposite. Because it stretches you. And there's millions of people out there who think the same as I do, and lead the same lives.

TH People, who in the past might have gone into normal jobs, can't, because those jobs don't exist now. They have to look at different ways of operating.

BEZ I meet people who come from different backgrounds from me, from privileged backgrounds. But what I realise is that we're all the same at the end of the day. We've got the same problems, the same thoughts, and the same human feelings. When I was younger, I wouldn't have accepted that. But now I'm 33 and I see these things. I'm really into being human, and developing being human to the maximum. Every-one suffers the same things.

TH A lot of people's problems come when they imagine that others are better off than they are.

BEZ There's different sorts of wealth, pal. There's financial wealth, which is like you don't have to worry about the little things. But you can be just as fucked up being a millionaire as you can when you've got fuck all. Money won't give you any mental security – that comes from the people you know and socialize with. And I believe in God, even if He's only a particle out in space somewhere. The human mind is the most powerful tool, but for me it's like a particle that's the meaning of life. Without this particle, nothing would be here. If you don't believe in God, and you try to deny it, there's a little place in your mind that tells you there's a God, or else you wouldn't be denying it.

TH Does that mean you're spiritual?

BEZ Spirituality is a different thing altogether. The powers of the planet and the universe are spiritual to me. I'm an anarchist and I hate any form of authority or control. I realise that authority is an essential part of life, but at the same time I fuckin' hate it with a passion. I hate the Tories, I hate the Labour Party, and I'd probably hate the Liberal Democrats if they ever got in power. But to me, it's the hate that keeps me going. I've done some bad things, things I feel slightly ashamed of, but under the circumstances I had no choice.

TH How do you get to that point, of being confident and courageous enough to do what you want to do?

BEZ 'Cos basically I don't really care what anybody thinks about me. I'm happy in the knowledge that I am what I am and there's nothing I can do about it. I'm willing to stand my ground and fight like fuck about it if anyone wants to say anything about it.

Tim Roth

by Tom Hodgkinson

IDLER 22 · WINTER 1999

THIS WASN'T THE BEST INTERVIEW WE EVER DID. TIM Roth just wanted to talk about his new film. At the time I thought that it was possibly an interesting read because we were discussing the creative process. But when I read the piece now, it seems a bit boring. What follows is a short excerpt from the original.

★

When Tim Roth turned up at an Idler party, we couldn't resist the chance to ask him for an interview. Roth was in the closing stages of shooting *The War Zone*, his debut as a director. It's the story of a highly dysfunctional and incestuous family, based on the book of the same name by Alexander Stuart. The book focuses on a 15 year old boy called Tom. Roth wanted to do the interview with his Director of Photography – DOP in filmspeak – the highly rated Seamus McGarvey. The DOP is the director's right hand man. He sorts out the lighting and the angles, leaving the director free to concentrate on the actors. We did the interview at midnight at the wrap party for Roth's picture.

TH Is this the first time you two have worked together?

TR We literally hadn't met before. I was interviewing DOPs for the film and I was in the process of casting the crew – I cast the crew like a cast the actors. I had a guy in America, an extraordinary DOP, who I've worked with before and who I wanted for the film. But he's LA-based and it was a bit weird, he's an older guy, a little guy in his seventies, and extraordinary film maker. I had just worked with him in an independent film and the word was we should see other people just in case. So I saw the top dogs and people who were interested about making a film about this subject.

TH So how did you know what you were looking for?

TR I didn't. I had absolutely no idea. I wanted to find someone who would inspire me. It's very easy to find people who are qualified, but that's not the issue. My experience as an actor, watching directors work, especially first-time directors, was that if you don't find your 'marriage', you're screwed. He got the script, he got the idea. We sparked and that took care of it for me. We have a marriage. It was always what was told to me – find your DOP, because if you don't, you're fucked. And that's why DOPs get fired, I think, and that's also why editors are the next in line to get fired very quickly.

TH Is acting less intense than directing?

TR It's shorter, for me it's always been shorter. I'm an actor. So it's quick. I'm in and out in about eight weeks. If I'm working in America, for example, and I have an accent, I do three weeks preparation on the accent, then I turn up, shoot, an I'm out of there in six, seven weeks. It's all independent films – I've done two studio films, which are pretty dull. What was interesting for me was that I've been on this for two years and I've only just wrapped – and it's not over yet. I still have 16 weeks of post-production. Then I deliver the film. Then it's still not over. I have to sell the film.

TH So this is actually one of the most intense things you've done ...

TR It is. And it's considered very short in the grand scale of things. I was shown the book, read it, decided to make the film and within two years I was shooting it. That's really quick. I came over here to pitch it to financiers and within my first meeting I was being offered money. And I was turning it down because I wanted to find the right people to do the film.

TH That sounds like a luxury.

TR It was, but it was also scary because I knew that my name attached to it was what was selling it. Not the story itself. So you distrust the initial response.

[Dixie, producer, comes in]

DIX Tim, you've got to do the awards, sorry to interrupt.

TR You're going to have to ask your last question.

TH That whole business side of it – the pitching and so on – was that something that was new to you?

TR It was brand new to me, but in a sense it wasn't, because as an actor you pitch yourself all the time. I would go into a meeting with Dixie or Sarah Radclyffe [producers], with absolutely no fucking idea of what to say, and by the end of it I'd get some money – or not. Winging it, that's part of the process. I'm better at it now. OK. I'm gonna go and hand awards out.

John Gray

by Tom Hodgkinson

IDLER 23 · JUNE 1998

W E COTTONED ON TO JOHN GRAY AS AN IMPORTANT figure in contemporary though, quite early on. When I did this interview he was a professor at LSE, but he has since quit to follow the life of the freelance scholar. He has become much better known lately thanks to his book *Straw Dogs*. I enjoy his continual questioning of the myth of progress and liberalism in general.

★

TH What I've enjoyed in your work is your discussion of the collapse of distinctions between Left and Right, the changes in the world of work, and also the emergence of this almost libertarian populace, especially among young people.

JG The key thing, I think, is that liberal thought hasn't begun to understand the present. It's not that we should engage in futurism. The key thing is to understand the present, and the present is changing much faster than our thinking about it. Most of our organising ideas come from the 19th century or from the Puritan post-war generation, from 1945 up to the late Seventies. Very few politicians engage with the reality of events now. One example is the emergence of a deeply liberal youth culture. It's not an ideological protest — it is just the way they live. It's not even an issue. It's neglected or not understood.

TH And you don't suddenly understand it by inviting Oasis into No.10.

JG I think the relationship of all governments with this libertarian youth culture is profoundly uneasy. The bottom line is that it's a relationship of incomprehension between the generations. I'm told that people in Russia who were young when the Iron Curtain came down are different people. And also most politicians want to placate the values of what they perceive to be the swing voters. A better guide for politicians than focus groups is what tabloid newspapers and advertisers think about. They probably understand the idea that there are a large majority of deeply conservative citizens out there, is a gross caricature.

TH The stereotype of the '*Sun* reader' or the '*Daily Mail* reader'.

JG Yeah. But the *Sun* reader or the *Daily Mail* reader might not be the *Sun* reader or the *Daily Mail* reader. I wouldn't be at all surprised, for example, if legalizing cannabis is advocated by the *Daily Mail* before the government. People as astute as they are are more likely to pick up what people think. They have a continuous reason, which is readership, and they're constantly surveying it. And they learn from experience. That's harder for governments.

That's one big change in which political parties are miles behind reality. The other is the unpackaging of beliefs. Not everyone who is libertarian about drug use is a liberal on crime. Not everyone who is a staunch advocate of gay rights is against capital punishment. So the idea that beliefs come in easy to handle packages may have been true once, but not now.

TH It's more practical too; people are having to do that in order to live, as the world is changing so quickly.

JG Exactly. If people have a pick-and-mix approach, it's based on something: their own needs, their own circumstances, their own experiences, rather than taking it off the shelf as a ...

TH ... as a ready-made thing. For me, it's part of the move towards people trying to control their own lives, because the established patterns, or patterns that other people try to impose on them clearly don't work. Like the world of work, the 'jobs' model doesn't really work, so you have to retreat and make your own with your friends.

JG Someone who invested ten years of their life, in the sense of not spending and not consuming now, but postponing all that to a later point, will be doing something which is much more of a gamble than was true in earlier generations. If you spend ten or twelve years of your life preparing to be a top-flight accountant, you might get the job you want, but then you're fired three years later.

TH Or the company collapses.

JG Disappears. Or even whole occupations. There are going to be no bank tellers. Many areas of the economy – whole professions – are just shrinking or disappearing altogether. They're wiped out either by technology or competition. So someone who thought that knuckling down for ten years of grind and self-denial, laying up a fortune for themselves later on, is making a mistake. The changes in the world of work have been far more profound than have been generally recognised. It's not only our opinions coming out of their packages, but also partly because of sheer competition, you can now gain more control over your life.

TH   A lot of our generation prefer that. We like the idea of going in to an office and just doing the work in a few hours, rather than spending half the day dealing with office politics.

JG   Yes, then you can go to the pub or whatever. So it's not only that economic necessity is forcing people out of wage jobs – although that's happening – it's people like yourself who want more control, more leisure – and more money. And you do that by contracting yourself out, in other words, doing jobs in the old-fashioned sense. A job in its original sense meant a packet of stuff like a bale of hay which was moved around – a particular task, which you do at your own pace, as fast as you want, in any way you want, when you want. For many people that makes a lot of sense. I think what standard politics hasn't faced up to is growing individualism. On the Right they *thought* they were individualists, but their individualism meant banging people into standard homes. The Left is starkly anti-hedonistic. They have the idea that doing things for pleasure, or playfully, or for their own sakes, or with no ulterior motive – is a waste of time.

TH   It always amazes me that parts of Labour assume it is the dream – it is what everyone wants. That a job will suddenly solve all our problems.

JG   It may be because of the roots of Labour. The model socialist institution is the factory. And that doesn't fit into what's going on now. But there are also people who don't think in terms of career structures, steps and stages, but who want a secure position which pays moderately and has a certain social respect. Like those which existed in the old rotten days of municipal socialism, ironically. There are many public spaces that have become dangerous, because they're empty and uninhabited after a certain time. It's considered a waste of resources to have human beings tending them. I think that's a mistake. If there are three people on the railway station all the time, and they're doing various things like making the tea, and they've got walkie-talkies, you'll feel safer.

TH I sometimes feel lucky having started work in a recession. Any earlier, I might have signed up in an ordinary job and not had an interesting life.

JG It would be better if people saw work as a set of experiences which they use for pleasure, for income, for personal relationships, for self-development. The more fluid the better. That's the way I look at it. There are still a lot of loose ends in society that should be got rid of. The standards, if you apply for a mortgage, say, only apply to a shrinking number of people. Their idea of what makes someone trustworthy is primitive. It arises from the age of industrialism and the factory, when clocking in, being there week after week, year after year, being loyal, turning up, being obedient was what made people useful. But it's not what makes people useful now. You're more useful if you say; 'I'll do this work for three hours then bugger off to the pub', rather than sitting there twiddling your thumbs, being frustrated, at the end of your tether.

TH But people who have a totally free life – artists, pop stars – can go a bit mental.

JG Being an idler is too austere a profession for most of the species. It's too difficult. You find as you get older you're increasingly capable of genuine idleness! You need the recurrent anodyne of work and routine. A really subtle culture would see work as a medical necessity or a regime of health.

You can learn a lot from other animals. They seem to establish habits when they can. If they're hunters, they sleep a lot, they don't work unnecessarily.

TH Koala bears sleep for 16 hours a day and the rest of the time they're stoned on Eucalyptus leaves.

JG You'd need a very strong underlying culture, probably religious, which governed the process of being stoned all the time, why you're stoned, what you do when you are stoned. You can actually do stuff when you're stoned, explore different symbolic motifs and so on. To do it as a form of individual playfulness is astonishingly rigorous over time and, inevitably, most of us aren't up to it. I think it was Oscar Wilde, or one of his characters in *The Picture of Dorian Grey*, who said: 'Not for me the vulgar pursuit of happiness, but rather the heroic life of pleasure'. He recognised it to be tragic. But why make a tragedy of your life? Why not gravitate to more balance? But to create balance is terribly difficult. There's nothing to guide you. Most of the ruling ideologies of work, or what you should be doing with your life, are ones that very few people take seriously and they're obviously ridiculous. Equally, the experimentation you see going on around you is experimentation in emergent territories. All you can really do is improvise, improvise the balance of routine and flexi-life. Work and play is a hackneyed distinction, isn't it? We're compelled to improvise, just because of the fragility of routine in our lives. Even when you want them, the routines aren't there.

TH You have to create them yourself.

JG Much more is self-invented about people's lives than, I think, has been true ever, or at any rate in recent history. Being the author of your own life – you talk to a professional writer – is bloody difficult. People always welcome others taking over the strings. Large institutional authorities, be they political, religious, medical or psychological, don't have the answer. Such vast machines are not supple enough, or smart enough to give any useful advice. It devolves on each person separately.

TH What do you think governments should actually do?

JG In some areas of social and cultural life government should retreat. But there are some things they can do. There is an important need for strong, well-functioning public services: public transport, NHS, good education – preferably not only in schools but throughout life. A rather forgotten figure these days – I don't know why – is Ivan Illich, a very interesting man in my opinion. Education doesn't just mean schools. Providing strong public services, is one of the things that makes the individualism of the economy and life nowadays not just tolerable but congenial. The whole point of civilised life is to be able to saunter. To be idle you've got to feel safe. Otherwise you're anxious, a fugitive. People look to rural life as a model. Rural life is important but it's a complete mistake to think of it as a model for us. The model now is city life made congenial and relaxed. To achieve this, the state should just have a light touch ...

TH Let the river go where it wants to.

JG Yeah, and maybe even have locks here and there, to moderate the turbulence. Create pleasant areas to take time off from shooting the rapids of the modern economy. It means having limited practical goals for what you're doing which enable people to be more relaxed, to be more inventive, to be less harassed. To enjoy life more.

TH Are you optimistic about that kind of government ever happening?

JG Well, I have a reputation for not being terribly optimistic about anything. I wouldn't be completely hopeless about it. But it's in the nature of government to view the risks and dangers of life as problems to be solved, and evils as things to be removed, rather than as human experiences that people have to learn to cope with. Especially now, when everything is being revolutionized. But to have a rigidly libertarian approach seems to me to be silly. I don't think, for example, that all drugs should be legalised for everyone. What you're looking for is a mixture. To me, the prohibitionists and libertarians are in the same camp, in a certain deep way, which is 'we want something and this is how and this is the only way.' The idea that an Indian tribe is going to have this absolute right to smoke crack, something they've never heard of ... it's ridiculous when you think of it, as ridiculous, but less maligned today, than prohibition, which is the natural governmental response to everything. It takes a very subtle and educated government not to intervene, when they see something that's judged to be evil. In pre-modern societies these things were handled by myths, religion and magic. There wasn't a God-given right to do whatever you want. It was handled by shamans, by rituals. There was a local wisdom. Now that's been abolished, partly by Christianity, partly by modern Puritanism.

TH   Are the people who are attracted into government the kind of people who want to impose their will on others?

JG   Maybe, but it's also because of voters. Voters want solutions. If government turns round and says, 'this is dangerous, but there's not much we can do about it, there will still be tragedies' – that's not what most voters want to hear. So I don't blame the politicians, they're just reacting most of the time. Most of what people call social problems aren't problems. They're either things that are being solved already, or they're evils which have been created by stupid interventions, or they're just features of life which may be terrible, but are not going to go away. Take 'The War Against Cancer'. One of the reasons we have cancer is that we live such a long time. It's like saying, 'The War Against Death'. Why make an unnecessary tragedy out of something that is perfectly natural? Why not just see human life in the same way that in some earlier periods of history people have done, as something which has various phases? Death is the end but it's not necessarily a tragedy. The main thing is that life has been well spent. Partly in idleness.

David Soul

by Louis Theroux

IDLER 24 · SUMMER 1998

ISEEM TO REMEMBER THAT I MET DAVID SOUL AT FILTHY McNasty's. Louis jumped at the chance of interviewing him, and produced this very funny account of their meeting, during which he accused Soul of being henpecked. Afterwards Soul told me how impressed he was with Louis: he's a very special guy, he said. David himself is a lovely man and unlike many actors, he has something to say.

★

I drive to my appointment with David Soul in a car I bought only the day before, a 1993 Yugo Tempo with 35,000 miles on the clock. I got it at Used Car Supermarket in West London for £500 pounds. It was missing its passenger-side seatbelt, so I shunted the passenger seat all the way forward to make more room in the back where the seatbelts are fine. After the interview, David asked for a lift to a shoe repair shop on the Edgware Road.

I warned David that my car wasn't fancy. He said he didn't mind. The photographer climbed in back, and before I'd had time to adjust his seat, David was in front. This was the first time I'd had two passengers simultaneously, never mind that one of them was an international television celebrity, one of the biggest stars of the Seventies, and a byword for spectacular cop show car chases. As I pulled out, I looked over. David's knees were around his ears. 'I've got Hutch in my Yugo!' I kept thinking. He looked so funny all scrunched up that I started laughing out loud, lost my concentration and nearly hit a parked car.

We'd spent the afternoon running errands for David's partner, Alexa

– picking up groceries, drink, some dry cleaning – and then chatting in David's local pub. David lives close to Warwick Avenue tube and everyone in his local shopping arcade knows him and calls him Dave. It was the day of the gay pride rally, and one of the barrow boys in the local greengrocers said, 'I'm surprised you're not in Hyde Park.' Another one said, 'Dave, this girl's got a question for you.' 'Excuse me,' said the girl, with a slight continental accent. 'Do you have some free cardboard boxes?'

David has lived in London for the past two years. He said he enjoys the sense of community. 'I know the people in the neighbourhood and I like that. It's always great to belong somewhere.' He's about to star as a washed-up surfer in a stage production called *The Dead Monkey*, which opens at the Whitehall in September. When I met him at lunch-time one Saturday, he was wearing dark glasses, chain-smoking and looking slightly unkempt. He was friendly, a little distracted. I'd hoped to get a walk round his flat; I'd brought my guitar so he could teach me the chords to his 1977 hit 'Don't Give Up On Us Baby', which I dimly recall seeing him perform on *Top of the Pops* when I was seven. But it wasn't to be. 'I don't think we're going to have time to do anything that creative,' he said.

After we'd run Alexa's errands, David disappeared inside his flat to drop off the shopping. He came out five or so minutes later wearing a hangdog expression.

'Well, we fucked up,' he said. 'We didn't get the right stuff so she's going to have to go out and get it.'

'What did you not get that you were supposed to get?'

'She said, "I can't use this hamburger meat!"'

'I was going to say something. Because what we got are patties.'

'Well, she said they had hamburger meat but they don't.'

'So you have to take it back?'

'Mmmm.'

I don't know why, but I took this as my cue to lower my voice, and say: 'She's got you by the short and curlies.' David seemed affronted.

'How's that?' he said. 'I bought it. She's not dressed. I'm going back that way. Might as well pick it up.'

'Yeah, I guess you're right. Yeah, quite right. Take it back.'

'Short and curlies. What do you mean, short and curlies?'

'It's just an expression.'

There was a long pause and just the sound of our footsteps on the pavement.

'Do you … can I ask you about the play you're working on?'

We dropped off the frozen hamburger patties at the grocer's. David got his money back. Then we hit the pub, where I stood David a white wine spritzer.

LT   As someone who has lived such an amazing life and who has been at the top, what have you learned? Are you pleased with the way you handled things?

DS   No, but I've stopped flagellating myself for my mistakes. I've started to accept them.

LT   What were your mistakes?

DS   Myriad of them. A lot of them weren't my fault. That's a very important recognition. Some of this is not your fault. You can be making a fuck up because you haven't learned anything. Who is ready for that kind of high-powered high-visibility bullshit? Not me! So it's not like you ease into it. I have an easy style with people, I've never had a problem with that. But it's a hell of a lot different to deal with once you have the success that I did experience back in the Seventies and early Eighties. I didn't know how to handle it. I just didn't know. It scared the shit out of me.

LT   Didn't know how to handle what exactly?

DS   I didn't know what to expect from anybody. 'What do you fucking expect from me?' 'What do you want from me?' 'What is it?' You play a game. You go along. You play according to their rules. Then something else is expected of you, and somebody says, Hey, this all goes with it! But I mean I'm not getting anything out of it! 'Get these cameras out of my face!' What right do they have to go and inveigle their way into my house and into my life? It's none of their business! You know and: [nerdy voice] 'That's the price you pay for fame'.

LT   How could you have handled things differently? I don't mean in the sense of looking back and saying you have regrets. I mean in the sense of … what I'm trying to get at is what you've learned. How does one conduct one's life? Do you know what I mean? It's one of the hardest things and no one's really giving us the answers.

DS   If there's anything I've learned it's really to — rather than to put things in terms of external success or internal failure, the two extremes, is to learn to acknowledge and accept yourself for who you are. And I think that is maybe the most radical thing I could suggest at the moment. The most difficult; the most simple and the most difficult. We're not talking about blame or guilt or fear or success or a new set of clothes or a new phase of life or a new lifestyle. That's not what it's about, it's about accepting yourself and living with that. And I think that's what I didn't do … Particularly in this business, you're only as important as your last record or your last hit or your last great story, or your last television show or your last this or your last that. Celebrity is a lot like ice cream, you know, it melts and then you've got to live with yourself. [Chuckles ruefully.] And I think to be able to accept that, with the greatest awe, is the key. It's not a big wise statement but it's the only thing I know of to talk about.

LT At the pinnacle of your fame you were probably one of the most recognisable people on the planet. What was that like? Was it awful? Fantastic? Mediocre?

DS Frightening. It was all those things. It was exhilarating, it was frightening, lonely. It was frustrating. Thinking, that's not who I am, guys! This is who I am. Not that guy. Am I what you think I am? Or am I what I know of myself, you know? Never having the courage or the balls to be able to say this is who I am. Wanting to please everybody. Because they expect you to please everybody. So I tried to please everybody. But I couldn't do it. If you don't do it then you're a bad guy. So I'm a bad guy. But I look back on it. It's 30 years now I've been doing this. And one thing I can tell you is that I'm as excited and as passionate about what I'm doing now as I have ever been. And it's because I love what I do. So tomorrow is another day, another opportunity. And it feels good.

LT Does the size of the audience matter?

DS It does. It does from the standpoint of the industry – the business itself. But I'm not part of that. I'm in it, but I'm not of it. I'm in it but it doesn't define who I am. So if I'm in it and my show isn't as successful as it would be by the standards of the television network to be running it for ever and ever, the show's going to get cancelled, it's not the end of the world. If I make a record that doesn't sell more than x number of albums, it's not the end of the world. That's the way I feel about it.

LT So then what are the things that are of value in the world? You can say, I'm in this world because this is how I ply my trade, as an actor and a singer, but it's not going to be my life because that would destroy me. But what is your life? How do you enjoy your life? Is it relationships? Is it your friends?

DS It's all those things.

LT Is it your car?

DS No. I don't own a car. Don't own a house. Don't own anything. It's about good experiences. I've lived all over the world. It's an appreciation of the experience of others, the way they view things. I get new life and new breath from diversity, someone different from myself. I love it. It really keeps me alive. That's my ideal. You've got to be willing to look around to say where are my opportunities, what are my choices?

LT I'm reading the *Tao Te Ching* at the moment, and it sort of says, if you want to be happy then don't try and be happy, kind of thing?

DS There's another one. What do you want to be in life? I want to be happy, I want to be happy, I want to be happy, I want to be happy! You push push push push push. Happiness, it seems to me, is you kick back and you say 'I'm happy!' It's not something that you make, it's something that you realise, that you come to. And it can be in a moment, it can be in a relationship, a day or a lifetime, but we're not always happy, so why do you try to be happy? It's trying! Trying! Pah! Don't!

LT How is it living in London?

DS Before ending up here I lived in New Zealand and Australia. Both were work-related. And then I went to France for a year, and I did a film over there. Then I got an offer to do a play here. It was part of a circuit. I'd had it with LA and I think LA had had it with me. And I probably did the right thing by leaving. I'd kind of burned it at both ends.

LT In what sense?

DS Well, I'd been used up to a large degree by the business. There was no more attraction. I had done too much television to be working in film. They didn't want television people working in film. There were some questionable behaviour patterns on my part. The way I was perceived, the bad boy image.

LT People thought, oh we don't want to hire David Soul – he's bad news?

DS Yeah, that kind of stuff. I've always pressed for quality work. I know there were a number of producers that when I came walking into their office were like 'oh shit, here he comes.'

LT Really? So what about say Steven Bochco [creator of *Hill Street Blues*,

NYPD Blue]?

DS Steven's a great friend of mine.

LT You couldn't go to him and say ...

DS I wouldn't do that. I'll do it another time. I'll do it when it's right. Yeah. That's exactly what I hate about LA, relationships... so much of this shit is based on who you know, opportunities based on that. I suppose I could go knock on his door and say, Steven, I'm here, I'm available to do a job. But the networks are run by kids. It's a whole other era. I now probably have a better chance of going back having been away. Because I'm still very viable – they don't quite know who I am anymore, but they know me from their childhood and there's still the vitality there and we haven't seen him around. But what I've done in the meantime is fill it with theatre, sort of utilising one thing that LA did give me which is international visibility, whether it's France, Italy, Spain, Hong Kong, China, Japan, South America. But it's very important for me to do theatre because that's where I come from. I came here for that. And Alexa was with me and she needs to do something and it becomes important that she contributes.

LT How does it feel doing *The Dead Monkey*, which seems like an exciting project, compared with what you were doing in the Seventies, early Eighties. Better, worse, different?

DS Different. A different time of my life. I've been there, done that. It's not everything it's cracked up to be. It's not. By definition. It can't be. There's only a handful of people that control 12 to 15 to 18 million dollars per picture. And this business chews you up and spits you out pretty fast. And if there's an award given it should be for persevering. You know? And I'd rather, at the end of my life, be able to say, I chose something, I took an opportunity by the tail, and have lived my life doing that. I mean, the sale of the records, being a top-notch artist, terrific. But it's not something that lasts. And I've found a lot more satisfaction doing things that I enjoy doing, like this. I mean, we're producing! We're not just acting in it. We're producing it. No actor in the West End produces their own shows!

LT If you had the Seventies to live over, would you do the same self-sabotaging stuff?

DS No, because you're defining that after the fact. See, I didn't know what was happening when I walked into it. I don't have to answer for that. And I don't need to be questioned by that. This is one of the insipid things that the press does. They categorise your past behaviour as if that's who you are, thereby judging you by standards they themselves don't live up to. It's just stifling. It's just [mimes choking].

LT How do you decide who you are?

DS I think we talked about that before. You accept yourself, you know. I mean, I hate the kind of focus in the last couple of days since that World Cup game where Beckham kicked that player. That was a dumb, stupid thing to do. That's all, guys. That's all.

LT Don't give him a hard time!

DS Yeah, that's all, a dumb, stupid thing to do. Now what are you going to do? You've got headlines everywhere. I mean, come on! Give me a break! That's one thing I hate about this country. It's so provincial, because it's an island, it's small, and everybody knows everybody else's fucking business. It's none of your fucking business! You know? It's small and contained and provincial. But fight against being small and provincial! Live and let live! Acknowledge that it was a stupid thing to do and move on.

Satish Kumar

by Jay Walljasper

IDLER 25 · 1999

IWAS PUT IN TOUCH WITH JAY WALLJASPER BY MY FRIEND
Joshua Glenn, who at the time was working on the *Utne Reader*. I
knew of Satish and loved his magazine, *Resurgence*.

*

I am clambering up a hillside in the rain, green expanses of Cornish
countryside to my left and magnificently rugged coastline to my right,
trying to keep up with Satish Kumar, a 60-year-old former Indian
monk who once walked halfway around the world to promote disar-
mament. All of a sudden a giant boom pierces the air. It sounds as
though the world's most horrible thunderstorm is headed straight for
us. I stop dead in my muddy tracks, speechless and shaky. So does
Satish ahead of me and his wife June Mitchell, right behind.
'What in the world is that?' I yell, searching the skies for lightning.
'The Concorde,' Satish and June say in unison.
'It often enters England right here on its flight from New York to
London,' June explains. I look up toward Satish, who's frowning in the
direction of the plane. For a man whose lifelong mission has been to
help the world realise there is more to life than being rich, being fast,
being worldly, and being technologically advanced, this surely must
pose a reminder of what he's up against. The peace of his pastoral home
is often invaded by the supersonic roar of an energy-guzzling aircraft
rushing upscale passengers between world capitals.
I watch as Satish shifts his attention from the sky to the splashing sea
and picks up the thread of our interrupted conversation. 'Wandering
and drifting in nature is one of the things that replenish me,' he says,

striding again toward the peak of the hill. 'It fills me with energy to keep doing the things I want to do.'

Satish, who can be counted among our most interesting social thinkers, needs considerable energy to accomplish all the things he wants to do.

For several decades he and June have edited *Resurgence* magazine out of a postcard-perfect stone farmhouse bedecked with ivy and surrounded by flower and vegetable gardens. The magazine, which is now working to widen its tiny North American audience, has been called 'the artistic and spiritual flagship of the Green movement' by the *Guardian*. Satish also directs a college devoted to holistic principles of learning, an alternative school in his local village and a publishing house... all of which he founded. He lectures all over the world on assorted topics, and will be touring North America in February and March to promote the new American edition of his fascinating autobiography, *Path Without Destination* (Eagle Brook/William Morrow).

Satish Kumar has set out to do nothing less than make the modern world more aware of the beauty, mystery and connectedness of all things, and less fixated on hierarchy, competition and bigness.

Unlike many crusaders for worthy causes, Satish and June actually live the simple life they celebrate. She receives a modest salary from the magazine and he from the college. The mortgage on their house and two acres of gardens and flower patches is held by a trust of *Resurgence* benefactors. By almost any economic standard of the modern world they are poor, yet it's hard not to envy this way of life. Their centuries-old cottage lacks central heating but is still as comfortable as any place I've ever stepped into, outfitted with authentic editions of the rustic elegance in furnishings, kitchenware and art that *Good Housekeeping* strives for. Much of their food comes straight from the garden. The long table in the middle of the wood-beamed kitchen feels like the centre of the universe, the place where friends and family gather over Satish's Indian dinners and June's desserts, drinking local cider and talking for hours on end.

Gary Snyder, Wendell Berry, psychologist R. D. Laing and Gaia theory founder James Lovelock, are among the guests who have enjoyed Satish and June's bright hospitality. While most of the magazine's work goes on in a converted stone barn a few steps from the front door, the house's living room doubles as Satish's office. He sits down at his old wood desk and we begin to talk.

'My major idea is that we need to change consciousness,' Satish says. He is a small man, wiry and dapper, with a grey goatee and intense brown eyes. 'We live under the power of Modern Consciousness, which means that we are obsessed with progress. Wherever you are is not good enough. We always want to achieve something, rather than experience something. The opposite of this is Spiritual Consciousness. By that I mean you find enchantment in every action you do, rather in just the results of your action.

'Spiritual Consciousness is not a particular religion,' he tells me, 'but a way of being.' Explaining its tenets in Path Without Destination, he translates a chant that Gandhi composed for morning and evening meditation: Nonviolence, truth, nonstealing / Sacred sex, nonconsumerism / Physical work, avoidance of bad taste / Fearlessness, respect for all religions / Local economy and respect for all beings. / These eleven principles / Should be followed with humility, care, and commitment. 'These principles are not do's and don'ts,' Satish writes. 'They are not vows; they are aspirations and inspirations. They are like resolutions which are made on the eve of a New Year ... They could be used as resolutions for the new millennium.' While such sentiments might strike you as completely quixotic as we enter the new century more completely in the thrall of technology, commercialism and globalisation than ever before, his longtime friend Richard Boston counsels that Satish is not someone to underestimate. 'His gentleness is accompanied by a will of steel. His schemes are apparently absurd in their Utopianism, but turn out to be quite practical. He is a great deal more hardheaded, shrewder, more canny than he appears at first.' I know what Boston means.

A small but important part of the reason I'm in England trailing Satish through a rain-soaked landscape is to understand how I came to write a column in Resurgence for absolutely no pay. I depend on freelance writing to cover a major portion of my monthly budget, but when Satish, whom I'd never spoken to before, asked me to write the magazine's 'Letter from America' column I immediately answered 'yes' without even thinking to ask about money.

To say 'no' to Satish, who speaks in an elegant and melodious flow of Indian-accented English, feels like turning down some prestigious and hard-won honour. No one published in Resurgence has ever seen a penny for their labours, and the list includes luminaries like Gary Snyder, Vaclav Havel, Wendell Berry, Vandana Shiva, Thomas Moore, James Hillman, Susan Griffin, Matthew Fox, Winona LaDuke, Ted Hughes, Fritjof Capra, Ivan Illich, Noam Chomsky and Prince Charles.

These are some of the same names that teach courses at Schumacher College, the academy of spiritual and ecological education that Satish founded in 1991.

Named after E. F. Schumacher, the visionary economist whose groundbreaking bestseller *Small is Beautiful* was based on articles first published in *Resurgence*, the college offers students of all ages three- and five-week courses on subjects like 'Psychology and Spirituality' or 'A New Economics for People and the Planet'.

Housed in a 14th-century hall on the Dartington Estate in southwestern England, Schumacher College offers people from around the world the experience of immersing themselves in the process of learning – discussing new ideas in classes, over dinner, while washing dishes and out in the orchard by moonlight.

Satish's remarkable success in enlisting people's goodwill and financial help for his numerous projects seems to arise from a highly developed set of skills he's honed out of a unique life of rebellion, spiritual reflection and political action. At age nine, against the wishes of his family, he joined an order of Jain monks (a religion with spiritual tenets akin to Hinduism and Buddhism) and spent the next eight years wandering across India, depending on the kindness of villagers each day for meals and a place to sleep.

At 17, after reading a book by Gandhi (although reading was forbidden among the monks), he decided to join the campaign being led by Vinoba Bhave, Gandhi's successor as leader of India's village movement.

He helped organise strikes among farmworkers of the untouchable caste, and then became an editor at a newspaper of the Gandhian movement until he was sacked for criticising some prominent Gandhians' plans to build a complex of fancy modern office buildings – a stark rejection of Gandhi's own programme of simple living.

Later, as he recounts in *Path With No Destination*, he was sitting with a friend at a café, looking over the newspaper and noting that the famous British philosopher Bertrand Russell had been jailed at a ban-the-bomb protest in London. It was 1962, and people at breakfast tables all around the planet were uneasy as they learned of the latest round of nuclear sabre-rattling between the United States and the Soviet Union.

But no one else undertook what Satish and his friend Prabhakar Menon did. Inspired by the 90-year-old Russell's deep convictions, the two of them vowed that morning to make a pilgrimage, bringing a message of peace to leaders of the world's (then) four nuclear nations.

They set out a few weeks later and walked most of the way from Delhi to Moscow to Paris to London to Washington with no money in their pockets.

They befriended many people along the 8,000-mile journey who offered them food and shelter, including Martin Luther King and the Shah of Iran as well as hundreds of peasants and factory workers.

The two of them snuck away from their government hosts in Moscow and eluded Soviet police all the way to the Polish border, engaged in a long discussion about human rights with an East Berlin border guard, were held four days in a filthy Paris jail cell and deported to England, where they met up with Bertrand Russell, who raised money so that they could take the luxurious Queen Mary ocean liner to New York.

Martin Luther King welcomed them to his home in Atlanta, and Satish had a gun held to his head by the owner of a lunch counter in Albany, Georgia, who did not want to serve a brown-skinned man. They met with representatives of Nikita Kruschev, Harold Wilson and Lyndon Johnson – but not Charles DeGaulle – and gave each of them a packet of tea from a woman they met in Armenia, who said that leaders should brew a pot of tea before making any decision to fire missiles.

Upon returning to India several years later, Satish continued to promote land reform issues and also became involved with humanitarian work among refugees fleeing a bloody civil war in Bangladesh, which led to an invitation to visit London and speak at the opening of a photography exhibit about the disaster.

That's where he met June Mitchell, a librarian speaking at the same event who had done relief work in Bangladesh. Soon the two of them were living together in London with a baby son, making plans to move to India. But one day while taking his daily walk Satish bumped into John Papworth, an English peace activist who had accompanied Satish around the United States on the last leg of his peace pilgrimage and who later founded *Resurgence* magazine. Papworth was leaving soon for Zambia to become an adviser to President Kenneth Kuanda, and insisted right on the spot that Satish take over the editorship of *Resurgence*.

Although Satish had no formal schooling, only a limited command of written English, and no visible means of support, he took the job, which paid nothing.

'I didn't like to ... refuse something that was coming to me by fate,' he explains in his autobiography. 'I decided to put off my thoughts of returning to India ... I should have known that life does not operate on the basis of plans, no matter how rational. My nature is to let things happen rather than make them happen.'

It is this spirit of Taoist detachment that, when paired with Satish's own undeniable determination, adds up to a very powerful personality – a man toward whom the universe seems to bend a bit, a figure from whom seemingly impossible ideas sound somehow less impossible, especially when you consider the simple sensibleness and fundamental appeal of what he has to say.

'Fragmentation is at the heart of Modern Consciousness,' he says as we sit at the kitchen table eating fresh-baked tarts and sharing a pot of Earl Grey tea. 'You divide knowledge into subjects, you divide people into categories. But I think there is something more to the world than what you are able to measure, analyse, and quantify. In Spiritual Consciousness there is a dance between what you know and what you don't know. The place of mystery is an essential ingredient.'

Seeing the universe as something that flows in cycles rather than following a path of linear progression, Satish believes that Spiritual Consciousness will eventually replace, or at least counterbalance, Modern Consciousness.

'Modernity is very powerful,' he admits. 'It has the media, the corporations. Yet there seems a discontentedness in many people today, despite all the glamour and achievement and technology and wealth. There is a sense of the loss of meaning. That's why people are coming to embrace a different kind of consciousness. And of course the pollution, the crime, the poverty and the ugliness.' Satish freely acknowledges that he chooses to live in the midst of the modern world and knows it is not always easy to resist its pull. That's why no matter how urgent the duties of the day, he spends two hours every morning meditating, chanting and reading, and takes a walk every day with June – and sometimes with their daughter Maya, a college student studying art, and son Mukti, a filmmaker and sailor.

It is also why *Resurgence* is published in Hartland, an out-of-the-way farming village near the west coast of England.

'Out of my office window I can look at blackcurrants, redcurrants, plums, apples, greengages, quinces and raspberries growing in the courtyard,' he says. 'After a morning of editing we go to the garden and pick the vegetables for lunch. When it's a beautiful sunny day, we'll say let's go outside. No editing today. People tell us we are very inefficient and naïve,' he says, a sly grin crossing his face.

'I say, yes, we are inefficient and naïve but we are happy. You keep your efficiency and we'll keep our happiness.'

'Change is always a surprise,' he continues. 'Look at the fall of the Berlin Wall and the end of apartheid. When I came to England 25 years ago, if you stopped in a restaurant and told them you were vegetarian, they would panic, "What can we feed you?" Now 14 per cent of the British population is vegetarian. Even one of the pubs in Hartland has vegetarian curries on the menu.'

Last year, Satish turned 60, an age by which many Indians have renounced their worldliness, given away their possessions and retreated to a mountaintop. Satish has no such plans. He says he's content with his life exactly as it is. He says he's accomplished all he ever hoped for. But then, scratching his goatee and wiggling a bit in the kitchen chair, he admits that he has thought of writing a book about Spiritual Consciousness and ecology. And moments later, he adds that if he could ever find the time he'd love to revive the Arts & Crafts movement – a movement led by socialist poet and designer William Morris in the late 19th century that rose up in favour of fine craftsmanship, humane working conditions and simple unadorned beauty in architecture and everyday objects.

Although he is now sitting perfectly still, looking serene in his usual dignified manner, I sense that his mind is rushing ahead with thoughts of more projects to tackle. He looks over at me with a warm yet intense gaze and says, 'Let's take another walk. The rain has stopped now. The coastline will look splendid in the afternoon light.'

Iain Sinclair

by Tony White

IDLER 26 · SUMMER 2000

THE LONDON EYE WAS JUST ABOUT TO OPEN, AND TONY White, novelist and *Idler* lit ed, suggested taking Iain Sinclair up there for a ride.

★

Who would be the tour guide of choice, I thought, for a press freebie on the London Eye? Why not Iain Sinclair, the novelist, satirist and psychogeographer, who's taken his occult-obsessive explorations of the Capital into the bestseller lists. He hadn't, I discovered, been up on it yet. So I made him an offer he couldn't refuse.

Sinclair arrives bang on time. A wave in the crowd and there he is; taller than I'd remembered, big black waxed coat, bag slung over the shoulder. He looks around. 'Fabulous day. You managed to blag it, then?' he asks, gum stretched between teeth and tongue. He'd relocated his meeting for a 'Shakespeare's London' radio documentary to the South Bank so he could stroll along the Embankment for this. 'Shakespeare's London?' I ask. Curtain Road? Southwark? Coaching inns? 'Yes. A chance to wander around, talking to people.' I draw out an anecdote about the artist Jo Joelson, who does lighting design on the side, and tell Sinclair about her work in Tokyo last year on an indoor replica of London's own replica Globe Theatre ...

'Artificial London light? Didn't realise until I started working with Marc [Atkins, photographer] how many different kinds of London light there are. There's the dull grey that everyone expects, but that can change spectacularly in seconds. London's prey to all these wildly contrasting micro-climates at any one time. The weather can just sweep in and suddenly bathe everything in clear light. Like it is now, and then, just as suddenly, it's gone. Something else entirely. Since I've been doing the M25 work I think that Heathrow has an effect too. Must have. All those jets constantly coming in. It's like they create their own weather: a kind of Ballardian microcosm.' He looks up at the wheel. 'Should see a fair bit of it from up there.'

I mention the work Sinclair did in the novel *Radon Daughters* on Luke Howard, the East End chemist who corresponded with Goethe, and developed the cloud classification system that's still used today. I'd read somewhere recently that vapour trails have now joined cumulus nimbus etc. as a bona fide cloud form.

'Atkins,' he says, 'has a thing about vapour trails which form an "X". Where two cross over. They're everywhere. These bloody great alphabetic signs in the sky.'

We're due to rendezvous with 'Atkins' next to County Hall in ten minutes or so – he's going to be doing our pictures today. I'm straining my neck to keep an eye out for him – I have no idea what he looks like.

'Don't worry,' Sinclair says, 'You won't miss him, he's about six foot eight.' He looks at the slowly descending capsules between us and the river. 'Wonder how long till someone does a remake of *The Third Man*,' he offers.

In fact, Atkins doesn't show. At the press office, a woman asks me if I'm from the *Idler*. 'Marc can't make it,' she says, 'So he asked me if I could come down instead. I'm Sarah.' BA took so long to confirm our tickets that Marc had assumed it was off.

As we walk across the Embankment and get waved through security it starts to rain; a sudden shower that magnifies the sun's glare off the river in every drop. Sarah marvels at the light, and Sinclair starts telling her about the Tokyo Globe.

He points at one of the capsules. 'They look strangely sinister, don't they? As if you'd get sealed in there and gassed or something. Then sucked out through those big vents under the seat.'

'Have you seen the hatches on the bottom?' I ask, pointing at two trap doors.

'Yes, look,' he says. 'I'm sure that one was full a second ago.'

Our capsule glides slowly along next to the asphalt. I'm expecting us to have to break into a run, to make a leap for it at some critical moment, but boarding the Eye is less dangerous than – though compa-

rable to – jumping onto the running board of a big bubble car that's
doing one mile an hour.

As the doors close behind us, Sinclair takes the bag off his shoulder
and squats down to retrieve his Super 8 camera. 'Thought I may as
well,' he shrugs, switching it on and nestling the finder against one eye.
He points it through the glass and fires a burst of frames at the Palace of
Westminster opposite.

'So why has no one else invited you up here, then?' I ask.

'Well it's not that no one's asked, actually. A few people have, but I've
been so furiously busy finishing the book that I haven't wanted to do
any journalism. And now the film has taken up the whole of the last
two or three months. You're lucky, you timed it right.'

I remember that I'm supposed to be interviewing him. That was the
original idea – how I swung it. Doesn't work in practice. I'm not
stupid enough to fire questions at him and stick a microphone under
his nose. I'd rather let it all sink in. I'm playing with fire here, anyway
– I'm well aware of this. Christ! Look at Atkins. If that's how he
describes one of his friends in a book, how would someone who really
pissed him off fare?

I look down at an oil slick spreading along the river between a string
of orange pontoons and Hungerford Bridge, then turn to look west.
I nod in the direction of Vauxhall. It's too far away to see whether he's
at home, but we know that Jeffrey Archer's place is there, and we're
approaching penthouse-altitude.

'Should be entering the Archersphere any second,' I suggest.

I get a laugh. 'That's a good name for London; the Archersphere.
Would have been, anyway. It's amazing, you know. There was a
review in the paper today – another book of some sort. Did you see it?
The thing is, I think Archer only ever had enough ideas, or energy – or
enough material – for maybe one book. At a pinch. But he can't stop
writing the things. I just don't know why he's got this compulsion to
write more and more books when he's got absolutely nothing to put in
them.' He nods at County Hall, obliquely invoking last year's disgrace.
'Bound to be doing loads of them now.'

It's destined to become a truism, but this wheel fucks your sense of
direction. The river seems to be spiralling around us. Chelsea's there?
I look towards what I think is the east – I'm way off, Canary Wharf is
practically behind me. Planes for Heathrow seem to be going north.

Sinclair has the same problem.

'Look at that insurance building, the kind of Egyptianate one, in Finsbury Square. Amazing.'

He lines up his forearm with the Telecom Tower.

'See the Post Office Tower. Now go along three, below and to the right of that green one.'

'Ah. So what's that dome thing below it?' I ask. (I notice that we're both saying 'above' and 'below' as if we're looking at a picture.)

'Must be Smithfield. Yes, it's Smithfield, I'm sure of it.'

Wait a minute, I think. Then it dawns on me. 'Christ, no, it's the British Library reading room.'

'What? Oh, hang on.' He squats down to rummage in his bag again, and comes up with a pair of glasses. 'That's better. Yes. So that must have been the Senate Building.'

I turn and try to take a bearing from the three towers of the Barbican, to try and find Smithfield. But I can't.

We're not the only ones who are confused, though. At that moment the stewardess comes over. A couple of the other passengers are asking where Buckingham Palace is. 'Look,' says the stewardess, 'you see the river?' She's not pointing at the river. She's Australian, and every sentence is a question. The couple both nod. 'Follow the river up? You see, there? Follow the river up until you see a kind of gold thing?' They nod again. 'Behind the gold thing? That's Buckingham Palace.'

Sinclair and I exchange glances and raised eyebrows. What kind of disinformation is this? That's not the river, for God's sake. It's the duck pond in St James's Park.

'Look at that,' he says, nodding down at Whitehall. 'Vast amounts of real estate. It's hard to visualise just how much of it they own. But up here you can see it all. It's the best view of it I've ever had. See that?' He's pointing at the Shell Building now. 'Used to be able to go up there. Had to pay. No point now.' He turns and shoots another few 8mm rounds. Tracer fire invisible but implied. We're at bomber height, and Sinclair's still got Big Ben in his sights. Best view of London you'll get without going back in time and joining the Luftwaffe. A small storm is coming in over – what? – the Berkshire downs? Can we see that far? It's changed the light, though, already.

A defunct office block beyond Waterloo carries a banner offering apartment conversions, which could only be seriously visible to passengers on the Eye. Reminds me of that Saatchi & Saatchi advert back in '89: 'First over the wall'. Six months, I think, and every roof will carry a hoarding for this captive audience. I'm glad we're on it now, when rooftops are just rooftops, not advertising opportunities.

'It's a leap of the imagination compared to The Dome,' I say. 'You don't have to fill it with something, because there's all this stuff,' I wave my hands in the general direction of outside, 'already here.'

Sinclair starts waving his arms around too. 'What's great about this is that it has absolutely no agenda. You can't impose what people will see. It's up to you; completely open. And it seems that people have completely accepted this. They should have just left the dome empty – just come and see this space, this great thing – instead of filling it with loads of tat. I haven't been on the Jubilee Line yet, but that's part of the problem. I mean there's no interest in useful tube lines, the Hackney Tube extension, say – and that area of London's crying out for it – but they'll build the Jubilee Line extension to make it easy for people to get to where they don't want, or need, to go. The best thing would be if you just got off the Jubilee Line and there was a staircase up into the Dome and then you turned around again and came straight back home.'

He turns and shoots more footage of the Houses of Parliament as we approach the apex of our revolution. From this angle it feels as if we're on a rollercoaster; a curve of track above us, and beyond it the void. I almost expect the car in front to disappear, but gravity has no special claim on them, or us. Sinclair looks back at the car behind us.

He laughs out loud. 'Even up here, look! Even up here people have got to be on their mobiles!'

We both laugh. 'I'm on the wheel!' we say together.

As we approach the platform, I can't believe the ride is over. 'That was the fastest half-hour of my life.'

'Was it really half an hour?' Sinclair asks.

At the exit is a booth selling computer generated images of punters in the capsules. It's unstaffed at the moment, so we both take a 'British Airways London Eye'-logoed mini-carrier bag from the pile on the counter instead.

'A souvenir!' I say.

'Yes,' says Sinclair. 'Should give these out before you get on. Look,' he opens it and mimes puking, 'British Airways sick bags!'

David Nobbs

by Jonathan Coe

IDLER 26 · SUMMER 2000

JONATHAN COE IS ONE OF MY FAVOURITE CONTEMPORARY
novelists. In fact, he is probably my favourite: sharp, funny, intelligent. So the idea of sending him to interview Reggie Perrin writer
David Nobbs seemed too good to be true.

★

Jonathan Coe, author of the seminal satire of the Eighties, *What A
Carve Up!* meets David Nobbs, author of the seminal satire of the
Seventies, *The Fall and Rise of Reginald Perrin.*

My train is running 22 minutes late: a source of irritation at first,
but in the end I don't mind because I realise it gives me the perfect
opening line when I see David Nobbs waiting for me at Sheffield
station. 'Morning, David,' I say. 'Twenty-two minutes late: defective
junction-box at Chesterfield.' He recognises the catchphrase at once
and smiles.

Nobbs is used to having his own jokes quoted back at him. *The Fall
and Rise of Reginald Perrin* had a startling influence on the national
psyche: not just the name of the central character but even whole
chunks of dialogue have become lodged in the public consciousness.

In Plymouth, for instance, there is a restaurant called 'Veggie
Perrin's' which boasts 'no cock-up on the catering front' on its premises. As we pound the streets of Sheffield looking for a suitable interview venue, I tell him that in the Landmark Trust holiday properties
to which I periodically retreat for writing purposes, they have log
books in which people are supposed to record their impressions: the
last one I visited contained the simple entries, 'Great – Tony Webster'

and 'Super – David Harris-Jones'.

But Nobbs's writing is more than just the sum of his catchphrases. He is also a novelist of enormous distinction; a fact which his publishers' thumpingly jokey covers and his high reputation as a TV gag writer tend to obscure. Nobbs's early novel Ostrich Country is an absurdist gem which also manages to satirise the Nineties fads for nouvelle cuisine and food-combining 30 years before they came to pass, while his later books have a tenderness and an eye for detail and a range of human sympathy that is notably lacking from the work of some Booker prizewinners.

When David Nobbs wrote to me a couple of years ago and asked if he could adapt my own novel *What A Carve Up!* for the screen I could hardly believe my luck. Other novelists have to make do with fly-by-nights like Stoppard and Pinter adapting their books, but I'd got the real thing. The mélange of comedy, melancholy and social comment I'd attempted in that novel owed its existence to him, if anybody. Who better to dramatise the tragi-comic excesses of the Thatcherite Eighties than the man who had caught the spirit of another era – the *weltschmerz* of the Seventies suburban commuter – with such lethal accuracy?

JC *The Fall and Rise of Reginald Perrin* seems very much of its time. TV comedy of the late Sixties and early Seventies is obsessed with the notion of the commuter, the little man in his bowler hat and his pin-stripe suit, getting on to the same train every morning and living a rather dull, circumscribed life. You find that figure in Monty Python and you find him in Marty Feldman. Have you any idea why that was?

DN A lot of people were doing it and they were all so clearly identified visually: the rolled umbrella; the way they dressed. But there's no City look any more and I think that's one of the reasons that Reginald Perrin seems to be so of its time. However, seeing it again, it was extraordinary how very relevant and up to date a lot of it was: all about Euro rhubarb and the fact that country people aren't living in the country because they can't afford it. Other things, certainly, are dated. The behaviour of his wife, for example. Her peculiarly bland and servile attitude, just being there to cook meals and never complaining about anything: that struck one as much more extraordinary now than it would've done in 1976.

JC In the second series, though, she became his business partner.

DN Somebody did attack me for the attitude to the wife and then, of course, later on it all changed. They should wait till they've seen the whole thing really.

JC Have you been following the stuff in the papers about Internet companies floating on the stock market? There's a parallel there with what Reggie was doing with Grot. In both cases people are making huge amounts of money by selling something which isn't really a product.

DN I think there is a parallel. It's interesting. I hadn't thought of it until you mentioned it, but it's nice when you do an interview and you learn something [laughs]. I think the funny thing about satire is that it's very difficult to get beyond the real thing, and if you wait 20 years you'll be behind the real thing as the world gets more and more absurd. It's a very interesting parallel, yes it's extraordinary how much money they're making, and extraordinary how much money Reggie made.

JC Are you on the Internet?

DN I'm not on the Internet. At the moment I'm a Luddite through laziness.

JC Did you know there's a Reginald Perrin page?

DN Yes I do, and it's very nice to know there is.

JC But it's American, strangely.

DN It gets shown on public service endlessly in Boston and New York and one or two places. I met a man in a bar of a London Hotel – from Idaho, I think – and I said my name was David Nobbs and he said 'Not the David Nobbs?' He said, 'I didn't get where I am today by being in a hotel in London with The David Nobbs.' It turned out all his students did these catchphrases, and there was this little pool of fans somewhere in mid-America.

JC What do you think of British TV comedy today?

DN It's a very difficult question for me to answer. I have to be careful because I don't watch a lot of television. I find the constant rudery depressing, and I find the shit and fart jokes endless. I find too much sex, I find these things not put in a particularly funny context. I always say farting isn't funny in itself, but it's funny in a wedding reception, or a dinner party or in church. I watched an episode of *The League of Gentlemen* but I watched one that was particularly revolting, with exploding dogs and everything. I couldn't quite take it. People tell me if I'd watched any other episode I'd have loved it.

JC Comedy these days has lost its inclusiveness. Anybody between the ages of 18 and 65 can sit down and get something out of Reggie Perrin,

whereas something like *The League of Gentlemen* will only appear very
funny to a rather restricted age group. And it's kind of baffling and
unpleasant to anyone older. One of my happiest memories of Reggie
Perrin is watching it with my grandfather when I was 14 or 15 and he
was in his seventies.

DN That's absolutely right, and I think it rather reflects life. There's a great
gap between the youngsters in their café bars and the older people in
their pubs; the youngsters in their clubs and the older people in sedate
hotels in the Cotswolds. There's the series with Geoffrey Palmer and
Judi Dench on Sunday evenings which goes on forever and is loved by
old people and is very successful. No young person would watch that
and old people wouldn't watch the other ones. I think that is a shame.
But repeats of *Dad's Army* still cross that divide brilliantly.

JC The generation gap and the disenfranchisement of the older generation
was a theme you took on in *The Legacy of Reginald Perrin*. How did you
feel that series worked out?

DN It didn't work out. We had great fun making it, it had a marvellous
point to make along the way but it just got to it too slowly. I think I
overestimated – not for the first time – the strength of my characters.
I didn't think I needed a particularly strong story. I'm sad about it
because it did build to a marvellous climax with the old people's march.
And of course it was a terrific gamble without Leonard Rossiter. It was
a cheek to do it and it didn't come off.

JC Reginald Perrin is full of character actors who probably can carry a
series by themselves. Geoffrey Palmer, who is a bit player in the first
series of Reggie Perrin, went on to become one of the biggest sit com
stars.

DN Yes. It would be nice to think one pushed him on a little bit. Of course
I took him on myself into a starring role in a thing on Channel Four,
called *Fairly Secret Army*. Another cult show, but a smaller cult [laughs]
and the sad thing with that was that I loved the character and the way
he talked so much that I didn't give him enough storyline in the first
series. I had a strong storyline in the second series, but it was a bit late.

JC Reggie is someone that young people today feel drawn to and feel sympathetic towards. There is a tremendous 'fuck you' attitude about him.

DN Absolutely. There is a moment where he's going to give a speech at the
British fruit seminar and this chap talks about how British food can be
no more or no less competitive than the society in which it is raised,

and he looks at him and gives a little laugh and says, 'Really, that is uninteresting,' and he did it brilliantly. That is saying 'fuck you', but I hope it's saying 'fuck you' more wittily. I love saying 'fuck you', but I don't want to say it just as 'fuck you' every time.

JC I love your feeling in *Reggie Perrin* that there's something magical about trios of lines. There's a moment where CJ is pitching terrible ideas at Reggie, and with each one Reggie sits there thinking to himself, 'Oh my God,' but what he says out loud is 'Wonderful, CJ,' until the third one, when he thinks to himself, 'Wonderful, CJ' and out loud says 'Oh my God.'

DN Someone at the BBC said, 'You can't do that, it's just too complicated' and then somebody else said, 'Well, we can dub those things on later' and Leonard Rossiter wasn't having any of that. We had endless trouble at the beginning of the series with the timing of the Hippopotamus going across the screen. He refused to have it cheated or edited in, he said the look on his eyes must entirely reflect what he had seen and he must see it. He was a perfectionist. They had to announce its start about eight seconds before it came on. It had to be perfectly timed, and it always was.

JC Was he a demanding person to work with?

DN He was a demanding person to work with, but not so much for me because ... it sounds immodest, but it was a pretty good product. Once he said, 'This scene doesn't work at all.' And we all sat round and I said, 'We're not going to rewrite this scene in committee. I'll go home and deliver you a better scene tomorrow.' He was quite frank about the scene not working. I once criticised him, I said, 'Leonard I don't think you're saying that line quite right,' and he said, 'Oh. How would you like me to say it?' I told him, and he said 'Well, your fervour impresses me. I'll do it the way you want it.' And he did it the way I wanted it and there was an enormous laugh, and I said to him, 'I was right wasn't I?' and he said, 'No, you were wrong and so were the audience.' That was his attitude [laughs].

JC Which, would you say, gives you more satisfaction as a writer: the pleasure you give to readers of novels, or the pleasure you give to or have given to television viewers?

DN The great thing about giving pleasure to viewers is that you actually hear the laughter so I suppose that is more instantly rewarding. I once read that my books are very embarrassing to read on public transport because you roar with laughter. So imagine my joy at seeing someone on the Northern Line reading one. I stayed on long beyond my stop to hear him roaring with laughter. He never did. He got sunk in deeper and deeper gloom [laughs].

JC But they are melancholy books. The ending of the first series of *Reginald Perrin* and the novel is quite downbeat. Elizabeth and Reggie are together again but he visits his ashes and has to wipe a tear from his eyes.

DN Yes, it all comes out like that. There is a lot of sadness in the world, obviously, but I do get great pleasure from life, and sometimes I think it would be nice to write something of total pleasure and optimism. But it just doesn't come out like that. I don't think it ever will.

JC Was the process in the Seventies of getting an idea from the page to the screen easier than it is now?

DN It was so much easier that it's almost impossible to talk about it. You didn't have the layers of command, so you actually saw the person who made the decision. That's the key factor. Now you just don't see the person who has the say so, and you don't really know why they say yes or why they say no. I long for the simplicity of the old days.

JC Your creative efforts are being thwarted or held up by exactly the sort of bureaucracy that Reggie Perrin was satirising.

DN I suppose that's one more irony in a very ironic world.

JC What were you more bothered about as a writer when you were younger? Getting the jokes in?

DN Getting the jokes in and showing people how clever I was and therefore occasionally failing to be clever most dismally.

JC I was re-reading your very first novel the other day, *The Itinerant Lodger*. It's very different from the rest of your work. Were you a Beckett fan at the time?

DN I was a Beckett fan at the time and I wrote plays, I was into N. F. Simpson and the theatre of the absurd, and I think it shows. I think the book stands up moderately well and that I did manage to show some of my own voice. I wished I'd shown more but it was a first novel. The publisher's reader actually recommended that it should not be published because it was a load of drivel, but they ignored Alan Coren's advice.

JC Has he ever spoken to you about that?

DN I've never spoken to him. I admire him and think he's terribly funny, but we've never met.

JC   Do you think that if you pitched *The Fall and Rise of Reginald Perrin* today as a six episode comedy drama about a man having a nervous breakdown and faking his own suicide, it would get made?

DN   Well, it's very difficult to say. Probably not, and I'm sure that's the answer you want me to give, and it's the most interesting answer. Things are made that are unusual and off the wall, but it's much harder.

JC   I should ask you something about *What A Carve Up!* What has it been like working on that for the last couple of months?

DN   I bought your book really because you'd written such a nice comment on the cover of mine, I thought I must read one of Jonathan's. I was riveted by it. I thought it was a marvellous book and, as you know, I asked you if it was being adapted and now I finally have the chance to adapt it. I've enjoyed doing it enormously. I think it's very punchy, I love the anger and the drama as well as the marvellous jokes, and I just hope somebody makes it, and makes it soon and makes it well.

I switch off the tape recorder and we go looking for lunch, finally settling on an inexpensive pizzeria where, in tribute to Reggie, I am sorely tempted to order ravioli, followed by ravioli and ravioli. It wouldn't be the first time, David Nobbs tells me, that a fan has carried his devotion that far.

Relieved that the formal interview is over, he radiates the quiet contentment of a man who is now enjoying a happy second marriage, a well-earned tranche of repeat fees from the BBC, and the gratifying sense of having created a fictional character who is still, almost 30 years on, well-known and well-loved by the British public. Not many writers can boast as much.

Two weeks later I am back in a Landmark Trust property on the South Coast, wrestling with a new novel and, of course, the even more challenging task of writing something memorable in the property's log book. A quick flick through the previous entries and I see that somebody has got there before me:

'I didn't get where I am today by writing in log books …'

Patrick Moore

by Alex James

IDLER 28 · SUMMER 2001

WHEN WE ASKED SCIENCE-LOVING, MARS-EXPLORING Alex James whether he'd like to interview Patrick Moore for the *Idler*, he responded 'Oh yeah! Jim'll fix it!'

★

PM So, what's the purpose of the interview?

Patrick Moore is fixing me with his observing eye and I wonder who is going to be interviewing who. I'm on a couch in the wood-panelled salon of his part thatched house in Selsey on the South Coast. Sunlight is streaming through low windows and there is immense calm and room for thought. There's so much to look at. We're surrounded by comfortable chairs and musical instruments, mainly xylophones. There's lots of stuff in here, but it's not clutter. Photos of heavenly bodies, drawings of aliens. There's nothing further removed from *OK!* and *Hello* magazine but this is my idea of a dream house. Here is a man who's written over a hundred books and decoded the cosmos for generations.

AJ The boys at the *Idler* like the idea of your observatory – it's the ultimate shed, where you can go to build your dreams [loud laughter] ... well, that and a light airy chat about the Universe at large.
PM Right you are, right you are.
AJ I'm a musician and ...
PM Do you know Brian May? He's a highly qualified astronomer, an astrophysicist, he's an expert on interplanetary dust, he was on *The Sky at*

Night with me. Oh, no I don't like their music, not my kind of music. I've written quite a bit of music ...

I had noticed some hand-written sheet music at the piano.

PM Oddly enough, can't move my right hand, suddenly went on me. Relic of the war. Friends' wedding next year. Wanted me to compose them a wedding march. Sat down at the piano and thought 'All right, I'll write the piano score down.' Played it though and that's the last time I could play sadly, I can never play again.

The music is still there to behold as you read this and the drama of the situation is almost theatrical. It's quite a romantic image for me. I'd already noticed he can strike a pose for the camera, much better than I can. He pads off whistling cheerfully and quietly to himself and presents me with a CD of his music performed by an enormous orchestra. It's called 'Moore Music' and it kicks ass in the style of Souza. He's quite the Renaissance man: fanatical cricketer, composer, scientist.

AJ Do you think art, music and science all merge into one thing at a certain level? Science is a methodology for approaching the truth in the same way that art is.

PM [Pleasantly] True enough, true enough. You have to be creative to do good science. You've got to think for yourself, that's the whole point. I'm totally art blind, I couldn't draw this cup if I lived to be a hundred [he surely shall]. No idea about art [guffaw].

AJ I'm sure that most people feel they have no capacity for science, in a similar way, you know, people generally think they can't draw or sing or do maths. Anyway you do all your observing in the visual range!

PM Most, if not everything that we know about the cosmos is through the analysis of electromagnetic radiation, and you probably remember from school that light is just one type of electromagnetic wave. In recent decades whole new branches of astronomy have evolved around observing different wavelengths. Radio waves are the most sophisticated means of communication we can conceive at present. Light waves tend to get absorbed by Brian May's cosmic dust but long wavelength radio waves penetrate space unhindered and are what we expect sophisticated civilisations might be using to try to communicate with us.

Patrick had been hoping to make a long series of observations of Mars this year, but the arm business has scuppered his chances. The phone rings and he wanders off, apologising. With immaculate timing many different clocks start whirring and boinging the hour and I enjoy a magic moment. He returns with his little cat.

AJ [Nervous] Well, we're standing on the shores of such profound mystery.

PM [Eyebrow fully raised] We are indeed. There are lots of things I'd like to know, we won't know in my lifetime, but when I think of what we didn't know 60 years ago, we're now batting on a completely different wicket. It's been an amazing period.

AJ [Tackily, possibly] What's the single most amazing thing?

PM [Graciously] I think the realisation that the universe is so...vast. When I was born in 1923 we thought our galaxy was the only one. Now of course, there's thousands of millions. We had all the distances wrong. The real crunch came with the electronic revolution – photography replaced by electronic aids – CCDs. All our ideas about the planets were very largely wrong, we thought Venus might be a world covered with water and there might be life – Ha! Far from it.

AJ Still, there's an outside chance of life on Mars.

PM There may be very primitive single-celled life on Mars, probably is I think. I think we shall soon know. But certainly nothing so advanced as a blade of grass.

A bewilderingly intelligent scientist I met at a cosmic cheese and wine do a couple of years ago had explained to me that life that's evolved elsewhere may have been generated in a completely different fashion – not involving DNA, so we've certainly got lots to learn. In fact half of the matter in the universe is apparently undetectable – we know it's there as we can see its gravitational effect on galaxies. Physicists believe we are moments away from a paradigm shift as devastating as relativity. Newtonian and Einsteinian and Quantum theory are all re-developments of the same processes. The quantity of the knowledge we have is growing at a faster rate than ever. Observational work and reconceptualisation go hand in hand. Often all possible conclusions are mind numbing and there is no need to sensationalise. Bertrand Russell noticed that when you ask, 'Are we alone in the Universe?' either conclusion is daunting.

Alex James and Patrick Moore contemplate the heavens. [Julia Hember]

PM We could have a man on Mars in 20 years if we wanted. No atmosphere though, we could never live there.

AJ We could have a roof on it. I heard somewhere that the sun may have an invisible partner that it's orbiting.

PM We'd have found it by now – there may be another planet out beyond Neptune, but an ordinary planet.

AJ What about the Oort cloud? Thinking about that helps me go to sleep.

PM Ah yes, strange place, they're about six million million miles away, these Oort things – ice particles – it's where comets come from. We landed on the surface of an asteroid a couple of months ago. Eros. Absolutely amazing. Look at that – cats sound asleep. This time last year I was hoping to play cricket ...

AJ So there was a great surge of technology with the moon shots and we were doing everything we could to throw ourselves into space – what happened?

PM Things seemed to calm down with the manned flight programme for two reasons. First, the Russians are essential in this, and they ran out of money. The Americans made a mistake in that they put all their cosmic eggs into one thing, the space shuttle, and they used solid fuels and that awful Challenger disaster. The one thing Werner von Braun told them not to do. That held things up completely. It'll get going again, the international space station is up there now. The un-manned probes to the planets were amazing in this period. We've now contacted all the planets except Pluto. Amazing pictures back from the whole lot!

AJ And the moons …

PM Io, Europa, Callisto, Ganymede. Titan will be next, 2004. We'll find out if there really is a chemical ocean, there may well be.

AJ A lot of moons, no?

PM Well, only four big ones on Jupiter, one big on Saturn – five medium; no really big one on Uranus – five medium again; and one medium with Neptune; unless you count Pluto, which is an oddity; but Jupiter's four and Saturn's one, they're the only planetary size.

AJ Do you feel any scruples about going into space – isn't it a military sector anyway?

PM Not now, let's face it. The first shots were military, but we have to go into space, or we'll stagnate.

AJ Isn't the military the engine that drives the technology that builds it all?

PM Not now. When von Braun was building the V2s in Germany, the RAF bombed it. I wasn't on that raid, but I might have been. Five years later me and von Braun were having lunch together in New York.

AJ Before things can really kick off, we need a new form of propulsion technology.

PM I can't see where that's coming from. In the solar system we can do it with our rockets. If you're going to go further, I don't think any propulsion system will do – you can't go as fast as light for various Einstein reasons. Getting to the stars has got to be by some non mate-rial means, and when you start to talk about space warps, teleportation and mind travel, it's all pure science fiction, but no more than television would have been half a century ago. Don't ask me how it's going to be achieved.

AJ I've been trying to visualise what shape the universe is. Are we perched on the three-dimensional surface of a hypersphere?

PM Impossible to say. We're certainly a few dimensions short. You know, Einstein couldn't have answered that question. I know because I asked him.

AJ Right.

PM I think that there are beings out there that are cleverer than us, for sure.

AJ Shit.

PM They're too far away. Radio waves are too slow. You can't go faster than light and there's no way round that.

He has no family, his girl was killed in the war and like the piano business, that was that, he's never had another. Perhaps this has given him the space to become what he is, it's hard to imagine how someone with a family could be quite so devoted to their work, he's spent thousands of hours mapping the moon from his back garden – 'show me a crater and I'll tell you which one it is.'

He's never lived in London, never fancied it. He's got his thing and let the world beat a path to his door.

After some more coffee we wander round the garden with its temperature gauges, vines and roses. Birds are singing and it's idyllic.

There are several telescopes in various domes all built for him by Fuller of Farringdon Road (always worth a visit). We enter the biggest shed carefully and as the roof glides back with mechanical precision he swings a perfectly counterbalanced telescope through 180° and I realise this is where he spends his time, it's all his machines for finding out what he needs to know. We point her at the sun and project a few sunspots, there's quite a lot of magnetic activity today.

Astronomy is an ancient profession, but here's someone who's cut a swathe for himself. Can you name any other astronomers? Far Out Geezer.

Bill Oddie

by Louis Theroux

IDLER 28 · SUMMER 2001

LOUIS' INTERVIEW REVEALS A RAW, VULNERABLE AND SELF-
doubting side to the former Goodie and TV nature enthusiast.

*

Bill Oddie and I are sitting in the back room of his house in Hampstead
on a rainy afternoon in March. We are surrounded by the comfortable
furnishings of a suburban Bohemian existence – warm cushions with
lots of tiny mirrors sewn into them, wicker tables, an African mask,
sundry musical instruments including a drum kit, and a poster of
Prince wearing nothing but a pair of tiny black underpants. I have been
a fan of Bill's since childhood, when I was obsessed with *The Goodies*.
But when I approached him about doing an interview, I discovered he
had just come out of hospital, where he was being treated for depression. Nevertheless, he was still keen to talk, about both his career and
his illness.

LT I wanted to interview you because I was an enormous fan of *The
Goodies*. When you're young and impressionable, you form a deep and
intimate connection with people on TV. What made it more powerful
with *The Goodies* is that – as far as I'm aware – it's never been repeated.

BO Yes. It's a slightly sore point for all three of us. I don't want to whinge,
but it was a sort of 30-year anniversary-type-thing last year, and a lot
of people said, 'Well, why aren't the BBC doing something?' And it
was weird because a guy called Robert Larson fixed up a night at the
National Film Theatre for us to go and chat to the audience, show a
few clips, that sort of thing, and he sold out in a day! You know, there
were four or five hundred people there and some of the young chaps

Louis Theroux and Bill Oddie in Bill's garden with gnomes. [Julia Hember]

from the various comedy shows. Then Tim went to Australia and they had a Goodies convention.

LT   So it was really big in Australia?

BO   It still is! I did a Michael Parkinson radio show the other day. He's just come back from there and he said, 'Why don't you go back to Australia because you're always on there?'

LT   Do you see any money from that?

BO   Very little, very little.

LT   So it's not enough to live on?

BO   [Laughs] It's not enough to buy a cup of coffee! It's almost funny because you vie with one another as to how low the cheque can be. You get a cheque from six series being sold to Australia, and it's 50p or something like that. It's nothing.

LT   How many series of *The Goodies* did you do altogether?

BO   I think it would be about ten.

LT   How many on BBC and how many on ITV?

BO   There was one series for ITV but we virtually did a series a year for the BBC for ten years.

LT I read somewhere – there's a Bill Oddie fan site, where I read about an appearance at a convention you did somewhere in Britain – I think it was Torquay...

BO I went because Robert Ross had written this book. He was selling it there and he asked me to be a guest for the weekend at this thing – and it was, you're quite right, it was Torquay – well done. [Laughs] They took over the whole of an ancient holiday camp for the weekend, these delegates; and there were about 500 of these people – and they were very nice.

LT All different kinds of people?

BO [Laughs] Err, nope. I'll put it this way, it's a mixture between a convention and going to Lourdes – they were mad, they were dotty. It was a bit strange. They were ever so sweet.

LT Well I think there's ways of being diplomatic. They're just people who are fanatically interested in certain TV shows.

BO Yes, you could put it that way.

LT Every age and gender? That's what I meant: all sorts of people in that sense? All men?

BO Probably more men than women.

LT Slightly geeky types?

BO You said it.

LT That's all right, I consider myself to be a geeky type.

BO You haven't got a mad T-shirt and about 25 books under your arm.

Bill begins talking about his role as the musical brains behind The Goodies. I know he composed the theme music ('Goodies! Goody-goody yum-yum!' as well as the hit single 'Funky Gibbon') and I have brought my guitar along in the hope of jamming with Bill. I am surprised to learn he plays barely any instruments except the drums. He said he used to compose by humming into a tape recorder.

LT So you don't even know what the chords are?

BO No, I don't.

LT So you'd go like this is the song – *oooh oooooh*.

BO Yeah.

LT Did you literally hum that into a Dictaphone?

BO I'm afraid I did, yes.

LT And *Funky Gibbon* was number one, wasn't it?

BO Not quite. It got to two in some charts and four in others. What I
    always used to do was start from a rhythm. I would put that on the
    tape, so I would literally be going [beats in time on his knees] at
    the same time with that bit going during it and then I'd say 'I think the
    bass should go like this, dum dum de dum dum dum'.

*I ask Bill about his Prince poster. Bill reveals himself to be a huge fan, dating
back to the time he first saw Prince perform, in 1979, during the* Dirty Mind
tour. Bill talks enthusiastically about side five and side six of Emancipation,
Prince's triple album.

BO He's just so damn prolific, and I think that's where he got lost. Maybe
    he doesn't care. He doesn't have to. I really don't know. I don't know
    how you judge that sort of person as a person. I don't know if there are
    any rules that apply.

*Just then, Bill's wife Laura pokes her head round the door. She asks if she can
introduce her friend, Sally. They've been writing together in another part of the
house.*

LO [To Louis] You're not being horrible are you?
LT No, no! I don't think so. Am I?
BO No he's embarrassing me because he remembers Goodies things.
LT Yeah, I'm a huge Goodies fan. Well, I would say that everyone my age
    – I'm 30 – was obsessed with *The Goodies*.
LO So do you remember all the scripts and stuff?
LT Yeah!
LO Wow! Really?
LT Well I was surprised when I went back and watched it, I was surprised
    how little talking there was in a lot of them.
BO Our favourite ones are actually the wordy ones.
LT Because I dug it out – there was *Shoot Out at the OK Tearooms*.
BO Oh yeah. Yeah. Yep.
LT [Correcting himself] *Bun Fight at the OK Tearooms*. [General laughter]
    And *The Goodies and The Beanstalk*. That was good. In my mind at the
    time, it was: Oh, my God! What brilliant TV! And it still stands up
    actually.
BO It's not too bad that one. I have seen that one.

LT I mean, so inventive.

LO Loads of special effects, weren't there?

BO There's a lot in it. There's a lot in it.

LT That was a really good one.

LO Was that Alfie Bass?

LT&BO Playing the giant.

 S I like Alfie Bass.

LO No, that one was really good.

BO [Quietly] There was a lot in that one.

LO&S Anyway we'll leave you to it, come on.

Laura and Sally leave the room.

BO [Whispering] Yeah. Sally is a writer. And Laura and she work together
    on children's programmes at the moment. I mean, Laura does all sorts
    of different things.

LT [Whispering] So Laura was ...?

BO [Whispering] On the right.

LT [Whispering] On the right.

BO [Whispering] Right to you. Yeah. Yeah [Laughs]. There aren't any men
    in my life, thank God. I've got three daughters.

LT We should all be so lucky. So as I was saying, the one benefit of not
    having *The Goodies* episodes repeated is ...

BO You've got that memory!

LT Yeah, you've got that memory. It's like an irretrievable golden age of
    youth.

BO I think there's a lot of truth in that. You have your own vision of what
    a programme was like. I don't know, I've always likened it to a pop
    group. I think we produced images like hit records, a visual equivalent.
    So people remember the giant cat ...

LT Tandem bikes ...

BO Yeah exactly, you've got these little images, and you don't want that to
    be blown. So in some ways I agree, but having said that, it was quite
    hurtful ... I was talking to Tim last night, and we were saying – I think
    we all had a bit of a downer in the last year and I just happened to have
    the extreme version, I got clobbered – I mean, I don't mind saying, I've
    got clobbered by clinical depression – for about a month and err it was
    – [To Laura, who is leaving the house] Bye bye, my dear! See you soon!

LT [To Laura] Bye! [To BO] How did that come on? Is that something you've had a history of?

BO No, no, it was, um … you know, I'm happy to talk about it but you become a bit of a depression bore if you're not careful because you do need to talk about it, I mean it's a terribly serious thing.

LT Yeah.

BO I mean, it's life-threatening, because half of bloody suicides are clinically depressed, and now I know what it's like. OK, I may have had a negative streak in me for a long time. I always have had. Even as a kid, I know I was fairly cynical, sceptical and stuff like that. But it was there, it was part of my character, and it never felt like despair or anything. I mean you don't really know. You could get it like you get flu!

LT Yeah.

BO It's as simple as that, you can get it like you get flu and suddenly, early January … one morning … still school holidays, didn't have to get up, Laura had gone to work early and I was just lying in bed and I started getting really bad anxiety attacks and finding myself begin to shake, and feeling absolutely miserable.

LT Just pottering about the house?

BO I was still in bed. I couldn't get up at first, and I had about two hours like that. Then I tried to get up and I was feeling really shaky and I thought, shit, something's going on here.

LT So it was really a physical thing then …

BO Oh absolutely physical: shaky, hot and cold. I went to the doctor in the afternoon. I knew there was something really wrong, and I just found myself breaking down in tears with the guy instantly. I couldn't talk properly. I said, 'Well, I'm not sleeping properly,' and this, that and the other and he said, 'Well, you're showing all the signs of depression.' But – and this is what you have to get into your head – it is a physical ailment, a chemical imbalance.

LT So it's really got nothing to do with what's going on in your life?

BO Not necessarily, no. It tends to have a trigger of some sort but equally – I mean there's books all over the bloody house, like this [indicating a book on the coffee table, Coping With Depression]. You hear of other case histories. Sometimes people get it when they're successful, or just after a huge success … in my case I think there were a few slightly stressful things, or things that had been on my mind more or less right the way throughout the year.

LT Professional?

BO Some of them. And the trigger was the most ridiculous thing, 'cause there's usually something which tips you from just being kind of morose ...

Bill talks about being caught on tape by a police camera, doing 80 in a temporary 50-mile-an-hour area, some time in September. He has been involved in road safety campaigns and regards himself as a conscientious driver. The idea of being disqualified from driving began to prey on his mind.

BO No matter how much I told myself there's nothing you can do, it will probably be all right anyway, go and tell them what happened, you honestly had no idea you were speeding, you need the car for work and all that sort of thing – I couldn't get it out of my head and it completely obsessed me. And there were other things, like the insecurity of work.

LT I was going to ask you about that. As someone who's on TV myself, I'm aware of the insecurity of being a TV presenter. And things are going well for me at the moment, but I'm always aware that there's not that much longevity in the business. I wonder if that played any role in what you went through?

BO I think it did without any doubt. Tim, last night, he said, 'Yeah, I got really depressed last year'. It was like nobody had taken any notice. I mean, we worked for somebody like the BBC for ten years. We had a couple of bloody Silver Roses and Montreux Award bollocks, and huge audiences, and you think, Ohhh, come on! Some producers actually put up the idea of doing a Goodies evening or a repeat thing like 'I Love the 70s'.

LT Yeah.

BO And I was interviewed for all these bloody things and I was on all the damn programmes talking about it but they never showed any of it. [Laughs] There was one tiny clip but they never showed a programme, and I think that actually niggled away as well. But it was mainly the insecurity. I was filming the wildlife series, the one I made last year, but in strict terms I had no work for this year at all, not at all.

LT You looked at 2001 and just saw this big empty space.

BO Absolutely.

LT That must be terrifying.

BO It is. As the years go by you get all the more resentful of it, and more and more nervous about it. You shouldn't think about the insecurities. As you've said, you're doing great at the moment and please God let that continue, it would be deserved. When I was your age, we started *The Goodies*, and we used to work from year to year and they never signed us up for more than one year at a time, but we never thought about it.

LT Did you make good money at the time?

BO No, no, we made more switching to ITV because they gave us a three-year contract. Although we didn't go through the whole three years, we probably made more from that contract than we did for the whole damn series we did at the BBC.

LT Really?

BO Yeah, so it was pretty awful.

LT But as far as the job insecurity goes, it's obviously something we all face – but I mean, I've enjoyed watching your bird-watching programmes.

BO Thank you.

LT It seems like that's quite a regular thing for you.

BO It may seem an odd thing to say, and I'd say it for this magazine, because I probably wouldn't say this anywhere else – but I have the image on the bird programmes – I know this from the letters I get – for being incredibly enthusiastic, and very relaxed and stuff like that. I do ad lib it all, you know, none of it's scripted in any way. I'll have a few noted down before I do a piece, that sort of thing. Anyway I get these letters, saying: 'I love the fact that you seem to love what you do, it's all so natural.' But I know that I'm acting, to a considerable degree.

LT Yeah.

BO It might be take three, say, and I know that it's a performance. I actually find that strange to cope with. This is what I really need to, as they say, 'deal with'. I think, 'Yeah, but I'm acting this really' and they think, 'Oh, he knows so much about it!' Well, some of the things I do, and some of the things I don't, you know? I know about birds, but with other things, the other animals, I want it to play for real but I don't know that much about them. But I can *look* as though I do, if somebody gives me a page of notes five minutes before. So it's, 'OK, have a look, yeah, got that,' and I'll look as though I know exactly what I'm talking about, and I feel – cheated is exactly the right word, because that's what I feel sometimes. I think, 'Why am I giving myself a hard time, because that's what a presenter's supposed to do?'

LT   Yeah, that's the job.

BO   The job of a presenter is to try and look as though you know what you're doing, or admit that you don't in a funny way.

LT   I do the opposite which is occasionally make it look — it sounds like self-flattery — but make it look as though I'm slightly worse at something than I actually am. Like in the rap programme, my free-styling is actually not too bad — [Bill laughs] but they said, 'Oh no we're not using any of that because it's not funny' — so they had to use all the bits where I was really bad [Bill laughs again], so there's a certain phoniness that comes with it.

BO   Yes but that's the job, isn't it? So I don't know why it bothered me.

LT   Does it bother you still?

BO   Yes. Increasingly throughout the year I kept thinking that, it's almost like saying [pleading and chuckling] 'But you don't know—' you know? 'I'm really bleeding inside,' and 'It's not real.'

LT   That's right, that's right: 'It's a lie!'

BO   That had been gnawing away for a long time. I intend to, without going mad on it, try and get some constructive therapy of some sort. Also age begins to worry me, I can't pretend it doesn't. Also, you've seen my taste in music and you know my attitude to things, particularly music, and if I've been doing a talk in the theatre — I do these illustrated talks …

LT   About wildlife?

BO   Yes. So, say the theatre decided to put some music on, and sometimes they'll put some nice classical stuff on and I just want to walk out at the beginning of the talk and say: 'Turn that fucking shit off and put Prince on!' [LT and BO laugh for ages]. I'm sure half the audience would go [deep intake of breath] — because somehow the wildlife image and the countryside should have nice music.

LT   You should come out to 'Head'. You know, the Prince track.

BO   Yeah, [laughing] definitely, I listened to that time and time again when I got the album.

LT   I'm going to make another frivolous suggestion.

BO   Please do.

LT   You could pitch a show, which you could present, on depression. Having experienced it first-hand.

BO   I don't want it to become …

LT   A new hobbyhorse?

BO Exactly, yes, that's exactly right because you can't help talking about it.

LT Yeah, then you'll be acting about talking about acting.

BO Exactly, you need to talk about it. Almost therapeutically. Whether you're talking to a therapist or not. I mentioned it on this Parkinson radio interview. I didn't intend to, but in between playing records, he'd got some research about the fact that my mother was in a mental home, which is true, and I hardly knew my mother at all. I have two or three memories. He said, 'Do you worry that that might be genetic?' and I said 'It's funny you should say that, I've just had a nasty turn—' And he said, 'Do you mind talking about it?' and I said 'Well, OK, just a bit'. I don't remember what I said, it was only a few weeks ago.

LT Was it Radio 4?

BO Yeah. Quite a few people rang up – people I know! – who had written to or rung me saying, 'Yeah, actually I have that; there was a thing in the paper about how John Cleese gets it.'

LT Yeah, I was going to say, John Cleese is known to suffer from it.

BO I mean John's always been pretty obsessed with self-examination. He's been through 500 different therapists by all accounts; I mean he's married three of them, or two.

LT Yeah that's right. All American apparently.

BO Yeah, that's the way to do it, you don't have to pay those fucking great bills then! [Laughs] That was a horrible shock, anybody out there who thinks they've got medical insurance just check the small print! It probably says: 'Does not cover psychiatric.'

LT Really? And at what point, when you went to see the doctor, did it become clear that you needed to go into hospital?

BO It was – you're really told, the key thing – this is horribly heavy really – it's when you start mentioning the dreaded 'S' word, suicide, and er, the way the doctor put it to me was I'd got to the stage where I was almost catatonic. I was just lying in bed.

LT And this was after you'd seen the doctor for the first time?

BO Yeah the first time he'd put me on an anti-depressant, which is perfectly standard. It really is no more different than if you'd got acid indigestion in your stomach, here's a pill that will balance that out.

LT Yeah.

BO And that's what an anti-depressant is, but it does unfortunately take about three weeks to start working, and during that period you can have side effects from that medication which includes things like terrible hot sweats, and your mouth goes all dry. I literally got to the state where you just can't get up, you just stay in bed all day, and you start having really black thoughts, and at some point the doctor will visit you and they will say: 'Are you thinking about suicide?' Strictly speaking, the answer to that was 'yes'.

LT Really?

BO You are thinking about suicide, which is slightly different from saying 'I am thinking about committing suicide'. You do because you can't see any way out. It doesn't matter what they say. They keep saying to you, 'Hang on in there, it will pass, I absolutely promise,' and you just say, 'It doesn't mean a thing to me, I can't believe it.' And unfortunately when they say 'are you thinking about suicide?' you have to say 'yes'. I wouldn't do it, but it just begins to go around and around in your head, you can't think of anything else. It is at that point when your GP will say 'I think you ought to go into hospital.'

LT So you were actually in hospital when *Bill Oddie Goes Wild* was going out?

BO Yes. I was either in hospital, or in bed or in misery – all three mainly – and it was such a fucking waste. The producer would ring up and say 'We got really good figures for yesterday' and I was just going, 'Yeah, so?'

LT So that didn't bounce you back at all?

BO No.

LT It didn't bring you up one infinitesimal amount?

BO Just a tiny little bit yes.

LT That's what amazes me, is how I can be depressed and someone will go, 'I loved that thing you did ...' and I'll go, 'Oh, OK, I feel better'. It's slightly embarrassing how narcissistic I am in that way.

BO No, no, no, no, no. Listen: everybody's like that, it's nice, of course it's flattering – it's beyond flattery though because you are actually entertaining somebody, you're giving them something. If you do a programme which people want to stay in and watch, you've contributed some happiness to their lives, you know. You do that, and I know I have done ...

LT Exactly.

BO You go through exercises when you come through something like this. You write down the things that you are proud of. I've been connected with four programmes during my life which affected people's lives, or lifestyle, or enjoyment of things. The first one was the radio series, *I'm Sorry I'll Read That Again* about 15 years ago, and it was, well, very big really, and masses of people have said, 'Yeah that was what the Goons was for me.' *The Goodies* was obviously another one where people have said, 'Yeah, I was brought up on that.' One is a rather strange one, it's just personal satisfaction. I used to have my own programme on Jazz FM, in their relatively early days. On Sunday mornings I had three hours which I programmed, playing music which wasn't strictly jazz. We called the programme, *Yes, but is it Jazz?* because I'd play anything, like world music. And the other one is the wildlife programmes. I got a bloody great pile of letters, I feel terribly guilty not having answered them. Really nice letters, people saying, I love the programme, it made them go out and do something. Or from old people saying, 'I can't get out any more, you just took me for a walk out somewhere I used to go.' They're beautiful, really, and I have to tell myself that. But boy oh boy, do I have to tell myself that.

LT Well, I think you should be very proud – it sounds patronising but I really enjoyed all the wildlife programmes as well.

Julia, the photographer, says something about taking some pictures outside.

LT Do you want us to go out there?
JH Well, it's a bit cold and rainy.
LT I want to see the frogs, but you're only wearing slippers.
BO Yeah, that's all right.

It's still cold and raining and Bill's only wearing slippers, but the three of us wander out into Bill's little back garden to look at some wildlife and have our photos taken. Bill has said we might see some frogs in his pond but there are none visible, only a grey squirrel on Bill's feeder and Bill and Laura's collection – 20 or 30 strong – of garden gnomes. Bill's slippers start getting damp and we head back inside. We go upstairs. Bill has a wall of personal memorabilia, including his original sketch of the three principal Goodies characters. In the interest of creating an engaging photograph, I suggest that Bill looks at me through his binoculars. Bill says no, and we all laugh because the idea is so ludicrous. During a lull in the conversation, I mention that I was a keen bird-watcher as a child, but that I got bored seeing the same birds over and over again. Bill says, 'I know what you mean.' We go back downstairs, and Julia leaves.

LT So how are you feeling now? The big picture?

BO Much better – I think it takes quite a bit of time before you lose the fear. You have to do a bit of therapy – but you know you just get little bits of anxiety things, the sort of thing that most people get anyway. But when you've been through something like that you worry about it: 'God, am I relapsing?' You might in the future have to face the possibility that it could happen again.

LT And are you going to have to stay on medication?

BO For a while. That's just the way you do it. I'm probably working more than I should, but it's almost impossible not to. I try to say no, but it's probably better to be working, so I think the prognosis is reasonable [laughs].

LT You know that quote about how 'what doesn't kill you makes you stronger'.

BO Yes.

LT Any evidence to believe that might be the case?

BO Yes, I think there is some truth in that. It's made me think about my attitudes to things, because I know my negativity thing is a danger, and I know it's a bring-down for other people. Laura, for example, is a very positive person and I know it must get on her nerves for me to be negative about things. I've got a very unsociable streak in me as well, and it's made me think about that. Just try and be a bit more affable with people when you just pass them in the street, you know, instead of just saying hi, stop and pass the time of day, that sort of thing.

LT Really? Because, well, it's the first time I've met you, but you seem very affable.

BO Socially, I'm deeply inept most of the time, and I'm not being self-deprecating, it's true. I mean it's partially historical: I was an only child, brought up at the edge of Birmingham. We had little social life at home, it was just my dad and his mother. I really never developed terribly good social skills. I've always been terrified of going to parties.

LT How funny. So rather than that you'd tend to opt out and say 'Oh no, I'll just chill at home' and listen to CDs or whatever?

BO Yes, absolutely that. I think one of the things that sort of struck me, relevant to the sort of chilling out and that sort of thing, I jotted this down the other day, it's sort of my Oscar Wildism.

LT Yeah.

BO There's a thin line between solitude and loneliness. You can bird-watch in crowds but I don't, and I spend a lot of time on my own. Obviously I had to when I was a kid. I wasn't weird in that sense, I mean, sport was my main thing at school, so I had a social side there. But I do spend quite a lot of time on my own and I like to think that I'm strong in that sense – that I can manage on my own. But I don't think I can. I don't think I have been able to for years and this has brought it home to me: the fact that there isn't quite such a solid base as I'd like to think. I've always liked to think I was terribly together [laughs] and I'm fairly organised. I work hard and everything like that. But one's more vulnerable than you realise, I suspect, underneath.

LT It's funny: as well being on TV – I mean I'm on TV but I'm also a watcher of TV – I see someone on TV and I think they must be naturally outgoing and gregarious.

BO Are you?

LT Not really, no.

BO No, so you know it's not true, see?

We talk for another few minutes, then I say goodbye. Julia is still outside, packing up her kit. She asks Bill for an autograph. Seeing her, I do the same. When Bill has gone I look at the inscription. It says: 'To Louis. From a fan! Thanks for remembering!! And so young too.' A month or so after the interview, I called Bill to see how he was doing. He told me the BBC were renewing his wildlife series and he'd had other offers of work, including a TV segment about going on retreat in the Scottish town of Findhorn. He sounded much improved.

Alan Moore

by Jonathan Ross

IDLER 28 · SUMMER 2001

HIS IS THE SECOND INTERVIEW WE PUBLISHED WITH
Alan Moore. This time we asked Jonathan Ross to interview
him, knowing that Ross was a huge fan. He readily agreed.
Reading it back now, I am surprised to see that Ross seems to be a fan
of the anarchist intellectual Noam Chomsky.

★

Alan Moore is the greatest comic book writer alive today. This isn't
me being deliberately cute or contentious – it's about as close to a fact
as you can get when dealing with opinions. In just about every
respectable poll of the comic-loving community – like The Harveys or
the recent *Comic Buyer's Guide* poll – Moore comes out on top – and
normally by a very long shot. I think I might even venture that he is the
greatest comic book writer ever, in the history of the medium. In fact,
I'll go further. He is the greatest living comic book writer that ever was
or ever will be, until this beloved and much derided medium inevitably
dies out from apathy, or collapses under the weight of too many overly
muscular men in tights trying to save the world.

If you don't know much about comics – and chances are you don't
because you're a hopeless waste of chemicals who buys *FHM* when
your *Idler* pals aren't looking – then here's all you need to know to get
started. Moore writes comics. He writes comics that successfully take
the essential ingredients of whatever genre he's working in – old style
superhero, gothic horror or science-fiction adventure – and he twists
and teases them out of shape and into something utterly new and completely intoxicating. He took *Swamp Thing*, a so-so monster-mystery

book, and made it into a dark, weird love story. He fooled around with Superman and actually made that dullest of dull bores into a fantastic riff on what a day in the life of a super-powered freak would be like, if the bad guys really did use their immense powers for evil – and not just that mischievous tomfoolery that we all knew would never lead to them ruling the world. With *Watchmen* he gave us a dystopian take on the whole super-hero genre. And most recently, with *Tom Strong*, *The League of Extraordinary Gentlemen*, *Promethea*, *Top 10* and *Tomorrow Stories* he has produced – from scratch! – a whole new comic company that is so far ahead of the competition in terms of skill and craft and originality that it has caused grown men to fall to their knees in comic shops and sob like middle-aged babies with gratitude. Or maybe that's only me.

So when Idler HQ asked me if'd like to meet the great and beardy one, I rushed at the chance like Charlie Sheen at a porn starlet. But – and this may surprise you – I felt nervous. Not a feeling I'm overly familiar with, having met and interviewed – well, almost everybody since the bird of fame and good fortune first alighted on my shoulder about 14 years back. But Moore was a different proposition. Here was someone who I didn't want to entice pearls of wit or wisdom from, didn't hope to hear amusing or bitchy anecdotes about his peers. Here was someone I just wanted to sit near and bask in their presence. So what follows is a sort of messy record of the meet as we ate at Momo's Moroccan restaurant in Heddon Street, just around the corner from the very phone booth that David Bowie camps it up in on the sleeve of *Ziggy Stardust And The Spiders From Mars*.

Alan is, unsurprisingly I suppose, just like his writing. In short, he's not what you'd expect. Tall, bearded, long-haired and dressed all in black with a long, silver-topped walking stick. A casual observer would write him off as a goth or mystic, a new age feng shui nut with a taste for herb teas and early Hawkwind, a lover of underground comicana and hardcore adult stuff that would confuse and confound the fan boys and have their parents calling the social workers out. But he's none of those things. Well, actually he does rather like herb tea and as for his feelings about early Hawkwind I suspect that, much like you or I, he has no strong opinion one way or the other. But here he is on the need for mainstream comics as a way of introducing new ideas into a tired format – I asked him about the style of his girlfriend Melinda

Gebbie, who draws the strip 'Cobweb' currently running in *Tomorrow Stories*.

JR I love the art in 'Cobweb'. It's a really, really weird style for mainstream comic readers to see.

AM This is what we wanted. The idea behind them is that mainstream comics are pretty clearly going down the toilet. You get people like Gary Groth and Fantagraphics who will applaud that, but I don't think they quite realise the implications. The thing is that no comic shops can stay open selling Acme comics, From Hell or any of these books, worthy as they are. You've got to have The Uncanny X-Men there and you've got to have Spawn and all this stuff for the shops to stay open. If mainstream comics go down the tube, it pulls the rest of us along too. So it seems to me that you could invigorate mainstream comics so that you wouldn't have to separate comics out into mainstream, independent, underground, alternative: because it's too small to categorise like that.

JR So you disagree with that phrase that we all got so tired of seeing a few years back: 'comics: they're not just for kids anymore'.

AM 'Comics have grown up.' Me and Frank Miller have got a lot for answer for, it has to be said. When I did *Watchmen*, I thought, great, people are going to feel compelled to look at the clever storytelling involved and they'll feel compelled to match me or better me in coming up with ways for telling stories. But instead, it seems what most people saw was the violence, the grimness, the layer of atheist pessimistic politics that was glossed over it. That's what got regurgitated and recycled with the Vertigo books.

JR It's still happening.

AM Well, one of the main things I've got against Vertigo, and there's some great books that Vertigo do – but the thing I find a bit of problem is that their atmosphere, their ethos or whatever, seems to be based on the bad mood that I was in about 18 years ago. It's not even their bad mood. I was in a bit of a strop, you know, about politics in general, because of the Thatcher years.

JR It was a bad time, yeah.

AM And that might have coloured my outlook somewhat, but I don't see why it should colour everybody else's in exactly the same way.

JR I'd have thought you'd have got it out of your system with that thing you did with Bill Sienkiewicz, *Brought To Light*.

AM I did, yeah.

JR I always thought that looked very cathartic.

AM I thought that was one of my best works. I'm glad you remember it, Jonathan.

You really have to get hold of a copy of *Brought To Light*, the best and most unsettling piece of Chomsky-like political truth telling I've ever seen, and one of those books which hits you – SMACK – between the eyes with the potential that the medium has.

But here's another thing about Alan Moore that I really want to share with you. He's a genius. He really is a fucking Grade A once-in-a-lifetime inspirational talking-in-tongues genius. And of course being a genius means that his ideas and his approach and his methods have been stolen and appropriated and homaged by just about every lesser talent who trails in his wake. It also means that there's a legion of Moore devotees like myself who pore over every panel of every book he's worked on – and of course he has his fair share of unofficial websites on our glorious Internet which comes in handy when you're trying to ensure you catch every last reference that Moore crams into his work.

JR So what about the Alan Moore mythology that exists out there? I went on the Internet and had a look at a couple of the Alan Moore sites – it is a strange place to go unchaperoned. There's a few guys out there who take quite a scholarly approach to your work, and almost see it as their job to be librarians or collaters of it all.

AM There's one bloke who analyses *The League of Extraordinary Gentlemen* – and it's just one bloke – I thought it must be a team of literary fellas.

JR And he picks up all your references. I get the feeling from your books that not only have you read a lot, but there's a continuing quest for knowledge.

AM I've always been absorbing information in one form or another. I got chucked out of school when I was 17 which is more or less when my education started.

JR You were expelled?

AM Yeah. The way that school seemed to me was that there was an overt curriculum – reading, writing and arithmetic – and a covert curriculum, which was more or less punctuality, obedience and the acceptence of monotony. In a lot of cases it seemed that school was like aversion therapy. It wasn't there to teach you knowledge, it was there to put you off learning. You'd associate learning or reading with work and you'd associate work with drudgery. This is why most people are happy to just sit down in front of the television at night. 'I'm not actually doing any work, therefore I must be having a perfect time.'

JR Being entertained, it's a passive thing.

AM Yeah. Now, I was shunted out of school when I was 17. The headmaster, he took against me, I'd like to think that it was a class thing. He wrote to all the various colleges around and said, don't take this kid because he's a corrupting influence on all the others.

JR Bastard!

AM Well, I was 17 and I was a pretty hellish 17 year old. But, I was only 17! He wrote to all the employers telling them not to give me a job. That was mental, but I was forced back on to my own resources and started to read voraciously and learn and filled my head with various stuff and it's all back there in a soup and I'm putting more stuff in there all the time. I read very quick. I sort of suck 'em in – it's just gone in to the general silage vat in there and it will ferment and maybe it'll evolve into something in twelve years time.

JR What I hate about a lot of modern comics is that they are relentlessly dark, and they never step outside this template. Whereas even in *Watchmen*, for example, I'll give you an example of something which I remember finding genuinely inspirational and educational. One issue, you tell a story as if it appeared in an old pirate comic book. It loops back into the history of comics, which I only found existed after reading that. At the time you opened the eyes of this young fan boy to what comics had been once, and maybe could be again.

AM *Swamp Thing* is probably more of a template for the Vertigo books than *Watchmen* was, but with *Swamp Thing*, you've got all these stories which are really horrible, really grim and really depressing, but then you'll have these little stories like the *Swamp Sex Issue*, a love poem more or less.

JR Yeah, some of them were quite light.

AM In a way it's crueller, if you give people a love poem they'll numb out and switch off, it keeps the horror fresh if you …

JR … give a little taste of sorbet in between the death and desolation.

AM You feel the pain much greater.

JR It's making me want to go back and re-read *Watchmen*. Beautifully done, sir!

AM I don't know whether it's *The Sopranos* but recently I've found myself really getting hooked on the mafiosi.

JR I haven't watched *The Sopranos* yet, I'm embarrassed to say, because I missed the beginning of it, and I didn't want to come in halfway through so I've now got them ready to watch, and everyone raves about them ...

AM It's Shakespeare, it really is. I mean I'm very, very hard on most television work, and most film work, but *The Sopranos* is like Shakespeare. The characters are so wonderful, the writing is terrific. I envy you.

JR You don't smoke, do you?

AM I'm quite happy at the moment. I'm trying to stop the drink. I decided that, it was really because I was bored with drink and I wasn't having any fun with it anymore and I felt the same thing about smoking.

JR Are you sociable in Northampton? Do you go out much? Or do you pretty much stay at home?

AM If you asked that lady on the radio [I had mentioned on Radio Two that Northampton was home to the country's foremost comic book writer, much to the bemusement of the lady who had phoned in from there to win a Ricky Martin CD], 'What about Alan Moore?', she'd say, 'Oh yeah, that bloke with the walking stick and the beard, oh yeah, lovely chap, got a note from him the other day, know him very well.'

JR Is it not misanthropic anyway, the desire not to mix?

AM Possibly it is, as you may have noticed, I'm partly deaf. So you'll have to excuse me.

JR What, in both ears?

AM No, only that one, and I'm practically blind in that eye and practically deaf in that ear so it balances out ... One of the reasons I stopped drinking is because I don't like pubs, and background noise and it gets a bit diffficult ...

JR They get very noisy ...

AM ... and also I think that during the Eighties, the conventions, that put the wind up me a bit.

JR There was a period when *Watchmen* was huge, and you were like God. The Great God of Comics. I remember you coming out and people went nuts. It was like a rock star, or deity, it was that sort of insane level of adulation ...

AM Yeah.

JR That must have been strange for you anyway, but what did fans want from you, what was the exchange between you?

AM Um, I don't know... I mean I'm a very untidy person, I can't be bothered shaving most mornings. However, this does seem to give a certain messianic gloss ...

He stares at me in a Manson sort of way. Charles, not Marilyn of course.

JR Especially if you do that with your eyes, Alan!

AM Yes!

JR No, I like it, keep it going, it's good!

We spoke about a lot of other things, and comic books and creators too obscure to inflict on you. I dropped Alan off at the station and went home to re-read every one of his books that I could dig out. Reading back through the transcript of our meeting I realised that I could have asked him a thousand better questions – could have probed and got to grips with the inner man, could have eased out his hopes and dreams, lingered on his regrets. But fuck! It was Alan Moore! You're lucky I managed even one semi-coherent sentence. Now if only the *Idler* can get me an audience with Elvis I'll die happy tomorrow.

Neville Hodgkinson

by Will Hodgkinson

IDLER 28 · SUMMER 2001

Tom was 13, he got involved with a meditation group called the

HIS IS AN INTERVIEW BETWEEN MY BROTHER WILL AND our father Neville. The theme Will explores here – the effect of my Dad's spiritual awakening on our family life in the Eighties – is the subject of his new book, *There Are Yogis in the House*, published by Blue Door in 2014.

*

Parents are embarrassing. It is the duty of every good parent to make their teenage offspring shrivel up into a tiny ball of pure I-wish-I-didn't-existness at least once a week. But having your father become celibate and join a strange religious order just as puberty hits is a few notches up from dancing badly to 'Hey Ho Silver Lining' at Uncle Richard's third wedding.

It's taken a while to realise that Tom's and my father is actually a brave man who has been entirely true to himself. When I was 11 and Tom was 13, he got involved with a meditation group called the Brahma Kumaris, whose central beliefs are that the soul is eternal, that time is cyclical, and that we can return to our natural, soul-conscious state through meditation, contemplation and study. Soon our parents were sleeping in separate rooms and our father was inviting crowds of softly-spoken sari-clad yogis to our semi in Richmond – that's when he wasn't being discovered by our friends meditating on the kitchen table at four in the morning. As our mother has said, rather than losing her husband to another woman, she lost him to God.

He's been faithful ever since. These days he lives a communal life with other BKs at a retreat in Oxford, and in order to understand his choices better, I went down there with a tape recorder and a few questions.

WH What was your life like before you became involved with the Brahma Kumaris?

NH Fairly frenetic. I'd been working for four years as medical correspondent for the *Daily Mail*, which was a very intense job — it was a demanding paper, Liz [Mum] was getting her career going, and you and Tom were growing up, so it was hard to balance everything out. I couldn't put a stop on the work — it took everything out of me and left me completely dry. I never switched off. I was doing well with all that drive, but it wasn't sustainable. I was 37, and felt that I couldn't carry on like this. I felt hollow inside. Looking back, there was a negative component to working that hard — it was an ego-driven thing. All my identity was in my work and family. If I saw a big byline in the paper I'd feel a temporary release from my driven state, like a fix. The next day, if my story hadn't worked out, I'd feel completely deflated.

WH So your well-being was in the hands of other people.

NH Totally. And on the family level too. The very materialistic outlook I'd lived by for many years was leading to Liz and I being very self-indulgent. Instead of using time constructively, we'd use leisure time to go hunting for new pictures for the house, for example — it was all about acquisition, about finding external ways of defining ourselves.

WH So what led to the life you're living now?

NH I'd started to understand the importance of the mind in determining our health and happiness, and I gravitated towards doctors who were treating patients at that kind of level. Medicine was in a critical state at that time; a lot of doctors had felt that they'd just become pill-pushers, and this problem in medicine reflected the problem in myself. Around this time I'd become interested in meditation through meeting doctors who were suggesting it as a relaxation technique. One of these doctors invited me to a press conference with a visiting swami from an eastern meditation school. After the talk they did a little chant, and in the silence that followed it I had an extraordinary experience: my eyes were closed, but a golden red light seemed to open out from my forehead. This shook me profoundly. I remember walking the streets for about two hours afterwards. Back in the office, I tried to analyse it away scientifically — I looked up *Gray's Anatomy*, thinking that it might have been caused by an electrical discharge between the two halves of the brain. But I couldn't get away with that. A couple of days later I handed in my notice at the *Mail*.

WH But at this point you still didn't know about the Brahma Kumaris.

NH No. I got a freelance job to cover a health conference, and I met a young woman who was involved with the Brahma Kumaris. Something about what she said struck a chord, and I wanted to meet the sisters of this movement. Liz and myself met them and the contrast between our reactions was very great – Liz went there as a journalist, sitting at the centre and scribbling notes, but I was entranced.

WH But weren't you suspicious of this spiritual movement, having avoided any sort of religious life up until then?

NH I had a very negative view of religion and the things that have been done in its name, but there was a yearning in me. From the age of 13 on I'd decided that there was nothing, it was a fantasy, but the interest was always there. My initial reaction to the BKs was that there was something beautiful both about them and what they were talking about, although I couldn't initially understand the ideas about the soul and the supreme soul, and a cycle of time. My belief system then was a materialistic one and wouldn't allow for these beliefs, but I kept going because the experience of meditation was so good – I'd fly into these beautiful experiences of an innate wisdom that seemed to bypass the intellect entirely. The shell of my materialism was pricked by this needle of truth, even though that truth didn't make sense to my intellect.

WH At this stage we were living a very conventional life – semi in Richmond, Volvo in the driveway. So did this spiritual discovery suggest a new life?

NH No, there was no suggestion that I should take myself off and stay on some mountain.

WH But you have taken up a very ascetic lifestyle now.

NH Many years later. But some things started to change straight away – a vegetarian diet, celibacy, no drinking. These were put to me as options to improve the experience of meditation.

WH Wasn't celibacy a problem?

NH No, because Liz and I had been together for 20 years, and that side of life had become rather empty for me, like a need rather than a loving relationship. Liz was immediately interested in celibacy from a feminist perspective, even though she wasn't getting the pay-off of meditation.

Sex had in any case started to become an issue between us, so celibacy actually improved our relationship.

WH What was the reaction of your friends to this new life?

NH They thought I'd gone mad. One was very anti – he had another friend who had gone off to something he saw as a cult, and when I was expressing this interest, he thought it would ruin my life. He bombarded me with documents about cults and so on, and I felt that this showed a great lack of faith in me, frankly. It seemed more to protect himself, rather like a smoker when one of their number gives up. I'm afraid I didn't respond very well, and the friendship faded away. Other good friends expressed concern too.

WH But not Mum?

NH No, because she had that genuine respect. She appreciated the spiritual input, and saw that there was nothing cultlike about it. I understand concern about cults, because there's such a hollow in so many people's hearts they can be easily exploited by someone with selfish motives, but I felt that these friends never questioned me about what was going on, it was just a reaction, whereas Liz was open about it. Although she was always the interested journalist, never the participant.

WH But she ended up getting irritated with it, or more to the point, with you.

NH Yes. I see now that in order to fill with the positive qualities that had somehow drained from me, I needed to give my heart to it. I wasn't making a success of living in two camps – as the journalist and the family man, and as the soul searcher.

WH I didn't like it when you drifted around in white and talked in a soft voice.

NH When I was like that it was because of what I'm trying to explain: on the one hand I was attracted by this but I wasn't truly doing it. It's not a question of giving up work and family, but transforming your relationship with them, and become more giving and less needy, dependent. But I had a lot of dependencies, especially with my relationship with Liz, and that was stopping the soul from really receiving the repair job that it needed. So I talked about it too much, to try and talk myself into it, in a way.

WH Also it justifies it more, if you manage to get your family into it.

NH That's right, because of the insecurity. It's another form of ego, a false identity. The whole game is to shift the locus of identity from outside things like car, house, job, family, money, and to move it to an inner place. To identify yourself as a soul-seeking yogi is just another trap.

WH I also didn't like the forced, superficial trappings of the yogi life – white women feeling they have to wear saris and so on.

NH I agree. They can be offputting to say the least. We've learnt a lot over the years.

WH So these days, you live in a yogi community and live that life fully. What's a typical day now?

NH Get up at 3.30AM, first meditation is at 4 until 4.45, which the residents do as a group. Then I'll have a shower, a bit of study, sometimes I'm on early morning reception duty. Then at 6 there's a further meditation; at 6.30 we have a class where students come from the surrounding area, and that lasts until about 7.30. Then breakfast, and off to a fairly typical working day. For me that means my writing, and I help with the life of the house – I might get some vegetables, run someone to the airport, look after a guest.

WH So how have you benefited from the meditation-based life?

NH Professionally, my motives have become more positive, which is a great strength. I am far less stressed by ups and downs. Spiritually, the hollow that I used to feel has gone. I feel I am much more genuinely giving in all my relationships.

WH Do you never miss the old life?

NH When I first came here I did feel a gap – I was spending my time strengthening my relationship with God, but I realised that I had still been taking a lot of support from work and family. Living here has enabled me to become charged up internally through the yoga, and over the last two years I've come to a new level of naturalness and happiness.

WH But in this pursuit to live your life on a soul-conscious level, surely you have to do something with it, or it's just selfish. What's the ultimate purpose?

NH To become better able to be giving, creative and constructive with one's relationships with other people, work and the world. How that is done varies from person to person. My lifestyle is an exceptional one – there are only 20 of us living here, while there are thousands of people following the yogi life in a more conventional way, with jobs and families. But my case was such a needy one that this intense experience is what was required. I may not be here forever – I like it here, I love the work and the people, and the fact that we have something like 10,000 guests coming through every year, so it's not isolated – but I may have more to offer to journalism still.

WH Do you not miss the cultural life?

NH Many people nourish themselves spiritually through cultural life, but the path I've chosen concentrates on this relationship with what we call the supreme source of consciousness, and rebuilding oneself through that relationship, and doing what one can to share that with others. I see films on long-haul flights and I'm always rather fascinated, but I often found television and film exploitative: it grabs you and draws you in and leaves you drained. I think I have something of an addictive personality, and I was always a bit of a sucker for that, and grateful to be away from that. I did read the first Harry Potter book recently, and thoroughly enjoyed it, but it's not the centrepiece of my life to be doing those things. Often they're more of a comfort zone than something that is going to make you strong and independent.

I've felt a lack of intellectual questioning with the Brahma Kumaris in the past. That's a fair point, and that's changing, as people become more mature about this. There's much more debating going on. We've also had a number of conferences on science and consciousness recently, where we've been looking at the views coming out of quantum physics and the areas of science where some frontier thinkers are suggesting that the material explanation of the world simply doesn't work. We can build jumbo jets and have hip ops, but the suggestion that consciousness and our sense of individuality is simply a creation of brain function has no scientific support – there's nowhere in the brain that gives that sense of self. Also, some interpreters of quantum physics are suggesting that the human observer is not just involved with material reality as it unfolds, but that the human is fundamental to it – consciousness may precede what happens at the physical level. This kind of thinking is providing a useful bridge between science and spirituality.

Will Hodgkinson's book *There Are Yogis in the House* is published by Blue Door in 2014.

Penny Rimbaud

by Tom Hodgkinson

IDLER 29 · WINTER 2001

I FOUND PENNY RIMBAUD TO BE HUGELY INSPIRING BECAUSE, in Socrates-like fashion, he questions every single bit of received wisdom that one has. He doesn't believe in any of the normal stuff: the emotions, empathy, psychology – they all come in for a right pasting. Penny went on to become a great friend and also a contributor to the *Idler*.

★

Julia and I arrive at Dial House one crisp bright morning in September. Jeremy Ratter, AKA Penny Rimbaud, co-founder of anarcho-punkers Crass, and of the Stonehenge Free Festivals, and winner of a Beatles art competition on *Ready Steady Go* in 1963, is up on the roof. It's nice to see that a champion of DIY culture is still doing it himself. He is in the process of re-tiling the entire thing, a job that has been put off for something like ten years while he has been fighting a nasty court case against the former landlord. It's a case he and housemate Gee – artist, illustrator, architect of the Crass iconography – have just won. In February 2001, a friend lent them the £150,000 they needed to buy the house and they have now made over the property to a trust. They plan to develop the house and garden as a creative retreat, or 'centre for alternative globalisation'.

Rimbaud first moved to this little corner of the Essex countryside over 30 years ago in search of a quiet place to think, which was in striking distance of London (it's just a short cab ride from the house to Epping, last stop on the Central Line). The then-derelict cottage, with its acre of land, became the home of Rimbaud's activities. It developed into a commune which attempted to live out the ideals proposed by first hippy and then punk. They really did tune in, turn on and drop out, and then they really did try to create anarchy in the UK.

Crass, notably, was a hugely influential project. Rimbaud has said that he was always more interested in ideas than in rock'n'roll, and it was this thirst for new ways of thinking that led Crass to sell over two million records in the late Seventies and early Eighties. They popularised the anarchy symbol, and turned on a whole generation of young people to radical political thought and the ideals of self-determination, truth, art and freedom. The records still sell: indeed, the eight members still share an annual income of over £60,000 a year from record sales.

We sit down at one of the innumerable benches that dot the garden and drink coffee. The sun comes out. I tell Gee and Penny of the recent progress of the *Idler*, of our so far successful experiment in independent publishing. Gee believes it is much the best path: to stay independent, to avoid public funding, avoid being bought out. Rimbaud, shaggy of hair, calf bleeding from a roofing wound, smoking roll-ups, starts to talk of how, at 58, he still dreams of breaking the mainstream.

PR I always refer back to *Big Sur*, Kerouac's book that he wrote after *On The Road* was published. It's a huge trail of disillusionment. It's stupendous. It was his last book, I think, and after that he sunk into drink and despair. He had this dream that *On The Road* was his message to the world, and it did, in time, have a profound cultural effect. But it was too late for him to realise it, benefit from it. It had no effect on him. I think it's one of the most beautiful books ever written, because there's no aspiration, no hope left. It's just raw Kerouac. I've been attempting to write coming from there, wherever that is. My most effective piece of work is what I've just finished. I wrote it whilst we were going through this court thing, so I wrote it when I didn't know I was writing it and I ended up with a book. It's the first book I've written outside myself. I've always tried to do that but never succeeded, and now I know how to do it.

TH Rather than start out with a plan?

PR I had a thing that if I started trying to reason, and therefore started understanding, I would erase it. If I understood it, it wasn't valuable. There are huge passages of ridiculously stupid pornography which doesn't even interest me. It doesn't turn me on or off. It's just so bland. Very odd.

TH Dr Johnson said that if you write a sentence and look back on it and go, 'oh, that's quite good', that's a sign that you should cut it out.

PR Definitely. If one writes a sentence and it remains a conundrum or a paradox then there's a value because it means you're on a trail, you're walking down a path. The only time I didn't was when I wrote *Shibboleth* [Rimbaud's highly readable and enjoyable autobiography, which I thoroughly recommend], which I regret in some ways. AK [the anarchist publishing house] wanted me to do it and and I'd always wanted to tell the story of Wally, my friend who set up the Stonehenge Festival. That was the way I justified it – to tell Wally's story properly. [Following the first Stonehenge Free Festival, the life-loving, positive Wally was eventually arrested by the police, sectioned, given massive doses of largactyl, almost made into a vegetable, and died after a supposed suicide attempt. Rimbaud believes it was murder].

TH Shall we have a wander?

Gee takes us for a tour of the abundant garden. I've never seen so many sheds in my life. This is great, because as any idler knows, sheds are invaluable spaces for reflection and contemplation. One of the sheds is Penny's home: his desk and his bed are in there. Another is being made into a studio with a bed. Another houses the bikes. Another shed has been made into a writer's retreat, complete with stove and kettle.

GV We used to have goats but they all gradually died, of old age. And we were on tour so much with Crass that we didn't get any more. That mound up there [pointing to a grass mound topped with silver birches which looks like Teletubbyland] was from earth out of the barn. The legal thing has taken up a lot of time and energy. And they put a ban on us doing anything on the house. It was leaking everywhere. We'd done it for 30-odd years, all ourselves. We said, either you do it, or we'll do it and send you the bill. They'd said if we touched the house, they'd take us to court for breach of the tenancy agreement. Now we're dealing with the problems caused by two years of leaking. Everything is chaos at the moment.

To the side of the house sits the vegetable patch, where Penny and Gee grow almost all they need for their vegetarian diet. A most remarkable feature of the garden is that every few yards there seems to be a bench, or seat, or table. It's a philosopher's paradise: go for a stroll, get hit by a thought, and you'll be able to sit somewhere beautiful and cogitate further. Every tree stump has been carved into a sculpture; every fence post likewise. There is an overgrown pond and four huge pollarded trees, so symmetrical and evenly-spaced they look like an artwork. The garden is like a condensed version of a Capability Brown stately home garden: built for quiet repose, packed with follies, hermit's caves and grottos.

Penny now takes us on a tour of the house. It is a magnificently wonky jumble of rooms, about 14 in all. Tongue and groove walls and wooden floorboards, stained-glass windows and plants are everywhere. There are sitting rooms, studios, guest bedrooms. The black-painted floorboards upstairs slope steeply. It's cosy and spotless, ceilings are low and the overall effect is that of several well-loved old boats tied together. You're reminded of Kettle's Yard in Cambridge, or Barbara Hepworth's studio in St Ives. We walk past carvings of Punch, made by Steve, former lead singer of Crass, a Jack-in-the-box Buddha and a giant Warholesque poster of Rimbaud the poet. The walls of the bathroom are made from old wine box crates, varnished. Needless to say, all the work has been done over the years by Penny and housemates. We sit outside again and smoke more roll-ups.

TH Was your intention with the house always to establish a centre or base from where you could do things?

PR Yes. Gee and myself found the place and I moved here on my own and I got a couple of fellow teachers from the local art school. I wanted the quiet and the solitude so I could work. I was increasingly getting people visiting and hanging out and I saw the potential of a place where people could do that. It offers me quiet and solitude, despite the fact that there might have been 15 people living here at one time. The other agenda, the public one, is the running of the house. The idea is to preserve the cultural and historic heritage of the house, and also to act as an educational and creative centre. It means we become a charity so we don't have to worry about tax things. We don't want any of that.

We've managed to get away without it by not existing for a very long time.

TH How do you manage to not exist?

PR I really don't know. Not even through being evasive, really. When I resigned from teaching I got called into the tax office and I said that I'd retired and that I wasn't going to work ever again, which isn't strictly true. They were quite snotty about it at first and then they just accepted it. The tax people did catch up with me with Crass ... but I suppose it's through just not taking any interest. I remember sending silly answers back to censuses and things and the result of that was that one didn't hear again.

TH Was it simply a lack of interest, or was it a confidence that you got from somewhere?

PR It's a Micawberism, really. It's been quite interesting living with Gee all these years. She comes from a help-your-neighbour type working class family. Her way of survival is pure Micawberism – something will turn up. My form of Micawberism comes from the other end of the social scale where you went out and took it because it was yours. I suppose there's a social sort of confidence which Gee has from being a street kid, and I have from being whatever a street kid isn't. I'm a blagger. Gee will look in terms of pennies creating pounds, and I will look in terms of thousands being broken into pennies. Neither of us have ever had any money, probably never will have. But that doesn't matter, we survive. I'm wary about talking about it, but things do turn up. Whenever I've really been up against the wall something or someone is there. The only time I've been in real schtuck was on a mountain – I didn't know where the fuck I was, I didn't have the right equipment – the clouds just opened for a split second and I saw someone down the hill, and realised if they were there, then I could get there too.

TH When you go 'I give up' that's when something happens. Apparently pinball players are looking to get into this state – they call it the fugue state.

PR You could apply that to everything. That's what real jazz is about, real writing – it's when people have gotten out of the way. It's almost like knowing that once you start instilling any form of intellectual value in all the good things in life, you'll start destroying them. Like shooting stars, you only see them through the side of your eye. I think I've lived my life by that principle. You asked how I've managed to not exist. I'm very able and capable at putting on the pantomime in the physical world, but I don't feel involved in it at all. I'm not concerned by it at all. I'm not concerned by the events of last week [11 September], they do not touch me. They concern me politically and intellectually and I'll make some effort to inform myself if I think the information will be worthwhile. Which it generally isn't. Which is why I don't read newspapers, watch the television or listen to the radio.

TH You can get infected by anxiety. Our friend Brian Dean has a project called Anxiety Culture. He believes we're kept in a state of anxiety because it leads to the notion that you can free yourself from your anxious state by buying things. The Twin Towers reminded me of that, because suddenly everyone is full of worry.

PR I've always been convinced that the whole anxiety thing is totally linked with capitalism. I had the notion of a society for banning people from consuming media. Members would wear a red star. If you see someone with a red star reading a newspaper in a café, you can go up to them and upbraid them and they will be banned for life.

TH I go through phases of not reading the papers, and it certainly does remove a whole level of anxiety from your life. *Vogue* and the glossy mags are also depressing.

PR Well, I get sexual anxiety from them. From the newspapers I get social and political anxiety. It's ten years since I made my vows and my mental health has improved a millionfold. And I'm no worse-informed, which is interesting.

TH Where does your information come from?

PR Firstly it comes from common sense and secondly it comes from the shooting star theory, and thirdly, well: I have a friend who has developed curlean photography so he can scan the body for energy fields, it involves the use of crystals. He's a gorgeous person, very serious and academic and comes up with these crazy ideas. I was going to contact him because I have the distinct impression that beards that haven't become proper beards – two or three days stubble – act as receivers. I had to shave this morning. I was definitely feeling anxiety, nervous. It sounds ridiculous but I'm going to ask Harry whether he might do some research into this.

TH I suppose you do feel better when you've had a shave. Like when you've a hangover.

PR It certainly does make a difference. As a result of not being media-

Penny Rimbaud at Dial House. [Julia Hember]

exposed – I mean, I don't even answer the phone – I don't have those energies floating around. And so I have become very conscious that those energies start to float around when I'm unshaven.

TH Have you been quite druggy and hedonistic in the past?

PR No. I've never been druggy and never been hedonistic. I did have a series of very extreme experiences about 25 years back. At the time, the drug culture was really big. I'd smoked a bit of dope when I was at art school but I didn't use drugs. It was pretty much like what people described as acid experiences, which certainly gave me a different sense of reality.

TH   And that came just from wandering around?

PR   It just started happening to me one day and lasted about a week. Suddenly I was able to understand any language. I could see round things: if I was looking at that tree, I could actually see it in its entirety. It was very powerful indeed. I wasn't particularly worried about it, but I did need someone to help me, and a friend who was heavily into the *Bhagavad Gita* at the time sat with me day and night and he enabled me to come back. But I came back through a particular mystical path, which was his. I realised it was a bit of a cul-de-sac, as I think all spiritual explanations are. It wasn't so much that it utterly changed my life – it was when I came alive. Up until then I was a sort of puppet performing an operation in a world. Since then I've had no physical attachment to the world.

TH   Attachment is what Eastern religions are trying to get you out of. But it's quite a hard concept to grasp, because people confuse it with love.

PR   A lot of my work has been an attempt to redefine things like love. I do regard all human emotions as theatre. I don't believe in the emotional world. Which doesn't mean I don't have them. But when I do, when I'm operating in that field, I acknowledge that.

TH   Don't you have emotions to make you feel alive?

PR   Yes, but they don't. And that's why people are so addicted to those forms of behaviour. Actually they do the reverse. They make you feel dead. They confirm your deadness. I mean, this sounds so Zen-like, but there's only one moment of existence that has any relevance whatsoever, which is now. There's nothing else. If we carry any past or future burden into that moment then we are removing ourselves from any true expression. The only real music or writing comes from that position. The moment you impose any self-consciousness, then the thing becomes self-negating. You end up becoming an Archer.

TH   Did the idea of having a job ever interest you?

PR   No. I think I wanted to be an artist when I was six or seven. In my terms an artist is everything: a philosopher, a writer, a painter, a sculptor, a roof-builder. And that's how I realised I wanted to live my life. And not only did I always want to be like that, I always was like that. You can't want to be anything, can you? You are or you're not. I was fortunate to recognise early on what I was and what I wasn't. Which is why, in scholarly terms, I was such a desperate failure.

TH Because you wouldn't fit the agenda?

PR I just didn't believe it.

TH Why do you think it's so rare for people to create a life for themselves where they are self-determining?

PR Well, firstly because rationally the odds seem to be against you. I think also because most people's conditioning is so hideously divisive. In that sense I was very fortunate to have had spectacularly good parents. My father loathed everything I did, but his strength in his own belief allowed me to become the person I was. Fear is the other factor. The whole anxiety culture. As far as the media goes, as long as I can remember, the question is not 'what is this person saying to me?' What's interested me always is 'why is this person telling me this?' The information is irrelevant. Why this, out of the millions of things a person could say? That remains the basis of my whole dialogue.

TH How do you define work?

PR My definition of work is something that you don't want to do. People who come to visit cannot realise that because I don't put on a uniform and go somewhere, that in their definition of the word, me sitting on my arse or sleeping on my bed is actually part of what is a 24-hour-a-day work process.

TH You don't see a separation between work and play?

PR There is none. People think I am extraordinarily fun-less, that's because I don't think laughter is an expression of fun. I think that laughter is a form of rather unpleasant hysteria, a little bit like tears. I suffer from both. Generally speaking I drift quietly in the middle of the two which is where the real fun is. I think laughter and tears impose your own response on the situation. By imposing your response you're cutting off the very thing you're responding to. Our idea of love denies the very thing that we actually pertain to be moving towards.

TH Which is?

PR The very conditions of what we generally define as being love, are in absolute contradiction to love. The concept of possession and ownership is such a vulgar disregard for what the feeling should be and is. The whole idea of fidelity as somehow an expression of love and devotion to an individual person – why, or how I can't imagine. If you love someone you assume that the world must love them, so therefore how could you possibly become jealous at anyone else trying to do what you might be doing, which is screwing or holding hands?

TH But jealousy is a real emotion.

PR Well it isn't actually. I don't believe in real emotions because I don't believe that emotions are real. Emotions are purely reaction and no reaction is real. It is a re-action. One shouldn't talk about 'reality', maybe one should talk about 'ality'. The reality that people talk about isn't the 'ality', it's the 're'. We tend to talk in 'res' all the time.

TH So why are emotions such a major part of people's lives?

PR Because of an utter barrenness. They are the expression of the world's emptiness.

TH So you're talking about a life of total self-responsibility. That how you have chosen to work and live, your illnesses, your emotions – these are things that people actually choose to do. Why is it that people feel so victimised, that they blame their problems on external things?

PR Because they're incapable of taking on the responsibility themselves. They don't want to take responsibility. The simple fact is that ... I don't actually care what happened in New York last week because I acknowledge my responsibility and complicity in it. If I wasn't aware of that as an obvious outcome of what's happening then I'd be upset. It's people's paucity of mind that gives rise to their emotional response. The deeper the emotion the greater the paucity of mind.

TH When you say you feel complicit, what do you mean?

PR We orchestrate what we perceive, to whatever degree we've developed our own awareness. I'm more and more aware that we must create the world around us. There is no other reality. What we understand, what we include and what people bring to us can only be governed by our understanding and our perception of it. Therefore in something like the New York thing, I had to agree to be involved. I could be in another situation where I would be forced to be involved, through my paucity of mind.

TH Surely you feel sad that lots of people have died?

PR I'm not in the least bit sad, and I can't pretend that I am. Why should I pretend that I am? There's millions of people dying today, and millions will die tomorrow. People do die. If I was sad at my mother's death, then that simply would have been an expression of my paucity. That I hadn't realised, that I hadn't fulfilled, that I hadn't lived my life. It's generally acknowledged that our intellectual life is, if you like, controlled or at least defined by capitalist interest. I think it's quite horrible that our emotional life is equally defined by the same interests.

TH As in Princess Diana?

PR The awful thing about that was the denial of one's ability to even realise one's own feelings, whatever they might have been. Because you can't, against the undercurrent of this ghastly theatre. I have been fascinated by the Holocaust, but recently I got bored with the whole thing. I thought, it's just one fucking great smokescreen. It prevents us from seeing how the society we're now living in came about. We don't look back through history to the Imperialist programme which spread out of Britain to America. We're only able to go back 50 years and then get hit by the Holocaust. It's like a steel curtain against history.

TH If you keep going on about the Holocaust it lets you off the hook for …

PR It actually removes your own complicity.

TH And if you throw flowers on the monument after the death of Princess Diana, you're saying, 'look – I'm a human being.'

PR I think more than that, it's actually a degradation of human feelings, whatever they are. And I don't know what they are. At present I'd be happy to say that all emotions are a sham. Who the fuck cares? It makes no difference whatsoever. On a practical level it's a useless gesture. One's own grief or one's own humour does nothing but express your own grief or your own humour – so fucking what?

TH In that case, why do anything?

PR I don't think the Lord God said 'Let there be light', I think he said 'Let there be words' because we have fabricated a world around words, everything is idea. It's actually that paper-thin. It's that gossamer-thin. I use that word because the prophylactics of human experience are the very thing that deny us human experience. Emotions, the intellect, are all processes by which we are denied our existence. They are the prophylactic between ourselves and ourselves. I'm not an academic, therefore I can't sit and write great philosophies, but I have thoughts which are philosophical and whether they are expressed musically or through painting or through the word, they're my attempt to rewrite the programme. I'm reprogramming.

TH And that's what Crass was about?

PR That's what my part within Crass was, yes. We're very much regarded as being a political band. Well, I have had no interest in politics ever in my life. Neither have I ever been in the least bit worried about whether or not someone's going to drop a nuclear bomb anywhere in the world including here. I have written that the boil on the end of my nose is always infinitely more worrying to me than an atomic bomb. My part in Crass was the use of commonly accepted icons, mythological features – be they wife-bashing or atomic bombs – to undermine emotional process. To me the bomb is an emotional and physical icon that can be used to sow a seed of different awareness. The interesting thing about Crass is that continuing to this day the major response is 'thanks for changing my life'. Not, 'thanks for the great music' or 'thanks for the fashion style'. What people mean by that, is 'thank you for allowing me to question my own existence'. I have no doubt that that was the power we had.

TH At the *Idler* we get letters from people saying, 'I can't believe it: I thought I was the only one who thought this way, I've found out I'm not alone.'

PR So that's why one does things. And one actually can't not do them. I can no more not write than I can not make our own bread. They're all part of the same process. Of being a person. Because otherwise, why be a person?

TH So you've never had any sense of career.

PR Oh no [laughs], absolutely not. Or of ... I have no sense of being. I have no sense of identity, I have no sense of myself. Which might seem a bit strange as I consider myself quite skilled and adept at the theatres of life and very articulate with them. But I genuinely am unable to have a picture of myself. Which is lovely. A mirror means nothing to me, although I am visible in a mirror. But I don't recognise anything about me in that image and I'm absolutely incapable of imagining of what I might look like or might be.

TH So you couldn't sit down and write a description of your personality.

PR Oh no. I have none. I know I have no personality.

TH What does that mean?

PR It doesn't mean anything [laughs].

TH Well, obviously in some sense you do have a personality.

PR No I don't. I don't have any integrity. Most people like to believe that their personality is something to do with an integrity. This is who I am, this is my presentation. Well, I have no presentation with any continuum. If other people choose to create personalities and identities for me, then that's their business. My lover is someone who shares the same principles and attitudes to emotions and personalities, which is why I'm able to have an affair with her. It's been an affair for 25 years, but it is like an affair because I don't know her. I've never known her and I will never know her.

TH Are you saying it's a trap when people try to get to know each other?

PR Oh utterly, yeah. I couldn't know anyone. To attempt to get into someone's head is an utter violation, is rape, really. We're committing acts of psychic rape 24 hours a day. And I recognise the absolute preciousness of existence and I respect that. And just as much as I respect it in other people I respect it in myself. So I leave myself alone.

TH You don't beat yourself up.

PR No. I don't believe in psychology, I think that's an utter sham. I don't believe in essence. I don't believe those sorts of things if they're attached to ideas of individuals and personalities.

TH Like who is the 'real' Victoria Beckham?

PR And I have to say that the real Victoria Beckham exposes herself every time she appears on the front of a magazine. In a somewhat old-fashioned way, I do believe in the lines on the face, and that the eyes are the mirror of the soul. I haven't met Victoria Beckham so it's a bit unfair, but the number of times I've been exposed to her pictures when going to buy my tobacco, makes me somewhat fear for her soul.

TH I worry that I get an ideal for living confused with bourgeois aspiration.

PR Well, I sometimes worry that I cunningly set up my bourgeois comforts under the protection of the open door policy. Here I am living in one of the most beautiful places I've ever been in my life, of a particular type. Very, very comfortable. I mean, I don't have any money, but that doesn't seem to worry me. There's lots of nice food in the vegetable patch and people often go to France and bring back lots of tobacco. I'm very comfortable, thank you. But actually I'm just as happy to be sleeping in a plastic bag at the top of a mountain as I am sleeping in my own bed. I don't really care one iota. I see things in the material world as being a practical consideration, and I include people in that equation.

Colin Wilson

by Louis Theroux

IDLER 30 · 2002

COLIN WILSON IS THE AUTHOR OF 'THE OUTSIDER', THE
book that was to see him praised by the critics as a young genius
one day, only to be savagely discarded the next. He lives in
Cornwall with his wife Joy. Louis went down to visit him with photographer Zed Nelson, and the interview Louis wrote for us sparkles
with his characteristic mix of intelligence and humour. Colin Wilson
suffered a stroke in 2012 and can no longer speak.

★

In the week leading up to my encounter with Colin Wilson, he and I
exchange emails regarding arrangements. He invites me to visit him at
his cottage in Cornwall, since he is too busy writing to come up to
London for an interview. The photographer and I can stay the night, if
we wish. 'We could manage beds in the "chalet" we use for guests,' he
says. 'That fucker Humphrey Carpenter was the last to stay in it last
November and he went on to write a foul vicious piece in some book
on the angry young men – treacherous little shit. Let us know times.'
    During my stay with Colin and our hours of conversation, I notice
he is occasionally given to these sudden angry asides. It's odd because
most of the time his mood is happy, almost beatific, and a good deal of
his writing has been on the need to cultivate a positive attitude.
Driving to his house, the first evening we are with him, Colin is
talking equably about the religious poet Thomas Traherne when he
suddenly breaks off to shout: 'You learn to drive, you cunt!' at an
oncoming car. Colin is an enigmatic – in some instances baffling –
character, which may partly explain the strange position he occupies in

English letters. Having been heralded as a literary genius aged 24 by such luminaries as Cyril Connolly and Philip Toynbee upon the publication of his first book, *The Outsider*, in 1956, Colin's subsequent career and his hundred or so books of philosophy, psychology, criminology, mysticism and fiction have met with a protracted diminuendo of mainstream critical interest.

When I was growing up, my parents kept several of Colin Wilson's books on their shelves. My mum had a copy of *The Occult*, his compendious study of the paranormal. My dad gave my older brother a copy of *The Order of Assassins*, Wilson's survey of serial killers, for his ninth or tenth birthday. In a way, Wilson blighted my childhood, since my brother, after reading the book, rejoiced in telling me about a murderer nicknamed *Jack the Stripper*, who would choke prostitutes to death using his penis – not something you absolutely need to know about as a seven-year-old. But maybe as a result of that childhood exposure, I have an abiding interest in Wilson, and a belief that whatever his foibles as a writer, his work deals with some of the most interesting areas of human life.

I travel down from London by train one Saturday afternoon, with *Idler* photographer Zed (known as 'Zik') Nelson. After a four and a half hour journey, we get off at St. Austell and catch a taxi to Pentewan. Colin is waiting for us at the bar in a pub called The Ship. He is wearing a dark polo-neck jumper and a houndstooth jacket, with an open bottle of white wine and some bar snacks. He was 70 last year, but he's still got all his hair, which he wears swept across his forehead in a rakish parting. In matters of personal style, he is still the Fifties student existentialist. With him is his wife Joy, in a cardigan and trousers, a bright-eyed and sprightly woman, roughly the same age as him. She is bespectacled and birdlike, with full blonde hair and a trim figure that belies her age. They have been together for nearly 50 years.

We drive back to the pebble-dash cottage they share, and where they brought up their three children, Damon, Rowan and Sally, all of them now grown up. The overwhelming impression is of books everywhere. Colin says he has more than 30,000 books.

cw This is the guest bedroom, which as you can see contains as many books as all the other rooms. This is the Philosophy section behind you.

LT *The Killer* [a novel of Wilson's]. I read this one at University.

CW Yeah, that's a good edition.

LT With a Bacon painting on the cover.

CW Yeah, it's a complete new edition, they cut out some stuff for being too filthy.

LT I really enjoyed that one. Did that get good reviews?

CW [Laughing] I don't know, I don't think it got particularly good reviews; none of my books have got particularly good reviews.

LT Well, *The Outsider* and *The Occult* did, didn't they?

CW Oh yes, *The Outsider* did and *The Occult* did, but basically I'm quite an unpopular writer, you know. Some Japanese said to me, 'Ah, Mr. Wilson, in England you must be as famous as Charles Dickens', and I said, 'In England nobody's ever heard of me.'

Colin and I retire to the front room, while Joy prepares dinner. There's an African grey parrot on a branch that's hung up on chains. Every wall is covered with jerry-built bookshelves – near the parrot, the shelves have plastic screens over them to protect the books from its ravages. There are also children's toys, video tapes, books and magazines piled higgledy-piggledy on the floor and a tray of condiments on a coffee table.

We make ourselves comfortable, Colin in an armchair, Zik and I on the sofa. Colin is now wearing a blue neckerchief with white polka dots – he says he is susceptible to sore throats; it has the effect of making him look slightly roguish and nautical in a way I can't put my finger on.

Unbidden, he begins talking about the sequence of events that led to the publication of *The Outsider*; how he conceived the idea for the book one Christmas on his own in a bedsit in London, and began writing it during his spare time at the British Museum, while he slept in a waterproof sleeping bag on Hampstead Heath. With several chapters completed, he sent a copy of the work in progress to the publisher Victor Gollancz.

CW Within ten days I'd got this letter back from him which to my astonishment said, 'Do let me see the rest of this, it sounds like the kind of book I'd be interested in.' So of course I was dizzy, like F. Scott Fitzgerald running out onto the street stopping people and shouting,

'My first book's been accepted!' And he said, 'How have you read so much by your age?' and I said, 'I dunno, I've never done anything but read.' And I said, 'And anyway, apart from that, I'm a genius.'

LT Did you say that?

CW Probably.

LT Really, you think you said that?

CW That's how I got Joy in the first place, I said 'come up to London with me, I'm a genius.' She claims I grabbed her by the ears and banged her head against a wall.

LT That's funny. Do you have a conviction that you are a genius?

CW [Immediately] Of course, yes, I pretty obviously have, but I mean it doesn't make me conceited at all. I mean Shakespeare knew he was, it says so in the sonnets... I think the trouble with someone like T.E. Lawrence was that he was a genius but he didn't know it. He didn't believe in it.

LT Really?

CW You've got to believe in it, you've got to be certain of it. And I'd spent so many years you see in this bloody working class environment, knowing that I was cleverer than anyone around me and yet not at the same time being able to do anything or impress anybody. I'd write long stories and teachers would read them and say, 'Well you know this is all very impressive but you're using too many long words' and all that kind of thing and finally you get a feeling of total humiliation and get so used to being kicked and people saying you're no good. And then sometimes you wake up in the morning and you've written something brilliant the night before and you re-read it and you think 'My God! I am a fucking genius!' And you realise you've got to have this self-belief.

LT Of the books you've written do you feel there are masterpieces? If so which one?

CW Oh yeah, I mean *The Outsider* obviously, most of the *Outsider* cycle actually, about six books, and then *Mind Parasites*. *The Space Vampires* came almost as a dream literally.

LT That's the one that was turned into the film *Lifeforce* [horror/sci-fi film that came out in 1985 directed by Tobe Hooper].

CW Yeah that's right, and then books like *The Occult*. *Beyond The Occult* is my best book. I'll give you an essay I wrote called 'Below The Iceberg' which some Japanese publisher asked me to write, you know write about your best book ... But of course unfortunately this terrific amount of publicity that *The Outsider* got, I mean just non-stop publicity you know, like Elvis Presley famous ...

LT It was 1955 wasn't it?

CW Yeah, well '56. Suddenly of course the critics got sick of this fucking angry young man stuff, they'd just had enough of it and so when my second book, *Religion And The Rebel* appeared, I'd had so much publicity, non-stop, they all leapt on it and stamped it on the floor.

In the ten years after *The Outsider* appeared, Colin published 21 books; seven of them were part of an 'Outsider series' in which Colin developed a philosophy which he describes as 'new existentialism'. In a postscript to *The Outsider* written in 1967, Wilson writes about his lecturing on these ideas in America. 'Their reception by audiences of American students all over the country convinced me that I had not been too conceited in suspecting they constituted a kind of revolution in philosophy.' It strikes me as rather wonderful, the idea of a struggling author in remote Cornwall solving the major problems of human existence, and founding his own branch of philosophy, which he is confident will sooner or later be accepted as orthodoxy by the mass of universities and academics. Colin seems genuinely baffled by the ascendance of French philosophy – Foucault, Derrida, *et al* – in the Sixties and Seventies. He says he spent two years getting to grips with Derrida – 'I was determined to crack this fucker.' He adds: 'One shouldn't be impressed by Foucault. In fact, these French Post Modernists are all of them absolute cunts.'

Still, he says the experience of being ignored as a writer was dispiriting.

CW During my middle life I did book after book that I knew to be bloody good and got few reviews and only just managed to keep scraping along. And some friend of mine occasionally ironically quoted this thing about some writer whose books predeceased him and you think, Oh God, I hope that doesn't happen to me.

LT That's right. I think that's in the introduction to the edition of *The Outsider* I was reading where you said someone said that Colin Wilson's ideas predeceased him as an author. In other words that you'd outlived your ideas and that ... it's not a very nice thing to say is it?

cw   Oh well, I mean there have been many worse things said. I mean I told
      you about that fucking cunt Humphrey Carpenter thing.

Ah, the Humphrey Carpenter situation. It seems Carpenter came
down to Cornwall to interview Colin for a book he was writing about
the Angry Young Men. Joy was out that evening, so Colin cooked him
a slap-up meal of oysters and smoked salmon and venison with vintage
wine from the cellar. They had a pleasant weekend together – though
'I did notice he fell asleep when I was explaining about the New
Existentialism,' Colin says (he woke him by talking loudly). 'So off he
went and he said, I'll send you what I've written, and I said, OK, fine,
and about a week later came his book with an introduction describing
coming down here to see me, but then the rest of the hook was already
written! And the bit on me was a shitty, nasty, vicious bit which was
really designed to say, Well, *The Outsider* was a flash in the pan and anyway it's no fucking good.'
      Carpenter and Wilson entered into a vigorous correspondence. 'I
said, Look, you fucking cunt! Read! Try reading the new postscripts of
the new *Outsider* and you'll see it's saying something! It's not just a jack-
daw picking up thousands of other writers ... I said, you're a bit of a
bastard, you're a Bishop's son – he's the son of the Bishop of Oxford –
and I said, how could you do a trick as dirty as this? To write to someone, claiming that you want to interview them for a book that's already
written in this vicious and dismissive way, you'll sit and eat their food
and all the rest of it and still write as viciously as this? And anyway, he
sort of said, oh well you know. So I said, if you ever come near here I'm
going to kick the shit out of you.'
      I find myself wondering how bad it was, whatever Carpenter wrote,
and whether I should be worried on my own account. Funnily enough,
I have met Humphrey Carpenter, and he struck me as a nice chap, and
not the least bit malicious. Joy comes in and serves us a delicious meal
of steak where we are sitting. I am still curious about her relationship
with Colin.

  lt   Colin said that when he first met you he said you should go with him
       because he was a genius.
joy   [Laughs] Well, I suppose he did try to persuade me.
  lt   Was that his chat-up line?

JOY Not really, well I don't know, perhaps it was … It was either take it or leave it, that line, wasn't it?

CW She was a very gullible girl fortunately.

LT Did you not think he was a bit of a weirdo, Joy?

JOY Well, not a weirdo, you mean a sort of crazy kid or something?

LT Well just insofar as a bit intense, burning with a sense of his own mission, his claims on posterity.

JOY No he didn't mention that. He had ideas about things, literary matters and things, really a lot of literary …

CW But then you see I was really lucky you see, because I said to her 'I'm a genius' and then *The Outsider* came out and everyone was saying it.

Colin goes to bed at nine every night and it's getting close to that time. Joy talks on the phone to Colin's family in Leicester, where they're having a 'boogie-up' (as Colin calls it) to celebrate the sixty-second birthday of Maureen, who is the wife of Colin's brother Barry. 'I've got Louis Theroux here,' he says. 'He wants to know how many times a week I screw Joy.'

Zik and I stumble off into the darkness to find our chalet. It may be the wine, but I reflect how much I enjoy coming to Cornwall, with its palm trees and balmy evenings. It's like being abroad. The chalet has a fifties boarding house feel. There is an electric blanket on my bed, and a bar heater and an electric blow-heater. Lino floors with colourful slightly folded carpets. Stripey candy-coloured light fabric curtains, slightly distempered looking. Again, books everywhere. Hardy, Beckett, Hugh Walpole. The complete works of Henry Williamson, who wrote *Tarka the Otter* and was tainted with charges of fascism. Off at one end, there's a little kitchen; off at the other end, is a bathroom. I tug the cord for the light switch, and it stays dark but the shower comes on.

Colin has given me a book, a hardback from 1962: *The World of Colin Wilson* by Sidney Campion, which I read until I am ready to sleep.

Next morning, Zik and I have Crunchy Nut Cornflakes in the chalet, then I venture back down to the main house. I loiter awkwardly for a few minutes before Colin appears. He's been up since five reading and doing his journal on tape. 'I've got two or three hundred tapes, so someone after my death will have to transcribe them all,' he says. His computer screen is broken; he is going to phone one of his sons for advice.

We go down to the basement, where he has his study.

LT How many days a week do you work down here?
CW Every day.
LT Every day of the year. Wow.

Bookshelves everywhere, all the walls, books on the ground, discarded shoes, slippers, a huge waste-paper bin, a daybed, manuscripts, tapes, computer disks piled everywhere. 'Could do with a little bit of a tidy up,' I comment.

LT I was reading *The World of Colin Wilson* and it talked about a cocktail party up in London and I got the sense that you had a jolly time.
CW Well that's the problem you see: you become famous overnight, which I quite literally had, then indeed you're invited non-stop to cocktail parties, publisher's parties and all kinds of things and it's all very pleasant and jolly.
LT You can turn the invitations down of course ...
CW Well, as I said, at 24 you don't, because you're anxious to get to know what life is all about. And you think perhaps you're going to meet a very important person, who'll give you brilliant ideas and so on, which you never do.
LT Well, this party that you talk about, it's got Stephen Spender and Iris Murdoch, Herbert Reid, John Osbourne ... it did sound like quite glittering company.
CW Yes. I got to know them all pretty well, at the time of *The Outsider*, Iris had an obsession about sending me to University, she thought quite wrongly that what I needed was to train my mind because *The Outsider* she thought was all over the place. Obviously far from making me write better books, it would have crippled me.
LT So then in coming down to Cornwall you remove yourself from their society, isn't that something you've missed a little bit?
CW Not really, no, because I could see them whenever I went to London, And quite apart from that anyway I don't really terribly like mixing with other people, with so-called equals, because what I'm doing is following on from what everyone else is doing anyway. I'd realised from the beginning that what I was doing was in its way completely unusual, nobody else I ever met was remotely interested in the things

that interested me, that is to say in the notion of people who don't fit in simply because they've got this kind of innate sense that they need to evolve to a higher level. I realised at a pretty early stage that that's what I was talking about, human evolution, and that what I was really saying was that man is on the point of an evolutionary leap to a higher stage, and what's more he's nearly there. He's very very close indeed, and so that's what *The Outsider* is really about.

Two years after *The Outsider* appeared, an American psychologist named Abraham Maslow wrote to Colin. Maslow had been studying healthy, happy people, and had discovered they shared the quality of having moments of inexplicable optimism, which Maslow termed 'peak experiences'. Wilson seized on this idea as being a solution to the problem of the outsider – that these ecstatic states were the natural condition of mankind, if only we had a proper perspective on the world.

LT Now what can you do to try and induce a peak experience in yourself?

CW Well that was the great question for me. The question that I've spent my whole life trying to answer. Obviously the one answer was to try to get the mind to, as it were, shrink. You see, Graham Greene played Russian roulette with a revolver, when he was terribly depressive in his teens. He'd put it against his forehead, spin the chambers, pull the trigger and when there was just a click he'd look down the barrel and the bullet had just slipped into position – and he said it was as if a light was turned on, and suddenly he saw that all life is absolutely wonderful. Now if the cunt had gone on recognising that, he would have written totally different books. Instead of these bloody stupid depressing books which he actually did write. I met Greene once in New York and I immediately saw what was wrong with him. He sort of said, 'Well of course, when one wrote *Brighton Rock* one felt completely different' and it was quite obvious that you'd got this sort of upper class lack of self-belief, which you tend to find among the aristocrats because they've all been trained so much to be modest and so on.

LT Well how did that relate to what Greene had said about *Brighton Rock*?

CW Oh, it's this fact that he kept referring to himself as 'one'. Anyway what I was going on to say was clearly there's a good way of inducing a peak experience. The only problem is that it's a bit dangerous [laughs].

LT It is, isn't it?

CW Greene did it six times and managed to get away with it, but he said gradually the effect lessened. Now I thought well now think about it, what actually happened when Greene did that, I thought well there he was in this state of boredom, no will, as if your spring is not broken but is loose or unwound, then he points the gun at his head, pulls the trigger and suddenly his whole being goes, 'Aaarrgghhhhh!' expecting to die in a split second, and then there's just a click and he goes, 'Phhheeewww'.

LT Yeah.

CW And it's this terrific 'Phhheeewww ... Aaarrgghhhhh! ... Phhheeew-ww.' So the mechanism is the peak experience. Now it's very difficult to achieve the kind of concentrated tension which Greene achieved with Russian Roulette, but in point of fact you can, if you choose to concentrate very hard. I mean you simply take a pencil, you hold it up against a clear background like the ceiling and you concentrate and you really concentrate, you behave as if that pencil was the only thing in the world, you really concentrate your mind on it, and then you relax completely until you can see the rest of room around the pencil and then you concentrate once again and then you relax once again and if you do it about 12 times and it begins to hurt you behind the eyes ...

LT And it really works?

CW And you find if you push yourself it really works ...

Joy appears. 'What are you doing, breakfast?' Colin asks. 'I'm not doing anything until I'm told,' she says. I say I've had some cereal in the chalet. Zik asks for some toast.

LT Can you give any more specifics on ways of making that happen? Like, I'm not inclined to exercise very much but sometimes if I have done some exercise it does give me a general feeling of well being. Is that a bad example?

CW No, no that's a good example because what you're basically doing in exercise is as it were winding yourself up like a key in a spring to a greater degree of a certain kind of positive in a tension and that's the important thing. The other thing of course is that it is possible to do it, simply by focussing and concentrating the mind, and I tend to do that every morning. I do it for five minutes and once you've got used to this, quite suddenly you slip into another mode.

LT   How do you focus it, you don't mean by looking at the pencil?

cw   I don't look at the pencil. I do tend to use the muscles of the face and concentrate like that.

LT   In the way you tell it's self-initiating, but I don't know if it's peak experiences or not but thinking about moments in life that seem somewhat bordering on the spiritual or the fulfilling, it can be just contingent on what the weather is like, whether the sun is out, whether it's a particularly balmy temperature. Sometimes you're on a bus and you get a view across London, you have a moment of elation and hope and feel like actually everything is fine, everything is going to be all right.

cw   But that depends completely on the degree of natural, inner positive tension that you already adjust to.

LT   So you have to be open to that?

cw   Yup, because you notice that if in fact you've had a series of bad things and you're hung over, then that doesn't happen, it doesn't happen because the charge on your battery is so low there's not really enough to give a spark.

LT   As far as an evolutionary leap, it seems to me that we're further away from that than ever, in that all the forms of power in the world, like consumer culture and governments and industrialisation, militate against those sorts of habits of life.

cw   But you're talking once again about the external factors that cause the problems. And when you think that the world is so full of all these awful things, once again it's your thought that's doing it. What you've got to recognise is how far you are capable of that complete switch yourself. What actually causes the emotion is something inside you and when you get these feelings on a nice morning something inside your brain, a little muscle, and it's that focussing that gives you the peak experience.

Once in my teens I looked at a windowsill which had been painted green and just something about the paint mildly interested me, and as soon as it mildly interested me, and therefore I focussed in on it, I got a little peak experience. Exactly like holding your prick and doing that [makes wanking gestures] and actually feeling a sort of pleasure, only the pleasure was coming from the windowsill instead of the mental image of the opposite sex.

Incidentally masturbation is of incredible importance because no animal can masturbate. Human beings are the only animal who can envisage a member of the opposite sex and carry it right through to orgasm. Now that's quite an extraordinary thing to do.

LT We're the only ones who can do that?

CW An ape cannot focus on a mental image long enough to stabilise it. It just dissolves away.

LT You hear about bonobo monkeys giving each other blow jobs, and wanking ...

CW ... not on their own.

LT We should think about going out for a little walk, shouldn't we? Yeah, now first of all I've got to ring my brother, I also want to ring my son, to ask him about the problem with my screen.

A short while later, Colin, Zik and I climb into Colin's Land Rover. Colin's two dogs climb in the back.
　　There is a seatbelt.

LT Well, I might risk it and not bother.

CW [Faintly admonishing] Well, I'll put mine on, because it's illegal not to.

After a trip to the post office, we drive down to Goran Haven, the small fishing village which Colin and Joy's cottage overlooks. At Zik's instigation, Colin drives on to the beach. We get out and walk around and Zik takes some photos. A young woman calls out to Colin – she points out that just a few feet from where her toddler is playing on the sand Colin's dog has done an enormous shit. Colin and I spring into action: we get a plastic bag from a nearby newsagent. I buy a pack of Revels so the newsagent doesn't feel exploited. After Colin and I have scooped up the shit, he lets out a groan: the dog's done another huge shit down on the grey rocks closer to the sea. We clear up this one as well.

LT We dealt with that all right, I think.

CW I think we dealt with it rather well [laughs]. I'm afraid that is the kind of challenge that life consists of, a whole series of things like that. And you notice that with every challenge, you can either go, 'Urrrgh' and let out your energy, or do the opposite ... Anyway, let's get moving before something else happens.

But our adventure isn't over yet. Up on the cliffs, where the road is only wide enough for one vehicle, we get into a stand-off with an oncoming car. Colin drives off onto a field and we attempt to get past that way – but our opponent begins reversing the way he came, as we ride alongside over the tussocky grass. Ha ha! This is better than the road!

ZIK Are you allowed to do this?

CW Not really. But this is National Trust land. And I know that National Trust bloke. Now that silly cunt, she's still going along there. I didn't think our little trip was going to be quite as adventurous.

LT They think we're just joyriding.

CW Chesterton said, 'An adventure is only an inconvenience rightly considered, an inconvenience is only an adventure wrongly considered.' You cannot survive without adventure, and since the aim of civilisation is to prevent inconvenience, we're obviously doing something wrong. Whitehead said civilisation cannot survive without adventure.

LT That's the contradiction we were talking about earlier. Modern man with all his material needs being satisfied but none of his spiritual needs.

We head back to the cottage. I sense the outing has taken it out of Colin.

We are close to the end of our time. Zik and I have a train to catch back up to London. Colin and I retire to the front room, him in the armchair again, me in the sofa.

LT You said in your introduction to *The Outsider* that your only real regret was not being able to take advantage of the sexual opportunities that you were presented with at the time.

CW Yes, you suddenly get the opportunity of going to bed with a girl at every literary party. They'd say, come on back to my flat. But of course I was with Joy by then. But it's just as well, because you realise how easy it would be to get involved with entirely the wrong girl, and what's more, since girls are like sticky buds which stick to your clothes, to imagine that you can have a whole series of – mind you, Graham Greene made a very determined attempt to do that. He decided at a certain point in his life: no more marriage, I'm just going to fuck every girl I want to. And he did for the rest of his life. Just had endless affairs.

LT Seems like a lot of work.

CW Not if you enjoy fucking.

LT I mean dealing with the emotional ramifications.

CW One girl wrote of Freddy Ayer that she decided to give him up when he had seven mistresses, and there wasn't a night left for her. Freddy was like this. And so was Philip Toynbee. Just wanted woman after woman after woman. That's all very well, but what I realise as I get older is that sex is fundamentally an illusion that takes you in. Rather like the siren song in *Ulysses*. He orders them to tie him to the mast, and when they pass the sirens he screams at them to untie him. Sex does that to us. We do things that we would not normally do, and the result is that you get yourself into these awful situations. When I look back on my life at the number of girls that I've been greatly tempted to get involved with, even since I've been with Joy, and haven't, I heave a sigh of relief. Because every one of them would have been a waste of time. It's like having a permanent desire to try new ice cream. But once you've tried one ice cream you've tried the lot. Well, maybe two ice creams.

LT That's right, you don't want to go through life only ever having had a single partner.

CW You don't want to go through life only having a single ice cream! But then again, when I was fairly young I didn't. At the time I first knew Joy, I gave her quite a lot of heartache, because in spite of the fact that I didn't go to bed with lots of girls at parties, I did to some extent take advantage of what was on offer. After *The Outsider* came out, and even after we moved down here to Cornwall, but I'm glad that I never got any permanent involvement. And what's more, I was always so relieved to get back to Cornwall and Joy if I'd been in London for a couple of days misbehaving myself. Such a pleasure to be back in my own home. And once Sally came along, and I was 30 when that happened, I quite suddenly decided to stop misbehaving completely. And this was obviously because having a pretty sweet little daughter gave me the essence of femininity in a little bottle.

LT That's a little troubling, isn't it?

CW Well, not really. There was also the feeling that if anything happened to Sally, whom I absolutely adored, I would have felt it was my fault, if I'd been misbehaving … I adore Joy and always have, so intelligent and good-tempered. She's much too nice a girl for me. On the other hand, she didn't expect to get a genius. She was about to get married, she would have a been a nice ordinary middle class housewife, and I think she had a more interesting life with me than she would have otherwise.

LT Freddie Ayer was asked if he had any regrets and he said he wished he'd had sex with more people.

CW Well yes, it goes the other way. John Betjeman said on television – he was a great friend of ours – he said I wish I'd had more sex. But he didn't have a lot of sex, he wasn't a Freddie Ayer. But Freddie Ayer wasted his life, and the result of course is that his philosophy is shit.

LT You don't know that he would have been a better philosopher if he'd had less sex.

CW I suspect probably.

Soon after, Colin drives Zik and me back to St. Austell, to the station. He says we're welcome to stay any time we're in the area.

As much as I enjoyed my time with Colin I leave him feeling puzzled, for reasons I can't quite put my finger on. When I read through the transcripts of our conversations, I'm struck by how little he actually engages with my questions – they seem to be unwelcome interruptions to what he has to say. Some of the time, he might as well be delivering a lecture. But I reason that it's this same faculty of self-assurance, of having an unshakeable commitment to his own muse, that has allowed Colin to work for 50 years in the wilderness without much in the way of mainstream acknowledgement and still less remuneration. And if he seems somewhat aloof and detached, what do you expect from an Outsider?

Chris Yates

by Kevin Parr

IDLER 30 · 2002

IDLER DEPUTY EDITOR DAN KIERAN'S FRIEND KEV WAS AN angler and a huge fan of legendary fisherman Chris Yates. He asked whether I'd be interested in an interview, and I said, absolutely. Chris is an outstanding human being, a real philosopher, and he went on to contribute to the *Idler*, and to write *How to Fish* for Hamish Hamilton.

★

Photographer, author, editor of *Waterlog* magazine, but foremost a fisherman, Chris Yates has been described in angling circles as a 'legend in his own lunchtime', not least after the capture of a British record carp, but his enigmatic and private nature has confused many, who label him eccentric and mildly unapproachable. This latter attribute perhaps affirmed by his initial response to my request for an interview.

'Are you interested?' I said.

'Not really,' he replied, 'I'm not interested in anything that resembles work.'

Fortunately an *Idler* interview is far from real work and I soon secured an invitation to his cottage in south Wiltshire, with the promise of a pub lunch, afternoon tea and a damn good chinwag.

And so here I am, sitting on a sofa in the most glorious of clutters that is the study of Chris Yates. By one wall a wood burner, which is lit and toiling, on another a huge bookcase that represents five decades of collated paraphernalia, Chris' desk and chair on the next wall, and finally my sofa. In between the structure is an organised mess of journals, nets and at least a dozen fishing rods – all hand-made split cane, and all probably decades old. Chris is a single parent of four, and in the next room are two of his children, both sick and off school, but both seemingly content with my presence. Due to this unforeseen bout of illness the pub lunch could be out of the equation, but Chris is a tea freak, and the second cup is on its way.

CY And I forgot to strain this one.

KP Is that mine?

CY Yes, but there's proper tea-leaves in there, you can see them – of course, I remembered to strain mine ...

KP As you would.

CY You can have some fruitcake – it is your cake.

KP No, it's yours.

CY Well it's my cake now, but it was yours ... I'll cut a couple more slices ... and you should add that we were going to go to the pub, but as this is now 'children's hospital', we can't go and leave the patients. Besides I'm actually quite glad we're not going to the pub ...

KP It's definitely off the agenda?

CY I think for the minute it is, well an hour. It's half past one already and, besides, this is a much nicer atmosphere, here in my study. If we were in the pub there'd be clanking about and thinking about what to eat and all that is too much ... trouble. [Laughs] It's never too much trouble deciding what to drink, though, but when you want to have a quiet chat, it could be a bit distracting with all these people coming in from the fields and the woods saying: 'Hello Chris, ya seen any big fish recently?!' [Pause] No I haven't. No, I haven't seen a big fish for over a year. Fishing-wise, it's been a very bad season.

KP Yes, likewise.

CY Very few carp in the summer – but I did catch my best salmon.

KP [Excited] Did you? Where was that?

CY It was on the river Tana, in Finnmark, the most northern salmon river in Europe, which flows into the Arctic Ocean ... and that was in August. I was in a boat, a little narrow wooden boat.

KP Wow.

CY It's probably the best Atlantic salmon fishing in the world, on the river Tana, it's simply unbelievable. The river flows through Finnmark – that's Lapland, but they don't like being called Laps, and I discovered this after a few black eyes. Using the wrong words out there is just bad

news. Anyway, I was willing to put up with the fact that it was meant
to be the best salmon and trout fishing in the world. I thought, yes, I
can put up with that if I can get to the grayling. Because I'm not a great
fan of salmon and trout.

KP No.

CY They are pushy sorts of fish, always jumping about and being far too
flashy and showy.

KP Definitely – and they're a bit thick as well.

CY Incredibly thick – because they're like a cruise missile, with the same
amount of intelligence, in that they just keep going, no matter what
you throw at them, they keep going. Whereas the carp, the carp is the
grandmaster of chess. And a barbel ... a barbel is a little strange, but
they are mysterious in a way that salmon are not, they don't seem to
have too much intelligence but they move in a different way.

KP Absolutely, there is more art in catching a barbel than a salmon.

CY Indeed, but back to the summer in the far north, I was going for the
grayling, that's what I really wanted, but there were so many salmon in
the river I couldn't get through them to catch the bloody grayling.
Every time I cast out I caught one of these stupid salmon – although I
did manage a twenty-one pounder.

KP So has no one tapped into this gold mine, and exploited the tourism?

CY I think a lot of people have known about it but they keep quiet.
Germans, and quite a few Swedes were over there, and erm, Americans.
But it's got to be the most productive salmon fishing in the world now,
in fact the world record was caught there – eighty pounds – which is a
bloody big salmon.

KP That's the size of your desk!

CY Yes. [Laughs] It's a big silver tourist, but they just don't appeal, not
really, they don't do anything for me. And they are just tourists, you
know, they come up river, look around, and go back off to sea again.
Some of them don't make it on the way back, though. They get bored
and just roll up and die – just like real tourists. [Laughs] They've got to
be on the move all the time, they can't sit still.

KP And they're not even supposed to feed in freshwater.

CY That's it, to catch them you just provoke them – that's all you do.

KP But I'm sure they would get a little hungry going up river – in contemplation of what they are about to do, which is shag.

CY No, it's just a conditioned reflex. They see a little thing like a fish flash by and they just snap at it. Maybe like a well fed person going for a little piece of pudding.

KP Or a second piece of fruitcake.

CY Or maybe even a third piece of fruitcake.

And so yet more fruitcake is consumed.

CY [Through a mouthful] But, as we were saying, apart from the salmon fishing and trout fishing in places other than England, it's been a very poor season. And yet I haven't really minded. I think, perhaps, I'm going through one of those crises that people go through, every now and then, where suddenly fishing has become slightly less important, because there are all sorts of other things going on. It's like you've reached a fork in the stream, and you think it looks good one way, but it doesn't look at all fishy. And yet I might find something a bit unusual, where it's shadowy and murky, and that's where I've gone – I've gone up this little side-stream, which is a backwater in life, and I don't know where it's going to lead but I like it, and it's completely unknown to me, where I am at the moment. I think it's the first time in my life where I haven't actually been fishing regularly for over a year. I haven't been out that often, and yet I've been discovering a lot of new things. It's as if I've discovered – blimey, I can do other things in life, other than fish! [Laughs] It's exciting. So, I think that's what's happened to me – it could be a mid-life crisis, I'm not sure, though I've always been rather dubious of the term. I think it's just a bloody excuse for someone who's got bored of one thing and thinks they are too old to take on something new – I don't think you're ever too old to start something new.

At this point Chris was summoned next door to the children's ward, where the patients required food and drink. I took advantage of this opportunity and nipped outside for a cigarette and a nose around the garden.

The Yates' residence is certainly idyllic. Set against a steep wooded bank on one side of a valley, that offered views of classic Southern downland, grazed by sheep and quartered regularly by buzzards. The garden itself was kept as a cottage garden should be – low maintenance naturalization. Overgrown, strewn with discarded toys and fashioned wooden weapons (the bow and arrow, I later discovered, was one of Chris' efforts), with a worryingly unprotected well near the front door, and no apparent boundaries with the countryside. It was refreshing to see well trodden paths cutting into the trees behind the house; Chris' children certainly made the most of their spacious habitat, and didn't need 'Tekken 2' or 'Pokemon' in order to stretch their own imaginations.

KP   During the Seventies, when you spent half of your life fishing at Redmire pool, did you think to yourself: 'My goal is to catch the biggest carp ever', or did it just happen like that?

CY   No, No. At that time, the fishing at Redmire, which was probably the best carp fishing in the world, was restricted to ten people who were allowed to fish it. It was incredible that I managed to worm my way in. Actually it was a pretty low trick I played to get in, but I won't tell that story now, I'll save it for another day.

KP   Did you feel less pressure than other people actually to catch fish?

CY   Definitely. I didn't need to be fishing; I just needed to be at that place. But other people, who had proper jobs and less time, felt the need to catch fish. They had to make it worth their while, whereas I didn't care. And to make it worth their while, they were always talking of the monster fish. I was happy to talk about the monster, but I think I was the only one not really concerned about catching the record, because that was just a dream. And while I was happy for that dream to swim around my head, I wasn't that keen on making it a reality, because I so enjoyed absorbing myself in the very special atmosphere of Redmire. It was a magical place. The others, though, were very keen to catch the record and become the new Dick Walker, who had held the record since 1952, so it was odd when I broke the record – smashed it to pieces – because I was the one who perhaps least wanted it. Of course I did want it when it ended up in my net, and I saw it – I was thrilled – it was a huge event in my life, but it didn't change the way I thought about fishing.

KP   So after the leaves fell in autumn, what would you do?

CY   As a child – when the fishing stopped, we would find other things to do with water. Making boats, building dams, splashing around, but not in the winter. In my teenage years, we used to build rocket boats, through the winter we would be designing them, and then during the closed

season, when we went out to spot fish, we would round off the day by
having a little regatta.

KP So what were the boats made from?

CY Carpet tubes – packed with sodium chlorate and sugar, and we fixed
fins to them so they looked like sharks. Some of them would be doing
30 or 40 miles an hour, bouncing along the lake: born, born, born and
then BANG!! They would explode, and of course because they were
made from carpet tubes, they would always either blow up or burn up,
and all our hard work would be gone. We sometimes put passengers in
them too, normally freshwater mussels, but once we had a toad as a
pilot, and I'm afraid he probably didn't survive the experience. But we
wanted something that would last, something that we could re-use. So
we considered developing an electric motor. A friend got hold of an
oxyacetylene cylinder, we sawed the end off it, and we decided to test
it in my parents' garden. So we dug a hole, filled it with sodium chlorate and sugar, and fixed a long fuse, which ran behind a bank in the
garden. We surrounded the launch site with bits of old iron mongery,
to absorb any big flash, and there was also a garden roller and a windshield from an old scooter I had. Then we lit the fuse, which made a
lovely noise, a soft roar, and flames leapt from it, we were thinking,
'This is gonna be good.' But suddenly it stopped, and I thought, 'Eh?'.
There must have been five pounds of rocket mixture in the cylinder
and it had only been going for a few seconds. What had gone wrong?
Then there was a fizzing sound, like someone struggling with the top
of a warm bottle of beer, and all of a sudden the most fantastic explosion, which shook the garden. The garden roller, which must have
weighed a few hundred pounds just went high into the air over a labur-
num tree and landed on my neighbours' lawn with a dirty thud. The
windshield simply disappeared, and the top of the cylinder vanished
through a red streak into the ionosphere and came down miles away.
There were bits of earth and turf coming out of the sky for a long time
afterwards, and the bang was so loud it registered 1.8 on the Richter
scale at Greenwich.

KP Bloody hell!

CY And the Home Office came round the next day, and we were in serious,
serious trouble. So after that we decided to stop building rocket boats
and go back to passive fishing.

Don Cox

by Laurence Rémilia

IDLER 31 · WINTER 2002

FOR OUR 'REVOLUTION' ISSUE, IDLER CONTRIBUTOR Laurence Rémilia travelled to the South of France to meet Don Cox, former Field Marshall of the Black Panthers, now living in exile.

★

Donald Lee Cox is the only high-ranking member of the Black Panther Party still in exile. Seven years in Algiers, 25 in France. The past 12, he's spent in Camps-sur-Agly, a hamlet 'in the heart of Cathar country' in the South of France, about an hour's drive from the Spanish border. It takes me the best part of a blustery September day get to the nearby village of Saint Paul-de-Fenouillet. From there, Don Cox drives me to his home along the tiny, sinewy road cut through the Gorges of Galamus, pointing out the cave once inhabited by the hermit Saint Antoine. Upon arrival, he shows off the idyllic spot he's retired to – nestling on a steep incline, the 25-home hamlet overlooks a half-dozen mountain peaks – as well as his home, a converted barn. That's where he spends his evenings, indulging in his hobby: looking at the stars with a heavy-duty telescope.

A tiny bit of background: in the autumn of 1966, Huey Newton and Bobby Seale meet at Merritt Community College (Oakland, California). In October the two campus activists form the Black Panther Party for Self-Defense (BPP) and are quickly joined by others. They raise money selling *The Red Book*, quotations from Chairman Mao ... They become involved with the local black community, advising people of their legal rights. Soon, the movement gains national visibility. Its clashes with police make front page news; photos showing the best-dressed revolutionaries there's ever been (their uniform: black leather jacket, beret and trousers, not forgetting the gun frequently on display) are everywhere. By September 1968, FBI Director J. Edgar Hoover is calling the Panthers 'the greatest threat to the internal security of the country,' and his unit is doing its best to eradicate the BPP. Its Counterintelligence Program (COINTELPRO) encourages the in-fighting taking place within the Party. By the early Seventies, the Party is in tatters, all but ready to become nostalgia-fodder for a variety of 'demographics' a couple of decades on.

Early evening, we sit down to a meal in the spartan kitchen. As we talk, I busy myself with picking every piece of meat off the pizza he's prepared, having failed to mention that I'm vegetarian. This doesn't seem to perturb him.

DC I was born in 1936, in Appleton City, in the plains of Missouri and when I got to fourth grade, we moved to Cedalia. After high school, an uncle gave me a ticket to come to California. We couldn't even dream of going to California; that was the land of milk and honey. I went out there, met a girl in San Francisco and she got pregnant. I got a job at a printing place, and I worked my way up and became the boss. At the time I was apolitical, but very conscious of all the troubles there were for blacks.

LR How did you get involved with the Black Panther Party?

DC They had some articles in the paper, and I was curious about them, with the guns and whatnot ... That sounded different from all this civil rights stuff I'd been hearing about. We got a very unofficial group going – this was in the summer of '67 – and finally, we got Huey [P. Newton, co-founder of the BPP] to come and speak to our group. He gave us work to do, in San Francisco. I thought that was strange, you know, 'cause I looked up to them like they were from outer space ... I made contact with a couple of people I had confidence in and we started moving. We did our first job on the anniversary of a policeman killing a black man in San Francisco; we knew they would make the connection because of the date. We tried to find the policeman that shot the kid, but we couldn't. We found the station he was transferred to, so we just got one of them. Well, he wasn't killed, but he was very ... scared. That was our first action.

LR   And the violence escalated.

DC   When Huey was shot [on 28 October 1967, in Oakland; during the altercation, BPP Defence Minister Newton and fellow Panther Gene McKinney are arrested, while a police officer, Herbert Haines, is killed and another wounded], all of us was just destroyed, figuring that he's going to get the death penalty... So the group that I was with, two weeks after they moved on Huey, five of us retaliated. Nobody knew what the hell was going on, you know, the police or anybody...

LR   You still had the day job at the time?

DC   Well, by December of '67, the San Francisco police department asked for a special budget because of the guerilla activities being perpetrated against them. We were moving fast, hard, trying to catch up with the other people and in fact we was out there by ourself, but we didn't know that at the time. We kept on working for about a year, and then Bobby [Seale, one of the Party's six founding members] came to meet us and asked me to be on the Central Committee. And finally, in '68, in Berkeley, we organised a big rally that all the national leaders of the Black movement came to; it was very successful. After that, I quit my job, to open the office in San Francisco. That's when I started my full-time political activities.

LR   And you were never arrested?

DC   No. What happened was, I was dealing with the East Coast and there had been a lot of repression in the City of Baltimore. So I went there in June to try to straighten some stuff up, to try to put the Party back together again. But by the time I got to the door of the Panther office there, somebody came and said, 'Don't come in.' I said, Why? They said, 'There's a pig in the closet.' I said, How long's he been in there? He said, 'Three days.' And it was about 105°C. It was hot, really hot. I said, Oh shit. So I knew that for me it was over.

LR   A pig in the closet?

DC   They caught one that had infiltrated the party.

LR   And they dealt with him there and then?

DC   Yeah. So he eventually was killed. They found his body in a park in December, and when they found out who he was, they came right to the Party to try find people that would talk; they'd give them immunity, and they would be a witness. So one of them, soon as he got his immunity, he sent me a cassette and told me the whole history. That was two weeks before they started arresting people, which gave me a chance to hide. This was in May of '70.

LR By then the Party was in a bad way?

DC Well, it was pretty strong, getting bigger and better until Huey got out of prison. He didn't get out until August ['70]. I was in Algiers then ... But everybody was happy, [thinking] his getting out of prison was going to change everything; when Huey got out, it was, oh, Christmas all across the country.

LR But I was under the impression that there was already a lot of in-fighting prior to his release.

DC Yeah, but nobody knew about anything like that at the time. Then, everything was pretty cool, as far as the public was concerned.

LR In early 1970, you pop up in Tom Wolfe's 'Radical Chic' article [Wolfe's snide account of a fundraising party for the BPP held at Leonard Bernstein's Park Avenue duplex on 14 January 1970].

DC Yeah, yeah. I was pissed off! Because the night at the Bernsteins', there wasn't supposed to be no shit going on. But he had a tape recorder, and then he wrote all this stuff around it, got it out. We talked to him; he considered he'd done us a favour ... But we didn't need him at that time, we didn't need that at all. All across the country, editorials, cartoons ... 'Cause they wanted to make sure that those kinds of people didn't support us [Cox brings out his clippings file, and hands me the article in which he's portrayed as a 'Parlour Panther' and shown leaning 'up against a fuchsia wall'].

LR That must have got a lot of people talking.

DC There was a group of these things [fund raisers] organised for us, but because of all this publicity, they were all cancelled. In '70 or something, Tom Wolfe was in town; I heard this dude talking about this thing, and it was him. He was saying how he had gotten us all that attention. But at that time, at that date, we were known and getting articles around the world, didn't need him for that. Oh, I was pissed off.

ALGIERS

Back then, Algiers was a Costa del Sol for left-wing extremists on the lam, thanks to the Boumedienne government wanting to emphasise its revolutionary credentials. It was only natural that as the decimation of the BPP was underway (28 dead by December '69), it became a port of call first for Minister of Information Eldridge Cleaver, granted asylum in August 1969, with other Panthers joining him the following year.

LR When exactly did you head for Algiers?

DC When they started looking for us. I went underground immediately when he informed me that they were going to be doing that. Without knowing when, or anything, I didn't want to leave, so I stayed for two weeks, but then when they started kicking down doors looking for me, that's when I split. It took me a couple of days because I didn't have a reservation.

LR Eldridge Cleaver was already there?

DC Yeah, he was the only one. He and his wife, and the kid. But he was invited to lead this delegation to Korea and left about three weeks after I got there. About a week before he left, they [the Algerian government] gave us a facility, so I dealt with creating the BPP 'Embassy'. I didn't even have to think about money as Eldridge had money from the books he was writing, and he was using that to finance everything. And the day after he got back, we had the grand opening [3 September 1970] ... See, at that time, Algiers was very revolutionary. Not necessarily because of its own politics, but because it accepted all liberation movements from all over the world. There were about 90 of us from different movements and different countries there.

LR Was there a lot of contact between the different groups?

DC Yeah. That first summer, it was terrible. Five nights a week, you were going out somewhere. And you can't refuse an invitation.

LR So there was the Embassy opening ...

DC There was problems with Eldridge already. We'd discovered, when he was gone, some of the stuff that had been going on. He had killed a person in Algiers. It was lowdown, non-political shit. Just some jealous crazy man, 'cause of his wife ... We had the opening Friday, he moved his stuff off Saturday. He didn't have any dealings with us, and we didn't have any with him until November.

LR So you basically kicked him out of Algiers?

DC Well, he was going out with a young girl. Fourteen- or fifteen-year-old girl. Okay, she was looking fine. Oh shit! But she was only fifteen years old. When I get to Algiers, I didn't know. I'm going to school with him at noon to pick her up. [Laughs] All these other men in these cars, picking up ...

LR Their daughters!

DC Their daughters, yeah! [Laughs some more.] And we're picking up this girl! Oh shit! But I didn't understand any of that at the time ...

LR That didn't have anything to do with the killing.

DC No. I used the opportunity of him being gone to get that girl away from there. Well, when he came back, and he saw that she couldn't come there anymore, he left.

LR And then Timothy Leary shows up [having escaped from a US prison on 12 September].

DC Anybody American [coming to Algiers], that was our responsibility. We were sort of like an Embassy. You wanted in, you had to come through us. But with Leary, the press found out he was there, and it was a nightmare. Hundreds of journalists, from all over the world, all trying to find him … The government panicked. They just wanted us to get out of their country. It was okay to come back, but they just wanted the attention to be drawn on him somewhere else. We decided we'd have to get over in the Middle East somewhere, let the shit cool off before coming back. I was the one whose job it was; being the Field Marshall and everything, whenever there was any travelling to do, I had to deal with it. I took him to Beirut. Well, that turned out to be a fiasco … We were in the hotel where the Middle East press corps stayed; we didn't know that at the time. They got the word of Leary's coming, so they were running all over town trying to find him, and he was there in their hotel. They finally caught him, in this toilet … And we were really concerned about the [Lebanese] government fucking with us. I asked Eric Pace, a fairly well-known journalist from *The New York Times*, what was happening. He said, 'Well, you don't have to worry, but someone from the government will come and ask you to leave.' When I heard that, we decided we'd just go to the airport at about four, five the next morning and wait for the first plane to Cairo. When we get to the airport, everybody was looking at us. Finally, I got to the news-stand, all the newspapers, Leary. I mean, headlines that big, photograph of him on the toilet, you know. Oh, it was terrible.

LR You were never tempted to just dump Leary?

DC Oh, no, no no. That was my responsibility. So, we get to Cairo airport. Again, what seemed like hundreds of journalists. We got Leary through to the transit area, and the government said, 'OK, relax, you're safe now.' So we did. We had to wait three or four days to get the plane back to Algiers, and all the pressure was off by then. Oh, it was terrible.

LR But the other Arab governments accepted you?

DC You should see the stories they put in all the papers the next day, about us being arrested and all this kind of shit. We were free, but they told them a bunch of shit and we had terrible stories in the papers.

LR They put disinformation out about the relationship between them and you?

DC They didn't want to admit to the world that they were friends with us. So we finally got back to Algiers. Huey was calling the next morning. He was going to be on a live talk show, on television, and he was going to call Algiers, 'cause there seemed to be rumours going around that we weren't getting along anymore. And he was going to call, and that way we could talk, and let everybody know that everything was fine. [March 1971, Newton uses his appearance on a local SF TV show to expel Cleaver and the whole of the International section. In February, Cleaver had called for Newton to stand trial and for Chief of Staff David Billiard to be expelled.] So when we hung up the phone, we said, this is it.

LR Reading your article ['The split in the BPP' in *New Political Science* vol. 21 #2, June 1999], the split seems to really affect you.

DC I was really disturbed by Huey's actions. I had never imagined something like that happening. That knocked me off my feet. I was pretty upset about that. I had to start thinking about the fact that maybe everybody wasn't as perfect as I was hoping they were.

LR That article is described as the epilogue to *Maiden Voyage*, your unpublished memoirs.

DC The title is from Herbie Hancock. When I first started, the first meeting with the young dudes in San Francisco, the first time we all got together, that was playing and that was the favourite album among the group: *Hancock's Maiden Voyage*. I wrote everything in '80, just to get my memory down. I just sat down at a typewriter every day, for 12 hours a day, till I got it all down. But it's not organised. It hasn't got any kind of form at all.

LR That split has been qualified as being between those wanting guerilla action, and those wanting community action.

DC Well, it wasn't a question of community action. He [Huey] wanted just to do away with all of the guns and everything like that. But instead of having a meeting and talking about it, he just started moving on people. And so the people that were on the other side, the leftist people, well, they started doing actions right away. I went back to the

States, clandestinely, and stayed six months. I tried to talk to them [the East Coast Cleaver faction] and say: Hold it, we've got to get certain things together in order to be strong, there was hardly anyone left. Within about a year, everybody was gone: dead, in prison ... I'd been part of a group [in San Francisco], and everybody was busted except me. It was bad, man. So, as of then, I put an end to that and started being by myself.

FROM ALGIERS TO CAMPS-SUR-AGLY

A small nervy cat darts in to eat from the plate Cox has left out for him. It's sheer black and as I observe it, I recall the title of a 1977 book about the movement, Reginald Major's *A Panther is a Black Cat*. Cox explains it's one of two cats he has, that he's never given names to either of them, and that they're only allowed indoors to eat. He says he prefers them wild.

LR You headed back to Algiers.

DC Well, I didn't know where else to go. All of a sudden, here I am, by my-self. So I went back to Algiers. But as an individual. All the political, organisational stuff was over.

LR That was the beginning of your personal exile.

DC And I stayed in Algiers until April '77, which is when I left for Paris. Soon as they passed that 'Charte Nationale' and started all that religious stuff, I got out of there. All the men in the community, I'd been speaking to them, and all of a sudden, nobody's saying nothing to me anymore. And Friday, the Mosque, you can't move in the neighbour-hood. I mean, it changed, just like that. Scared the shit out of me.

LR Why Paris?

DC It was the only other place I knew. I was prepared to go to jail. I didn't take any luggage with me, and knew the passport had been changed so much, it had a hole in it ... But I had to get to be in France in order to ask for asylum.

LR You had no charges pending against you?

DC No, no. So then I just had to start learning how to live by myself. It was hard. I was doing photography work, 'cause that's what I was doing in Algiers, working as an industrial photographer. But after a while in Paris, I had to get out. It was too far North, I didn't relate to that. So, I came down here and first time I saw it, I decided I was going to settle down here. And I bought this place. But I only started living here full-time in '89.

LR Is it frustrating, observing the States from here?

DC It's terrible. I could never have imagined it could be as bad as this. Well, it's been frustrating, in that shit's going on and I had no way to stop it or change anything, that's what really destroyed me. I've been gone 32 years.

LR You're never going back?

DC Oh no. I wrote a book after Newton got out, a sort of a training book on guerilla warfare, and I used a couple of our actions as examples. I did that without thinking about it at all... I would never go back... You know, I would never be at peace with that system over there. I'll always be at war. I'll never give up, never go back. I mean, I might go back clandestinely, but officially, I will never go back. It's over for me.

Dave Stewart

by Tom Hodgkinson

IDLER 32 · SPRING 2003

I WENT TO VISIT DAVE STEWART, WHO WAS ON THE POINT
of launching his new arts centre and club, The Hospital. It thrives
today. At the time he was living in a groovy flat on Seven Dials.
Very successful, very dynamic; yet he seemed troubled at some level.

*

Ahead of the launch of his multi-million pound arts centre, The
Hospital, musician and entrepreneur Dave Stewart chats to Tom
Hodgkinson.

Dave Stewart's first brush with the music business came in 1967.
At just 17, he signed to Chris Blackwell's then-fledgling Island Records
label. He has never had a job since, and cuts an inspiring figure when
you realise that he's always managed to combine commercial success
with experiment, risk and creative freedom. We went to visit him in his
minimal central London pad, all white walls and stripped floors. The
sitting room has a Starship plasma television set into the wall. It's from
here that Stewart runs his many projects, two of the latest of which are
the Artists' Network, a sort of fair deal record company which aims to
give artists greater control over the commercial side of their work, and
The Hospital, the multi-million pound Covent Garden arts centre that
he is opening in March 2003, with partner Paul Allan, co-founder of
Microsoft, and one of the world's richest men. After a photo session
on his spacious roof terrace during which Stewart talks of the various
bureaucratic frustrations he's experienced over the six years he's spent
trying to get The Hospital up and running, I ask my first question.

TH So you've never been attracted, seduced or victimised by the conventional world of work?

DS I had a job once. I was meant to be moving furniture in Sunderland into the new Civic Centre, and it was great because they employed us for a week and no furniture turned up. But what we did find out was that they'd built something else under the Sunderland Civic Centre and I believe it's a fallout shelter for the Royal Family and members of state. We'd wondered why we were getting an incredible Civic Centre that seemed to cost millions.

TH And that was your only job?

DS Yeah. Then I had a record stall. I was one of the first people in Camden Market. There were just four stalls in the beginning. One of them was run by Julian, my Zen Buddhist stepfather from Brittany. He was the champion idler of all time, he never touched money for about 30 years, but he found everything he ever wanted. He would read the *Times*, because he knew people at this place threw them away before they got on the bus. Then he knew of a particular shop which threw out their croissants at about ten o'clock, so he'd have a nice croissant. He inherited a houseboat from a great aunt and it didn't have an engine. But he didn't want an engine. He used to just float around. He would put a sign up on his boat 'game of chess wanted' and just sit there for four hours waiting for someone to come up and say, 'Yeah, I'll give you a game of chess.' He used to write tons of crazy slogans and have them round his neck. In fact how my mum met him was an incredible story. He'd been married I think three times before. He'd heard that his wife at the time had met this woman called Sadie, my mum, at college in London and that she was an amazing woman. He was obviously thinking, 'How can I get to meet this Sadie?' and then he heard she was coming to tea. So he thought, 'I'll try and meet her before she gets in the house.' So he went and wrote on his billboard sign – 'The ice caps are slowly melting' – this is in 1967 – 'we're all in danger of being flooded, for more information ring this number.' So my mum was walking down Rosslyn Hill in Hampstead, walks past, reads this, goes back and goes, 'Excuse me, there's some mistake; that's my telephone number.' He says, 'Sadie, I've been dying to meet you.' He was the *crème de la crème* of idling.

TH There are these people who somehow manage to live this very free, almost aristocratic life, without any money at all.

DS He lived like that. The painter Souza gave him a painting, and I remember he was really annoyed because Julian had found a frame – he never bought anything – but the painting wouldn't fit in the frame, so Julian sawed the end of the painting off with Souza's name on it, and this painting's probably worth £150,000 or something like that. For years and years Souza was really, really annoyed with him. One day he came round and said, 'Forget it, I absolutely love you. I like the fact that you weren't bothered about the price of it.'

TH Because he was never going to sell it.

DS Yeah. And he had incredible adventures like some kind of flotsam. Once he disappeared for a few weeks. My mum was really worried. It turned out that he'd floated somewhere and someone had asked him on board because he was fantastic at speaking and he'd ended up at the Rothschilds' wedding party on a barge. They'd invited him somewhere else and flown him here and there. He wrote haikus, one of which was translated from English into Japanese. It was: 'This dunked biscuit, will it, won't it reach my mouth?' That's total Julian, I can imagine him pondering it.

TH That's beautiful isn't it?

DS It's totally in the moment. He found this electronic chess game, which he'd play for a few hours, then he'd look at his watch that he'd found in some dustbin, and he'd say, 'It's about time they threw out this garlic sausage, round the corner.' My mum used to get fed up because he'd invite people round for dinner and she'd make dinner and he wouldn't allow her to make anything for him because he'd only eat found things.

TH The art of foraging.

DS But his idea of being in the present wasn't all philosophising and med- itating. He'd also be like, 'You get this bottle of red wine and you drink it as soon as you wake up, and it'll last you about four hours.' One of the Eurythmics' very first B-sides was me and him. He was meant to read the alphabet in French and the track is called 'ABC Freeform'. He was so drunk he couldn't remember and he kept going backwards and forwards ...

TH He couldn't remember the alphabet?

DS He kept going backwards and forwards and forget where he was up to, so I put this crowd noise from the Albert Hall on, and as he stumbled backwards the crowd would start to cheer a bit, and as he got to the end they'd start cheering wildly.

TH So you had this character in your life ...

DS ... since I was about 16 or 17. I introduced everybody to him. Bob
Dylan would come and say, 'Let's go round and talk to Julian,' and
Julian had no idea who Bob Dylan was.

TH So do you think you'd have done what you've done without him?

DS No. There are certain people throughout my life that, although I was
thinking a certain way, affirmed it, and said, 'Yeah, that's OK'. Another
one was Conny Plank and also Holga Czukay, the bass player from a
group called Can who are a German underground group.

TH Is he the guy that talks about how something quite limiting, like having four strings on a bass can actually be very creatively ... er ...

DS Yeah, there's a saying where the less you have, the more imagination
you use ... anyway, he was Stockhausen's star pupil, and he was a perfect idler because he'd be going, 'I want to make these really strange
recordings, I haven't got much money but I really like living well.' So
he went to teach at a Swiss finishing school, because he thought, 'If I
marry a really wealthy daughter of a family then I could be kept and do
my weird music,' which was what used to happen back through the
centuries. But he ended up getting caught up in Can. The first
Eurythmics album had him playing on it and Marcus Stockhausen,
Stockhausen's son. It was called In The Garden and Conny Plank
produced it. He'd produced Devo and Kraftwerk. That's how I learnt
about recording. In studios you're always made to feel like you're a
dunce by the engineer, and you're not allowed to touch the board.
When we were making the Sweet Dreams album, we didn't make anything that was anything like what was going on, you know. So our
video had me and Annie [Lennox] and we had a cow come downstairs
into the room, we were in what looked like a boardroom; it's based on
Buñuel and Salvador Dalí sort of imagery. And of course the record
company were up in arms ...

TH Really, it just didn't compute?

DS No one in the record company thought we'd be successful at all. In fact
Sweet Dreams arrived in America by import and some radio station in
Cleveland was playing it and that's how it started to become a hit. We
sent this video off to America and the next thing we knew it was constantly being played and people were discussing it: is that woman a man
or that man a woman? Then it went to number one. But that was completely born out of Canny Plank, and it even says on the album cover,

credit Edward de Bono, Julian my stepfather and Conny Plank. Things do get born outside of this hothouse of fashionable turnover stuff. That's how people like Tim Burton come out with something that's got nothing to do with anything. Or like the B52s came from Austin, Texas, or Beck, or bands like The Specials from Coventry. The more successful they get the harder it is to …

TH … copy what you had in the first place?

DS Yeah. I've tended never to go into some complacent situation, so I'm always making it really hard for myself. And Annie and I did that. Normally a band would have a hit album and then go: 'Let's record the next one in the Bahamas,' but we went and hired a youth club in the suburbs of Paris, I think it was £1,200 to rent it for eight weeks. There was a room like this with people playing table tennis, you know, French kids smoking, and they didn't believe we were making a record. We went there every day and made the album.

TH So how did you come up with that notion to go there?

DS Well, we really liked Paris but we didn't want to spend a load of money in a recording studio because we'd already made the first album on an eight-track. We said, 'We've still got the eight-track, why don't we just take it somewhere?' The *Sweet Dreams* album cost about £5,000 including the equipment, and the next album cost about £12,000 because in the end we went to LA and we put Stevie Wonder playing the harmonica on it. So every time we did it we decided to do it in another quirky way, and I'm still doing that … Just now with Jimmy Cliff, we went to Jamaica and ended up in this tiny place in the middle of a kind of jungle, this hut studio, and then we went into the hills in Kingston. And we wrote and recorded some stuff and we brought it back here and it was sort of, you know… 'Necessity is the mother of invention', that's it. And of course after you've sold 50,000 copies you're already into profit, so what happened with Annie and myself is that lots of groups around us were selling albums too, but they didn't seem to have any money. We were doing OK: we were buying a flat in Paris or a house in London or whatever, and they were still going 'How do you do it? We're still paying off our debt to the record company'. And that's one of the reasons why I started the Arts Network, now called AN.

TH Is that related to The Hospital?

DS It's a different project but it'll cross over in parts. The idea is to empower the artists. It's a 50–50 share, but it's transparent so they get to see where everything is spent. So they can go 'Fucking hell! Wow, it costs us that to do that! We'd better not do that again,' and also they have shares in the company itself so it's in their interests to try and keep the costs down, and not hire limos all the time. I mean the worst example of this is Michael Jackson, who's got five studios on hire all the time, limos everywhere and doesn't turn up at any of them. His album cost £25 million or something and it's shit. Have you ever seen MTV Cribs? It's this ghetto fabulous thing where rap artists get their royalties and go mad. They buy mansions and five sports cars and then they invite MTV in their house and go, 'This is my marble whatever ...' and then a year later they go bankrupt, which happened to TLC. They don't understand that the money they've been given ...

TH   Is a loan ...

DS   ... is a loan and it's going to be recuperated at a very bad rate. You see, the record companies were the pushers and the artists were the cash junkies. The artists bought a lifestyle that they start to really get used to, which can happen to anybody, and then all of a sudden they realise: 'Oh hang on, for three years I'm not going to get any more because they're busy recouping what they gave me, how am I gonna pay my mortgage?' And then the record company goes, 'Oh, well maybe you need another advance.' So you get the next advance but now it's like, can you just sign this for another three albums, so ...

TH   So before you know it you thought you were being free and now you're in slavery to a big corporation ...

DS   That's why Prince wrote 'Slave' on his cheek. Tim Burton tells this great story about when he was trying to get the money for *Edward Scissorhands*. He said he would be sweating in meetings. He'd go, 'It's a love story, with Johnny Depp and ... [under breath] the hands are scissors ...' and they'd go, 'I'm sorry?' He said there'd always be one bright spark that would say, 'What about one hand scissor and one hand normal?' They wanted to compromise everything ... The pyramid becomes upside down. It's the same in music where you get single after single on MTV, R'n'B ones, where every video is in the desert, and cost $3 million. That's just Coca-Cola saying, 'We're not going to advertise in your show unless there's a certain amount of quality and money spent on the look of the overall show, the videos that are in it.' So then you get all these weird people dictating what the art should be.

TH   So did you suss out all this quite early on?

DS Well the very first time I got really worried was when we'd had a couple of big hit albums, and then RCA changed the head of their company in America. This man came along called José Menendez and I was told he came from Hertz Rent-a-Car. He wanted to meet us. He was the guy who got killed by his own children, the Menendez trial. Remember his kids murdered him and his wife?

TH Bit of a dysfunctional family then ...

DS Slightly. So this was the guy who would now be in charge of our career in America. I got a bit worried when we were selling three top ten singles, selling out stadium tours and our albums were peaking at 900,000. Whereas Tom Petty who was doing similar stadium tours was selling four million albums, so where were the other three million going? Probably being printed in Colombia or somewhere, and sold on the side.

TH So he could have been selling millions without putting them through the books?

DS Oh yeah, that happens all the time. That money gets put into the soft porn industry and then it's laundered through another company, like a talcum powder company and then it comes in back through Mexico. But I started to get worried when I knew the new head of our company was coming from Hertz. As you would if the *Idler* got into this massive thing and then a new CEO was coming from being the head of whatever, a meat-packaging factory, well actually that might be quite cool ... so that was a very odd meeting, I must say.

TH Did he appear crooked?

DS Just very scary, powerful. A big suit, firm handshake, gleaming teeth, tanned sort of guy that didn't know anything about music, not one tiny thing, but he was trying to say the right things, and it was just a scary experience. We can't talk about names but the president of one of the biggest music companies in America is a known mafia person, and he owes me money, owes loads of people money and you know you'll never get it. A friend of mine gets sent a gun every Christmas to remind him that he's never getting it.

TH So it's pretty hard to work with all of that while still doing exactly what you want.

DS Well yeah, it is very difficult. Also, trying to get other artists to understand what's going on is quite difficult as well. I can understand a person saying, 'I don't want to know what's going on' so they can just do their thing. And secondly, when you tell someone how it works, it's really so horrific that they think, 'Oh God, why do I want even to enter into this?'

TH There should be some kind of counselling advice centre for young pop stars.

DS Well, it's funny you should say that because one of the things I've started is a sort of private bank called Artists Bank. Normally, artists will get a record contract, and they'll get an advance of £50,000, but they haven't got a bank account yet, or they haven't a clue about paying tax, but in a year that album might sell a million, like Miss Dynamite, and they've suddenly got a cheque for £780,000, now what do I do? They'll have a manager and a financial adviser, but it's amazing how many people don't ever ask to see the biog or the credentials of their financial adviser, and anyone can call themselves a financial adviser … people like Sting, even though they're really wealthy, realised only recently that they've been ripped off millions. Also, how many artists made a record that did reasonably well, then realised they didn't have any money and were back working in Pizza Hut?

TH What about the relationship between letting things happen organically and planning?

DS Well that's the good thing about The Hospital. I'm of the opinion: build and they shall come. So no, you can't create false situations by ringing up so and so and getting him and everyone else … but you can build a place and see what happens. That's what Chris Blackwell did, and it's funny because it's come full circle. There's a press announcement coming out today that Artists Network and Palm Pictures and Chris Blackwell are all joining together. So now – it sounds mad – we have a bank, a church [Dave's Crouch End recording studio is a converted church] and a hospital.

It would be a great idea for the *Idler* to have a thing at The Hospital. Like a once a week *Idler* tea or once a month *Idler* dinner or something, where you also get to interview the various people that come through, Dennis Hopper or whoever. It's great for the artists that are coming there too, as they don't necessarily want to do interviews with straight papers … I can hardly believe that The Hospital will be open in five to six months. I wasn't expecting so much bureaucracy. But you know, it's all really about reality and responsibility being the path to freedom.

Zadie Smith

IDLER 33 · SPRING 2004

What time do you get up?
At the moment I have a job, so 8A.M. Normally, 10:30A.M.

Do you leap up or lie slumbering?
I employ the snooze function.

Do you smoke and drink, and if so, how much?
Only weed. Supposedly I am a non-smoker, but I can suddenly smoke
40 cigarettes in an hour if I'm nervous, talking to somebody very clever
or posh. A half bottle of white wine per day, and if in London, a cocktail or two on the weekends.

How many hours work do you put in on an average day?
Normally three; when a book is going well sometimes ten or more; at
the moment because of almost-real job, about six.

Do you take holidays?
See above. My work does not really justify the taking of holidays.
Often unsure what day it is, for example.

Where do you live?
Normally Kilburn, at the moment, Boston.

Where do you work?
Normally in a small room in Kilburn, at the moment, Harvard
University.

What are you three greatest pleasures?
Eating/sex, reading, writing.

Do you like money?
I never ever check my balance or do anything sensible regarding investments, accountants, etc. I find the mention of money very depressing. But I love owning 6,000 books – so in the end, I must like money.

Are you happy?
Very. But I've always been like that. I'm only unhappy if something really shitty happens, like a death. I find it hard to be depressed. It depresses my friends that I'm like that.

How many hours do you sleep at night/day?
I have to have at least seven. But during the winter I frequently fall asleep at around 3 p.m. for three hours. Except now I have to teach. I have to teach in about 20 minutes.

What are you reading?
Aleksandar Hemon, *Nowhere Man*. He's coming to read to my class tomorrow.

If it came to the crunch, would you choose money or art?
Art. There's no contest. Even now that I have money I don't know what to do with it. I just buy books and shoes, books and shoes.

What have you been thinking about?
Buying a house.

Who are your heroes?
Vladimir Nabokov, Zora Neale Hurston, Franz Kafka, Virginia Woolf, Shakespeare ... I don't know ... Fred Astaire, Jimmy Stewart, Iris Murdoch – heroes are complete bullshit, though, aren't they?

Any advice for young people?
Make sure your lubricant is unscented. Don't join fashionable 'schools of thought'. Read everything.

Do you like to go a-wandering?
Not really. I can't stand travel. And I like to walk, but only routes I

could walk blindfold – from Kilburn to Hampstead Heath, for example. Or from Admiral Nelson to Bar Italia.

What is paradise?
Sancerre, novel, beloved's head in your lap.

Grace Nichols

by Christiana Currie

IDLER 33 · SPRING 2004

T HIS LOVELY INTERVIEW WITH POET GRACE NICHOLS
was carried out by Christiana Currie who was doing work experience at the *Idler* at the time.

★

Five hundred GCSE students nestle in the comfortable surrounds of
Central Hall, their minds transported from the London squall and
carried to exotic places, rich with colour and filled with sunshine.
The gentle Caribbean tones of Grace Nichols lull the audience to the
rhythm of a heartbeat, awakening senses to the pulsing of nature and
the flourish of passion.

'Idleness is part of life,' Grace told me with a curling smile. 'For me,
it is important that I am totally at ease before I set about a poem ... my
most creative ideas happen when I am in bed during the daytime. For
example, I was in bed when I found my first inspiration for *Fat Black
Women's Poetry*. As I was dozing, I thought how wonderful it would
be to celebrate the Black Woman. No effort required when you are
relaxed and easy.' A woman after my own heart, I thought, as the veil
of guilt surrounding my own lifestyle was lifted a little. The Successful
Woman is a prevalent archetype; she is dynamic, she is strong-willed
and she is someone we all know. But what of the Idle Woman? What
of the woman who prefers to amble forward, to leave behind the dusty
power-suit and take life in her saunter?

'As a woman, and as a poet, much of my daily life is based around
choice. The choice is only ever between two things, organisation or
creativity. The options are clear and simple: do I get up now and clear

the breakfast table? Or do I stay in bed and think a while? As a woman and a writer, these are my two considerations. It is always my choice to attend to creative tasks first, they are far more urgent.'

Grace's smile broadens further, and I expect she is musing on the same thought as I am; the moment you decide not to tidy up is a beautiful thing.

Grace Nichols, poet and author, was born in Georgetown, Guyana and spent her first 25 years living and working in the West Indies. The inspiration for her first novel *Whole Morning Sky* (1986), came from her childhood experience of Guyana's struggle for independence during the 1960s. As a teenager, she became interested in political journalism and chose to study Communications at the Uni-versity of Guyana. Her assignments took her to the most remote areas of the country, where her experience of local community spurred an interest in Guyanese folklore and the further investigation of American Indian myths and the ancient civilisations of South America. Grace became fascinated by the vibrancy of tradition, and recognised the importance of preserving the legends of time-honoured cultures still to be found throughout the Caribbean. This, together with her political concerns, indicated the direction in which Grace's creative work would develop.

In 1977, Grace moved to Sussex, England, where she now lives with her partner and fellow poet, John Agard. Her first collection, *I is A Long Memoried Woman*, was awarded the 1983 Commonwealth Literary Prize and subsequent works have achieved similar acclaim. Her best-known collection *Fat Black Women's Poetry* is a bestseller both in England and the United States. Grace Nichols' important contribution to the GCSE syllabus and independent writings on Caribbean litera-ture made her an expert in her field. It was her third collection *Lazy Thoughts Of A Lazy Woman* which was to be the focus of our discus-sion, and is perhaps, my favourite of her books. Grace's good humour and generosity of character simply oozes from the poems in this collection, which Grace describes as being 'homespun'. She divides her attention between light-hearted observations and some important messages about cultural difference. Her short poems 'Dust' and 'Grease' are celebrations of the dirty kitchen and all things mouldy. Seeking to alleviate the pressures of being an organised person, Grace elaborates on this concept: 'There seems to be a "must-ness", there is a feeling that we "must" be tidy, we "must" be organised, or else ... or else something awful will happen. I have never thought that I "must" write a poem, I just do it when the time is right... Similarly, I have never thought that I "must" wash the saucepans, as I shall do that, too, when the time is right. It is not natural to behave according to demands we place upon ourselves.' I enquired as to whether or not the poem 'Grease' was a picture of her own kitchen. Grace smiled again, and with an amiable air of smugness she replied, 'Yes'. 'People forget that life is to be enjoyed. They forget everything they are needing and wanting can be found just outside.' Grace gestured over to the window, where city life swung below. 'The flowers on the trees, and walks in the park, it is all there for you.' She thinks for a moment, and chortles, 'It is like the advert on telly, with the poem, and the swan. "What is life, if full of care, we have no time to stop and stare." It is true. Life is idle, in the sense that it grows before it dies, but nothing else "must" happen, apart from love and enjoyment. Let things be, we must sit back and watch sometimes. Ideas will come.'

'There is a blissful side to small things. Mould and mildew, they are blissful things, they ask for nothing, they are harmless and yet they represent an important chapter in life's process: decay. There is nothing wrong with slowing down and losing shape, it's the same with people. Everything is affected by nature.'

After my meeting with the poet I went home at once to lie down. Once in position I read the first paragraph of my favourite poem by Grace Nichols, 'The Body Reclining', a message for the lovers of a horizontal life:

> I sing the body reclining
> I sing the throwing back of self
> I sing the cushioned head
> The fallen arm
> The lolling breast
> I sing the body reclining
> As an indolent continent.

Barbara Ehrenreich

by Tom Hodgkinson

IDLER 33 · SPRING 2004

MOST LEFTIES ARE FANS OF HARD WORK, SO IT WAS great to see the fabulously witty agitator and journalist Barbara Ehrenreich stand up for idling. This short interview was conducted by email shortly after the publication by Granta books of Ehrenreich's *Nickel and Dimed*.

*

I was blown away by *Nickel and Dimed*. In it, American social commentator Barbara Ehrenreich works as a cleaner, waitress and shop assistant and reveals the routine indignities and poverty endured by millions of Americans at the bottom of the capitalist ladder. It's also very funny and a great read. But her book presents a more subtle line than the familiar liberal plea for full employment with slightly better wages and slightly better conditions. There's a more radical agenda here, one which questions the basic wisdom of the Work Ethic. There follows an email conversation with BE, and two extracts from the book. Her latest project is a volume of essays called *Global Woman* which, like *Nickel and Dimed*, is published in the UK by Granta. We can't recommend her work highly enough.

TH Do you consider yourself to be an idler?

BE My embarrassingly late response may have led you to believe I am an idler, but this is not true. I do lots of things, some of which are actually work, and in fact find it hard to sit still for very long. Does riding my bike count as idling?

TH Don't worry about being late – I have built a generous margin for error into our deadlines as I know what you writer-types are like. Do you ride your bike for pleasure or to get from A to B?

BE I ride for fun, but would happily use my bike for general transportation if it were safe – *i.e.*, if there were enough bike trails. It maddens me that we have to pay to exercise at a gym when, in a normal world, exercise would just be a routine and unnoticeable part of life.

TH We're great fans of *Nickel and Dimed*. It seems to debunk completely the idea that 'Hard Work' leads to health and happiness. Why do you think it is that wealth and technological progress in post-industrial nations like the US and the UK have led to more work, and not less?

BE Probably some deep lingering Calvinist sickness. I can recall how in the early 1960s there was all kinds of concern about what people would find to do in the new post-industrial, leisure society we were about to enter. Now of course Americans work harder than ever: the poor-to-middle class ones, because they'll starve otherwise; the rich ones because busy-ness has, perversely enough, become a status symbol. I think one of the great social struggles of this decade (or, alas, century) will be to reclaim our right to leisure. Everyone should be an idler.

TH That reminds me of Dr Johnson's quote 'every man is, or hopes to be, an Idler' (1758). The ultimate purpose of the busy, he says, is to be idle, but sadly almost no one ever gets there. Perhaps we need to start de-industrialising ourselves? Or at least ridding ourselves of consumer desire?

BE I suppose you are aware of the big historical change *vis-à-vis* idling: at one point, aristocrats did it with pride; now the rich at least pretend to be busy. Sometime in the 1980s I wrote a column on the 'cult of busy-ness' and how it's become a status symbol. I don't know how to counter this, unless we could get some celebrities to engage in serious public idling. By the way, there are times when idling is a real and necessary skill. Last week I found my plane had been delayed by three hours at Dulles airport. I actually felt a kind of pleasurable anticipation as I plotted out my idling strategy: half an hour walk through the D con-course, visit to D concourse bookstore, compare iced tea at various food outlets, window shop in B concourse, study the kinds of people who eat at Cinnabons (sweet rolls) and compare them by social class, weight, etc. to Au Bon Pain eaters, read novel, etc. I could barely get it all done in the three hours allotted.

TH Could you give us a brief outline of your routine, if you have one?

BE Yesterday I worked for about three hours and would have done more
    but it was not very compelling work. Did errands, went kayaking,
    talked to friends on phone, made dinner for other friends. I've been
    struggling for years against my own Calvinist inclination that a day
    hasn't been properly lived without a few hours at the computer – and
    I'm happy to say that I'm winning the struggle. My two-year-old
    granddaughter has been a big help. With her, following an ant for
    15 minutes is a perfectly legitimate activity. Or throwing all the stuffed
    animals out of the crib and then throwing them back in while scream-
    ing 'Teddy can fly!' And similar projects.

TH Three hours a day – that seems about enough. Our proposal for uni-
    versal happiness is the Three By Three idea: three hour day, three day
    week. I wanted to ask about women and work: it seems to me that
    feminism encouraged women into the workplace, but now they are
    there, they might be realising that it's not that great. Is being enslaved
    to a boss any better than being enslaved to the home?

BE It depends on the home – and the boss. Most women, probably like
    most men, would like some 'balance', as we're always saying these days,
    between work and family or work and whatever-you-choose-to-do. In
    the 1970s, when feminism was coming to life again, that really seemed
    possible, because in those days, work generally meant eight hours a
    day. Now professional and managerial people are expected to work
    about 12 hours a day, and the poor work two or three jobs. This is not
    what we early feminists had in mind! That's why it's so important – for
    both sexes – to launch a serious movement to reclaim our time. I see it
    as a movement that could cut across class lines and raise profound issues
    about capitalism, bureaucracy, and the meaning of life. More and
    more, as a public speaker and agitator, I find myself talking about this.
    It's just crazy how much Americans work – as if we'd never had the
    struggle for the eight-hour day! Enough! I'm off to idle.

Joanna Blythman

by Dan Kieran

IDLER 34 · WINTER 2004

FOR OUR 'FOOD' ISSUE, IDLER DEPUTY EDITOR DAN
Kieran went to meet the author of *Shopped: The Shocking Power of British Supermarkets.*

★

We love supermarkets. We must do because 80 per cent of the food we eat in Britain comes from them. Supermarkets have made food cheaper than it used to be, we have more choice today than before they were here and they've made shopping much more convenient. Or have they? Not according to Joanna Blythman.

DK We loved your book. But reading it was terrifying. Did the things you found out shock you?

JB I thought I was going to find problems with the way the supermarkets operated and I went through a phase of being shocked. One farmer who had literally to chip leeks out of a frozen field on his hands and knees with a chisel to prevent his company losing its supermarket contract. I remember going back to the car thinking, 'Oh my God, it's so awful!' But then I just became used to the horror of it, so now I take it for granted that supermarkets behave in this way. The suppliers are so feudal. I'm not very business-minded, but when they say to you they're growing hundreds of acres of vegetables for a supermarket but they don't have a contract ... I thought, doesn't every business rely on contracts? I just didn't know anything about it. But that's when you start to realise where the power lies.

DK You say that ready meals have had a huge impact on whether people buy raw ingredients.

JB That is the most worrying thing. When the older generation is gone there will be almost no one alive other than butchers who know what a properly hung piece of beef looks like. It's like a chain of knowledge that's being eroded because of the way supermarkets have changed how we eat.

DK My gran says, 'You don't realise how many different varieties of apples there are.'

JB Supposedly supermarkets give us this fabulous choice and before supermarkets we were in this state of rationing. It's quite a psychological achievement when you look at how narrow the choice really is. There is a choice, but it's not a qualitative choice. The real variety, the different crops that we used to grow have all gone. Very few people have challenged the supermarket idea that they provide choice.

DK The other thing that supermarkets have managed to persuade us is that they're cheap. How do they get away with it?

JB I think we just don't challenge it, we don't have time. But also it's quite cunning. Supermarkets sell cherries, for example, in 350 gram packs and they seem bigger than they are. When you get them home and you take the lid off you can't believe how few cherries are actually in there. But they'll have a few things, like bananas, which will be really cheap to help create the idea that everything else is. Unless you buy the really heavily processed foods, things like baked beans, you'll find that supermarkets are actually much more expensive than small shops and markets. In medieval times the centre of civilisation, the big populated areas, was the cathedral and now it's the shopping centre. And have you noticed how they always have very pretentious architecture?

DK Do you think there's much hope for the future?

JB I think there is. I use the analogy that it's like being in a bad relationship for a long time, you know, you suddenly wake up one morning and you look at the person and you think, 'I've been with you for ages and actually I've realised this morning that I really hate you. I'm now re-running all the things that I thought I liked about you over in my mind and I've realised I actually hate them and they really get on my nerves.' I think people are beginning to feel this way about supermarkets, they're beginning to realise that there is an alternative. I think it's on the edge and it can change. Particularly the way these enormous supermarkets just keep getting built, people are beginning to feel, 'Oh my God, not another Tesco,' which is the way it's going. Every petrol station is run by Tesco, their local convenience store is run by Sainsbury. I don't think that British consumers are up for that, even if they don't care about food, or they don't know about food very much. People care very much about the High Street, their locality, and their town not being exactly the same as every other town, it's so alienating being in a place which is just the same as every other place with a Sainsbury's.

DK   Maybe that's the answer, you've got to prove to people that there is an alternative.

JB   But we've got to encourage the people that are hanging on, the independent shops, the butchers and bakers. We have to say, 'We are committed to you, we are going to make a point of supporting shops like yours.' Because we're at a tipping point now, it may seem as though supermarkets have it all but there's still 20 per cent of the market that they want. Thankfully we've got a lot of Asian shops with alternative, fantastic produce who make a tremendous contribution to the independent sector. But if people could transfer just 5 per cent of their total shopping budget to greengrocers, butchers and bakers it would make an enormous difference. We have to send the people that are still here a very clear message, 'Hang around because we want you, we value you.' Even if you only change small things, like don't buy your newspaper from a supermarket, get it delivered. Every time you buy a bottle of wine don't buy it from a supermarket, get it from the off license. Even shops like Oddbins and Threshers are petrified of supermarkets now [both chains have since closed down]. But if we don't support these shops they will vanish and then we won't have a choice about where we buy our food. And in whose interest is that?

Raoul Vaneigem

by Laurence Rémila

IDLER 35 · SPRING 2005

I
T WAS VERY EXCITING TO GET AN INTERVIEW WITH THE
well known Situationist philosopher. Vaneigem could be called the
grandfather of punk; in the Fifties he and his cohorts graffitied 'ne
travailler jamais' on the Paris walls, and wore ripped clothes with slogans scrawled on them, in the tradition of the Cynical philosophers,
who wore rags to signify their disdain for worldly matters.

Laurence Rémila meets the great philosopher and writer, one of the
prime movers in the Paris riots of 1968, now living quietly in Belgium.

*

He's been dragging round the reputation of being one of the lynchpins
of the *International Situationiste* for over 30 years. Raoul Vaneigem's
Traité de savoir vivre a l'usage des jeunes generations (*The Revolution of
Everyday Life*) was published the same year (1967) as his *compagnon de
route* Guy Debord's *La Societé du Spectacle*. It was one of the texts that
anticipated – sparked off, if you like – the May 1968 revolts, its dis-
course inspiring the *Enrages* of Nanterre, its words ending up on count-
less walls. And when giddy 1968 gave way to dazed 1969, he was out
(after eight years of activisim). A prolific author, he's since published
30-odd books.

Today, at 71 years old, Vaneigem is as radical as ever. He lives in the
Belgian countryside, refuses public appearances and face-to-face interviews (he will only answer in writing) and does what he's always done:
write for anyone who questions the way they're encouraged to live
their life. Here's a piece of advice for you, dear English-speaking
reader: get hold of his recent *Modestes propositions aux grevistes: Pour en*

finir avec ceux qui nous empechent de vivre en escroquant le bien public
(Verticales, 2004) – a fierce defence of our right to rip off the state – and
get that cute French thing working at the Tube-station deli to translate
bits of it for you. Just make sure to fare-dodge when you go.

LR Can one live without working?

RV We can only live without working. We only work through necessity,
to survive. Life starts when one stops working. Work is incompatible
with life which is essentially creative. Life is a permanent invention,
survival is nothing but a monotonous work of reproduction.

LR What do you think of the success of Corrine Maier's book, *Bonjour
paresse* (or even the work of the *Idler,* which has done a lot to promote
the idea of the benefits of idleness)? Is it a more accessible way of
approaching issues that concern you? Or simply a way of ignoring
them?

RV Yesterday, capitalism accorded the worker the leisure of recuperating
a little of his strength of production so as to be able to go back to the
factory and give the best of his energy. Today, when the modern
worker is freed from work-hours during which he has enriched the
ruling classes, he continues to increase the profits of the capital by
spending his salary and by becoming a slave in the supermarkets.
Leisure has become a work of consumption.

The advantage of idleness, is that it is not – unlike leisure – the ally
of work. It doesn't integrate the rhythm of labour, it is part of the
rhythm of life. It is through it that creativity ripens, that we get to
know ourselves, our desires. When we leave it – because prolonging it
soon turns to boredom – it doesn't incite us to throw ourselves in the
frenzy of work but rather to discover the pleasures of creating and the
art of creating pleasures for ourselves. One cannot live without idleness
and one cannot live through idleness (apart from making others work
for us, which turns the pleasure into ignominy). Idleness and creation
are inseparable, it is a good thing to remind ourselves of that as only
creativity can rid us of work, as there is only imaginative ingenuity to
subvert oppression.

LR You sometimes say you've been writing the same book for 40 years. As
you do so, do you consciously try to make it more practical? And how
does the start of this project, written 40-odd years ago, fit in with what
you've written more recently?

RV Every book is the product of its time as well as of an individual.
Radicality consists in seizing beings and things at the root, which is life.
My radicality hasn't changed. It becomes more precise as changes in the
dominant world show how merchant totalitarianism progresses and
how it produces, in the heart of its evolution, that which denies it. May
1968 sparked off a change in society that most people still feel confus-
edly today, though they are unable to formulate it, such is the force of
the inertia keeping our modes of thinking locked into the prejudices of
the past. One day though, we'll have to admit that May 1968 marked a
complete break with the majority of patriarchal values that had, for
several millennia, governed collective and individual ways of behaviour, all kept under the thumb of religious institutions, ideologies, the
army, the police, hierarchised power, paternal and marital authority.
Situationist ideas propagated the refusal of work and sacrifice, the
denunciation of ideologies, the rejection of all authority, by opposing
the primacy of life to survival, and by underlining the growing importance accorded to nature, to woman, to child, to creation, to desire. It
is this consciousness that I spend my time trying to reignite.

However, this consciousness, which could result simply from a vol-
untarist attitude, meets today – with the crisis caused by the mutation
of capitalism – the objective conditions that comfort it. What else have
we seen? We have witnessed, since the consumerism of the 1960s,
the accelerated development of a financial capitalism that, instead of
re-dynamising production by using a part of the profits, now only buys
stock to speculate. Confined to short-term profitability, imprisoned
in a financial bubble condemned to implode, this sclerosed capitalism
will give way, sooner or later, to a neo-capitalism that will discover, in
energies that are free and renewable, a new mode of production and a
source of profits that manages to avoid the threat weighing on petrol
supplies and on nuclear power stations, both of which are increasingly
contested. The emergence of a new re-natured agriculture and a
technological 'alternative', which prefers to ally itself to nature rather
than to pillage it, allows us to conjecture a possible going beyond this
merchant civilisation and the beginning of a humane society.

But such is the omnipresence of the spectacle – which considers that
what it doesn't recognise doesn't exist, that we only see the immensity
of the Titanic without realising its hold has burst. Almost all of our
field of vision is monopolised by the triumph of merchant totalitarian-

ism, resignation and servility, the nihilism of speculators, of fetishism and money, of fear and self-censorship.

The old capitalism founded on the pillage of natural resources and on financial accumulation in a closed-circuit will soon be shipwrecked. A new capitalism is here, which is supplanting it, and which we will have to fight because, under cover of privileging the quality of products, non-polluting energies, the primacy of the worth of usage and humanist values, it has no other aim but to perpetuate the reign of all that's mercantile. To limit oneself to vituperating the sclerosed shape, taken over by small-time speculators, while ignoring the new 'ecological' capitalism in development — with the firm intention of liquidating it too — it is to claim to destroy what is destroying itself and destroying oneself at the same time. It is to resign oneself, with cries of revolt and indignation, to sinking with the ship. For me it's a particularly morbid form of revolutionary imposture.

LR Is it important for you to address your works to high-school kids, to strikers, to well-defined groups of readers, as you have done with your recent works?

RV I'm the first person I address myself to. I try to disentangle the problems I find myself faced with each day and to solve them by integrating them in a global project of transformation of the world. I've made my longing for a life unceasingly more passionate the motor of a radical subversion. I don't suppose that my desires are those of each and every person; I simply think that many people are animated by a similar will for living and that, as a consequence, certain readers find in my texts an echo of their own preoccupations. It is neither the number of readers — nor their status — that interests me, it is the interest they take in my way of acting through picking up what they deem useful in my books and by discarding the rest. As for the accountancy of the passing years, it is time to do justice by recalling that if survival has an age, life is ageless.

LR You've lived in the Belgian countryside for many years. Do you feel cut off from the outside world? How do you act to be in touch with the problems of those to whom your books are explicitly addressed?

RV Everyday life is the only real territory that's ours to try and liberate. The fight for emancipation is an imposture when it strays from that territory and falls into intellectuality, militancy, thought separated from life, ideology. The questions people ask themselves about an existence from which real life is far too often absent are fundamentally the same the world over. The trouble is that they think they're solving their existential problems by cutting themselves off from them, by accepting bits of nonsense that populist and cronyist politics sell them unceasingly through the news and in media clichés. Where is the fighting spirit? With those who go out into the streets and shout slogans and then go home to relapse the following day into the same ruts? With the *casseurs* (breakers) who let off steam by defending the right to destroy in a society that already destroys everything including itself? With the socialist, Trotskyite, ex-communist, libertarian dinosaurs for whom the world hasn't changed any more than their sclerosed way of thinking? These people exist only by proxy, they accept to be nothing in a world that annihilates them. What's missing the most today, is the consciousness of both our creative richness and the possibility we have of creating situations that free us from our oppressions: the quest for survival-money, the need to work, the boredom produced by the spectacle of the living eviscerated, the falsification of desires, the frustration leading to hatred, the cycle of repression and release, the weight of archaisms.

I think that my aspiration for a radical change has some chance of meeting a certain number of individual resolutions which, through their specificity, go in the same direction. I'm certain that life always triumphs over the negation of life. In the absence of a conscience that's attentive to the will to live and to the mutations and social changes taking place, all there is, is admissions of failure. Never have the conditions for setting the basis for a humane society been so favourable and never have inertia, passivity, resignation, voluntary servitude and impotency triumphed so. The social struggles have given way to political populism and to corrupt face-offs in which the religious and nationalist old-timers lend their patched-up banners. Giving up is what many militants do best, who have never ceased to brandish them to salute just about any cause, apart from those that involve building their own lives. The social struggle has to re-invent itself. It should reject the archaisms that imprison it – political populism, bureaucratic trade-unionism, militancy, ideologies – and base itself on the conscience and individuals' desire for life.

LR Is it important to confront the fruit of your readings to the life of all?

RV What is important is that each person draws his knowledge from his personal experience and if a book or a speech can enlighten him, help him to live better or to eradicate that which is stopping him from living better, all the better.

LR In 1960/61, you discovered the strikes in Belgium, and it is a question which you regularly come back to. What's changed since the start of the Sixties with regards to this?

RV All reasons are good for stopping work but that isn't enough if we want to obtain more than the crumbs that your employers deign to throw you. Most of the major strikes from the past were about protest. They'd paralyse the system of capitalistic exploitation and exert pressure on it. They'd last the time needed for him to make a few concessions and satisfy a part of the workers' demands, these demands managed not by themselves but alas by trade-unionist *bureaucraties*. In exchange, the employers would obtain that they go back to work and it is of course from the exploitation of the work that they draw their profit, their plus-value. As for the trade unions, shouting victory, they'd consolidate their hold on the proletariat.

The old idea of a general strike that would overthrow capitalism and lead to a revolution has never been proposed with either conviction or pertinence. The communist ideology, this imposture bureaucratised by Leninism, claimed to regulate the revolutionary conscience for decades. We'll long remember the programmatic formula of the Stalinist Maurice Thorez: 'One has to know how to end a strike.' The point is, strikes were never revolutionary at a period where they could have been. Of course, they have improved the level of survival for the masses. But as beneficial as they were for the workers, the relative well-being it gave them would end up profiting capitalism itself which, from the years 1955–1960 on, started to draw the majority of its profits from the consumer sector rather than from production. Salary increases are directly recovered by the dominant system thanks to the proliferation of supermarkets. Slowly but surely, consumerism has devoured everything, including class consciousness. We've seen a market democracy be propagated on the model of big retail stores where each person has the freedom to choose a huge variety of products on condition he pays for them before leaving. The primary objective is to incite the consumer to buy just about anything just so long as the volume of purchases increases, the utility and quality of the products have decreased while the artifices of seduction aimed at customers, the techniques of promotion, that's to say the promotion of the useless and the parasitic, have unceasingly gained in importance. Information is nothing but advertising.

We are now prey to a populist system that governs politics and business indifferently, as well as corporate demands, religions and ideologies. There is a single demand capable of smashing this system that destroys all the vital sectors of society, it is the right to live, the right to create a milieu that facilitates and favours an existence that's truly humane. What I recommend are strikes demanding gratuity. Gratuity is absolutely antithetic to market economy, it is both a practical way of combat and a way of thinking that's in accord with this generosity of the alive that manifests itself in the feelings of love, friendship, solidarity or the pleasure of giving. It is this conscience of gratuity perfectly applicable in the primary sector that has to be propagated everywhere and stimulate invention. Have the trains, the metros, the buses running freely and you will provoke healthy emulation everywhere, you will awaken the creativity of each person.

The market for renewable energies is the driving force of this new capitalism that is emerging little by little and opposing its dynamism to the capitalism which, though still dominant, is sinking in stock speculation and is threatened by the rarefaction of fossil energies. However, even though they are seen as a source of profit, alternative energies currently in development implicate a principle of gratuity which it's up to us to brandish as a weapon against the new masters, whose exploitation is readying itself to take over from the one we knew before.

Corinne Maier

by Anne-Céline Jaeger

IDLER 36 · WINTER 2005

CORINNE MAIER'S BOOK 'HELLO LAZINESS' (2004) WAS A huge hit in Europe. A witty, acerbic and withering attack on the dead working life of a corporation, it clearly struck a chord with people. Later she published another bestseller called *No Kid: Forty Reasons Not To Have Children*. Soon after this interview was published, Corinne quit her job and retired to Brussels to write, read, teach and practise psychoanalysis. Her website is at www.corinnemaier.info.

Like most people working for a big corporation, Corinne Maier, a 41-year-old economist employed by Electricité de France, was utterly underwhelmed by her job. But unlike the rest of the conformist corporate bods, she actually voiced her frustrations. Not by pulling her line-manager aside during a meeting, or by writing a disenchanted email to the boss. No, Maier went biros a-blazing and published a book, which not only ridicules corporate culture but preaches a philosophy of active disengagement as well. Already a bestseller in France, her 120-page ode to sloth, *Hello Laziness: Why Hard Work Doesn't Pay (Bonjour Paresse)*, is now gaining momentum in the UK. A play on Francoise Sagan's 1950s novel *Bonjour Tristesse*, *Hello Laziness* is an antidote to the recent assault of career-enhancing self-help books. It's a battle cry for the 'neo-slaves' of middle management, which not only outlines why it's in your interest to work as little as possible but also demonstrates how you can corrupt the system from within without appearing to do so. Unimpressed with the manual, Electricité de France threatened Maier with disciplinary action. The union responded by taking her case to the media on the grounds that the corporation was threatening free speech. The outcome: phenomenal sales, appearances on TV and Maier got to keep her two-day-a-week job. Of late, Maier has been sauntering into the EDF offices, knowing full well that she is mocking her employer. Rather than fearing the sack, she is relishing the fact that the tables have turned and that after years of being used by the firm, she can exploit them in return. During her two days in the office, Maier, who is also a trained psychoanalyst, earns enough to live on. She spends the rest of her time dreaming up new book ideas.

ACJ Was going into conventional business ever a dream of yours?

CM Never. It just sort of happened. I was looking for a job and I found one in a big company and I took it. At first I thought corporations were strange places to be in, and as years passed I realised that working in one was a mistake.

ACJ When did you first think of subverting the workplace from within?

CM Every day at EDF I saw people who were pretending to work, but who in fact did nothing. There are so many people who do that without even realising they are doing it. They create the impression of being a team-player, they are nice with the managers, they speak the company's jargon, etc., but in fact they aren't doing any work. So I thought it would be funny to advise people to pretend to work but to do so consciously.

ACJ What are your tips for doing this?

CM When they tried to sanction me, my bosses accused me of reading the papers during meetings, but that was wrong. I work part-time, so I don't have to pretend that I'm working as I'm hardly there anyway. I don't pretend. That's one of the reasons they hate me. Nowadays, I do annoy them, but now I don't care what they think because I have enough financial backing thanks to the book. At times, I might have conversations with my colleagues about literature, and they can go on for hours.

ACJ Why don't you like your job?

CM First of all, I have to go outside. I have to ride my motorbike into the suburbs of Paris and I hate the suburbs. Secondly, I find the building I work in incredibly ugly. It's a depressing place. And thirdly, some of the people I work with are just so uninteresting. Also, I don't get on with my bosses. So I don't like going there. A few years ago, the actual work I did was still interesting because we had to come up with new ways of doing surveys and research. These days, it's all about productivity. We have to do more and more surveys. It's no longer about thinking analytically but about how many surveys you produce – even if these are done badly. It's less intellectually taxing. I have admitted openly in the company for some years now that the only reason I go to work is for the money. But you're not supposed to say that.

ACJ If you hate it so much, why don't you quit?

CM The fact that I still go there bothers my bosses and I think that's funny. I think that's a good reason to carry on going there. I want to annoy the company that has annoyed me for so long.

ACJ Don't you think it would be more revolutionary to stop working altogether?

CM I think it's probably more revolutionary to go in and pretend to work. But once I finish my game with EDF I hope I never have to go back to a big company. That's my career plan. At the moment I don't know how that game will end, and when that will be. But I'm curious to find out. I feel like I'm winning by going in. I don't see the point in quitting. It would be more fun to be sacked.

ACJ What does money mean to you?

CM To me money is important only in the way that it makes you more free in that you're able to say 'No' to the things you don't want to do and to people you don't like. I don't care about buying things and showing others that I have money.

ACJ How do you spend it?

CM At EDF I earn 1,500 Euros for 2.5 days a week. That's before tax. I have two kids so of course there are lots of things that need to be paid for. But generally I don't care about consumerist stuff. I have an old motorbike, a 20-year-old car, which doesn't go very fast. Good restaurants are important to me but that's about it.

ACJ What do you make of the of 'working more to spend more' bind?

CM In France we're lucky because we don't even have to think about how we should spend our money. The state helps us spend our money because the taxes are so high. I think it's fine for people to work a lot if they like their job, but if they don't, it's terrible. I just work to eat and to live where I want to live, which is in the 13th arrondissement in Paris, an ordinary neighbourhood.

ACJ What's the best way you ever spent your money?

CM Paying for my psychoanalyst.

ACJ How important is status to you?

CM I don't care about status. I've never wanted to be a boss. I don't like giving orders and telling people what to do. I don't care about social status or responsibilities. What I'm interested in is finding new ways of thinking or making things. I don't actually know any people who have a career. They must exist, but I don't know any.

ACJ To what degree were you inspired by the Situationists and Paul Lafargue?

CM I don't actually like Lafargue's book *The Right to be Lazy*. I think it's written in a really old-fashioned style. But I like the idea of defending workers' rights to be lazy. What I like about the Situationists is the way they wrote. Guy Debord had such a beautiful writing style and to me a beautiful style is always revolutionary. They weren't on my mind that much when I wrote *Hello Laziness*, but it's certainly a compliment to be named in the same breath.

ACJ What thinkers inspire you?

CM I like Michel Foucault, particularly his thoughts about power, which he outlines in *Discipline and Punish*. I also like the fact that he was fascinated by the study of marginality. He was interested in crazy people and prisoners. Lacan is another favourite of mine, as are Roland Barthes and Jacques Derrida. I love the French thinkers.

ACJ How would you describe your philosophy in life?

CM My motto is: *Ne servir a rien, ne servir personne*, which translates as 'Be useless, be a slave to no one'.

ACJ But isn't your book useful?

CM Books are not useful. It's important to have books as a collective, but if you think about it, most of them are bad, never read, inaccurate or irrelevant. I would put my book in that category. I'm surprised that people are buying it. I'm disappointed that they are buying this one. I'd much rather they bought my book on Lacan. But I guess the French needed to put a label on something they were suffering from. *Paresse* or laziness is now back in fashion.

ACJ How has your life changed since the publication of *Hello Laziness*?

CM Ironically, I work much more now than I used to. I do a lot of promotion for the book, so it's goodbye laziness for me. I hope it's temporary. But in some ways I can be more lazy now, as I can say no to things I don't feel like, such as writing books on subjects I don't care about, or making TV programmes with producers I don't like.

ACJ How has idleness improved your life?

CM I'm only lazy about the things that don't interest me. Laziness is the reverse of desire. When you don't desire something, you don't do it properly and you end up not doing it at all. It's a way of making a distinction between what you want and what you don't want.

ACJ What do you do in your idle time?

CM To me there is no difference between spare time and real life. So if I have things to do, I do them, and if I don't I think about what I could be writing about. I think the problem for most people is that they don't know what they want. I know that feeling well because I was there myself once. I started seeing a psychoanalyst years ago to deal with that feeling. I was lost. It really helped me find my way. It was a revelation.

Joe Rush

by Tom Hodgkinson

IDLER 36 · WINTER 2005

I'D MET JOE AT A PARTY, AND HE STRUCK ME AS A FAN-
tastically cheerful and talented person. The Mutoid Waste
Company had always been a legendary organisation to me. I remembered reading about their parties in the *NME* when I was 15. I
asked if I could interview him. He said yes, and it was a great joy to
meet this gentleman sculptor and adventurer, and hear his tales. Would
you believe he stole two fighter planes? Read on.

★

Back in 1984 artist and 2000 AD fan Joe Rush and friends had an idea for
making sculptures out of old bits of junk, the Mutoid Waste Company
was born, and a 20-year adventure involving giant trucks, the collapse
of the Berlin Wall, Mig Fighters and numerous run-ins with the
world's police began. We visited Joe in the yard he now rents in
Deptford, to where he'd just returned from a big show at the Glastonbury festival. We talked about the history of the Mutoids and Joe's
creative philosophy.

TH How did it all start?

JR It started in 1984. I started doing my own work in a little old under-
takers' office in a mews in Shepherds Bush. I would spend two weeks
on polystyrene carving and working on props, and that paid for me to
have my studio.

TH Did you go to art school?

JR No, I learned from my parents who were artists, and from people like
Brett Ewins of 2000 AD comic. He started *Deadline*, and was married to

my cousin, Victoria. This was when I was 15 or 16. The punk thing had just started and I was well into that ... the 2000AD guys were all ex-skinheads, like Mike Mahone ... it was brilliant. When I was 17 I was living with a 28-year-old stripper in Ladbroke Grove, which was quite an education ... then we busted up and I didn't know what to do with myself ... so I just stuck out my thumb and ended up at the Stonehenge Free Festival. Me and a fella called Willy X were the first two punks to walk on to Stonehenge that year. I spent the summer travelling with the Peace Convoy. Then I came back to London and was living in a house called Apocalypse Hotel which was in Frestonia in Latimer Road. Then I started putting the Mutoid thing together. I had a nervous breakdown, and quite a lot of things happened. By 1984 I had recovered, and I had discovered that I could make sculpture and I had this style thing going on.

TH How did you come up with the name?

JR I wanted it to be about mutants, people who were suffering from mutation or who were in a state of constant mutation. So 'mutoid' came from schizoid or paranoid or mongoloid, and was a description of a person who lives in a state of constant change. In 1985 we built the first truck, in the gardens of this independent state of Frestonia, which was a load of tumbledown houses with the gardens knocked into one. We were the thorn in the side of this hippie utopia with our house. The Clash were photographed outside it; it was quite a wild building. Somebody gave us a burned-out bus, and we turned into it this huge skull with eye sockets that you look through to drive, and with a rib cage done in metal and fibreglass, it was all open air. We were planning to take it to Stonehenge, but while we were building it the Battle of the Beanfield was going on. It became clearer and clearer that we couldn't go there. By the time we crashed out through the fence on this totally wild bit of illegal machinery, we'd decided to go straight to Glaston-bury. I think the police thought it was their conscience coming down the road. They just couldn't deal with it, it was so over-the-top and such a heavy image. They just turned their backs. They knew they'd done a wrong thing at Stonehenge.

We got to Glastonbury and I had a massive argument with Michael Eavis. We pulled on with the skull bus towing a big horsebox, with the *Ride of the Valkyries* playing out of it. We had a totally arsey attitude. We were trying to park up by the main stage. He came over with his

radio and I laid into him, he brought over his Hell's Angels security to
lean on me, and while they were leaning on me, they saw this centaur
coming out of a motorbike, the first Mutoid sculpture I'd ever made, a
character built of pistons and levers and engine parts. They were
intrigued by it, and said, 'What's that on the front of the truck?' And I
said, 'Go and have a look.' Suddenly it was just me and Michael Eavis
stood on our own again. He found me a space and we did our first
shows there. Then we came back to London and started doing the
warehouse parties. We squatted the old Caledonian Road coach station.
We had a piece of land in Latimer Road, a bit of nowhere land. Well,
we thought it was nowhere land but in fact it was the focus for a lot of
business. We ended up getting fire-bombed and I had my skull frac-
tured, and my lung punctured and set on fire and all sorts of shit.

TH Who did it?

JR Well, somebody had a vested interest in getting us off there but as to
who, it's not really worth speculating. They didn't actually get us off;
what did get us off was the fact that it was fucking wet and rainy and
we had no power. We were all sitting there wondering what to do. A
lot more had joined because we were under attack while I'd been in
hospital and it was obvious we were going to get hit again; my mate
Robin, who was a co-founder of the Mutoids, brilliant man, went out
into the street and grabbed everybody who needed a place to park
up ... and that became the Mutoid Waste Company. It was so chaotic
... it wasn't people I would have chosen but in actual fact that's what
gave the Mutoid thing its flavour. It wasn't really up to anyone to say,
'this is my creation'. It was total chaos. That was the magic of it; it was
creative chaos.

TH How did you fund yourselves?

JR We lived together. We'd give tours. In our Caledonian Road warehouse, we had a river running though the middle. It was actually a
flooded drain. We'd built ornamental bridges over it, a forest on one
side built out of car exhaust pipes, and gravestones made out of span-
ners. It was a weird inside-out world. People used to come in and we'd
give them the Graveyard Shift, which was a little tour, and then we'd
hit them for some money and then we'd got enough money we'd go
out and get a bottle of rum or something and all cane that. We lived on
scrap metal, we did videos for people. We built stuff for a Frankie Goes
To Hollywood video ... film companies would do shoots on the sites

we were on ... we built props for people ... and we didn't need much ... we were always surrounded by beautiful girls, we always had enough drink and drugs to keep us happy. We managed to eat. We were probably hungry most of the time, but we got on fine.

TH There was never a question of anyone going out to get a job ...

JR No, it was full-time work, to keep that thing on the road. People did come to help us, but the real hardcore crew had to work very hard. We were getting evicted every three months, which meant we'd have to break everything down, then we'd weigh a lot of it in for the metal.

TH How did you find the places to squat?

JR You'd check places out, get the trucks ready and then a few of you would go on a mission to crack it. To get the locks off, that was the hairy bit. Then suddenly, voom voom voom, all the trucks were in and you'd sit there waiting to see what happened.

TH Were you quite practical anyway, or did you learn by doing it?

JR The original Mutoid thing was probably about four different characters. There was Robin who was a mechanic and an engineer, and myself who was an artist. He had artistic leanings and I had mechanical leanings. So we crossed over. There was another man called Ricky Lee, who was a gypsy who used to run a scrap truck. He taught us about scrap metal.

TH Was the idea of using waste a deliberate philosophical thing or did it just happen?

JR No, it was more to do with the randomness of the objects. With waste, you can get something that's been beautifully manufactured, but which has no further use and which can be a lovely object. A spring or a bit of chain is actually a really lovely thing, and done right, it can look like the most beautiful piece of jewellery. People said we were talking about environmental issues, but in truth, we weren't. That wasn't our message. Our message was: be creative. And create just for the fun of creating, for its own sake, don't get hung up on whether you are an artist or not.

TH The objection I get when I raise these issues is: it's all right for you creative people. What about the people who aren't creative? What will they do in your idlers' world? Well, surely everyone is creative.

JR Yes, but the team I've got here ... Terry there has a brilliant eye for scrap, Tony there is a brilliant engineer and welder. It would be no good if we were all three artists ... on the scale we're working at, we need these different talents. We're all quite happy with our talents. What it is, you're gifted; these things are your gifts. It is a gift to you, to be creative or to be able to hear music in your head and interpret it or to take a photograph. Whether you choose to sell your gifts or work out what value they've got on the market is neither here nor there. You run the risk of jeopardizing your gift by prostituting it. It is your gift; it's given to you as a present. I think people get confused by that one. If there's anyone sitting there getting jealous about it, it means they've not really gone out and looked for what their gift is ...

TH But the current set-up, the job system and industrial system, doesn't offer people the chance to find their gift.

JR No, it doesn't. In fact, it actively discourages it. But people bind to that because they want the easy life. Right now, what we're doing really works. But there have been long periods of hungry, fucked up, argumentative times and I've wondered why we've kept on doing it. It's much easier to let somebody else do the thinking, take home your regular wage and sell your life off piecemeal. Everybody, I think, gets the sense that there's another world out there, but when you start to get into that world, it raises a lot of questions about what you've been told. You can start to get vertigo, you suddenly realise, you have to rethink everything. Most people scuttle straight back and never poke their head above the wall again.

TH I have found that, once you start questioning the world of jobs, then all the other structures seem to be similarly unhelpful to living.

JR I think the saddest thing is when people work all their life, sorting away their bit of pension, just to find that somebody's run wild with it and lost it all. To feel that you've been ripped off in that way at that stage of your life is a terrible thing to take to your grave, I think. But you can see that clearly in Wall Street: when Wall Street crashed, all these people came to the banks to cash in their life savings, and the money wasn't there, the bank was shut.

TH Money is just a balancing act.

JR Money is just a creative idea, like anything else. People with a lot of money understand that.

TH So ... you were real pioneers of the warehouse party scene.

JR Yeah, we were right early with that. By accident. We squatted the Kings Cross Coach Station, and these boys came in, and said, 'Oh, we were going to do a party here.' And we went, 'Oh, we'll do a party with you.' They provided the sound system and the music and did the advertising. And we decorated the place up ... we cut the tops of cars and put them in the drain to make it look really deep and somebody got a motorboat and put that in there and someone else made a water-skier on ironing boards ... we had this giant frogspawn from a film set and it got wilder and wilder and madder and madder ... the first party we did we had around 400 or 500 people ... the week after about 900 and the week after that we had to throw the doors open because people were being crushed.

TH   And all these things were completely illegal?

JR   Totally.

TH   So you needed a lot of courage ...

JR   When we were building our skull bus, people said to us, 'you'll never get this anywhere ... as soon as you take it on the road, you'll get nicked. It's got no windows, the steering wheel is just a bit of wire, it's got no tax, no insurance ...' But we carried on doing it in the face of all of this. Every time it got impounded, we got it back. We parked outside Buckingham Palace, we drove to Scotland and back. Our attitude to it was, the thing is so obviously illegal, that people will think it must be legal. We had a technique that the gypsies taught us, The Mumble, always having a explanation as to why you're in this vehicle.

TH   What's an example of it?

JR   Well, when Frank was on his way back from Glastonbury, the police stopped him and said, 'Is this your vehicle?' And he said, 'Don't talk to me about this vehicle, I've had it up to here with this thing! They sent me to Glastonbury to pick up the stage ... and look at it ... it's got no fucking windows, it's got no roof! I'm going to get it back to the depot and I never want to see the cunting thing again.' And the copper goes, 'Good luck, you'd better get on your way.' And that's The Mumble. You're always on your way to somewhere just out of their area, you're doing a kids' show, or it's on the way to the scrapyard. It's the nature of a policeman's mind that he works within a certain framework of rules. The other thing is that we really weren't a threat to anyone. And the police were quite impressed. Other people running warehouse parties would bar their doors to the police. But we would bring them in and show them around, just as though they were normal people. By the time they were halfway round, they were talking about stuff in the same way any other punter would ... we treated them as individuals.

TH So you don't have an aggressive 'them and us' attitude towards police?

JR No, not at all. Because I don't think it is 'them and us', I think it's just
us. And the further I've gone on in life, the more I've realised that's
true. At that time we believed we were an alternative society. But now
I think that actually we're just a part of society and people like us have
always existed. For us to go around saying we are an alternative society
is a cop-out.

TH You're the crazy guys coming into town, the troubadours.

JR Yes, that's who we are. When we got to Europe, we didn't have the
legacy of the Peace Convoy or the warehouse parties or the punk anarchy thing. They saw us for what we are, which is artists and showmen.

TH And when was that?

JR When Ecstasy came in, our thing was a bit superfluous. People didn't
need the big sculptural stuff to trip them out ... just a strobe light and
a beat ... Also, we had always wanted to go abroad ... so we got in the
trucks and moved to Amsterdam, to a giant squatted island. Some
English types had built a bar out of two buses ... they did a festival and
invited us out there. We built Stonehenge out of cars ... that was our
introduction to Europe. In England, we'd been getting so closed down,
the police were pursuing us across counties ... helicopters ...

TH That was Major's government, wasn't it?

JR Yeah, one of the fuckers.

TH But soon after that he started taking credit for the new creativity and
'Cool Britannia'.

JR I hate the lot of them. I hate politicians. There is something suspect
about someone who wants to be in a position to tell other people what
to do ... so from Amsterdam we went down into West Berlin when it
was a walled city. We drove 200 miles through the Eastern Bloc, a huge
convoy of bizarre vehicles, mutated trucks and vans, workshops. West
Berlin was incredible. We built this giant man leaning over the Berlin
Wall: his chest was a Volkswagen Beetle and his feet were bathtubs, and
he was on railway tracks, leaning out of the station which had been
bombed in the Kreuzberg, a really radical area. They thought we were
building a rocket launcher to go through the wall. The Mayor of West
Berlin, the Mayor of East Berlin, the American forces' representative in
West Berlin, the Russian military representative in East Berlin: all of
them came to Robin and told him that they didn't want this gift. He is
so pig-headed, that he did it anyway. And three months later, the wall

was down ... I ain't saying we brought the wall down, but we sensed that chaotic edge ... our man was a great smiley geezer, and in his hands was a giant chrome bird made of exhaust pipes called the Silver Bird of Peace. Finally we went to Italy for a theatre festival in a village called Santarchangelo. They liked what we were doing because they're really into their machines ... they loved the supercharged tractors with rhinoceros heads on them and motorbikes with tractor wheels on them. We had to do parades in the town, so we all drove in with wellington boots on our heads, riding motorbikes with caterpillars on them, three-wheelers with aircraft wings on them ... they just loved it. At the end we said, 'Do you mind if we stay on for a few weeks?' They said, 'If you ask us, we'll have to say no, so don't ask us.' Ten years later, the site's still there.

I eventually went back to Berlin, when the wall came down. I thought, 'I've got to get some of this.' It was the fucking biggest scrap pile on the planet. By the end we had two Mig 21 fighter planes, which we'd robbed off the airports. We built Stonehenge out of Russian armoured personnel carriers and tanks. The Russians were trying to get rid of this stuff and we were having the time of our lives, finding big eight-wheel-drive all-terrain vehicles in an old orchard, whacking batteries on them, writing our own number plates and just driving them straight into the middle of Berlin. Everything in East Germany was state-owned. When it collapsed, they just got out of their combine harvester in the field and walked away from it. They left all their tools on the factory bench and walked away. There were Trabants everywhere, full-size road diggers – we just brought it all in.

TH And how were you funding yourselves?

JR Well, we ran a bar in Berlin called House of Fear. We did it up with iconic Russian paintings, soldiers with missiles and sunglasses. The tables were made out of bombs, the bar was the front of a Russian truck, we put netting around it. After that I took the Mig fighters up to Potsdammerplatz and we started a big sculpture garden there. Eventually Spiral Tribe came to Berlin. We got on very well. We took the Migs to the Czech republic.

TH How do you transport a Mig fighter?

JR There's a whole book there! We had a huge transporter trailer that steered front and back, it had 16 wheels, and we had a massive Russian truck. The police roadblocked us as soon as we got out of Berlin but after a bit they just couldn't deal with it and they had to let us go. But it was the onset of winter, my girlfriend was pregnant, so I cut loose, jumped in a little truck and went down to Italy and the first child was born down there. He was born with a heart defect which meant that we had to stay close to a hospital. I started a thing called Mutech, a mixture between the Spirals and the Mutoids. It was a whole stage show with acrobats, dancers, drummers, video, sculptures, the lot, which was something I'd always wanted to do. We'd always had the feeling that we could transpose this chaotic thing into a tangible show that would say something very clear, and we did actually achieve that. Once I'd done it, though, it was pretty impractical to keep doing all that, on no budget, while trying to bring up two kids. I sold all the trucks and trailers, and moved back to England to be nearer a hospital. Now I've slowly started again. But instead of doing the huge great travelling thing, I work more on fine sculpture, and do big events like Glastonbury or Notting Hill Carnival.

Michael Palin

by Tom Hodgkinson

IDLER 37 · 2006

Winter We APPROACHED MICHAEL PALIN FOR AN INTERVIEW
because we'd seen him being interviewed saying that he'd
lived in the same small house since 1968. Despite his fame and
fortune, he'd never bothered to move. He had also just performed a
one-man show in the West End called *Forty Years Without a Proper Job*.
So it seemed he might have some wisdom to impart for those of us pursuing the idle life. We met Palin in his office near Covent Garden.

★

TH How often do you come into the office?

MP It varies, sometimes twice a week. I like the location here. Covent
Garden is up there ... Holborn and East London is not so far away and
you can walk down to Waterloo Bridge.

TH So you've just had your show, *Forty Years Without A Proper Job*, and
you've said recently in a TV interview that your life has happened
rather than being planned, that you had no burning ambition. It seems
that this idea has been on your mind.

MP The title of the show came from a practical consideration. This show
was going to be just about my life, so I thought, are there any themes
to it all? The fact is I've never really had a job. I've never signed a contract longer than six to eight weeks. So I thought, well, that gets me
out of appearing to be an expert on anything, or having to declare a
direction to my life. It really is pretty close to how my life has been.
Very fortunately I've managed to avoid the issue of getting a proper job
or deciding what I am best at or I'm good at. It goes back to my father
– he had been brought up in two world wars and through the recession

of the 1930s. It was a rough time, so after that the children were jolly well going to be comfortable and secure and follow a certain pattern, and part of that was *having a proper job*. I remember worrying throughout my education, as my particular talents lay not in any practical direction: I was not good at maths or mechanics or chemistry. I've always had a rather busy, productive imagination and that led more to things that you couldn't quantify as being useful such as writing and acting. Those were the areas where whatever talent I had, lay, so it was hard to reconcile this with my father's desire for me to *get a proper job*. But then I learned that my father, who was an engineer, had never wanted to be an engineer. He had wanted to be a church chorister, or church organist. He loved church music. He really wanted to be at Cambridge or somewhere like that and sing in the choir and his father said, 'No, you've got a get a proper job'.

TH And he passed that down to you, he hadn't looked back and thought, that was a mistake?

MP Well, we didn't really talk about things like that. He didn't say, 'Here's an irony, lad! There I am, trying to get you a proper job, and all I would have liked to be was this.' He steadily maintained that he was a working man, he went to work, he came back in the evening at the same time and all that ... so yes, I thought it would be a good title.

TH It seems that musicians and pop stars, often, are actually motivated by the fact that they don't want to get out of bed before lunchtime. That comes first. You sit in your bedsit all day on the dole and that gets you out onto a different path. Were you actually consciously motivated to do things that weren't jobs?

MP I was always insatiably curious about people and life, and I read a lot. The motivation was really just to try and reconcile the need to work with some particular talent and inclination. I had a fairly secure upbringing. Although my father didn't have much money, he did send me to a private preparatory school, and then I went away to Shrewsbury school. They provided a sort of structure. I thought that during that period something would come along, like puberty, but in terms of work, a desire to be an executive or work in a bank. You would wake up one morning and think, yes, this is what I have to do. But it never happened. I always enjoyed acting, which is a dangerously subversive talent in a way. You look at schoolmasters who are doing a perfectly good job and you become fascinated by the way they touch their left ear when they talk, or the way their trousers are very very very wrinkled around the crotch and things like that. These were the thoughts that came into my mind... I knew there was a financial imperative. My father had given up half his income to send me to school. So there was no question that he would support me. And just by a series of really lucky encounters I ended up doing two things: one was working with Terry Jones, who I'd met at Oxford. He'd left a year before me, and was writing a thing called *The Love Show*, a theatrical documentary about sex through the ages. He said, would I help him write it. It was an interesting project but paid very little. Then, quite out of the blue, a friend's girlfriend knew a journalist who was writing a new comedy pop show called *Now!* on TWW in Wales. Would I like to audition as a presenter? Without telling my father, I went up and I got this job. It was 1965 and it just involved introducing a lot of pop groups and doing rather bad jokes.

TH So that was a fantastic time for music.

MP Yes, we used to get groups there like John Mayall, Eric Clapton, the Small Faces, Georgie Fame, Alan Price ...

TH I saw *O Lucky Man* the other day ... a great film ...

MP Yes, a mess, but a mess you have to see. At that time it did seem that you were liberated from whatever had gone before. I was a provincial boy, born and brought up in Sheffield, so to come to London just at the time of The Beatles and Twiggy and Mary Quant ... it was the place to be. There was a feeling that there were opportunities to do something new and fresh. Although, the old hierarchies were still there. The BBC, which I ended up working for, on *The Frost Report* and eventually *Monty Python*, was run in quite a conventional way, by mainly men. It harped back to an ideal age of the Reithian Twenties or Thirties. Things were changing on one level but not on another. What was really happening was that young people coming out of university and art school especially, felt that they could do anything. But at the same time, people at the top level were saying, 'Not so fast, we're still in control.' So there was a conflict there that made things work better, for us.

TH If you imagine yourself at that age now, do you think things are less exciting ... are prospects better or worse for idlers today?

MP Aaaah ... It's terribly hard as I don't really know what's in the mind of a young person ... but I think that in a sense, when we did *Monty Python* there were far more restrictions against that form of expression, that sort of free-form comedy. You could be inventive but you'd go out late at night; if you got too popular you'd get censored for saying 'bum' or 'shit'... now there's a feeling that everything is permitted, apart from racial jokes. You can say what you want and that's left people a bit bewildered. There was such an establishment when we were writing Python in the late Sixties, and the Army and the Church and a very male-dominated traditional society was still in place. So we could have lots of jokes at their expense. We had censorship, the Lord Chamberlain had instructions on nudity on television. We were naughty, cheeky, mischievous little boys able to carry our naughty, mischievous ways into early middle age. I think the fact that *Python* is still popular among kids of ten, eleven, twelve is because they see something in it which is still outside the general run of comedy. Why that is I'm not quite sure, except that *Python* was a mish-mash: bits of film, animation, satire, pure silliness. The films were really well made, great credit to Terry Gilliam and Terry Jones for making them look so good. With *Life of Brian*, we always knew we'd have some problems because of the subject matter. The most serious act of censorship was when the head of EMI, who had financed the film – and we already had people in Tunisia building sets – suddenly read the script. 'Who's tricked me into this? We can't do this, absolutely not.' Refused to touch it. And that's when George Harrison came in. It was something like five million pounds, and someone said to George, 'Why did you do it?' and George said, 'Well, I just wanted to see it.' A very good reason, and of course, being a Beatle, he had a lot of money.

TH I've been reading the Abbie Hoffman and Jerry Rubin books, the Sixties underground heroes, and they always cite The Beatles as an influence. They pulled off this trick of being massive and also underground at the same time. And I suppose Python was quite similar. They were families, not individuals climbing up a ladder.

MP We both had a certain wariness of the world outside trying to market us or pull us in a certain direction, and for both Beatles and Python, the work that they did was only the important thing. If you were successful that was great, but it was about the work. You didn't bring in consultants to tell you what you should do, you didn't do audience research, as people do now. There were no showings for potential audiences saying what they liked. You did your own thing. The peer group was the little group you were working with. No one ever got in the way of that, all the decisions were taken by the group. So I think the reason why pop groups liked Python and why Abbie Hoffman liked the Beatles was that we seemed to embody an artistic freedom, a creative freedom. A creative freedom that was also successful ... you could see the Beatles going round the world being screamed at. It was like a very benign revolution. There were people of 16, 17, 18 who should have been at school going to airports shouting, 'We love you, yeah yeah yeah!' And The Beatles weren't manipulative. The sense people got of them being free spirits was true. And I suppose there was a certain amount of that in *Python* as well.

TH There were no precedents ... I suppose today that all comedy groups are going to have Monty Python at the back of their heads as a model, and every band certainly thinks about The Beatles.

MP There was no precedent, but we drew inspiration from certain areas. Spike Milligan's Q series was influential on the shape the *Python* shows took. Although *Python* was off the wall and unstructured there was actually quite a lot of debate in the early days about the form it should take. In the end we came up with the idea of the stream of consciousness, which got us out of all sorts of problems ... we had sketches that didn't end, suddenly cutting to film ... but that was inspired by Spike's series, he just did silly things. Having Gilliam, the American input, the animations, that was important. Graham Chapman was an odd character, rather distant, smoked his pipe, but came out with the most brilliant off-the-wall ideas. Having John Cleese, who looked the perfect establishment character, who absolutely represents authority, be completely zany and silly and able to send himself up ... it was all there. But what we felt at the time, was that we would have two or three good years and then someone else would come along and we would do something else. People weren't expected to last that long.

TH When it comes to money have you done things that later you wish you hadn't done because you did them for the money? Or has the money, though welcome, always been the second priority?

MP Ha ha, the idea is to get paid for something you really want to do! Yes, there were things early on. I did quite a lot of radio commercials just because they paid well and we needed the money. At that time there was no career path. As soon as John wanted to wind *Python* down we realised that there was no more *Python*. It was only after a couple of years of doing other things that we got the film together and it revived.

So right into the early Seventies, we were doing commercials, which I wasn't particularly proud of, largely because I had a glimpse into that world. Being asked to advertise something which you don't have any strong feelings about, a dog food or an instant coffee ... you were restricted in what you could say: you were generally working to a script that someone else had worked out. Everything seemed wrong about it. Instead of your peer group of five others you would have ten people squeezed into a gallery, saying, 'Can you do it a bit more Welsh, can you do it in a slightly higher tone, not Welsh but Welsh borders ...' You had people putting their oar in for no particular reason other than they were in the advertising business and they wanted to show that at the end of the day they'd done some work. That's a terrible problem. And I realised I didn't like doing these, I was a performing dog. But on the other hand we needed the money and I was grateful to be asked. Apart from that I've been fortunate in that from early on, I've had a considerable say in what I've done, as a writer and performer.

TH You say it's luck, but the existential idea is that doing and choosing are the same thing. So is it pure luck or are you guiding yourself into certain positions?

MP Whatever talent I had lay in acting and in writing. I noticed the comedy in life and the absurdity. Humour was the main reaction to things I saw around me. That was good because the sort of people you met had similar thoughts and tastes, and they were slightly subversive, they weren't the ones who said that life is terribly serious. I was worried about it at one time, someone at school said, 'Have you seriously thought about your life?' It turned out he'd become a Born Again Christian and I thought, there goes a good friend, but maybe I should be more serious ... maybe this flippancy is something I *should* grow out of. But it carried on and I made certain friends, people like a man called Robert Hewison, who I met at university. He was from London, very bright, really metropolitan, he was hip and I was a hick. But we got together because we had a similar sense of humour, we liked Spike Milligan and all that. I chose him as my friend and vice versa out of all the people I knew at Oxford. He made the vital decision of saying, 'Let's not just tell each other jokes, let's get together a half hour cabaret act and we can make money from this.' And I thought, 'Make money from laughing?' And I realised that not being serious *could* be a way of making a living. And by the time that I'd done a review at the

Edinburgh Festival, and David Frost had come up and talent-scouted us, I realised even more ... all I'm saying really is that the various connections I've made in my life and the people I've met have been very very important. Robert pushed me into performing which I probably never would have done because I was sort of shy, Terry Jones led me into writing after I'd left university. I've fallen into things because I've been there at the right time with the right people. I wouldn't say I'm a great one at taking the initiative. With the travel programmes, it wasn't me saying, I want to do travel programmes. It's just that when someone came to me with the idea of *Around the World in Eighty Days*, I realised that I loved travelling, and that this was a lovely way of not making a decision of what I really should do in life. And here I am, I'm 62 and I still have no real idea of what I ought to be doing!

Jamie Reid

by John Marchant

IDLER 38 · WINTER 2006

ART DEALER JOHN MARCHANT WENT TO SEE ARTIST JAMIE Reid, best known for his Sex Pistols artwork.

★

Spiritual descendent of post-Edwardian socialist reformer and Chief Druid George Watson MacGregor Reid, Jamie Reid takes ancestral sighting points as disparate as William Blake, Gerrard Winstanley and the Diggers, Tom Paine, Wat Tyler and Simon de Montfort. There is, however, a smokescreen around him that veils his persona and work. He gets ignored by the art world for being unmalleable and gets pigeon-holed by an increasingly nostalgic press who only want to feed on the corpse of punk.

Born in 1947, Jamie Reid was a founding member of Croydon-based Situationist-inspired graphics unit Suburban Press and was responsible for graphics and layout for Christopher Gray's *Leaving the 20th Century*. In late 1975 Malcolm McLaren asked him to work with the Sex Pistols, providing both image and political agenda. Following their demise, Jamie drifted through places and projects: BowWowWow, Paris, performance work, the Brixton squat scene. In 1987 *Up They Rise: The Incomplete Works of Jamie Reid* was published by Faber and Faber. Produced with music journalist Jon Savage, it documented his influences and works to date. Reid got increasingly involved with various bands and protest movements: No Clause 28, the Legalise Cannabis Campaign, Reclaim the Streets and Warchild to name a few. In 1989 he started a ten-year commission to revisualise and reinvent the interior spaces of both the recording and resting spaces of the East London-based Strongroom Studios using 'colour magic and sacred geometry' to encourage creativity and calm. He also spent five years as visual co-ordinator with the band Afro-Celt Sound System. He is currently finishing a heroically proportioned 6–700 piece project based on the Druidic calender: 'The Eightfold Year'.

We met east of Knighton, Powys, on the Welsh borders, at a spot fiercely contended in the wars with the English. It was here also in 1921 that the antiquarian photographer Alfred Watkins had a revelation about the hidden connections within the British landscape that he later wrote about in *The Old Straight Track*.

JM Jamie, you spend a lot of time now with your hands in the soil. Can you tell me about that?

JR [Takes out his trade tools and starts to paint.] It is part and parcel ... sowing, planting, growing, harvesting, nurturing. We are custodians of this planet ... the Garden of Eden, paradise on earth. We have mostly done our best to fuck the planet up. My work is deeply affected by my time spent working the land. Organic growth is integral to it. I'll spend hours gardening and then go straight into hours of painting, they merge and intertwine with each other. It really is at the heart of my spiritual beliefs: love and respect for nature and our part within it. I think you still have to explain what you think a lot of your painting work is about, because people can't get their head around it. I read an awful lot of Jung when I was 17 to 19. That was the same time I was into R. D. Laing and David Cooper and all that. Funnily enough that was all around that squatting scene.

JM And what about your belief system?

JR Lapsed Druid! When you actually open things up to ordinary people – I mean ordinary people who would never fucking be bothered to go to an art gallery or museum – and I think quite rightly in lots of ways ... I think magic has always existed to people of the land. They just knew. They didn't need loads of mumbo-jumbo ritual, they just knew ... because they fucking looked. And we can't see any more.

JM Alfred Watkins says that the people who laid out the Old Straight Tracks attained a supernatural aura because they had a knowledge that other people didn't. Isn't it natural for people to want someone to look up to?

JR As soon as you get pyramidical hierarchies the whole thing becomes corrupt. We've never lived in an age where people trust each other less. I can remember in Croydon, specifically in the early 1970s when we were doing Suburban Press, which was far from being elitist and was very involved with the working class, in that area, that was the first time ever we didn't have our doors open so it all started going then. But the whole Craig and Bentley thing really fucked Croydon. [The mentally ill Christopher Craig was hanged after his accomplice, the under-age David Bentley, killed PC Sidney Miles during a botched robbery in Croydon.] Then the police wouldn't go there. Croydon was very different then.

JM Have you done any of your own research into ley-lines? What they are, what they mean?

JR Only by observing and looking and seeing. A few years ago I was doing a lot of geometrical paintings. I tend to do them and then find the source. I knew about sacred geometry but it wasn't until I immersed myself in it that I realised what it was. In a way there was always that element of being self-taught. It's just such a fundamental element in everything – from primitive to the Renaissance to anything you care to name. You can see it reveal itself in front of your eyes in the landscape. You just immerse yourself in it – it's just a total experience where you completely lose yourself. It's the same as I feel when I'm actually working because I do go into a complete trance, which is why I can't talk and paint. It's very intense.

JM Were you ever a teenager?

JR I can't remember! Maybe I've never stopped being one. I think music's probably the biggest influence, from early rock'n'roll. Croydon was a really big centre of early Teddy Boys ... and the whole Bill Hayley thing had a massive effect. But I suppose more than anything the biggest influence was what was happening in jazz in America at the time.

JM Where was it coming from? Through the radio or through friends?

JR I was buying it as it was coming out. That would have been predominantly Mingus, Coltrane, Pharoah Sanders, Archie Shepp, Ornette Coleman. To me it was like a whole peak of 20th-century culture. It's never been surpassed. I also went to see a Pollock exhibition when I was about 16 without knowing anything about modern art and just found them like entering other worlds.

JM You describe Pollock's work as being like landscape painting.

JR It was just like fantasy worlds you could walk into and see what you liked. I loved the fact that they left themselves open to interpretation. And Blake. I was obsessed with the Blakes in the Tate. A lot of that I got through my father. There was always art and sport, and I was lucky enough to be really good at sport. As you know I was going to play professional football or cricket. I also used to go up to see Mingus and Sonny Rollins perform at Ronnie Scott's and Soho then was a big influence – at the same time Zappa, Beefheart and all that – it was an amazing period. There was a great element of experimentation. It was all part of a great belief in change, but I was brought up politically. My parents were diehard socialists and were very much involved in the anti-war movement, so I was dragged off to Aldermaston marches at an early age.

JM Your mother had problems with your Great Uncle George. She sounds like she was quite an iconoclast herself.

JR She was brought up in a back-to-nature environment and her dad wrote a book called *In The Heart of Democracy* so they were all involved with the socialist movement of the time. It was the death of the whole 50-year epoch of Victorianism. There was a massive interest in change both politically and spiritually, which is the thing that fascinated me about the Druid order. There was a great belief in access to freedom of knowledge, education, the whole alternative movement in medicine and health, and health foods, but they were as likely to be on trade union and suffragette rallies as be doing rituals at Stonehenge. It was all part and parcel, which is something I've really tried to continue myself.

JM Is this what connects the dots in your work, your wish to make people think that they can really enjoy this world?

JR To a great degree, yeah. I suppose on one level there is that element in a majority of my stuff which tends to be around painting or photography or bits of filming that I've done. There's an appreciation ... a great element of beauty in it, just seeing the magnificence of things. And there's obviously that other element – the political element: the punk collage, punk, whatever you want to call it, agit-prop, which is making comment about the evilness of the powers that be. I don't see any contradiction in the two but it's something that I do suffer from as an artist, in terms of the people who run Culture. I don't fit into one category. I would've thought that the whole idea of an artist is to be expansive, like an explorer going forward. Not stuck in a rut. If we're talking about influences John Michell is one. The man is like a modern-day wizard. I love him because he's so benign. Such a lovely person.

JM I remember you saying that computers were going to bring in a whole age of...

JR Backache and blindness.

JM No, you said there would be a new age of psychic connection between people.

JR I've probably got more cynical since I said that.

JM The London Psychogeographical Association is about to post a section on their website about Druidry. What's the connection?

JR I think we touched on it earlier when we talked about the whole period of say, the Golden Dawn and the early Druid Order in Britain. It was as much politically bound as spiritually bound. It was part and parcel of the same thing. If you look at the early trade union movement it was as much spiritual as it was political; but those things have become less and less apparent.

JM 'Ne travailler jamais': please discuss!

JR Well, our culture is geared towards enslavement, for people to perform pre-ordained functions, particularly in the workplace. I've always tried to encourage people to think about that and to do something about it.

Ronald Hutton

by Tom Hodgkinson

IDLER 39 · SPRING 2007

PROFESSOR RONALD HUTTON OF BRISTOL UNIVERSITY IS the *Idler*'s favourite historian. He has made merry-making one of his special areas of study, and is a brilliant speaker and writer. In books like *The Rise and Fall of Merry England* and *Stations of the Sun* he studies the festive culture of the British Isles and the various attacks on it by religions and states. This interview was printed in our 'Lie Down and Protest' issue.

*

Long-haired, mischievous and articulate, Hutton is very popular with his students. Indeed, the catalyst for going to meet him was receiving two emails from former students, raving about what a brilliant lecturer he is, and urging me to go and meet him. One student told me that during his lecture on Christmas, he would gradually blow out candles until he himself disappeared with the final candle. His students would then find him crouching under the podium. A scholar and a showman, I was told.

TH We're brought up to believe that the idea of Merry England is a myth, but the more I read the more it seems to be a concrete reality and fact. England was merry, the Protestants destroyed the festive culture and so I would say I'm anti-Protestant and pro-Catholic.

RH I think you can be anti-Catholic as well. The Reformation and the Counter-Reformation were two faces of the same movement by zealous Christians to tighten up Christianity and stop all this slackness and popular junketing. The Counter-Reformation is much the same thing in Catholic guise. In other words there is more centralised authority, there's more emphasis upon the Bible and more emphasis on the chief figures in the Christian religion, and a clampdown upon local saints and on the tendency of ordinary people to take religion into their own hands.

TH   Is this something that's been going on since 1100?

RH   It's more 1500 to 1600. It's part of a Reform movement which covers Western Christianity. It's the first big one that Christianity has had since the 12th century in which people who zealously want to get each other to heaven reckon that Christianity has got too slack, it's got too populist and popular. And people are enjoying themselves too much and not realising that they're probably going to go to hell as a result.

TH   This is a tendency in Western minds which grapples with the roustabout tendency.

RH   It's also the Bible. There's not much that's relevant in the New Testament. It's a bit hard to imagine St Paul in a booze-up, but he does say, 'take a little wine for thy stomach's sake.'

TH   'Eat, drink and be merry' comes from Bible.

RH   That's from Ecclesiastes, the great book that indicates you should enjoy yourself while you can, while being pious. But for every word in Ecclesiastes there are about ten ranted by the prophets. You need to read people like Amos and Habukuk [note from ed. I have now done this and he is right]. They are heavily against the kind of things that late medieval England enjoyed. Try to find the joke in the Old Testament.

TH   Is it very much late medieval England when things became really merry?

RH   Yes, for two reasons. One is that it's the great age of community. It's a time when communities are under pressure. You have plagues sweeping the land repeatedly. You have traditional ways in which you hold land and work together in the village going to pieces because the population is plummeting. So there's a huge new stress on holding communities together in other ways. And one very good way to hold them together is to encourage them to have fun together. But the aspect is a complete reversal of the Church's traditional attitude to merriment. The traditional attitude, which is found in one invective after another from the beginning of Christianity through to the·end of the 14th century, is to try and limit merry-making as much as possible because the consequences of getting boozed-up and sexy are almost unthinkable in moral terms. But towards the end of the 14th century the Church takes a new line and it seems to happen spontaneously because you don't get anybody organising a reform movement to bring it about. Its highlight is the 15th century. It is to co-opt merriment in order to pay for religion, in other words, to bring things like village feasts, dances and games into the orbit of the Church in order to make them into fundraising events. So before this, the way in which you pay for your Parish church is the way in which it's been done for most of the time since the 15th century: you have a rate, you get people to rent a pew, or the church even owns its own lands which produces rents. But all this goes out in 1400 when the major means of raising the cash to pay for the candles, the incense, the vestments and the upkeep of the building is to hold a party, a sort of church fete but on a big scale. And all sorts of ways in which people had fun before this without any reference to the church, except when the church condemned them, now get brought into the orbit of fundraising.

TH   Your own work is measured and academic but it's pretty obvious whose side you're on. You're pro-merry rather than pro-Puritan.

RH   Yes. That's because I'm agnostic and so I can't personally see the point in the Reform's message. Because I don't believe in a heaven or a hell, the question of trying to save people from one and pump them into the other is irrelevant to me. So I'd rather see them enjoy themselves on earth. Now to a devout Christian, this is of course the devil's message. And I accept that, but since I don't buy the contrary message then I clearly am in the position you suggest.

TH   It wasn't a cynical move on the part of the Church?

RH   Not cynical, it was sensible. If you follow their logic, and the logic comes out in their actions, then it's cheating the devil. The devil has set up things like boozing and dancing to lure people into sin, and now people are doing it in order to make Christianity more effective. The devil's been stripped of one of his greatest weapons, which is merriment.

TH   In Norman Cohn's *Pursuit of the Millennium* some of the medieval mystical sects go even further: to be really holy you have to free yourself of conscience, because conscience means you have the devil within you. So the truly pure can be free of conventional morality.

RH   That's a tiny minority view. What I see as more representative is the line taken by someone like Richard Carew, St Anthony, who was a Cornish man who writes about Cornwall at the end of the 15th century, at a time when merriment has become deeply controversial again. Now the Reformation was the rejection of the religion which the merriment was supporting. What the merriment was doing was funding a very material religion, a religion heavy in props, a religion heavy in beautiful churches, incense, lots and lots of ceremony, beautiful clothes for the priest. These were supposed to make people think of heaven more easily and get to heaven more easily. And the Protestant message is that the whole theology at the foundation of this is wrong. You need to scrap all the very things that the fundraising is supporting and fund preaching instead and so as they see it, the devil's scored a double whammy because he's actually corrupted Christianity itself and persuaded idiots to use his favourite weapons to support a wrong religion. He's almost got the jack-pot. So Protestantism gets rid of medieval Christianity itself along with the fundraising means that has supported it. So you're rejecting an awful lot together.

TH Clearly there's something in the Puritan spirit which doesn't like people enjoying themselves. So what comes first? Is it the resentment at somebody else's having fun which then turns into a religion or is it the religion that happens to have as one of its components an attack on fun?

RH It varies from person to person. But if I put my money upon a majority view I'd go for the latter. Perhaps I'm being too generous. But for an agnostic I do know the Bible extremely well. I have read every word at least once with great care. And it's not a manual for party animals. There's an awful lot of condemnation of merry-making from jumping around the golden calf when your boss is up Mount Sinai onwards. So people who read the Bible regularly and use it as their basic text are going to be put off church ales really easily.

TH Why has this particular period become one of your main areas of interest?

RH I think I got there originally because I was mesmerised by the English Civil War. Partly because it's the one time in the last 500 years when we've been really dysfunctional. And also because it's really glamorous: it's when we go to pieces and suddenly there's a violent resolution of traditional tensions all over the place which involves strongly marked characters, dramatic action, physical locations. It was riveting. I was interested in what made us rupture in the Reformation and again in the Civil War in a way we haven't done since.

TH What was the cause of the rupture? My line has tended to be the simplistic, Cobbettesque one that the Reformation destroyed 900 years of brotherly love. It was a huge disaster created by the tyrant Henry VIII. But presumably there must have been something in the spirit of the nation that made us ready for this sort of change.

RH Well, it's a lot of nations, because we came quite late to it. And after all Henry VIII can be downgraded to a bit player because he produced a Catholic Church not a Protestant Church. So his son Edward and his daughter Elizabeth produced our real Reformations. They're part of a package which spans the Continent. We get there after the Germans and the Swiss and the French and take up their ideas. We're in a corner of a big field. I think it's three things that happened physically and one thing that happened intellectually. There was a sense that the world was changing dramatically. It's difficult to believe the same things as your grandparents when the world isn't that of your grandparents. Now the Turks have bust into Europe, they're rolling back the borders of Christianity, so the idea of a medieval Christianity which is taking the world is reversed. Second, we invent printing which changes the face of communications, as big a revolution as the Internet now. Third, you have the discovery of new worlds beyond the sea into which we're expanding which give us a sense of manifest destiny to make up for the fact that Islam is munching away at the other side. And if I'd put in a wildcard I'd put in gunpowder which is blowing the face of warfare to pieces.

TH Warfare is no longer a noble battle with elegance and rules.

RH Well it was always pretty horrible. It was always a butcher's yard with things like the longbow acting as the projectile system. But now you have to have huge armies, you have to have vast fortresses and you have to have standardised weapons going in to the hands of soldiers and they have to be made in factories. You have to have munitions dumps so again, even in the way you defend yourself it's a new world. So you put that lot together and people are getting really quite badly shaken up. And the way in which Christianity responds to this challenge of novelty is to come up with new ideas of its own. And that's because the late medieval Christian Church was extraordinarily dynamic. It was throwing off new ideas all the time. It was rapidly developing. And it was part of the movement that we call the Renaissance. It's Western civilisation going into overdrive.

TH Was the Renaissance the flowering of medieval culture or the beginning of something new?

RH It was both. The Renaissance doesn't look like the Middle Ages. You can go back to the Middle Ages and find all sorts of antecedents for it. But there is a nationalism about, there is a new type of religion, that's Reformation and Counter-Reformation. There is a new style of communication, that's printing. There's a new concept of the globe, a new world, literally. The Reformation and the Renaissance are two faces of a huge renewal of European culture.

TH And that's really what Shakespeare is all about, world on the brink.

RH For someone who was a dyed-in-the-wool conservative, Shakespeare's dad was busted for Catholicism and Shakespeare probably spent time cosseted in a Catholic safe house in Lancashire when he was younger. It explains the sympathy with Catholics. It's very strange to find a Protestant playwright who looks with a kind heart on a friar like Friar Lawrence in *Romeo and Juliet*. Friars are seen as stormtroopers of the devil to a real Protestant. Shakespeare, like Ben Jonson, is somebody of really dodgy religion as far as a dyed-in-the-wool evangelical Protestant is concerned.

TH But wasn't he supposed to be producing propaganda for Elizabeth?

RH Yes, he also trims himself and he conforms and he is buried in his Parish church. Which he attended. He looks like a classic Church papist.

TH Isn't there also this new idea, as in *Dr Faustus*, that you are in command of your own destiny, rather than a more fatalistic attitude that had gone before? Isn't there a new arrogance?

RH It's more desperation. When you live in a world, in a community of Catholicism which has got the truth long ago, and it's just a matter of working it out in individual terms, then you don't have that acute sense of danger and need to pull yourself together and get on. But if you're part of a what is a minority religion, Protestantism, which the existing religion wants to exterminate, and is actually starting to do so: in 1580 half of Europe is Protestant, in 1680 one-fifth of Europe is Protestant – and Protestants are increasingly forced into this area of Northern Europe so it's a nation like the Dutch and the English who take to the high seas desperately and try and make cash out of the rest of the world in order to survive.

TH A bit like Jews who get pushed out and need to accumulate some money to provide safety.

RH Yes. I'd suggest a lot of the Protestant ethic is simply a survival strategy.

TH Because you're being attacked. Now the Puritans, where did they come from? Do you turn into a Puritan? Or did they come from outside and take over?

RH It's internal conversions. And it's almost a personality thing: you tend to find that white-hot old style Catholics become white-hot new style Puritans. I define the Puritans as the Protestants in England who couldn't accept the compromised Church of England. They wanted to have one which was far more radically Protestant. We do have the least Protestant Protestant church in the world, because of Elizabeth's determination to secure a quick compromise. A church that's Protestant but contains a lot of Catholic features, we still have cathedrals after all, and bishops and robes for the clergy. And we have bits of the service that look very Catholic, like making the sign of the cross and baptism.

TH Christening services have something like an exorcism.

RH Yes and that's the kind of thing a Puritan would notice at once and really hate. So Puritans are simply the Protestants in England who are not only unhappy with the compromise but actually want to do something about it. When you go back to the early modern period the Church of England is torn apart in a struggle between Puritans and those who loosely I'd call Anglo-Catholics.

TH Meaning?

RH Those who happen to like the Catholic features in the Church of England and either want to keep them or even enlarge them, and the Civil War is largely the showdown, the shootout. Each wins in turn. The Puritans as we all know win in the Civil War, hence Cromwell, the chopping down of the maypoles and the abolition of church ales. But then the Anglo-Catholics come back in a big way with the Restoration and the monarchy. And it's the Puritans who are forced out of the church for ever. They become the Presbyterians, the Congregationalists, the Baptists, later the United Reformed Church and of course the Quakers, who are the people who wear black hats *par excellence*, to show that they are serious about going to heaven.

TH The Quakers have a much more friendly image than the Puritans.

RH Well, not initially. Initially they are the stormtroopers of Puritanism, the most radical, the most reforming. It's just that they're turned upon so savagely by everyone else that they're forced to become pacifists and philanthropists and they do that extremely well. They've done it for 300 years and I think greatly enhanced our culture as a result. But they don't start out like that. They had a straight choice. Either they abandoned their radical views, or they persuaded those in power that they weren't a threat to them. And by becoming pacifists and suffering with extreme courage, without hitting back, they managed to survive.

TH And who were the Puritans who went over on the Mayflower?

RH They were extreme Puritans who couldn't stand the established church. They wanted to found their ideal Church in the new land rather than put up with a compromise.

TH And you see modern America as the result of that.

RH Modern America is the Puritan paradise. It's founded upon gathered churches, that is, churches that are not established by the state but paid for by the congregations. And communities form around them. There is a powerful ethic of the perfection and the improvement of the human race ...

TH Hard work ...

RH Hard work but also Evangelism ... interference, intervention.

TH And how do you see Benjamin Franklin?

RH I see him as a classic example of the connection between socialism and Puritanism, meaning that the great reformers and progressive thinkers of modern times have often had an evangelical Protestant background, especially in Anglo-American culture. And if you're looking forward to the Gordon Browns of this world, you'll find a lot of the socialist leaders are people with a background in Presbyterianism and Methodism.

TH Why do they end up as socialists?

RH Because it's a part of reforming and perfecting society. And there's an awful lot in the Bible that you can actually put straight into socialism. These same prophets who are ranting against having fun are often ranting against the tyranny of kings and magistrates, and ranting against those who oppress the weak and the poor. And I remember Jesus saying a few things on a mount about the poor and the meek which are grist to the socialist mill. And rightly so. So the very people who are paying closest attention to their Bible about chasing out sin may well chase out capitalism as well.

TH But The Sermon on the Mount is quite easy-come, easy-go. It's not about imposing your will on other people.

RH Yeah but read your Habukuk, the Biblical prophet. He's much more hellfire and brimstone against those who oppress.

TH When the Protestant preachers came along and ranted against the profligacy of the established church, the people must have been feeling resentful already for the ideas to take root.

RH Some felt resentful, others were happy with it. There's always been this split in the Church of England between those who go into a church and ill-humouredly note the stained glass, and the altar cloth and latterly the polished cross and candlesticks, and think they're an affront. And those who wish the sermon would end so they can get on with communion, because that's the main thing for them.

TH Going back to America, how would you say that Puritan project has turned out?

RH Huge success. Greatest power in the entire world. Again and again those who they face as mighty opponents seem to get overthrown without a huge amount of effort. In World War Two they find themselves useful allies at the right points and then the Warsaw Pact disintegrates which must be the hand of God.

TH I would see myself as pro-protest but then there's the unpleasant link between protest and reform and perfectionism and Puritanism.

RH Well it's the Sixties split, isn't it, which I remember all too well, between people on demos who had short hair and often beards, the men, and read their Marx and barked orders at you to get in line and told you what you had to believe. They didn't really seem to believe too much in democracy. And the long-haired rest of us who believed in individualism and choice were regarded by these snooty Marxists as self-indulgent traitors.

TH When you see the May Day riots of today what do you see? A medieval spirit? Or a reforming spirit?

RH The Middle Ages are big on riots and so is the early Modern period. I think it's very medieval. It reminds me of the May Day riots – Evil May Day – in which they're rioting against foreign businessmen setting up in London and starting to make serious money. And later on in the 17th century every Shrove Tuesday you get apprentices on the street rioting just for the sake of it. But their targets were very clear: they rioted against brothels, they rioted against people who charged too much interest on their loans and going for the icons of capitalism is in many ways a direct descendant from that.

TH Is it the spirit of Jesus turning over the tables of the money-lenders?

RH It is, but the great thing about the Bible is that it's so rich. The Jesus who flogs the money-changers out of the temples is the same one who tells you to turn the other cheek. On the one hand the Bible is an invitation to pacifism and quietism and on the other hand the Bible is an invitation to action. It all depends which fits your reading.

TH You can read the Bible to defend idleness or to defend the creed of industry. But Jesus tends more towards the idle.

RH Basically the Bible is a handbook for a peasant and small craftsperson society. If you look at Jesus's parables that's what he understands. He's talking about peasant proprietors and people who are actually making things with their hands. Jesus's attitude to the Roman Empire is to render unto Caesar his due, because Caesar is basically not the point, he's too high and far off.

TH It's about empowering the individuals here and now.

RH Well, I'd say the small man and woman.

TH The medieval ploughman saw Jesus as his mate and companion.

RH That's absolutely correct. The Old Testament is very much that of hill farmers. The king who nicks someone's vineyard is someone who has colluded in the devil's work.

TH That was an interest of Chesterton and Hilaire Belloc ... they were into the idea of Distributism, where every family would have its own plot of land.

RH My answer to that was that it was all a bit late. We've been so totally restructured. What we can do in present-day society is make the case that we can actually afford leisure as never before. So the movement to get us all to work harder than ever before and with more regimentation than ever before is totally unnecessary and artificial. We can do without it.

TH One of the things that motivates me in the *Idler* is a rage against the boredom of everyday employment.

RH It's a revolution that's happened in my lifetime. When I first went to work, as a civil servant in Whitehall, admittedly groomed for stardom since I had a Cambridge scholarship, back at the beginning of the 1970s, there was this sense of a kind of staple job that was laid out to leave the averagely productive person with a fair amount of spare time. It was up to you how you spent it. You could take longer lunch hours. Or if you were more idle than most, then the amount of work you were supposed to do would expand to fill the time, because you would work more slowly. If you were really ambitious you could ask for extra work, or you could catch up on your reading or file your nails. That's how people like Kenneth Grahame could be a clerk at the Bank of England and write *The Wind in the Willows* on the job. Slack was built in to what you were doing. That has all gone. We've had this revolution, everybody's been worked to the absolute limits and being checked up on the whole time. It's the age of assessment, surveillance ... partly it's the technology, you can survey people ... but there's this mentality that even if you can't you still need to issue questionnaires, fill forms, check up. Push, push, push. Clearly I'm an adrenalin-fuelled ambitious academic, so that sort of thing ought to fit in with me, and I'd rather see talent and ambition encouraged than squashed by drones, which was the problem with the regime 30 years ago, but it's still thoroughly un-healthy. I can see the results of stress all round me.

TH What about your students? Have they changed?

RH Yes, they work enormously hard now. In many ways that's good for me, but the number of stress-related ailments they're producing, the amount of actual damage to their minds, is disturbing. Students didn't have personal problems 30 years ago, save the very occasional unlucky one. But now they are a recurrent feature of the tutor's realm.

TH Going back to our theme of Protest and Idleness, what would your advice be to someone who wants to make their way in the world without becoming enslaved by the corporate megamachine?

RH It's very tough. Get together with like-minded people, read the *Idler*, and in your own life fight very hard for the right to work hard and by working hard create more space. In other words, fight as hard as you can to discourage those who employ you from observing that you've created some extra time by working extra hard and then filling it for you with yet more work.

Esther Perel

by Tom Hodgkinson

IDLER 40 · WINTER 2008

IN ORDER TO CHASE SALES, WE DECIDED TO DO A 'SEX' issue. I'd read an interesting book about sex and intimacy by a therapist called Esther Perel, and arranged to interview her about it via Skype.

★

Last year Esther Perel published a book called *Mating in Captivity: Reconciling the Erotic and the Domestic*. The work asks why sex can often disappear when couples get cosy and domesticated. It has touched a nerve and been published in 20 countries. Here she discusses love's paradox and ways to bring a sense of playfulness back into our relationships.

TH You are saying that sex is better when there is *less* intimacy. It's when you keep your distance and you don't merge: that's when things are more erotic.

EP The British were the first to look at the book from a particular angle which shaped it and defined it very differently. When the *Observer* came out, the *Daily Mail*, *Telegraph*, they all began to talk about this phenomenon: what happens to this generation that has egalitarian ideals in its head, contraception in its hand, lots of pre-marital sexual experience and comes to a committed relationship with an expectation of sexual fulfilment, and finds itself with very little desire for it or at least for their partner ... they don't understand it because they came with an expectation of sexuality to be an essential dimension of their relationship. Many of these couples are not in troubled relationships:

they are very good couples, but whose desire is flagging. They complain of the listlessness of their sex lives; they sometimes want more and they always want better, and what they long for is the sense of connection, renewal and playfulness that sexuality used to afford them, a certain intensity that gives them a feeling of being alive. Not the act itself. I'm interested in the erotic dimension: what helps people feel alive inside their relationship and in life in general. In that sense, the erotic is the cultivation of pleasure for its own sake. It's not measurable. The book was much less about sex per se and more about the ambiguities of desire and the quest for the erotic.

TH What factors do you blame for us having got into this position?

EP I don't know that I blame factors. I think that the idea of reconciling eroticism and domesticity in one relationship is new and brings with it a set of challenges. The idea that in the same relationship we want to experience grounding, meaning and continuity, as well as transcendence and adventure and novelty, is contradictory. We want respectability, children, family life, economic support, and at the same time we want that person to be our best friend and our confidant and our passionate lover.

TH You say that the partner is more fanciable when you see them in the distance and you get that glimpse.

EP I've asked this question in ten countries, give me a moment when you are most drawn to your partner? They say, when he plays with the kids, when she's giving a talk at work, when I see him play his instrument, when she does something that she's passionate and intense about. But it's not when they're looking at each other 10cm from each other, no longer able to distinguish the contours of the other, and not when they're that far when they can no longer distinguish them either.

TH Which makes sense, because for most people the most intense period sexually of a relationship is the beginning, when you're still separate individuals.

EP That's why in the beginning it's much easier for people to combine love and desire, than afterwards. It's not intimacy per se that is problematic, we seek that and I'm not an intimacy-basher by any means, what I am saying is that while love wants that kind of closeness, and love is about having and knowing, desire thrives on the elusive and needs a certain distance to thrive, and is about wanting, not having. In that sense it needs air, and many relationships today find it hard to maintain air between them, in part because of the romantic idea that believes in sharing everything, in cultivating transparency and basically in eradicating distances.

TH I like the idea of a more old-fashioned household. I read in books of Tudor history things like: 'I visited my lady's chamber.' The woman and the man of the house appeared to have their own completely separate lives, their own courts. They would come together at mealtimes. They had joint projects but separate bedrooms. That to me is a sexy idea.

EP In Jewish law, that's what people do: they sleep separately and they don't touch. Then they go to the ritual bath and they have two weeks where they are invited to be luscious and sexual.

TH That's an ancient idea?

EP That is the contemporary idea of Orthodox Judaism. That is the way that sexuality is regulated in traditional Jewish law.

TH Another great point that you make in the book is that some element of formality can actually be quite sexy: when you're first going out with someone, you make an appointment, go out for dinner, and there's probably going to be sex at the end of it. But established couples would find making a date for sex a difficult idea.

EP Unless they play it a certain kind of over-familiarity can numb desire. If we share everything it becomes harder to maintain a sense of lustfulness, it's too much of a taboo, we don't want sex in the family, therefore maintaining a separation or boundaries or privacy are elements that can nurture desire. On the other hand, we do live in a nuclear family, not everyone wants to have separate quarters; but the idea is that sexuality can be a playing field, a theatre, a stage, that actually allows us playfully to go against what we do in the kitchen between six and eight.

TH Didn't Benjamin Franklin say that once a month you should take your wife away to a hotel and treat her like a prostitute?

EP There was one couple I saw who was doing so. I don't advise, I describe what I know people do: the idea is that people can be more playful, more seductive, erotic, more pleasure-bound, in a space that is outside of their home. They can bring out different parts of their personality when they are in the space where there are no children and carers and responsible adults. And for some people, that's the hotel.

TH Are you French?

EP I'm originally Flemish-Belgian.

TH Right ... it's just that when I've visited France, they all seem to have mistresses ... affairs seem to be more a part of the culture than England.

EP I think people engaging in extra-marital relations in the US is no different from France. It's the attitudes that are different, not the statistics. Wherever women have more power and economic independence, their numbers are not that far off from men, either. The reasons for the affairs, and what they look for in them, may be quite different. In France there is a certain kind of understanding, and for the Italians, too, that indeed there may not be one relationship where you can find all. But you don't therefore separate. What I think is the difference between the Anglo-Saxon world and the Latin world has to do with the level of individualism. Some societies develop greater tolerance for divorce, while the other societies develop greater tolerance for sexual infidelity.

TH Does one go for a serial monogamy or stay with your main formal possibly sex-free relationship?

EP The idea that infidelities are always troubles or symptoms of disappointment in the relationship is an easy supposition but it doesn't necessarily bear true. And in societies where affairs are more tolerated, it's not that they think affairs are a great idea, it's just that they don't think they warrant destroying the family. Because they see the marriage as being not just two individuals – there are a lot of other people involved and you don't drag them into it.

TH You could argue that there's something self-indulgent about the ease and the willingness with which people divorce.

EP Yes, you could say that, or you could say that people who divorce are greater idealists, because when they divorce they don't question the model, they just think they chose the wrong person.

TH The triumph of hope over experience.

EP The divorce can be seen as an expression of how tenaciously they hold on to the model.

TH But don't you find that people fall into the same patterns in their second or third marriage?

EP Well, in the States first marriages have a 50 per cent divorce rate and second marriages have a 65 per cent divorce rate! What does this say?

TH So it's not the other person who is at fault, it's either you or the institution. Now, in some cultures, and in history, prostitution is tolerated, as it was for example in medieval Florence, where there were these bath-houses, where you went for sex with your wife. The bath-houses also had prostitutes. It was kind of accepted by the priests because they thought it prevented a greater sin, which was infidelity. That's another way of dealing with the problem.

EP You don't have to go to the Middle Ages. I was in Brazil last month.

TH The sex hotels!

EP Besides the sex hotels, I went to a place that until a few years ago was called The Silver Pussy. To that club the young man was brought by his brother or by his father, to be initiated by an experienced women. And at the same time as he was being initiated by her, he was protecting the virginity of the good girl he would marry later. Now he's not needing to go that club any more because the good girl is supposed to have pre-marital sex with him, and after she has a child, he's not supposed to go there any more either because they're supposed to cultivate desire as an expression of love in their own relationship. When people ask, are there societies where people have more sex, I say, yes: the ones where people have more children and the ones where women have less power. Yes! One, because sexuality becomes one of their main powers, and two because they don't have the possibility of saying 'no'. It's in emancipated Western societies where sex is merely a matter of desire, it's no longer operated by reproduction, it's not sustained by power distribution, so it's a question of: if I'm in the mood and you're in the mood and it happens to be at the same time. Therefore it requires that we cultivate desire and seduction and erotic engagement in the context of our own home in ways we never had to do before. It's not enough to say, I feel like it, and she obliges. He has to elicit her interest, he has to invite her and he never had to do that at home. Especially not when he goes to the prostitute.

TH St Paul says that the woman can ask for sex from the man if he doesn't feel like it, as well. It was the marriage debt, and either partner had to pay the debt if the other felt like it. Isn't there an argument that people should go through with it even if they don't feel like it?

EP I think you can make the argument: desire doesn't always precede experience. Sometimes it comes with it. Especially as we get older, we don't always expect sexual desire but we may have a desire for sex. The difference is that the sexual desire is internally prompted but the desire for sex is a response to motivations that are not always sexual in nature, such as: it would be nice, we'll feel good afterwards, he'll be in a better mood, I'll be relaxed. Give her the experience and then the desire will follow. She starts by thinking, why not?

TH How do you get them into that state?

EP They need to understand that this can be a pathway to desire. There is something very limiting in only seeing sexual desire as a physically based response ... she may want to engage in sex because she's having a fantastic conversation, because he's making her laugh, because he cooked her favourite meal. It has nothing to do with what's going on between her legs. That is one of the fundamental differences in pathways of desire between men and women. And that's why I make the distinction between sexual desire and desire for sex.

TH You talk in the book about a lack of desire being equally felt by the man and woman. But anecdotally in my experience, it's the men complaining that the women are not up for it. The men's desire hasn't gone away.

EP There's a number of things going on there. I think that for dads with young children, go back and read the chapter on parenthood. When women enter into motherhood they often find it harder to find the woman behind the mother, to reconnect with their permission for pleasure in the context of being responsible and loving for others.

TH There's a sort of saintliness ...

EP It's an inhibition about experiencing the selfishness that is inherent in desire, when you have the role of being carer of three little kids.

I think that committed sex is pre-meditated sex. It's wilful and it's intentional. It doesn't just happen. You make it happen. It's seduction. The reality of society seems to be that the man is still interested in sex and the woman loses desire. But in the therapist's office, we tend to see equal numbers. If a woman loses desire, it tends to be so expected that he's not going to bring her to therapy. But if a man loses desire, you may be sure they'll be in the therapist's office very soon, because the woman will worry about it, she will wonder about what's going on, she will want him to come with her to address this. So I can't only see it as an attribute of the woman. It tends to be more an attribute of the primary parent, the person whose sense of self has been totally invaded, if you like, by caring for the children.

TH So it's the mothering that's incompatible with eroticism. What do people do in relationships where this is not a problem?

EP The way I phrase it is to say that what eroticism thrives on — the novel, the mysterious, the unpredictable — is what family life defends against. Family life thrives in an atmosphere of consistency and routine, and those are killers of desire. But couples who have it can create an erotic space for themselves, in which they meet as adults, in which they go out ... not to talk about their kids ... in which they get dressed up, they go dancing. They remain playfully and seductively engaged with each other. Even if for a few years they have much less frequent sex, it's not a matter of how often they have orgasm or intercourse, it's really a question of how they remain erotically engaged with each other. They are not people who are constantly stroking their children and haven't touched each other in God knows how long. They don't just invite the children to come into bed with them and linger around in bed with them, but also find moments to be with each other. They are people who don't wait till 11.30 at night when they are beat but sometimes they decide to meet for lunch when they are dressed up and awake.

TH I sometimes wonder whether bed is not the best place for it.

EP Oh, bed is often the last place. It's often the place where they discuss all the realities of life, it's the place where they've already experienced a lot of rejection. I often tell people that they should look for other surfaces in their house!

TH In the maypole tradition, the dancing was followed by sex in the woods. I can't quite imagine that happening nowadays.

EP We're supposed to do it at home because now we have the permission to be wild in our house. But we realise that maybe being wild in our house isn't such an easy thing to do. And that many of us can be wilder when we leave the confines of this responsible, serious place that is called home.

TH Another thing that strikes me is how little we dance nowadays. In the 18th century, everyone had dancing masters. Dancing was a part of the everyday curriculum for schoolchildren. People danced every night after dinner.

EP I'm very keen on that. We need to develop pleasure not just in the bed but outside, and dancing and movement, and the sensuality and the physical contact, and the suggestiveness that comes from dancing. And it's usually the middle class that dances the least. If you go to the salsa clubs or the African clubs in New York, the only people who don't dance are the white people, usually, the white middle class.

TH Well, middle class morality is against things like that: the Puritans banned dancing, but the more old-fashioned cultures still do it. In Mexico they don't feel the need to go on holiday because they are celebrating all year round, there are constant festivals and parties, often religious in nature. And that would lead to more sex, I suppose.

EP Often it does. Music, movement: you can't dance and be unhappy. It's physical, it engages the senses, and it often invites a certain erotic connection. I look for ways to cultivate that erotic connection that isn't straightforward sex, but that induces the desire for sex. That's the erotic space. It's a space where pleasure is cultivated for its own sake, and sex can happen and often does, but it's not made for sex.

TH So you can't expect to go dancing just once and have sex.

EP Whatever it is that you choose to do that is physical and playful. With some couples it will be dancing; with others it will be taking hikes on top of the mountains. I tend not to give an explicit prescriptive. Instead I explain the principle. When you are dancing with your partner you are engaging with him in a completely different way than when you are in the house thinking about the cleaning, thinking about what has to be done ... You can't dance and think about what you need to do.

TH The book is coming out in 20 countries, right, and you've just visited half of them on a tour. Which cultures have appeared to you to be the healthiest?

EP Every country has its own problems and resources. I would like to say Brazil, but Brazil has its own complications. I think the book has had this kind of resonance because it speaks to a modern conundrum. I tapped into something long unspoken.

TH I always assume that other countries are doing it: Brazil is a non-stop sex party, so is France.

EP Well, England doesn't come from a tradition that understands that kind of seductive playfulness. People there seem to go back and forth between being shy and tongue-tied to being drunk and slobbering all over you.

TH Yes, that's our technique.

EP British people do not have a self-image as elegant and seductive.

TH But there could be a lot in common back at home, even between cultures that look very different when they're out.

EP Go to Brazil. You can see that there is a real attention to the erotic in the society at large and I can't imagine that it doesn't enter into the privacy of the people's homes. The country dances, the carnival: they understand ritual, costumes, fantasy. But given all of that, I still think that reconciling the erotic and the domestic is a challenge, period. In any country. And a paradox that you manage, not a problem that you solve with ten techniques.

TH We should be looking at it as a game, not a competitive sport.

EP For sure. The whole idea for me was to look at the poetics of sex.

Kevin Godley

by Paul Hamilton

IDLER 40 · WINTER 2008

IDLER CONTRIBUTOR PAUL HAMILTON, THE LEGENDARY drumming postman and culture vulture, gave us this fascinating interview with Kevin Godley of 10cc and Godley and Creme.

★

When Kevin Godley, singing drummer with 1970s hit factory 10cc, stopped collaborating with Lol Creme after their 1988 album *Goodbye Blue Sky*, he hung up his microphone to devote nearly 20 years to directing pop videos. In 2006, however, a new website appeared, quietly heralding his return to songwriting and singing. The new material was produced with 10cc bassist (and friend for 50 years) Graham Gouldman.

The *Idler* met the sunny Mr Godley on a rainy day in Soho to find out if his and Graham's new songs are more than, to quote one of his biggest hits, just a silly phase they're going through.

PH What's the worst job you've ever had?

KG I've never had a job.

PH You'll be 62 this year, fast approaching retirement age, and yet you choose now to return to music-making.

KG I can't even consider the notion of retirement since I don't actually work as such. I've got nothing to retire from. I do a bit of this and a bit of that. My life's been a series of lucky accidents: lucky for me, unlucky for practically anybody else. I suppose if I played the game properly I'd have been a graphic designer since that's what I was trained for at art school. The extraordinary thing about the baby boomer art school years is that it instilled, in everyone there, the belief that any-thing was possible, and not exclusively in art and design but in every medium.

PH After a few years in relative obscurity, you and Lol scored a Top Five single in 1981 with 'Under Your Thumb', a record stripped of your trademarks. No massed vocal harmonies, no exotic instrumentation, no crackpot unexpected middle-eights. It's a very straight story per-formed by a solo vocal and a synthesizer. It's almost a demo in compar-ison to your past productions. There wasn't even a video.

KG Yeah, we were on *Top Of The Pops* with smoke billowing out of my sleeves. Why was it a hit? A hit is something everyone wants to like, that's why it's a hit. Despite ourselves we hit that nerve. What hap-pened was we got a little home studio, a 16-track machine, set up in Lol's house. Thought it'd be fun to do it ourselves, and Lol could engi-neer it on a basic level. He was tinkering about with this synthesizer one day with a rhythm box chugging along when he came up with this riff. I said, 'That's cool', and started singing something. You see, if you haven't got a sonic template of 'How You Should Sound' then you're excited by anything that seems to work. That track succeeded at a very simple level, it didn't require a great deal of window dressing. Our sense of it was the more layers we took off, the more skeletal it became and the better it got. It really annoys me when people discuss the music of the Seventies: 'Oh yeah, man, Bolan, Bowie, Roxy, punk, Slade' and 10cc are always excluded. This is because of our total lack of Bad Boy Rebel credentials and, for some reason, not really taking care of our visual presentation.

PH Which is strange for ex-art students.

KG Exactly. We were not exciting to look at. We may have sounded like 400 Maniacs From Hollywood but we were Four Wankers From Manchester and therein lies the dichotomy. Most artists who are huge and 'significant' are so not merely because of what they're singing about, it's because of their personal mythology.

PH By the end of the Eighties you had become a vegetarian and got involved in environmental pressure groups like Ark. What brought this about?

KG I became a vegetarian because, I used to live in a house [Tara House, five glass pyramids in Chertsey, Surrey. Previous tenant: Keith Moon] which had a swimming pool, and every year, as in the classic Series One

Sopranos scene, a family of ducks would come and stay in the pool and then leave. One year the ducks flew away but left their smallest, a little duckling, behind. So we caught him, put him in a box with small holes in, took him to a bird sanctuary outside Chertsey. Phew, saved his life. Then we went out to Mr Chow's and had crispy duck. We thought, 'Hang on a minute!' It was like the veil had been lifted. I'd never been a huge fan of meat anyway, I just liked the sauces. So we just decided, 'Let's just not eat meat for a bit and see how we go.' That was 30 years ago. I'm still a vegetable. I became involved with the environmental pressure group Ark through meeting Chrissie Hynde who is far more extreme and radical than I am but wanted to reach ordinary people. A very diverse group of people got together to do something practical to change the way things are. We did pretty well until the Ark Organisation tore itself apart. Leadership squabbles. A real shame. What they were fighting for then is top priority all over the world now.

PH How choosy are you in respect of the songs you make videos of or the companies you make adverts for?

KG I would definitely turn down McDonalds or some other corporation that offends me, yes.

PH You couldn't be bought at any price?

KG No. Well, twenty quid and I'm yours! [Laughter] I don't really do commercials that often because I don't like the business. I'm the one in the Pepsi pre-production meeting saying, 'Guys, it's only a drink.' They look at me as though I'm crazy 'cos it's a way of life to them. To me it's not. Lol and I were asked by Herb Alpert of 'Tijuana Brass' fame to come up with a commercial for his new fragrance. We ended up passing because we couldn't take it seriously.

PH What was it called?

KG 'Trumpet'. [Gales of laughter] Who in their right mind would buy a fragrance called Trumpet? 'The great smell of Trumpet'. (Parp!)

PH How many videos do you make a year on average?

KG Not many. The business has changed radically because of YouTube. If you want to watch a video, click on YouTube and nine times out of ten it's going to be there. Which is fine, but record companies are rubbing their hands in glee because, 'Oh, Cheapo is in!' [Laughs] The record business at the moment is shooting itself very slowly in the foot. It ignored the digital medium when it arrived; it's unwilling to develop new talent; it's not geared to expanding and adapting. The upshot is people are losing interest. If they can't find something to excite them they'll look elsewhere … whereas [stentorian American voice] back in the golden years …

PH … it was a Way Of Life.

KG Hearing the new Beatles song or the next Dylan track was the best moment of the week. You'd queue outside a record booth, waiting to stick those headphones on and hear it. 'Oh, man!' Then you'd race home to wear it to death on the Dansette.

PH I'm not denigrating or demeaning your output with Lol, but what moves me in yours and Graham's new songs is the directness. There's none of the loopy deviations of your past songs, they cut to the quick. Do you think that's down to an awareness of mortality, a sense of time growing shorter and 'I can't fuck around now; this is what I need to say'?

KG That's partially it. Having been a writer, sporadically, for a long time, I've written in lots of styles. It can be so easy to write impressionistic lyrics that are merely part of the overall sound. But, right now, I don't want that.

John Lloyd & John Mitchinson

by Tom Hodgkinson

IDLER 41 · SUMMER 2008

W E WERE VERY LUCKY TO MEET THE MEN FROM QI, and even luckier when they agreed to guest edit an issue of the *Idler*. It became our best ever seller. I recorded a conversation with them to print in the issue, and that is what follows.

★

Behind QI, the television show and books, there is a serious philosophical remit: to end boredom and to rethink the way we learn. Here the two Johns discuss work, play, the horrors of school and the redeeming power of curiosity.

JL I'll tell you a funny thing about work. I met this guy, a school gate dad, just when we were beginning to do QI, at a dinner party and I was telling this group of six or eight people what QI did. This hedge fund guy, with billions in the bank, having decided to sell his business and retire at 40, leapt to his feet and shouted, 'How dare you try and tell me what I find interesting! You're a cultural fascist!' and I said, 'Sorry, Jeremy, what?' And he ran off into the garden. He came back and said, 'I'm sorry, it's just that ever since I gave up work I don't know what to do with myself.' He went back and started up another hedge fund and he's much happier. Getting the 6.30 train and making shedloads of money, because then he doesn't have to think about what matters. For some people work is an absolute crutch. I know because I gave up working. It was one of the things that triggered off the crisis that started QI. I was 42. I said to my wife Sarah, 'My life is so meaningless, so pointless, I'm so dull, I don't know anything. All I know is how to make television commercials about banks and lager. I've got to take some time off, I've got no ideas, I've got to recharge my batteries.' So I took three months off, and it was the most horrific experience, Tom, because I could do what I wanted but I didn't know what to do. I used to wander up and down the Fulham Road and think, maybe I should get a job as a waiter and not tell Sarah, you know, and tell her I'm relaxing, but work really really hard in someone's kitchen. And I went on an art class, I thought I must learn to do something proper, something meaningful. I went to this art class at Chelsea College of Art, and I walked in and someone said, 'What are you doing here?' I said, 'Well I've come to learn to draw,' and she said, 'I've seen you on telly, why would you want to learn to draw here? In this terrible dump?' I did four weeks of these classes, and she was really horrible to me, she said, 'Can't you see? Can't you see that the pomegranate should be next to the orange? What's the matter with you?'

TH What was wrong with her?

JL I don't know, she was pissed off, in a dead-end job, a lot of teachers are. They won't sit still, they won't let me just get through the hours. But it's like in life, the problems are the opportunities, as is often said. The difficult bits show you the way to something different and often so much better. Difficult children are a nightmare for schools so they think, let's just expel this person, because they're always late and they don't do up their tie. It's not, hang on, this person has got a really odd way of looking at things.

TH So QI really does have a radical centre.

JM What I think starts off with kangaroos' vaginas and the wives of Henry VIII ends up with trying to figure out why you're here. Because once you start to ask questions ...

TH We can definitely philosophise about why we are here, but aren't you also attacking the status quo in terms of the Government, business and so on?

JL It's not really about attacking people and certainly not individuals. It's about making people see there's a more interesting angle of looking at things. And actually, the research makes you very much less judgmental about things. I spend a lot of time researching tribes and languages in West Africa and I think to most people West Africa is 'Well, they're very black aren't they?' and they all speak a bit like Idi Amin. It's hot and sweaty and there are mosquitos, rainforests and Nigeria is very corrupt and that's about it really. They don't know that there are 500 ethnic groups in Nigeria alone. All the ships in the Nigerian navy are called hippopotamus, but they're all in different languages.

TH What I'm trying to say is those of us who learn about the world from newspapers and teachers are not told these things. But isn't there a reason why we're not told these things?

JL There isn't an evil lord running the CIA. That person, no matter how evil they appear to be, is just struggling through life. What we're trying to get round to is that if everyone was really interested and curious there wouldn't be these problems. These people would be a lot less powerful. I mean I think now, in general, people are a lot less able to put up with politics, people are ignoring it as irrelevant and not being to do with them addressing their lives.

TH When did it though? Did people ever think it was relevant?

JL They were more interested.

JM At the end of the Second World War a lot of people voted for Labour to get Churchill out.

TH I think people were interested in the 18th century, because you could actually see Pitt or John Wilkes walking down the road.

JL The Romans had no word for 'interesting', did you know that? Or 'boring' for that matter. The Industrial Revolution is about the time we get the words boring and boredom. It's work-related. When work is repetitive, meaningless, pointless, badly paid and dangerous, you need a word for this feeling that you get. As an agricultural worker, it may be very hard work but you've got the seasons, you actually know a lot about lambs and potatoes, so you don't need a word for interesting because it's what you do. This is the worky feeling, boring. Do you know the derivation of noise? Noise comes from 'nausea' and what 'nausea' means is the feeling you get on a ship, *naus* means ship, so nausea is that shippy feeling.

JM We still have 'noisome' which means irritating. But I mean … going back to work, there is the division between work and play, which is very strict in our culture. I'm absolutely sure that most of the creative work people do comes through the play state, not the work state. You need to be able to focus to get things done. But the creative state is when you're in that reflective state.

TH The Yequana Indians don't even have a word for work. One has started to come in, *trabaja*, from the Spanish but they don't have one in their own language.

JM The French word *travaille* comes from the word for torture ...

TH ... but the idea of work for them meaning 'a regrettable necessity' does not exist. It's all mixed up together.

JM In most hunter-gatherer societies very, very little work gets done.

TH But lots of philosophising.

JL There was this fantastic organisation I came across once called the Liberty Fund. There was this guy, in the 1920s, who was in agribusiness, and he had a huge fortune. He had an intuition just before the great crash in 1929 that it was all going to go wrong. So he sold all his stocks and then it all fell and of course he found he was the richest man in the universe. And his hobby was philosophy. He loved to talk philosophy. He couldn't stand other billionaires because billionaires are only interested in money, and yachts and stuff. So in order to get people to talk to he had to create this organisation and he paid people to be his chat friends. So he set up this Liberty Fund thing, and now it's a huge organisation and they run about 200 seminars all around the world every year. They pay you a thousand dollars and set you up in a nice hotel and then send you some reading material. Anyway I did it and I got sent *No Logo* and some Spinoza. There's always 14 people. You sit around a table and there's a chairman who might be some wonderful philosophy professor, like Steve Erickson, and he leads the discussion. And you sit there and talk, for no reason at all, about these interesting things. And over these three days you make friends for life. And you learn the most amazing amount, it's a wonderful thing. And these 14 people, I could go to war with them. They are wonderful people. And he starts by saying, 'You probably all think this is some CIA plot but it isn't. It's completely and genuinely for the sake of itself.' That's what we should be doing. I spent a day researching on Saturday, and John's the same, and you spend the whole day completely absorbed in discovery. You learn lots of new things. Like the fact that the white cliffs of Dover are made out of plankton. It's fascinating, and yet most people spend Saturday afternoon being bored, or angry, and it's a crime!

TH Do you think your television show has that effect on people, does it stimulate a new way of looking at things, and a new interest in learning?

JL No, what's really weird is we get no letters, maybe one a week if we're lucky. Almost no feedback. Very, very little. It's very odd. It's the way the establishment always gets rid of rebellion. It's by promoting it. That's what happens at public school. You get the worst boys and make them prefects.

JM It's like Oxford and Cambridge, you get the brightest people, give them somewhere nice to live, give them nice food, and they think: this is great.

TH You do get lots of radical professors at University though. I had at least one.

JL There are actually very few successful radical professors at University now. I would say there are no millionaire professors who are radical. It's like comedians. They all start off, Ben Elton, Billy Connolly, having a go at the Government but a few years later they start saying, 'Oh no, I never had a go at Margaret Thatcher, I quite like Mrs T.,' and now you've got Billy Connolly, friend of the Royal Family. These people are promoted out of danger so that they don't rock the system. And in many ways that's what happening to QI. We're getting very successful so we aren't seen as radical any more.

TH So how do you stop yourself becoming a caricature of your own work?

JL It is very difficult. When Douglas Adams was at the height of his fame he was very, very unhappy, very confused. He wrote these wonderful things with his great sense of humour and then he became all the people he parodied. Immensely rich and rather pompous. Mel and Griff did a wonderful parody of *Hitchhiker*, brilliantly accurate, pointing out that all the things he'd made jokes about, he'd become. He got really upset about it. Really, really angry.

TH I think Lennon did it quite well, he continued to be radical.

JL Do you remember how much people used to mock him for marrying Yoko and baking bread and all that stuff? You look at it now and he was right.

JM Why is it that so many people dislike John Lennon? Self-righteous, preachy?

TH I think people find it hard to deal with the apparent contradictions. Playing 'Imagine' in his mansion.

JL You know people say 'champagne socialist', well, so what? You'd rather people were champagne fascists would you? Surely it's a good thing? It's better to give something back than keep it all to yourself.

TH Have you read *The Man Who Was Thursday* by G. K. Chesterton? It's about a group of anarchists and these two guys are having this terrific row about the state of society and then one of them takes them down to this cellar café and says, 'Oh they do a wonderful Chablis here.'

JM I like proper old-fashioned anarchism, a persistent refusal to sign up. I certainly don't feel able to sign up to any political party at the moment. I hate this thing 'millions of people have died to sacrifice themselves for your right to vote'. No, actually, they sacrificed themselves for all sorts of reasons.

JL It is tricky, if you can't vote for anyone, again it's a very QI thing. It's because they don't have any interesting ideas. They don't. And they are all trying to guess what we want. Which is the other disaster of our culture. Instead of saying this and this should happen because it would be a great idea.

TH It's ridiculous. If you'd asked people in a poll in 1962 'What would you most like to appear in popular music?' no one would have said, 'Four slightly long-haired men from Liverpool'.

JM Futurologists predicted that the world would run out of food so they got that wrong because now there's too much food, but we can't get it to the people that need it, but no one predicted the Internet. It was all people living on Mars.

TH They're still going on about that though. Some of these futurologists running Facebook and all the rest have these ideas about going to Mars and living for a thousand years.

JL Even today the Internet seems, even though it's annoying sometimes when you can't log on in one second, utterly miraculous.

JM Well, what is miraculous, I think, is that the breakthrough in the technology came to saints. Tim Berners-Lee could be the richest man that has ever lived but instead he decided that he wanted it to be free. I get rather bored by the sandal-wearing Internet hippies saying no one should make any money from the Internet because that's never going to happen, but it is true that it is mostly extraordinary. It does undermine a lot of greed.

TH I think it stops people though. I mean instead of going on a march or attempting to recreate their everyday lives and deslave themselves, people are putting stuff up on Facebook.

JM I really think this social networking stuff is going to collapse under its own weight.

TH But it has 60 million people and it's going up all the time

JM   But of those 60 million 40 million probably hardly ever use it and think it's a load of shit. But who is 'the man', do you think, now? You know, 'working for the man'. It's really hard to know who 'the man' is. Is it global capitalism? Well, sort of.

TH   It's the man inside you.

JL   The man in your head is doing all the controlling, far more than MI5 or the CIA.

TH   There is stuff going on though. The word 'Papist' as in 'Papist Plot' was completely invented by the Elizabethans as a way of promoting Protestantism. It's like Newspeak. The authorities change the language in order to condition us.

JM   Like Al-Quaeda, we're all experts about Al-Quaeda now.

JL   The thing with Al-Quaeda is that it's become a thing because someone thought of the word. There is no Al-Quaeda network, well there is now, because people sign up to an idea, but that idea has been created.

JM   What does Al-Quaeda actually mean anyway?

TH   I don't know.

JM   It means 'the righteous' or something [it means 'The Base', Ed.]. It's like, Jihad doesn't actually mean anything like what we all think it means, but I've forgotten that too.

JL   In the Koran Jihad is the struggle to overcome oneself but it's misused to mean 'kill other people'.

JM   I didn't know the Koran was written in poetry. Instead of having the Gospels at the core of Christianity you would have Dante, or *Paradise Lost*.

JL   It's one of the good reasons to learn Arabic, of course, like learning Italian to read Dante. It makes it completely different to reading it in English.

JM   I did do that. I translated the whole of the *Inferno* when I was learning Italian at the same time. I had four months in Italy. But I'd come up with these Italian phrases which would be like Chaucerian phrases in modern Italian [laughs] because it's supposed to be the purist Italian. It was written about 500 years ago.

TH   So the success of the QI project, the books and everything, presumably that must all be cause for huge celebration?

JL   But all it means is that people consume it. It becomes part of the establishment.

TH   That was the precursor to all this, the 'dullness' of the 18th century.

They used the word bore to mean boring work, cant.

JM It's the same, cant, but again it's people who don't reflect.

JL There's no question that people must have had boring days and dull people but ...

JM It's vanity, which actually means emptiness. If you read Ecclesiastes, 'Vanity, vanity, all is vanity', and you replace that with emptiness or boredom, it works. All those great Roman satirists, like Juvenal, always attacked that venal, empty ...

JL We all, if we're honest, know the difference between an empty thing and something that somehow matters. You can do it in comedy. You can say, 'well, so and so, I suppose they're quite funny but there's no meaning' and we do it with programmes. We say, that's a good programme, because they matter in some way. It's very difficult to say, what's the meaning of meaning? That's why it's a pointlesss question to ask, 'Is the Universe meaningful?' because what does meaningful mean? But we know. It's another way of thinking. It's almost beyond intuition, you've tapped into something that you know is important, in some way, but you couldn't possibly say why.

JM There's a great Wallace Stevens line which says 'a meaning of a poem is another poem'.

TH But that doesn't mean you can't read critical essays about Blake or something.

JL A good piece of literary criticism is about an insight, isn't it? It's a connection, what he's saying here is ...

JM It always amazes me that the slowest moving part of any bookshop is the section on literary criticism. It's misnamed. In our bookshop we called it essays.

JL I don't know about essays. That's not good marketing. There should be a better word than that. There are a whole class of words that make you nod off, 'education' is one. But I mean, what could be more interesting than teaching children?

JM But as soon as you hear someone say 'education' you know the conversation is dead.

JL 'Religion', 'Environment', they're all the really important things ...

TH It's because they are co-opted. It's like 'Health and Safety'. It's been borified by Government.

JL But hang on, there you go! 'Health and Safety': what two more important things for human existence could there be? But we hate the very phrase!

TH   'Work and Pensions'.

JL   Aarrggghhh!! Please, please, no more!

TH   I suppose if you had a 'Department of Merriment in Everyday Life' it would become boring after a while.

JM   Merriment is fantastic.

JL   The Department of Merriment? I'd definitely go there. Imagine if they called the Department of Environment 'The Department of Delicious Food'.

TH   I don't know. I think it would quickly become very boring: 'Oh no, I've got a Delicious Food meeting, bloody hell, not again!'

TH   So in QI you try not to kick against the things you oppose because that will strengthen them?

JM   But it's a society that also has no confidence at all. That's the whole thing that consumer society is about. Buying things simply to make people feel better about themselves. What's wonderful about what we do at QI, and I certainly believe it has a definite spiritual impact on you as a human being, is you work on stuff and you learn stuff, and it's free. All of it is free.

JL   That's it really. You don't need money to be interested. A little bit of money for a couple of bottles of wine is very cheap entertainment.

TH   I've got a very pompous idea for a book called *The Nature of Things*. Things have a nature, so for example email, by its nature, tends to make people communicate in a kind of rude fashion. And if you write a letter with a fountain pen then it will have a different nature to one written with a scratchy biro. And you can take this idea out further…

JL   That's Plato's theories of forms, Tom,

TH   Is it?

JM   You're definitely right, it's like a difference between a hotpot and a frying pan. There's a determinism there.

TH   The heat from wood is different from heat that comes from gas or electricity.

JM   Those horrible fake glowing gas fires. This is going back to the point that there's this vast edifice of knowledge that's completely ignored. Of course we know a lot more now than they did in the past. I think we've probably forgotten at least as much. The stuff we've forgotten is the stuff we don't think is useful anymore, like what the wood from a beech tree is good for. Or planting by the moon, or whatever it is.

TH It's very hubristic to think that we're at a point now where we know more than we've ever known before.

JM Do you think we know more about raising children than we did 200 years ago?

TH There is the argument that Rousseau, in *Emile,* was reacting against quite a brutal approach to childhood. And people read Philip Ariès who said that childhood didn't exist in the medieval age. But every medieval historian I've read completely slags that book off. Some of the most intelligent people I've been reading about recently never went to school.

JL Really?

TH John Stuart Mill didn't go to school. He was taught by Jeremy Bentham and his dad. Blake didn't go to school. I'm going to do a great list of these amazing people who never went to school. Bertrand Russell was another and it can tend to produce a more independent mind.

JM Did you enjoy school, Tom?

TH Yes.

JL I hated it.

JM Sometimes I wake up now and think, however bad it is, it won't be as bad as that feeling you have about exams.

TH Now, what would a QI school look like?

JL A QI school, well, there would be no work for a start, it would all be play. Plato said that education should be a form of amusement, that way you will be much better able to discover the child's natural bent. The first few years, until eight or nine, is just larking about having fun. Then you decide, well this child is musical, this one is artistic, this one is good at science, and you only educate children in the things they want to know about. And by the time these people are eleven or twelve they'll be university level but all the other stuff, the Geography, History, foreign languages and so on, that's just fun. That's all stories.

JM Music, storytelling, doing stuff with your hands. That's how we interact with the world. There's that great line: you're taught for the first five years of your life to walk and talk, and for the next ten you're told to shut up and sit down. Kids figure things out so quickly when they want to. It's about trying to work with what's natural. And I know this.

JL I think music should be part of a compulsory core curriculum as it was in Classical times and all the way through the Middle Ages. But music is taught in the most banal, tedious fucking way by most music teachers, which is, 'You will learn the basics, you will learn to read music, hands up like this, no that's wrong! No, that's a C not a D, you stupid little boy, why didn't you practise?'

JM So what is this perverse thing in parents that makes them want to make their kids suffer in the way they did at school? Out of some belief that it's going to help them? The other thing of course is tremendous guilt because of the economic imperative that so many parents feel for not being around for their kids because they have to work.

TH I think a lot of it comes down to conditioning and brain-washing.

JM Well, it's collective madness.

TH I think it's planned.

JL Was it? It was certainly planned in the States. Coolidge in 1907 had a big thing about education and what it was for, and they divided the country into two kinds. The intellectuals and then the ones needed to operate machinery who they deliberately didn't want to have a high level of education because somebody's got to do the work.

TH Huxley says in *Brave New World*: 'we tried enslaving people against their will but that doesn't work. We've got to make them love their slavery.' That's the key. And these things are planned. We all know how we have meetings about how we're going to market our books, how we're going to hopefully manipulate people's minds by getting them to buy our books. Governments do that as well. It's like after 9/11 and everyone had to go shopping. The creation of a consumer economy was a deliberate thing. We've got to keep producing, we've got to stimulate demand.

JM When you say it's deliberate, it's difficult to know whether it's just an aggregation of a lot of people over a period of time.

TH An interviewer complained to me when I praised idling: 'But we've got to be competitive!'

JM But what does that mean? It's like fear of the sky falling in. It seems to me that you're competitive as a country if you've got good ideas. The whole country though, what are we talking about? The idea that living on an estate in Newcastle gives you any sense of kinship with the rest of the country...

TH Queen Victoria's Coronation was an attempt to get some patriotic spirit going, but before that people in the countryside barely knew who she was. These things are deliberately done. Like the show at

Crystal Palace, there'll be a public holiday so people can go and visit the great show and feel as though they are contributing to the commercial greatness of their country. It's propaganda. I think everyone underestimates how much we are manipulated all the time. We can believe it of 100 years ago or even 20 years ago, but we don't seem to believe it's happening now.

JM So we're all complicit in the end. One of the curious things now is there is nowhere you can go and be outside the market. There was a fantasy for a while that you could go to the Eastern Bloc, but actually that was all nonsense.

JL Who are the famous Victorian historians, Macaulay, Gibbon? Well, one of the facts on the QI database is that in the *Encyclopedia Britannica* entry on Edward Gibbon there is not one single interesting thing in the biography entry and he had the most fascinating life. You've really got to dig.

JM Gibbons were named after him.

JL No! That is so good.

JM It's better than that. The guy who first described them was Gibbon's best friend and there are two arguments, one was that they were called "Gib" because they looked like cats or Gibbons because of his best mate. What are you going to call a new monkey when you haven't got a name for them?

JL That is so brilliant. Now I don't understand how I lived, Tom, how I got through a week without having this sort of conversation. That's the wonderful thing about QI. It does you good when you hear that.

JM Some deep electrical thing happens. Humour, interestingness and sexual attraction, they're all … it is electrical. You know if you could see your brain the moment those little connections are made, 'yippee'.

JL One of the funniest things I ever heard on the *News Quiz* was this news cutting about this cleaner who'd been sacked from his job because he'd spent all day cleaning the elevator because he thought it was a different one on each floor. Why is that so funny? It's like John says, humour's about connection.

Jaz Coleman & Youth

IDLER 42 · 2009

THROUGH OUR TYPESETTER AT BRACKETPRESS, MR. BRETT,
I made contact with Youth of Killing Joke. We arranged things
for Youth to sit down with longtime creative collaborator Jaz
Coleman, and mull over the state of the world and ideas for change for
our 'Smash the System' issue.

★

Youth, known as Martin Glover to his mum, is a musician and record
producer. He has produced records for many bands including The
Verve, Embrace and Edwyn Collins. He is a founder member of Killing
Joke and also plays in Transmission. He is one half of The Fireman, an
electronic duo whose other half is Paul McCartney. Prague-based
musician Jaz Coleman is also a founder member of Killing Joke. He
studied piano and violin from the age of six and sang in cathedral
choirs. In 1989 Jaz began a study of Arabic music at the Cairo
Conservatoire. A permaculture enthusiast, he has invested in two eco-
villages, one in Chile and one on Great Barrier Island. Here Youth and
Jaz sit down in Los Angeles to discuss Permaculture, self-sufficiency
and transcending the system.

Y Clearly things are changing. Families, cities, the whole social structure
   is changing radically. How can we empower ourselves, and how can we
   look to our leaders to show us the way?
J I think what we're seeing with the banks going down and the economic
   collapse is that centralised government has gone broke. It cannot finan-
   cially support the whole country. London cannot support Manchester.
   So each area is going to become a sort of micro-climate: self-sufficient,
   self-reliant and with sustainable resources. The nuclear family – to

address the other point – is quite obviously breaking down. I think we need to reevaulate our education system completely. As far as banking goes and what we're learning, I think we will need to transcend the current system and study advanced systems of barter.

Y Can you ever see the systems of state control, governments around the world, relinquishing power and deregulating control to small communities and towns, so they can have their own currency and barter on their own terms?

J Yeah, I can see that time because it will make economic sense to governments to empower local areas so that they are self-reliant.

Y We have to build those communities outside of the normal structures of mayors and councils.

J And for us as musicians it means that the insulting idea of a 'fan club' is replaced by a network of like-minded individuals who share a philosophy, like The Gathering. So what was once a fan club, can buy up whole areas of virgin forest.

Y Have they done that?

J No, but it's a good idea.

Y Another good idea would be to suggest to fans that they could put a grand into the album, own a bit of the album, and the money they make from the album goes to a central fund that buys land.

J This is the kind of moral we want to show to other bands. So bands can link their shared networks and tribes, and create a system of arcs or villages worldwide.

Y Traditional roles have clearly changed in the last 30 years. And we're looking at families breaking down, problems with single parents, the breakdown of communities, isolation. How can we restore the harmony of families?

J I think we need to take our old ideas like Christianity and transform them into something more spiritual and plausible, because there's a huge gap. We're living in this very materialist society and our existing religions are failing people. Christianity is based on a fable that has nothing to do with the truth, and while I might go along with some of its ideas, for example compassion, it disturbs me greatly.

Y Where do we find the ideas? For me, I think we have to look back and look at our own native traditions, where we managed a rich and sustainable life for thousands of years.

J I think we need a new goddess worship, to link us with Gaia or Mother

Earth, which is, after all, where we get our food from. For me it's a sobering thought that all the faeces and shit from New York City is pumped into the sea and people complain about the price of fish. It's insane. The flush toilet is more deadly than the atomic bomb. We're shitting in our own food supply. We can fly to the moon but we can't keep our rivers and seas clean.

Y Do you think if enough people strengthen their own communities we could actually one day get away from central government?

J I think that the world we've come to know is coming to an end.

Y Globalisation, the free market, we're just beginning to get the consequences of these ideas.

J It's a double-edged sword, on the one hand the dream of a unified planet where there's no more wars has been entertained by many thinkers. But the reality is somewhat different. I take my perspective from being a New Zealand passport holder. I think the best people to look after New Zealand are the people from New Zealand. I certainly wouldn't like to see it as part of an Asia-Pacific political union. So, do I agree with the Rockerfellerist idea of abandoning nationalism for an internationalist system? No.

Y But the problem is the conflict.

J Man is very tribal by nature. I don't see how consolidation is going to work, where you've got an ancient culture like India. It won't fit into a 'one world' idea.

Y But nationalism is the infantile ego strutting around, putting flags up.

J One side of me is internationalist. It would be nice if we could achieve planetary consciousness, and this I think will happen. But then there's another side of man that I don't trust.

Y The great beast side of man is what you've got to balance, you've got to find some sort of harmony. You've got to find compassion: without compassion there's no soul, without soul there's just death.

J I like the idea of small nations, with their traditions upheld. One part of me is very reactionary: there are such things as cultural boundaries that exist on a map.

Y They should be reinforced culturally. It's politically that things get problematic.

J To a degree the two are inseparable. I really object to these European countries that are under an occupied status. Germany is still officially an occupied country... America is all over Europe. Is it necessary?

They could probably do with saving their money. In Prague 80 per cent of the population is against this new missile defence shield, they think it will inflame relations with Russia. But there's no referendum, the people aren't consulted and they just built it.

Y So you see eco-communities as a solution?

J Bill Mollison came up with the idea of Permaculture. It's the opposite of modern agriculture which is monoculture. This is a polyculture system, where everything feeds itself. Bill Mollison suddenly realised that behind this idea politics lurked, because he stresses that centralised government will eventually break down, and that each area must be self-reliant and self-sufficient. So, I've been studying all the advanced systems of barter that exist today. On the Great Barrier Island there's no banks, you can't draw money out, so people have an exchange system, but there are other advanced systems and one of course is Argentina. Argentina suffered under the Milton Friedman economic shock policy. Argentinians awoke one day, put their credit cards in the machines, and no money came out. All the banks were shut. All their savings and pensions had disappeared. They had to keep going and they devised an amazing system of barter, whereby for example, if you make a painting you exchange it for a coupon and then you can buy fish or shoes. I think we need a counter-migration to under-populated regions of the world. Away from the cities. Permaculture villages, which will say: 'in this community, we don't really accept banking'. Everyone should have a measure of land that is big enough to support them. We know when the goddess or god is with us, because we are plentiful, and we know when she's angry with us because we are without fruit or vegetables ... we must evolve into a fertility cult. I think we need to build sacred groves again ... our dead can be buried near these places, it can be a repository for our DNA ... the idea that couples should make love to celebrate the goddess at certain times of the year is a good idea. We have to change everything, including the existing religion.

Y Would you do it?

J I intend to.

Y Now what are you personally going to do about this, with your land in New Zealand?

J One thing that's brought a lot of joy to our island is the Wwoofa system, Willing Workers on Organic Farms. It's a superb system. It means that you can travel the world with no money. You do five hours work a day and you get all your accommodation and your food sorted out. Well, the ratio of male to female on our island was not in the male's favour at all, until the Wwoofa system, and then we had beautiful young Russian girls and the male population was a lot happier! So we have to take these existing frameworks and work with them so that people can feel free. Freedom is very important, and where you have these eco-villages, you have a sense of liberty, What worries me with the current trends is when we start losing our liberty. I was in New Zealand about three months ago, and I was shocked to see my daughter's friends being so politically aware compared to Brits. In New Zealand people are generally pretty eco-minded.

Y   Why are the young generation so apathetic?

J   I think they've got caught up in the 'me' culture of sticking their heads in computers and forgetting there's a life out there. Everyone wants to be famous. Whatever criticism we might have of our own education, we did at least have religious studies. But now it's lumped in with history and called humanities. Sometimes I get nihilistic and think that at least when we were at school, we saw England when the hedgerows were full and there were thousands of moths in the English villages and all that's gone. Until I got to New Zealand and found a place where I could see into the future. It gave me hope that everything isn't lost. We need to dream. In dreaming about it, you're halfway there. Napoleon said, 'beware of the man who dreams with his eyes open'. You're at school and you're looking out of the window and you're bored with the class. You're thinking of a more desirable reality, so you start visualising where you'd prefer to be, and eventually that comes true.

Y   Where I live in Spain there are a lot people who are self-sufficient.

J   I think things could get worse. The idea that everybody would have all their capital on a computer chip disturbs me greatly but that is the general plan. I think we have to try to live outside of this, I really do.

Y   I think a lot of that technology is inevitable and I don't see technology as being the issue. It's always an interface for other intentions. If we can have a sense of morality restored then that would be good. I'm an anarchist and I don't believe that people should be told what to do. But at the same time we have to protect our own collective interests.

J   That's why we have law. And I'm afraid I believe in law. We have to have law to protect freedom. But it is a problem as we move into a time where extremist elements could take power in large countries. It's been interesting being here in LA. People are frightened to speak. They're not free. This is like communism. I remember going to communist states and this is the same. People will not engage in debate. Which is ironic because Socrates told us that it is the duty of every citizen to engage in debate. While I have to respect the laws of another country, America was known as the bastion of free speech, and it's turned into the opposite. And not to point this out I'd be a traitor to myself. That guy in the bar last night said to me, 'You people from New York, you don't understand, that you just can't talk about things like that'. When pressed he didn't really say why. When it comes to all that 9/11 shit, my view is this: we all enjoy flying around on jets and going around in boats. It's the modern world. And whoever is in power, has inherited this nightmare that guzzles oil. You have to dig up Alaska whether you're a Democrat or a Republican. Because America imports 70–80 per cent of its oil, it makes it vulnerable, and in order for America to keep going at its current pace, it needs to expand its influence in the Eurasian oil fields. If they don't take it, then the Chinese and the Russians will move in. And this is real politics. The point is: 9/11 had to happen because the public were out of step with the reality, the beast, the machine, that we all enjoy. Brajinsky said in '98 that we need a new Pearl Harbour. Just as life follows art, it happened. It needed to happen if we're going to continue to enjoy this way of life. Public opinion had to be shifted. Democracy would never agree for example to putting more weapons into space. So an event like 9/11 was very useful for loosening up more money for defence.

Y But can you envision a world without war?

J I can. But I think we'd have to be honest about that element in man that creates war. I believe in a ritualistic approach to balancing these forces. I think we have to make the most of things. I read an article by Lovelock who did the Gaia hypothesis. He says enjoy yourself now because in 70 years time it will all be gone. He was very negative. It made me kind of angry. Because I found it defeatist. That's why it is necessary to dream. So for 2012 my dream would be to invite various artists to do commissions and come to Great Barrier Island to perform and exhibit there. It's called The Breakfast Club or the Concert at the End of the Earth. I've spoken to quite a lot of promoters and they thought it was a brilliant idea, and that would celebrate my 52nd year and I can't think of anything better to do than to set up an event to ritualise...

Y   To ritualise your birthday?

J   No! It's not, it's December 23rd.

Y   We can ritualise my birthday then.

J   Is that your birthday?

Y   Near it.

J   That's why you think you're Jesus!

Y   Don't get onto messianic complexes with me young man. I've been dealing with your flock all the last six weeks on this tour!

⟨❧⟩

Kenny 'Zulu' Whitmore

by Carrie Reichhardt

IDLER 40 · 2009

IMET CARRIE REICHARDT AT THE THREE KINGS IN
Clerkenwell. I told her I was planning a 'Smash the System' issue of
the *Idler*, and she suggested an interview with Kenny Whitmore.

★

Black panther Kenny 'Zulu' Whitmore has been locked up for more
than 31 years in solitary confinement in Angola, one of the most brutal
prisons in the US, also known as 'the last slave plantation'. He's held in
captivity under brutal and cruel conditions, in a 6x9ft cage. Zulu went
into prison with a fourth-grade education and a speech impediment.
He has not only educated himself for over 30 years, but has also helped
others within the prison complex. Zulu is deeply resolute.

Carrie Reichhardt is an artist and activist living in London. With her
partner she is in the process of covering the entire outside walls of her
house with ceramics and mosaics. They like to refer to their home as
The Treatment Rooms – the UK's only ceramic house of resistance.

Here Zulu discusses with Carrie, life, liberty, being idle and how he
still continues to smash the system.

CR For a man who's been held in solitary for more than three decades, you
must have come up with some interesting ways to be idle. What are
your preferred ways of passing the time?

KZW I am in this cage for 23 hours a day, but I make good use of my time. In
1980, Robert King [released from Angola prison in 2001 after his conviction was overturned], Albert Woodfox [still in Angola though his
conviction was overturned in September 2008] and I started an exercise

routine where we used to get up at 3:30 A.M. and work out for two
hours six days a week. Even when we were separated we kept it up. To
this day I still work out for an hour and a half six days a week.

After that I'll catch the *World News* on NPR [National Public Radio]
and/or meditate until breakfast, which comes between 6:30 and
7:30 A.M. Then I might catch the local news on TV Baton Rouge. At
8 A.M. or thereafter I set up my stand-up desk in the cell – my locker on
top of the table. I write and/or read until 4 P.M. If I am responding to
my many supporters, I write sometimes until 7 P.M. Legal work will
also pass the time.

I take short breaks throughout the day. I read a lot when time allows.
My absolute favourite book is *Native Son* by Richard Wright. Right
now I am reading *Silent Gesture* by Tommie Smith. He and John Carlos
were two of the most courageous brothers in America to raise the black
power salute on the world stage at the 1968 Olympics in Mexico City.

I get one hour on the yard three times a week where I and other guys
run behind the football for an hour.

In solitary confinement one must find something to keep the mind
active or risk going insane, as I have witnessed more than I would have
liked to. For me, everything I do is about self-discipline and continuing to educate myself.

CR You recently spent more than a year in the dungeon of Camp J
Disciplinary Unit; how did that compare with Closed Cell Restriction
[CCR or solitary confinement, where Zulu has spent most of his time
in prison]?

KZW Well, Camp J is the worst disciplinary unit in the system here in
Louisiana. While I was there, I smelled gas, Freeze Plus P [pepper
spray] and mace as regularly as if it was air freshener. Early in the
morning, the guards would gas someone at will. If someone passed out
because of the heat, they would get gassed. If the lady bringing medication said you did or said something to her, they would spray you
down like a cockroach and beat you. You must wear an orange jumpsuit, and when any female comes on the tier, everyone must have it
buttoned all the way up, summer or winter. The food is some shit you
wouldn't give your dog. It is very poorly prepared, and you get a small
amount. I lost 30 pounds in there.

CR Does the disciplinary unit have a canteen?

KZW Yes, once a week you can buy tuna, bread, chips, cookies, etc., but you are not allowed to have a plastic spoon or drinking cup in your cell without being written up for contraband, so you've nothing to use if you want to mix mayonnaise or mustard into your food. You can buy Kool Aid, but if you get caught with a spoon, sugar or a cup, you are sent to Level 1 to start all over [the disciplinary unit has different levels, which you slowly move up].

CR Did they have Yard Call?

KZW Yes, three times a week. You can only wear a T-shirt and shorts under the orange jumpsuit. You are fully restrained – waist chain, and leg irons. Only the leg irons are removed. During the winter months you are given a coat, the coat someone else has just run around the yard in, so I never wore one.

CR What about people's mental health?

KZW Camp J disciplinary unit has a large number of mentally ill dudes. On the tier I was on, I was one cell from a guy who screamed and hollered and talked out loud all the time. The guards used to gas him and have the entire tier sneezing and coughing with our eyes burning. It was a crazy situation.

CR Does the disciplinary unit allow visiting?

KZW Yes, but very few people let their family and friends come because the visiting booth is like 4 x 10ft with a screen separating you; no water nor bathroom. You burn up in there during summer and freeze in winter. Though they have an air conditioner on the wall, it hardly ever works; like the heater.

CR How is CCR, where you are now, different?

KZW Here in CCR you have more political prisoners in this building, which houses 111 dudes. CCR is long-term. Herman Wallace and Albert Woodfox of the Angola 3 stayed in here from April 1972 to March 2008. Robert King did 29 years. I have been held captive here in CCR since 1978, except for a 14-month stay in general population. Then I took my physical freedom [escaped] in 1986. I was free for 24 hours. I guess it's more than what others could expect. In CCR you get three days of yard in a jumpsuit. All restraints are removed. You have your own clothing: three pairs of jeans, three blue shirts, three pairs of socks, three sweatsuits, two winter caps and tennies [trainers]. You get two contact visits per month. Five visitors can come in at a time. We do not have a GED [General Educational Development] programme in CCR nor do they in any cell block. The food is better prepared, but like all over the plantation, we do not get enough fresh vegetables. We get powdered potatoes, old corn and a green salad twice a year – at Thanksgiving and Christmas; fresh fruit once a year at Christmas. In the dormitory where my brothers of the A3, Herman and Albert, are being housed, they have an inmate club with a deli that sells fresh salads, fish and other stuff. This is how I get fresh vegetables. But like anywhere in Angola, you are in prison.

CR   What are your top tips for 'smashing the system'?

KZW   It's going to take a collective effort by you the people. You need to petition your legislators and politicians and DEMAND change. You have more power than you may realise. Smash the system by saying no to new prisons and yes to new schools. Here in the US, more than two million people are incarcerated. The state of Louisiana Department of Corrections has a budget of nearly $700 million dollars to warehouse people for 40–50 years, with no sign of rehabilitation programmes. The American public is paying members of the pardon and parole boards up to $80,000 a year to deny people pardon and parole; voters need to make them put pardon and parole into practice. You hired the politicians – you are the employers; they the employees.

CR   How do you continue to fight the system from a 6x9ft cell?

KZW   I use my pen; I have made friends worldwide; I educate, educate and educate.

CR   What changes do you think there will be to the system with Barack Obama, a black man, in the White House?

KZW   By the American voters electing their first African-American to be commander-in-chief I truly hope it means that the country is finally ready to move out of the racist time-warp it has been stuck in for too many centuries, and we as a nation are ready to move forward.

On the criminal justice system, I think it would be unrealistic to think that Obama, after his first day in his new job on January 20, would go into the Oval Office, take his pen, and change a system that has been in place for the last 100 years. It ain't going to happen.

Obama has a full plate with the financial crisis – a crisis that was created by multi-billion-dollar banks, investment houses and the largest companies in the world: Bear Stearns, Merrill Lynch, Lehman Brothers, AIG. The sub-prime mortgage crisis has meant thousands of people have lost their homes. African-Americans were hit hard in this scam, and those homeless people are left holding a $700 billion bill to pay for the very motherfuckers who kicked them out of their homes. So Obama will first have to tackle the crisis that George W. Bush and his cronies created. But I do think that during his second term we will begin to see some changes in the criminal justice system with his choice of attorney general and the possibility of his appointing two new justices to the US Supreme Court. But let's wait and see.

CR What do you think is the difference between Angola the slave plantation and Angola the prison?

KZW The 13th Amendment outlawed slavery within the borders of the United States, but that didn't include prison. The day it came into effect, prison became the new plantation – they legalised it. Angola the prison has basically the same rules to govern its slaves as did Angola the plantation. The only difference is the name changed from plantation to prison.

CR Do you think that Obama really represents change?

KZW I am like most African-Americans in this country – I want to believe Barack Obama represents change, because he knows first-hand of African suffering in this country. I think he's bringing fresh ideas to the table, like sitting down with Iran's head of state without pre-conditions, and de-privatising the student-loan system.

But I do not want to pre-judge him in the way I and my comrades Herman Wallace and Albert Woodfox of the A3 have been. Albert recently won a new trial, and on November 12 [2008], a federal judge ruled that he be released on bail pending re-trial. But Louisiana's Attorney General Buddy Caldwell has pre-judged Albert to be a flight risk due to some unsubstantiated charges from 1967, and is blocking his release. So I won't pre-judge Obama.

Ona Move. Free Zulu, A3 and Move 9
Kenny Zulu Whitmore
86468 CCR, Upper C #11, LA State Prison, Angola, LA 70712 USA
www.freezulu.co.uk

Oliver James

by Tom Hodgkinson

IDLER 42 · 2009

PSYCHOLOGIST OLIVER JAMES IS THE AUTHOR OF THE best-selling *Affluenza*. He has also made many television and radio programmes on childhood. Here he discusses the importance of play, how the credit crunch might help us to spend more time with our families, and the innate dysfunction of politicians. We start by talking about my then recently published book, *The Idle Parent*.

★

TH *The Idle Parent* is really a mixture of two things. One was my own experience in having small children and finding it very hard work – stressful, sleep-depriving – and wondering why. And the other was a bit of D. H. Lawrence where he says, 'leave the child alone.' That hit me as real revelation. I thought, well, for one thing, that sounds like a lot less work! And if the child is more left alone, it will develop its own inner resources and self-sufficiency. So to leave them alone is good for the parent and good for the child.

OJ I think that it all depends what is meant by 'leave them alone'. For quite a lot of parents, that is exactly what they do: they just leave them in front of the TV. I imagine that what D. H. Lawrence was on about was something like the ideas of the psychoanalyst Donald Winnicott. He wrote on the theory of play. In a book called *Playing and Reality* he is very much about not trying to fill the child up with all of you and your stuff, but letting the child discover for itself about its own body and mind, and the relationship of those things to the 'not-me', to the external world. To learn that play and art and creativity happen in the place between me and not-me, the transitional space ...

TH Shouldn't it be easy: all you have to do to create that transitional space is to go into the next room and supervise them a bit less?

OJ Supervising them doesn't help, but on the other hand, playing with them definitely does. I went with my son Louis to Fundays yesterday; he is just four and has a very considerable fantasy life. It's a fantastic space: they go down huge slides and jump in ball pools. Our game is to take three teddies with us and torment them. He throws them down the big slide and I put on the voice of the teddies, who say: 'Oh no, it's terrifying, I don't want to go,' and he says, 'You've got to go.' And he takes great pleasure in throwing them into the pools. It would be much harder for him to get that kind of action going on his own. I suppose the argument of *The Idle Parent* is that the natural most healthy state for a child is to be in a state of fantasy play. That is utterly correct. Doing the fantasy play with them, led by them, and going where their fantasy takes them, and at the same time using your own imagination and childlike characteristics, that is good. Leave them alone, no, not in the sense of abandonment.

TH But some parents just can't stand to play like that. I think about my mother. There is nothing she liked less than playing with small children and taking them to the swings.

OJ I have the distinct impression that mothers very rarely engage in fantasy play with their children because they're so busy with the logistics. I look around me at Fundays, and it's full of fathers who really enter into it. I think around my friends and I notice that's very true: the men are more engaged with the fantasy play side of things than the women.

TH So we are agreed on the importance of play. But the whole weight of the culture is against it. What used to be called playschool, for example, is now called pre-school, in other words, the first step to taming and enclosing the children. They're preparing them for school. Primary school is a preparation for secondary school, secondary school is a preparation for university, university is a preparation for work. The state, ever since probably the Tudors, seems to be keen on a hard-working populace. The phrase 'hard-working families' keeps popping up, used by both the Tories and the government. Both parents are encouraged to be in full-time jobs; the child should be dropped off at nursery. Where is the time for play, for the children or for the parents?

OJ Well quite. What's been disastrous since the Second World War has been the hijacking of education by what used to be known as personnel departments but are now known as Human Resources. The invention of the IQ test I believe occurred in the First World War because they didn't have a way of classifying people and deciding what do with them, so they developed psychological testing. Then you have the collapse of the class system, or at least the illusion of a meritocracy is created, after the Second World War. The key point is that once you've said 'anyone can be Prime Minister', anyone can be a chief executive, there then arose the problem: but how the hell do we decide who? And this is the point at which education became essentially a method of trying to work out who gets the top jobs and the money. The whole premise has been that it's vital to educate the population in order to have economic growth. This is a premise that Professor Alison Wolf, in her book *Does Education Matter?* [Penguin, 2002] has disproved. That spending more money on education once you're a developed nation does not improve productivity in any way, shape or form. But nonetheless the whole premise of the system is that you've got to work your arse off at school in order to do well. And I think that play gets lost in that context.

TH And play shouldn't really be something that we have to pay for. But it's become commodified. There are these costly fun machines on sale, like the Nintendo Wii, which remind me of the ridiculous distracting sports in Aldous Huxley's *Brave New World*: centrifugal bumble-puppy and electromagnetic golf. You have to buy lots of toys. But play should not be in the arena of commodity. Kids really can play with anything: everyone knows the endless possibilities offered by a cardboard box. There is a nice essay on child's play by Robert Louis Stevenson where he reminds us how fantastically imaginative children are, and remembers he and his brother playing with their porridge, making it into desert islands. Literally anything lying around can be played with – twigs, dishcloths. Do we really need to be spending so much money on children? How do we escape from working too hard and spending too much money?

OJ The vicious circle is well-described in your book. Both parents work flat out in order to afford the things with which to distract the children that they're too tired to play with when they get home. I think that at the heart of it is the disinvestment of the domestic household economy, and which hopefully the credit crunch will reverse. But for the time being, women in particular now see the home as a kind of fuelling station for work.

TH And often a conflict-filled place. Parents get a job to get away from the dysfunctional family.

OJ The guiding light that *The Idle Parent* shines on this thing is the idea that at the heart we're far too invested in our work life. Is this not absolutely the right moment to be publishing the book? People can just wake up and smell the coffee.

TH Orwell said England is in a deep sleep. Maybe we are now waking up.

OJ The obvious solution to me, to the credit crunch problem is simply for people to work a much shorter week. And to have lower income. That is happening naturally. But unfortunately with workaholics like Brown and Mandelson and James Purnell in charge, it's hard to see that sort of solution being promoted. There's a golden opportunity for the Tories to say, 'Look, we've got a much better answer here.' I think also another key issue for the idle parent is what gender they are. In some regards more men spend time with their children than used to be the case. That is a real change and desirable. Whereas it's gone in the opposite direction for women. Women have been brought up to be Bridget Jones.

TH Yes, and then to go from party girl about town with witty companions and intellectual stimulation to sitting at home like a drudge must be very hard. But there are all sorts of avenues to be explored. One couple I know, both parents went down to a three-day-week each. So they had slightly more than one full-time salary, but they had four days each when they were at home mucking about with the kid.

OJ That's the way to go. Hopefully in 50 years' time, that's what everybody will be doing.

TH There's not much point in thinking that government will ever do anything helpful because it's in the nature of government to be hardworking, violent, bureaucratic. That's what Parliamentarians are like: ever since Cromwell, when the MPs went into work as normal at the House of Commons on Christmas Day. Cromwell took all the gambling, swearing and wenching out of the army. Is there any point in hectoring government?

OJ It's utterly hopeless. I think they are a self-elected group of workaholics who are completely addicted to the prestige of being admired for their status. They're people who felt powerless and inadequate as small children and who have been compensating for it ever since by trying to feel powerful or wanting to be perceived as powerful.

TH That means idle parenting will not produce the next Prime Minister.

OJ One of the great questions for any society, and possibly the most important question, is how you can have rulers who are emotionally well-adjusted and fulfilled people. Almost by definition in the English-speaking world, there's absolutely no way you're going to get them. In Denmark, I suspect that they do get them to a greater extent, because if you display any signs of narcissism, of me-me-me behaviour, you become a social pariah. People like Mandelson or Brown would be regarded as complete ...

TH The government is all over everything ... they are all over education. They say that they are preparing children for the workplace, to be efficient workers. The Number 10 website is quite shocking and offensive: they have a strategy for us for our whole lives, from birth to school to work.

OJ The logical conclusion of the whole thing will be when they allow McDonalds to administer their own GCSEs. Corporations provide qualifications. They make no apology for this sort of thing whatsoever. 'To survive in the global economy, we must ...'

TH *The Idle Parent* is about strategies of resistance. I want to show people that they are not alone, and also give some practical strategies to deal with these issues.

OJ Well in *The Idle Parent* you remind people that you can make up games, for example.

TH You can make up stories. As adults we become a bit useless and nervous, disabled. We are not encouraged to develop our own imaginations, because other people do it for you. I remember camping once and it was story time. But the torch had run out of batteries. So I had to make up a story. It was frightening, but once I'd started it flowed beautifully.

OJ I used to do that with my daughter Olive: I'd take a deep breath every time they asked me, because it requires such an act of effort, to think up a fantasy story. But every time I did, it was so rewarding.

TH We rely too much on books. When our baby was small we had so many of these parenting books. And the more you read, the more useless you feel. The more you are told what to do by an authority, the less you believe in the authority of yourself.

OJ I think there are lots of books that are useful, but I think that the whole shift that began with Gina Ford and *Supernanny* on television is wrong ... it's presented as being for the child, but it's actually about the needs of the parents.

TH What we've done is put Henry [my youngest son, then aged 4] outside the front door when he's had awful tantrums. Is that good?

OJ I don't think that's at all a good idea. You have to stay in the presence of the child and try to understand what's bugging it. It may be something simple. Stay with the child and keep calm. That's difficult because it usually happens at a point when you're tired, and you're dying to get out of there and go and have a drink or watch telly, you want a bit of downtime. That's why they're screaming, because you're hurrying them in order to get on with your evening. You're the one with the extra software and hardware so it's really incumbent on you to get a grip, take a deep breath and engage.

TH Isn't there a deeper problem here which is that nuclear families are by their nature dysfunctional?

OJ Yes, that's a good point and in *The Idle Parent* extremely well made.

TH When our first son was born, I remember thinking, we're not going to make any of those mistakes that other parents make. He's going to be calm, confident, happy and we're going to enjoy it. Three years later, there's screaming, door slamming, terrible scenes. And they seem to happen in every family, probably without exception.

OJ Yes, without exception. The idea that it could be any other way is ridiculous. Where does anybody get the idea that it could be any other way? You don't get enough sleep, you're hungry and that's because, as you say in the book, we don't live in collectivist societies. The grandparents, as you bravely spell out in the book, your own parents, simply don't contribute nearly as much as you would like. Grandparents have their own lives. It's grandparents' liberation, women's liberation and everybody is an individual.

TH My parents were of quite a selfish generation, liberated to the point of self-indulgence.

OJ This is a big difference between Western Europe and English-speaking Europe, where there are still extended families which they help each other in a way that ours don't. And there are places like China: I only met one person there who had been brought up by their biological mother. Every single other person had been brought up by their grandmother.

TH Actually my own mother was brought up by her grandmother, as her mother was busy running a shop.

OJ In China it would seem insane for the mother to stop work, because the mother is young, full of vim, able-bodied.

TH In the Ukraine the young girls will leave their two-year-olds with their mothers so they can come further West and explore work opportunities. So is that Chinese thing healthy?

OJ I think it's absolutely fine. I don't think there's any problem with it at all.

TH So the mother doesn't have to be with the child 24/7?

OJ Not at all. It's incredible what a good deal they get in China in early infancy, and I swear there will be much lower rates of personality disorder in Japan or China, because it's the first three years which is the foundation of it. Admittedly after the age of four they have an even more insane educational obsession than we have. But they're better prepared for it.

TH So what happens in those first three years?

OJ Well, it's child-centred care. They completely tune into the baby, it's feed on demand ... everything is done according to what suits baby. Which is how it has to be. That's how you become sane and independent. The great farce of modern parenting is the idea, 'oh they've got to learn to become independent from as young an age as possible.' Absolutely not. The way you become independent is by having your dependency needs met in your first three years. That gives you a very strong sense of who you are, and that everything will be all right, and you'll be able to withstand a great deal of things going wrong.

TH The Gordon Brown vision of things where babies are in full-time nursery from six months and the parents are both in full-time jobs is not going to provide that.

OJ Well, if truth be told, there are two things about that. One is, that in New Labour, none of them, man or woman, as far as I know, has ever looked after their baby. No one in the New Labour hierarchy has been left holding the baby or indeed throughout the élite. Funnily enough, I do not know of a single person in the New Labour élite who sent their children to a daycare nursery. They all have had nannies. So what's good enough for people on the sink estates and single mothers who are ripped apart from their children, is not good enough for little Tamsin or Tarquin. And then privately what New Labourites say is:

'actually, these single mothers are so screwed up, that the way to break the cycle of deprivation is to get the children away from them as soon as possible' – almost effectively adoption – 'put them in a day nursery where their educational attainment will be boosted.' Actually, this doesn't last; it can improve their cognitive faculties temporarily, but it then falls right away. They say: 'you don't realise just how badly these mothers are going to look after their kids. It's much better to get them away, get them working in Tesco's, contributing to the economy, boosting their self-esteem by getting some income while their kids are looked after by – oh, actually, by other single mothers who've left *their* children in a nursery! So badly paid women looking after children badly is all you get.

TH The other problem with government is that they see the situation as 'them and us'. The masses. They don't see themselves as in the same boat. 'We go out and help people, the government wants to help you.' It's just so patronising. All the good things that happen in the world come from the bottom up, from communities and individuals, not authorities. The good things are the things that people organise for themselves.

OJ Winnicot has the theory that 10 per cent of people are what he called 'democratic' personalities. That's as close he gets to someone who is nearly mentally healthy – and let's face it, nearly no one is – about 10 per cent are not 'me-me-me' people. They are genuinely trying to be supportive to other people. But they are not people who live for other people, they live for themselves. We all know those people: whenever you have dealings with them, you come away feeling more joyful and glad to be alive. And his theory is that society only keeps functioning thanks to these people. And none of them become leaders. None of them are workaholics, but they just spread a little dust around them. It might be the bus driver.

TH There's a danger though in going the other way, which is over-mothering, and this is another thing that D. H. Lawrence attacks, making a dependent, sickly, whining child.

OJ There is a large well-founded body of evidence on what's called 'over-controlling parenting', and it is undoubtedly very seriously bad for the mental health of children. It depresses them. It can actually drive them crazy if it goes too far. That's a particular subset of the general national phenomenon where little Tarquin has to be constantly improved from when he wakes up to when he goes to bed, when he's not left to play on his Gameboy. The over-controlling parent interferes with everything Tarquin does. With the perfectionist picky parent, usually love is conditional so Tarquin does not get any love unless he comes first. And he very rarely gets love anyway. The other sort of course is the earth mother who can't find an emotional life or identity of her own and merges with the baby. She goes on treating the child as a baby and won't let it go. Obviously that can lead to very serious mental illness if it goes too far.

If the child is an extension of the mother the mother can't allow it to separate and be independent. She is constantly fearful that something is going to happen. Not because it's got to be a success, but because the mother needs it to be dependent on her. From a psychiatric point of view it's real – it's always been there but it's exacerbated by the culture. Henry is four, and he enjoys helping getting the logs and finding eggs, and mucking out the stable. All the kids can lay the table. For most us now work is just sitting at a screen, which is not a very noble thing for the kids to copy. If they don't feel useful, then they'll sense that they're somehow an encumbrance, and that will make them whine. Rather than a welcome addition to the household workforce, which is how we should see children, we turn them into whining useless little princelings, hence all the fussiness with food.

It's a very simple but important point.

David Hockney

by Tom Hodgkinson

IDLER 43 · 2010

Iᴛ ɪs ɴᴏᴛ ᴇᴠᴇʀʏ ᴅᴀʏ ᴛʜᴀᴛ ʏᴏᴜ ɢᴇᴛ ᴛʜᴇ ᴏᴘᴘᴏʀᴛᴜɴɪᴛʏ ᴛᴏ
meet a living genius, so I was thrilled when David Hockney
accepted my request for an interview. I had read his book *Secret
Knowledge*, a beautiful account of the use of the camera in art from the
Renaissance to the present day. Art historians know that portraiture
suddenly became more realistic around 1400 to 1500. What Hockney
shows is that, in the 15th century, artists began to use lenses to project
an image on to a piece of paper, which they then traced to get a realistic image. That's why Renaissance art looks so photographic when
compared with medieval art.

It is Hockney's argument that the camera, in fact, far from being the
only realistic means of depicting reality, is only one of many, and a
rather boring one at that. It has come, though, to dominate the world.
Its rise in the Renaissance comes with a new way of looking at the
world: medieval art tends to look at objects from many perspectives;
the camera has only one. It is fascinating to note in the book that
Cubism, which was a revolt away from perspective and the camera-
based view, has more in common with medieval art than with art from
the 'realistic' period of the 16th to 19th centuries.

Hockney, who is 72, says that control of images gradually moved
from the Church to the mass media. But now he thinks that the mass
media is starting to lose control of the image. Could the image return
to the people, in that case?

I sent Hockney a copy of the *Idler* and he left a message on the
answerphone with the comment: 'It's all about images.' We fixed up a
time, and so one cold February afternoon I arrived at York station. A
few years ago, Hockney moved with his household back to Bridlington

in East Yorkshire, home of his mother.

I was picked up at the station by Jonathan, who is helping Hockney with the computer side of his new work. Jonathan has a smallholding nearby with his wife and son. He spends weekends at home and the week at Hockney's. One current project, he tells me, is a reworking of the French painter Claude's 'Sermon on the Mount' from 1656. They used a computer to clean up the original painting, thus revealing the colours and the light. Now Hockney is painting a new version of the picture for his upcoming show at the Royal Academy in 2012.

We arrive at Hockney's house after a drive of about an hour. Bridlington is a small remote town on the east coast of Yorkshire. 'We like it here,' Hockney had said on the phone. 'It's quiet. We are left alone.' His house is a Thirties double-fronted detached red-brick villa. From the outside it looks like any other house in the street.

Inside the house is a stylish and witty jumble of dark colours, flowers, little signs, paintings and books. There is a double-height atrium and a gallery staircase, which lends the house a theatrical air. Jonathan shows me into the front room, which is packed with books. By the door there is a pipe rack with a sign above it that reads: 'Smoking Area'. Hockney appears in a paint-splattered pinstripe suit with braces and a green polo shirt. He has the glittering, piercing eyes of Picasso and the same sense of mischief: the first thing that strikes me is that his face seems permanently on the edge of cracking into a smile or a grin.

Hockney explains that he lives here with his studio assistant, Jean-Pierre, and John, his partner of 20 years. He bought the house from his sister. Around the corner he has bought a gigantic 10,000-square-foot warehouse, just five minutes' drive away. He has a studio and a flat in Kensington but rarely uses it these days. 'I get too distracted in London,' he said. 'And to get a studio of this size in London, I would have to drive through half an hour of ugliness.' He is right on the sea, so he can get that feeling of open space that led him to move to California in the Sixties. 'Was it the light that attracted you there?' I ask. 'Yes, and the sex,' he replies.

When they feel like a break, Hockney and John get in the car and jump on the overnight ferry to Zeebrugge, catching the tacky cabaret on the way. From there they drive all over Europe. Hockney can't stand airports or trains because you can't smoke. In the car, he can smoke, and they can drive wherever they like. One favourite destination is the spa town of Baden-Baden in Germany.

He says he likes my anarchic writings, that he hasn't voted for many years, and that he is not political although he is interested in politics. He believes that we need beauty. He says that we all need both to take more personal responsibility for our own lives, and to be more neighbourly.

He tells me with delight about the 'Sermon on the Mount' project. He says that the original painting is very dark, but they discovered that it had been covered in soot from a fire. They cleaned it up on the computer. 'What attracted me was the sense of space in that picture.' I say that surely the subject matter was also interesting (I'm personally fascinated when artists return to medieval themes). And he says, yes, it is the great text on good ethics. He says he is not particularly religious but that he is very interested in religion. His mother was a strict Methodist. On his bookshelves is every conceivable sort of book: there is a lot of history and biography. There is Ted Hughes, Hardy, Evelyn Waugh.

I reflect that the rise of the camera in art coincides with the Reformation and a completely new theological attitude. We become more isolated after the Renaissance.

We go through into dinner and sit down in the dining room at an oval, polished wood table. The walls are painted dark red and there are heavy velvet curtains in the windows. Along the sideboard twelve candles have been lit, and a log fire burns in the grate. It is all very cosy and convivial. Hockney seats me at the head of the table and sits on my left. He continues smoking through the meal. He no longer drinks alcohol, and has a couple of alcohol-free beers instead. John serves up a delicious pigeon pie with mashed potatoes. We drink red wine.

Over dinner Hockney talks. He has an endless store of anecdotes and ideas, and speaks with great clarity, subtlety and humour. He remembers going to the cinema twice a week as a boy in Bradford, to see the Westerns. 'When I was thirteen,' he recalls, 'the man next to me put his hand on my cock. I've loved cinemas ever since.' He talks about the gay scene in Seventies New York: 'We used to go to the bathhouses. It was very democratic: everyone's a prostitute and everyone's a client.' But they were wild, he says. 'My friend would say, "David, is this heaven or hell?" And I said, "If you're asking, it's probably hell."' AIDS killed many of his friends and put an end to that scene.

Hockney talks about his love for opera and tells me I must listen to it properly. He says that you need to put some effort into it, and then you are rewarded. Not everybody, though, gets the point: he tells a story of taking Billy Wilder to the opera. The show started at eight. 'Afterwards Billy said, "During the performance, at midnight I looked at my watch. It said eight-fifteen."'

Hockney says that, for 50 years, he has done exactly what he wanted to do every day, and that this is the essence of being an artist or a bohemian. It's not about the money, he says. 'If you can live that sort of life, you are rich. I mean, sometimes I have been working for other people, doing set design. But I have chosen to work with them.' He says he has only really been unhappy once, when his partner Peter Schlesinger left him, in 1970. 'It's only when you're unhappy that you realise you must have been happy before.'

He is interested in all the arts and says that he was rather dismayed by Mick Jagger's attitude to opera when he met him at a party in the Sixties. 'He was very much performing the rebel pose, and sneered when I asked what he thought of opera. But surely as a singer, you would be interested in good singing?' And this is perhaps one thing that really marks Hockney out from most artists. He is interested in everything, whereas artists tend to be rather self-absorbed and often take absolutely no interest in other people's work whatsoever. Hockney is different; he is drenched in culture. He is also extremely well-read.

I say that I have just had my first bespoke suit made, and Hockney comments on the importance of good tailoring. He says he has always had his suits made, and he advises friends that there is no point going to the gym or on diets to lose weight. 'It's actually a question of good tailoring,' he says. 'Anyone can look good in a properly fitting suit.' He says that never have people in general been so badly dressed, and he includes Tony Blair, one of his hate figures. 'I was appalled that he wore just a lounge suit to the Queen Mother's funeral,' he says. 'He was trying to be like an ordinary person. But an ordinary person would have had the manners to go out to Moss Bros. and hire a morning suit for an event like that.'

He shows me to my bedroom. On the landing wall is his famous portrait 'Mrs and Mrs Clarke and Percy': can it be the original? My room has a huge brass bed, two comfy chairs by the window and 'a power shower', as Hockney points out with some delight. He seems to take great pleasure in enunciating each word, almost as if he is mocking them. It is the same when he tells me about breakfast arrangements. 'Take anything you like. It's self-service.' To get his voice, imagine a (funnily enough) slightly less camp version of Alan Bennett. A copy of *Secret Knowledge* has been placed by the bed. On the shelf is a collection of Evelyn Waugh stories. I take it down to find that the dust jacket is marking a page right in the middle of 'Scott-King's Modern Europe', a coincidence, as I had read that very story just before Christmas. It is about a Latin teacher who, having witnessed the horrors of modern Europe, decides that to teach Classics is more important than ever. I don't sleep very well. I must have smoked about 15 cigarettes since arriving; the room is hot and I am used to the cold, and my head is buzzing with everything I have seen and heard.

I come down for breakfast at half-past eight. The kitchen has black and white squared lino. It opens into a small courtyard garden, with pots and a barbecue. A couple of builders walk in and out. Jonathan comes in for his coffee. Hockney is sitting at the table on his iPhone, a black and white flat cap on his head. 'Morning!' I say. He tells me to help myself to toast and tea, which I do. The morning papers are spread out on the table. 'I'm drawing,' says Hockney. Sure enough, he is drawing the hyacinths on the kitchen table on his iPhone, with his thumb. Hockney is fascinated by the possibilities that are offered by the computer in terms of changing both how images are made and also how they are distributed.

After breakfast, Hockney drives me to his studio, which is around the corner. It is a vast warehouse on an industrial estate, with natural light that comes in through ceiling skylights. He shows me giant canvases of trees that he has been painting. He is going to paint them in each of the four seasons. There is also a giant reproduction of Claude's 'Sermon on the Mount', and along the walls are various new interpretations of the painting by Hockney. He says the beauty of such a large studio is that you can stand right back and take a good look at a large canvas. There is a scale model of the rooms at the Royal Academy which Hockney will take for his 2012 exhibition. I accept a cup of tea and a Camel Wide and we sit down to record an interview.

★

DH The invention of photography was the invention of chemicals to fix an image, meaning, it wasn't the invention of the camera. You can't name the inventor of the camera, but you can name the inventor of photography. Cameras are natural phenomena, really. But an optical projection of the world, which is what a camera does, is not really the way we see the world. Cameras just see surfaces, and we see space. I think photography might actually have made us see the world as very dull.

TH And how would the world have looked in the medieval period?

DH Well, I will point out that before that change [in the Renaissance] you had very few shadows. Nobody painted shadows. Chinese, Japanese, Persian, Indian; you name it, they didn't paint shadows. The Chinese might have said, 'Well, everything's a shadow.' I ask: do we see shadows? Well, we do and we don't. We can decide not to. In a way, it was the arrival of shadows that made me see that maybe this is optical, an optical technology, simply because it needed shadows. I was surprised that art historians hadn't noticed that. Most art historians are Eurocentric, they're very European-trained. I've always been interested in photography. A friend of mine was talking about art and photography, and I said, 'Henry, is photography an art?' And he said, 'I always thought it was a hobby!' Very funny, and there is some truth in it. Actually, for the early photographers, it was a hobby, wasn't it, because you had to be quite rich to do it. The arrival of photography slowly shifted power in the 19th century and created what we had for most of the 20th century, which is mass media. Technology did it. And technology is going to take it away.

TH That also coincides with the worst century there's ever been for totalitarianism and bloodshed.

DH You needed control of the media to be able to get away with what Stalin or Hitler did, or Mao, and you could: in the mid-20th century, if you controlled the media, you controlled all information. By about 1930 it was possible to do that. Now we're moving out of that time. It's probably now not possible.

TH But isn't the information still coming via big American companies like Google?

DH Yeah. They are a bit frightening. I read your piece about it [*We Want Everyone: Facebook and the New American Right*]. And I must admit, I wouldn't go on Facebook. If you want to keep your privacy, you have to be very careful. We do have a website, but I haven't done much on it, simply because I don't want to deal with people sending me things.

TH I closed down the *Idler* forum because they started getting nasty.

DH Yeah. I'm not sure that Internet democracy will be very good. It could be terrible, couldn't it? But there's a good and a bad side to everything; there's a minimum of two sides. There's always going to be a bad side and it depends how it's managed, I suppose.

TH Going back to the transition from medieval to Renaissance and later culture, most of those medieval pictures that you show in the book are absolutely packed with people, and then around the Renaissance you get the focus on one person. I think also of the difference between Joshua Reynolds and Hogarth: Hogarth has little characters all over the place, very funny and clearly not done with the camera.

DH Reynolds had a camera that folded up to look like a book, which is interesting, meaning it was hidden. He gave lectures saying that you shouldn't use it too much. He did it to get his likenesses, simply because it makes it easier and quicker.

TH Had you really seen that isolation of the individual subject before? It seems to come along with the camera.

DH Er, there are the Fayum portraits, which are about 2,000 years old. They found them in the desert sand and they are rather individualistic. The argument about the Renaissance has always been that it was humanism that did it. But my argument is that it is more likely to have been technology. For instance: the 'Mona Lisa'. Why was it really interesting? Well, one of the reasons is that it is one of the first paintings to have very, very soft shadows on the face; the edges blended. He obviously saw that through cameras; Leonardo talks about cameras. People see it and think there's something very realistic about it ... but you know, there is the famous story of when the Jesuits went to China. They were fascinated by China, and realised it was a very advanced place. The scholars ran it. One of them painted the Empress of China. When she looked at it, she said: 'I can assure you, the left side of my face is the same colour as the right side of my face.' Very good.

TH I don't get it.

DH She was talking about the shadows. The left side is the same colour. She didn't see the shadows. It's interesting: you start asking yourself, do I see shadows? The first dramatic use of shadows, in a way, is Caravaggio. I'm pointing out now that Caravaggio invented Holly-

wood lighting. It's very close to it. And if you think about it, the lighting had to be the sun, because it would be the only thing that would be
that bright. It's not talked about much. But if you look at a Caravaggio,
you rarely see a scene lit like that in painting, only in films, later.
Interesting subject, shadows. Interesting, yeah.

TH   The camera is not reality because it's only a tiny millisecond.

DH   I'll show you something. This is about the medieval world and the
difference. I did this diagram 20 years ago. In pictures, we know: that's
the world, that's the horizon, that's the vanishing point. The viewer is
here, and the viewer is an immobile point. And that, theoretically, is at
infinity. If the infinity is God, this and this will never meet. If this
moves, then this moves. That's perspective as we know it. But in the
medieval world, perspective is more often the reverse, meaning you
could see both sides of the altar. The altar would be like that, not like
that. OK, if you see both sides, that means you're in movement. You've
moved. That means that infinity is everywhere; God is everywhere,
including within you.

TH   Rather than the Puritan's distant point.

DH   We're stuck with this [the new way of seeing things].

TH   It's the same in literature, because if you think about *The Canterbury
Tales*, there are many points of view and many stories, all in one book.
And compare that with *The Pilgrim's Progress*, which is one lonely jour-
ney through the world. It seems a similar thing is happening in art.

DH   Absolutely, parallels, yeah. We've accepted perspective, and we think
everyone else has got it wrong. But they didn't. They didn't get it
wrong. Actually, there's no such thing. The Chinese use isometric
perspective. It means that all the lines are parallel. They don't meet.
Western perspective began with Brunelleschi in about 1412 in
Florence. He makes a painting of the Baptistry. Ten years ago, I'd been
thinking about this, and then I had a flash and it suddenly dawned on
me what he could have done. I realised he was supposed to have sat
inside the Duomo in Florence and made this representation of the
Baptistry which was in perspective. I point out that the Baptistry is an
octagonal building. It does have sides. We went there, and set up a
panel exactly the same size as his, and put it on an easel. And then, with
a five-inch-diameter concave mirror, projected the Baptistry on to the
panel. It acts as a lens and it will project back. You will point out that
Brunelleschi wouldn't have known this. Well, he would. Florence in

1412 was perhaps the most advanced city in the world, certainly very up to date with technology. Brunelleschi was very secretive and he was an architect, and in a way, this is the architect's way of looking at the world. The vanishing point makes it all the same time, it fixes it, whereas a narrative painter is telling a story: time flows. So there's no reason why a narrative painter would have devised perspective.

TH So the photograph is just a glimpse in time, and therefore much less real than a painting which is taking in a whole range of times and angles? [On the phone a couple of weeks later, Hockney talks about the use of perspective in crucifixion paintings. 'One of the first to use perspective was Masaccio's "Crucifixion", 1420. The crucifixion is an odd form of execution, because there is no before and after, no action. So you can depict suffering. With perspective there are gains and losses: you lose the narrative flow, but you gain a better feeling of the volume of the body.']

DH If you look at the medieval world and you look at the Chinese world at the same time, they have very sophisticated pictures. I found this out in a film we did about the Chinese scroll. I was fascinated by the different perspectives. I asked a scholar of Chinese art why China declined so much from the 17th century, when it was very, very well advanced, to the mid-19th century, when it wasn't. What had happened? And I was given two answers: one was that they'd lost their intellectual curiosity, which might have been the case; but the other was that there was superior military technology elsewhere, meaning more accurate guns and bigger ships, and so on. I immediately connected that with perspective, because when you set up perspective, you set up triangulation; with triangulation you can fire cannons more accurately, and that's what it was used for. The Chinese didn't have that technology; they'd rejected it, rejected it as not very human. Which is interesting, isn't it? They had rejected the idea of a vanishing point, because it makes you immobile. I think it was something like the 11th century. They were very sophisticated people, and their art is. I tended at one time to think that it was all a bit the same, like many people. Until you really get into it, and then you find that it isn't at all. I got very interested in Chinese scrolls. You look at landscape in a different way: you move through it, like we do [in life]. In a way, one of my interests in this painting ['The Sermon on the Mount'] was its depiction of a very big space indeed. It's very clever: it makes you feel you go round the mountain. I was attracted to it. You'll see it, and then think about it later, and what you don't realise is that you start cleaning the painting in your head. The subject is the Sermon on the Mount; Christ and his disciples are stood at the top; people at the bottom listening ... but that subject isn't that obvious when it's very dark like that but the space is obvious, and the space is very big ... I'm attracted to big spaces. From all of Claude's paintings, this is highly unusual, because you have deep space on the left and right side, and what's in the middle is closest to you, which is rather like a reverse perspective might be, whereas in most of his other paintings, the deep space is in the middle and the things close to you are at the sides, like a theatre set.

TH Cubism takes off around the same time as photography is developed.

DH Cubism was a rejection of perspective, and the first rejection for 550 years. In a way, it is saying, well, we don't see the world like that, we see it in glimpses, we put it together, we see with memory. Because we see with memory, we're all seeing something different, even if we're looking at the same thing. That's why cloning somebody ... would you clone all the memory in them? Can you? I doubt it. Meaning, you then wouldn't see the same things. But we tend to think we do. We don't ask these questions. We do have a visual culture, but it's not very critical.

Ian Bone & Ray Roughler-Jones

by Tom Hodgkinson

IDLER 43 · 2010

I WAS PUT IN TOUCH WITH IAN BONE BY OUR MUTUAL
friend, Jock Scot. I'd always found Bone's *Class War* magazine a bit
frightening, while obviously appreciating the wit, but Bone was
good and witty company. The third member of our converstional
group was Ray Roughler-Jones, old friend of Ian's and Portobello Road
legend.

*

When it comes to being a professional idler, I take my hat off to those
two grandmasters of anti-capitalist slack, Ian Bone and Ray Roughler-
Jones. Bone is best known for *Class War*, his provocative, aggressive,
anarchist paper, and his excellent biography, *Bash the Rich*, an account
of a working-class, bohemian life. Being working class for Bone is not
about slaving in the factories, but about pursuing a life of intellectual
curiosity, pleasure and freedom; in a sense, not working. Ray
Roughler-Jones is Bone's old friend, who I remember from my days
working at the Rough Trade shop in Portobello Road in 1990. Ray edits
the *Roughler* magazine and puts on all sorts of events in the W11 area,
often working with the actress Anna Chancellor, who starred in *Four
Weddings and a Funeral*. Another project is the YouTube channel
Roughler TV. He has been on the dole for about 40 years. Bone is
publishing Ray's autobiography, *Drowning on Dry Land*, on his indie
publishing label, Tangent Books. Another release on Tangent Books
is *Hartmann the Anarchist: The Doom of the Great City*, a story first published in 1892 and written by a 17-year-old public schoolboy called E.
Douglas Fawcett.

Anyway, I arranged to meet up with these two outstanding beacons of the idling classes in Mike's Café in Portobello Road. 'Blimey, this has smartened up a bit, hasn't it?' commented Bone when he walked in, well-dressed in a fedora and a nice wool overcoat.

TH Now most people think of anarchy as violent and aggressive. But to me it is all about voluntary action and independence. I have been talking [with Warren Draper] about an anarchy movement – called 'Anglarchy' – that is rooted in English literature, Blake and Cobbett, very practical, and not about smashing up the bus stops. Although there may be a place for that. What's your idea of liberty, anarchy, freedom?

IB Pretty much the same as yours: a world without work, a world of unlicensed pleasure. I certainly don't go for all that right-to-work bollocks. I see interviews with kids hanging around shopping centres, and all they want to do is sit on the wall all day and talk to their mates, and someone with a microphone goes: 'Wouldn't you rather have a job?' And they say, 'Yes, oh yeah, we'd rather have a job,' as a knee-jerk. But that's the last thing in the world they want.

TH The recent marches and demonstrations in London: they were marching for jobs. They had banners saying, 'We want jobs.' And there's this thing called the People's Charter, which says, vaguely, 'We want more and better jobs.'

IB That's just bollocks. It's mostly people on the Left who have this ethos, but the feckless working class doesn't want 'more and better jobs'. The Left has an image of the Jarrow Marches. My granddad was an unemployed miner in Scotland in the Thirties, at the same time as the Jarrow Marches. He was supposed to have had a job filling the pits in, but instead, there's a great photo of him playing cards and dominoes. The central question is, how do the working class become idlers, as opposed to those who can afford idleness, knowing others will provide their sewerage, drains, electricity, food, water and so on? There is a pivotal moment in Dave Douglass's new book where he writes about the return to work after the Miners' Strike: many miners deliberately sabotaged the pits in order to take redundancy payments. This unseen, unheroic working-class struggle for freedom from work is seldom recognised or acknowledged, so idleness as a class issue is not taken up, because the Left has a different agenda, with its Jarrow heroism.

TH One of my enemy figures would be Tony Benn. He has this idea of full employment and the working classes riding off to the factory...

IB In the Eighties the SWP organised the 'Right to Work' marches. Everyone had their little SWP bibs on. The kids who went on it were promised discos every night, sex, and all they got was Trotsky's Transitional Programme.

TH Do you ever hear that thing where people on the hard Left accuse anarchists of being bourgeois?

IB Fucking hypocrites – the SWP is entirely made up of people who used to be polytechnic lecturers wearing corduroy trousers... what's their working-class composition? Virtually nil, now. But I don't really care about people's background: it's where you are now. What you can't do is do both: be politically anarchist and retain all the privileges of the previous life. For example, George Monbiot, who has done the classic thing: Monbiot is so keen on allotments that he has seven of his own. But it never occurs to him there might be six other people out there. Have you heard his thing: 'The Land is Ours'? Yes, the land is yours: you fuckin' own it, you cunt!

TH Yes, but Simon Fairlie and *The Land*, though: that really is a good magazine.

IB Oh yes, well, I like all the anti-Enclosures stuff, the history of English radicalism. The poaching wars. There were huge wars in the 18th century between poachers and gamekeepers, with huge gangs on either side.

TH How have things changed since you two first came to London 30 or 40 years ago?

RRJ In Wales, signing on for us was a full-time job. The only people I knew who had jobs were people who were just about to have a court appearance. Nowadays, with the questions they ask you before you go on a medical, you can work out all the conditions to get on the sick... 'bad back' used to be the only clincher ... now, with the Internet, you can authoritatively claim to have the symptoms of Ebola virus and they'll sort you out sharpish.

TH And when did you both take against work?

RRJ It's just that nobody worked, none of our friends worked.

IB No one ever worked ... in *Bash the Rich* there's a story about 'turning to the working class' but we didn't know anyone who was working! We were all on the dole so we started a Claimants' Union, a union for people on the dole. We would fight to get you all your entitlements. The classic line was: 'If they get you a job, we'll fight your case'! There were all the jokes about what occupation you gave when you were signing on: Father Christmas, snow clearer and so on. One job I gave was 'Coronation Programme Seller'. 'What's that then, Mr Bone?' asked a puzzled clerk. 'Very long hours. On the day, you're up at five in the morning till all hours,' I countered – not mentioning I hadn't had the luck of securing such a position since 1953!

TH   Is it actually responsible to be claiming dole from the State?

RRJ Well, the less money they have to start wars.

TH   Is it easier now, or harder?

IB   It's just as easy. My son was sent for a job in Cashbusters in Bristol. How was he going to get out of it? I said, 'Well, first ask about unions. What sort of union is there?' Then the clincher – ask about paternity leave.

TH   So you advise your son on how not to work?

IB   Like a duck to water. He just didn't want to take a glorified debt-collection job.

TH   Does the skiving thing go back for generations, do you think?

RRJ It's not exactly skiving. It's hard graft to be on the dole. They never leave you alone. One time, we thought we'd better get a job. And we saw these dustmen in the pub in Swansea. They were always there at eleven in the morning. We thought we'd try that. We went down there. The interview was: 'What's your name? Right, you start tomorrow.' So we went the next day. Fireball XL5 was the name of our wagon. We said to the bloke in charge, 'Early finish, is it?' He said, 'Oh yes, you'll be finished by half past four.' We said, 'What about the eleven o'clock finish?' And he said, 'You've got to be here 30 years before you get that shift.' I remember running away from the depot.

TH   So even the prospect of working till four thirty just for one day was too much?

IB   Yes – we're fucking men of principle.

RRJ It's a tricky old life on the dole, because they don't leave you alone and they don't give you much money. So you spend the rest of the time trying to top up.

TH   Little businesses and things?

RRJ Or whatever.

IB   The critical problem for me has always been that capitalism needs a reserve army of the unemployed. What about the people who want to be unemployed? All these people who are broken-hearted because they can't get a job or are being made redundant ... so you might as well have people who want to be unemployed.

TH But capitalism wants the unemployed people who are desperate for a job, not the ones who enjoy being unemployed.

IB Remember the four-week rule in the seventies – if you were single and didn't take a job in four weeks they'd stop your money. A fucking disgrace.

RRJ It's tricky at the moment.

TH Are you on the dole?

RRJ I'm on the sick.

TH On the sick for what, though?

IB Bad back.

TH I have one friend who has declared himself mad.

RRJ Then they leave you alone completely.

TH Won't you both be getting a pension soon?

IB I've never paid enough subs to get a pension ... I was on the dole for years. And I had a job as a community worker. I used to go in and read the *Guardian*, make some phone calls and go on the Internet. I used to sit there reading the Annual Report for hours. I didn't even look busy. You're supposed to look busy. Most jobs you could do the work in about an hour, to be honest.

TH So this is all about using your intellect to become master of your situation?

RRJ The thing is, I'm always busy. I can't stay in the flat after eight in the morning.

TH I meet people who have taken control of their own lives and their work and been creative, and created an autonomous life, and I wonder, why is it that so few people do that? And it's not actually a class issue.

RRJ People are frightened.

IB People have families, so it ain't such a good rate to be on the dole as when you've got no dependents ... Even I had to work as a postie and a hospital porter for years when the kids were young.

TH Well, I've been in a nuclear family for ten years, and it can be hard to keep the energy up to stay freelance. Sometimes you think, this is too much hard work. Life might be easier if I just had to turn up in an office. And what did you do when you first got to London, Ray?

RRJ I didn't have a clue what I was going to do when I got here. I got a flat, I had a girlfriend at college, and she did what exactly what she wanted to do. She was career-minded. Her father was a professor and she had the work ethic. I didn't know what I was going to do. I went on the dole. And nothing much has changed since.

IB Ray was an accomplished shop-lifter in Swansea so was able to supplement his income.

RRJ I gave all that up.

IB Most people go round nicking big lumps of cheese, joints of meat and big Nescafé jars and hawk 'em round the pubs at lunchtime to get beer money, but ...

TH So you were exiled from Swansea, Ray?

RRJ Yes. I nicked a suit with an alarm on, got chased by a security guard, who got knocked down by a car but still got up and nabbed me. All the security guards used to say, 'Morning, Ray.'

TH You had political beliefs behind this.

IB I didn't want to work either for the state, being an anarchist, or for some fucking capitalist company. I thought I'd never work officially, but I could do stints on the dole and survive on fuck all money with no possessions outside of a bin bag.

TH It's a gentlemanly existence, isn't it?

RRJ This is from my book: 'On the third day, they'd got us working in the bowels of some huge silo thing ... falling brick fractures my arm and crushes two of my toes. I was lucky. Who said hard work never killed anyone? The twat.'

IB A mate of ours, John, worked as a ticket collector at Ladbroke Grove station; stood as Class War candidate in the Kensington by-election in '87. He never checked any tickets because he would read *Class War* or *The Sun* all day. After a while his Underground bosses said, 'We've been watching you for four hours, and you haven't checked one ticket. You've been reading a copy of *Class War* all day.' He brought a successful case saying he had been harassed. And then successfully transferred to the sick for years claiming stress!

TH Have you ever gone into a job and tried to rouse up the workers to rebellion against the bosses?

IB Well, always. When I was in the Housing Association once, I eventually got the sack for breach of confidentiality. There was some fiddling going on, and I told the local paper. They quoted me, an anonymous source, but then put my name in!

TH I thought it would be a good piece for the *Idler*, to get a young man to take lots of crap jobs and, in a sense, just behave like a dignified human being and see how long you last. And say: 'I'm ethically opposed to that. I can't do it.'

IB Cashbusters ... they're all working for debt-collecting agencies, pawn-brokers, call centres, charity muggers – all jobs offering mind-numbing boredom, and you don't even get the collectivity of signing on any more – it's all done from your computer.

TH My parents were in Fleet Street in the Seventies, and the workplace was something completely different then. Clattering typewriters, shouting, smoking. People worked together and it was fun. They went to the pub together. Now we are separated by the computer. Before Wapping, the unions had ensured that there were some good jobs.

IB The printers, or rather the Union Chapel, ran the show and got their members on about a million quid a week in the heyday of Red Robbo, fighting for jobs, the night shift at British Leyland used their engineering skills to build secret bedrooms on the factory floor where they could grab a crafty kip.

TH If there was something they didn't like in the paper, the Father of the Chapel would come upstairs and say: 'The boys ain't happy.'

IB All those big industrial jobs went. We went to a meeting called by Arthur Scargill ... one of the miners' wives went through a litany of family deaths and illness from industrial diseases caused by working in the pits and then said: 'I'll fight to keep the pits open for my children and my children's children!' A lot of the miners didn't want to go back. They were having a far better time on strike. They were meeting lots of women. They were going all over the country ... they were having a great time. There was an argument to say: 'Fuck the pits. We ain't going back underground.' After they went back, a lot of them systematically sabotaged the pits so they could take the redundancy money. It's always the middle-class Lefties who claim that the working class is desperate to fucking work. There's a whole lot of mythologised hokum spun by the Communist Party around the Jarrow Marches and South Wales Miners' libraries. And the proud working-class desire for self-improvement. In his top book, The *Intellectual Life of the British Working Class*, David Rose shows that most miners detested the communists because they were arrogant and bullying. The most taken-out book from Maerdy Miners' library was not *The Communist Manifesto* but *East Lynne*, a Victorian melodrama.

TH Can you generalise about what the miners did when the mines closed?

IB Turn to heroin! No, get on the long-term sick. They ran pubs. Many of them moved away and totally revamped their lives. After 25 years, few of them regretted moving from the pits, despite the nostalgic camaraderie.

TH Now what about the argument that says there is camaraderie in the workplace?

IB Well, there is, and solidarity. But people will find camaraderie in prisons or in the most desperate situations, you know. There is that camaraderie, but you find other ways of getting it outside the world of work. A lot of the miners found that difficult at first, especially with Thatcher intent on destroying a sense of community through her 'No such thing as society' speech.

TH The *Guardian* is the worst for this. The comments on their blogs are by far the most mean-spirited of all the comment-makers. They're the worst for calling for 'more and better jobs'. They're also the worst payers in Fleet Street. And it's full of hierarchy.

IB Well, they're all Oxbridge, aren't they?

TH Well, I am too! But it is Oxbridge-dominated.

IB The editor's daughter is on the payroll. When you see a young sprog in the *Guardian*, you know they're related: Barnaby, Josh and Harry... leave it out!

TH As an alternative to wage slavery, we want to do a 'Taking care of business' issue of the *Idler*, which will look at how to start your own small business. That is a realistic alternative. We are now running an online shop at the Idler as a micro-business.

IB For someone who is idle, you put in a hell of a lot of hard work.

TH As you can imagine, I've heard that comment a lot. Yes, we are quite productive. But at home, I work from nine to one and that's it, really.

RRJ If you are doing something that you enjoy, as he enjoys it, then you are idle.

IB It's like you said earlier, Ray: you are actually very busy.

TH Idlers are busy! You're more lazy in a full-time job. You just sit there waiting for six o'clock to come. Then you are too tired to do much beyond go to the pub or watch telly.

IB Do something to disengage your brain.

TH Jobs tend to be humiliating. You spend all day being told off and then you run to the tube. Then you can't wait for the tube journey to be over. Then you run home. What do I do now? Have a glass of wine and watch *Twin Peaks*.

RRJ The magazine I did, *The Roughler*, that was really hard work. It was a nightmare, and that was just a fanzine.

TH Yes, it is hard putting a magazine together.

IB The print costs have come right down. You used to go abroad to get stuff done, but you can get it done in this country now, cheap. The turnaround time is a hell of a lot quicker, too.

TH I've been looking at the pre-Reformation calendar. There was more fun. Cromwell ruined it and then Charles II reopened the theatres and the maypoles went back up.

IB Well, Charles II … The Ranters were against him.

TH When were the Ranters?

IB Well, around the same time.

TH But Cromwell hated the Ranters and the Diggers and the Levellers as well.

IB Winstanley … Ranters … Puritans … fornication … swearing … blasphemy – all that moment of liberation came out of nowhere.

TH Now, do you think it is always only going to be small groups who break away in this way, like you guys, or the Ranters? Can you imagine mass liberty, or are people just too scared to take that liberty?

IB A lot of them in jobs are doing what they want anyway…

RRJ Everyone's trying to be an entrepreneur all of a sudden.

TH Yes, but take postmen as an example. I know two posties. One had a heart attack and one was off ill from stress for months. And that's supposed to be a pleasant job.

IB 'When I get fed up I can climb higher – in time for my heart attack when I retire' – that's an old number called 'Right to Work' our band used to do.

TH All this ingenuity…

IB Sabotaging the production line has been a staple of workers' fightback throughout history.

TH Wouldn't it be better if all that ingenuity, energy and collective action was directed towards working for ourselves?

IB Not if it's useless production or some chinless fuckwit fashion-designer entrepreneur. And don't get me started on fucking farmers' fucking markets.

TH I don't get very far anyway in persuading people near me to boycott Tesco's ... what sort of spirit do you see in people compared to the late Sixties and Seventies?

IB There's very little fightback or imagination around at the moment. We are fed a diet of *Daily Mail* heath scares and panics: Don't go outside, you might get swine flu. Also in the Eighties, if you went on a riot and weren't nicked on the day, you got away with it. Now with CCTV and telly coverage, you can get nicked months or years later. No fun in that.

TH What about Climate Camp and all the rest of it?

IB I think that's just middle-class wank turning into green careers on environmental quangos. Climate Camp is the new Cowes week.

TH Well, what's happened to the working-class intellectuals, then?

IB A lot of them have been bought off, writing opinion pieces like in-house bits of rough.

TH Or they become stand-up comedians.

IB That's another lot – even the fucking comedians have all been to Oxbridge ... Sorry to say it, Tom, but they're all fucking at it. Everyone from the protest movement to the journos are Oxford or Cambridge educated – Tony Benn, Tariq Ali, Ken Loach ...

RRJ I interviewed Tony Benn. And I said to him, 'Tony, what about this story of Mrs Thatcher liking you?' 'Oh, that's in the past, we've got to forget about the past.'

IB I remember when Churchill died in South Wales. There were collections and some English villages raised thousands. Merthyr Tydfil raised half a crown, a couple of buttons. And some Green Shield Stamps.

TH But what's wrong with a good education?

IB Tony Benn, Ken Loach. I rest my case.

TH I wrote a chapter in one book about how anti-war marches were a waste of time. But my liberal publishers – who work with the organisation Liberty – wouldn't print it.

IB One of the problems with the anarchist movement is that it's lost its libertarian impulse and its hedonism. It doesn't vigorously oppose restrictions on liberty. We believe in free speech – opposing Griffin going on *Question Time* was fucking ridiculous, with people saying: 'I believe in free speech, but ... '

TH But a big part of the anarchist thing is to bust up racist marches, and so on.

IB Nothing wrong with a punch-up. I believe Griffin can have free speech but take the physical consequences if people don't like what he says. I used to admire Donald Soper on his stepladder at Speakers' Corner taking on all comers. Top geezer. There's a whole gamut of things … that's what I like in the *Idler*, that libertarian, English anarchy, an affection for place and roots. I love Frank Newbold's wartime posters: 'It's Your England – Fight For It' and Orwell's English socialist patriotism. A lot of anarchists are actually just boring leftists.

TH I like those creative things that actually add to people's lives, rather than the far Left whingeing. Which is also, in lots of cases, just resentment. And resentment is the wrong attitude.

IB Nothing wrong with a bit of resentment! Resentment and bitterness! The Yippees and the Dutch Provos showed you can be both bitter and funny. I can just imagine Monbiot on the train, saying 'Don't do that, Harry,' to one of his annoying sprogs who's annoying every other fucker in the compartment.

RRJ At dinner, the parents will stop the conversation so their child can interrupt!

TH We've been a bit guilty of that sort of thing. There's something wrong with my generation of parents. It's good to be ignored.

IB People give their kids ridiculous choices. Shut up and eat it! Would you like shallots? No fucking way.

RRJ If their mother and father are going out, the children should know they've got to behave.

TH Some kind of horrible progressive thing has happened. The word 'parenting' is a new word.

IB They're treated as young adults. But they're not and you need to take decisions for them.

TH State schools are pretty awful, because they have been subjected to successive progressive ideologies. That's why at home we are rebelling by learning Latin, by rote. So we are learning amo, amas, amat, amamus, amatis, amant.

IB Amabo, amabis, amabit, amabimus, amabitis, amabunt.

TH The future simple! You remember it. You were probably taught well.

IB I did O-level Latin. It's so easy to learn.

TH That's why you have a good brain.

IB Because of the Latin?

TH Someone like Boris Johnson did Classics at Oxford. He has that bluff exterior but he is a serious guy.

IB There was a story in the paper this morning that a woman was suing her boss for sexual harassment at work, and he had sent her a rude poem by Catullus in Latin. He claimed that she couldn't possibly have known Latin, but she did!

TH The old ways.

IB The old ways! I went to visit a kid at Summerhill School once.

TH How did you find it?

IB Oh, fucking awful. Half of them are Japanese, strangely enough, and there was a big row about stabbing a pet rabbit. They were having a debate about poor dead bunny but the young kids don't know what to think: what are your views on stabbing a rabbit to death, aged three?

RRJ Piers Thompson [a friend with kids] said to me, which camp do you think we fall into, Ray? I said, there are two camps. Either you tell your kids what to do, or you ask them what they want to do. If you tell them what to do, that's tough love. If you ask them, then you're a twat.

IB On the train, Jane, my partner, has no patience with middle-class twats letting their kids run amok: 'Stop these children coming up and pawing me. Harry, Harriet and Josh, you're going to get thumped in a minute.' She got off to a bad start, because their mater was reading the *Tatler*. Because she was reading *Tatler*, she thought everyone else had to look after her kids. After some strong words from Jane, the woman called the police … everyone was craning their necks – class war on the 5.20 outta Paddington!

TH This new attitude makes having children doubly more difficult than it was before. The men are feeling emasculated because the women ask for so much help and, naturally enough, turn to the nearest person around. There's not enough help from the wider family group.

IB Also other people used to intervene with your kids. Children are indoors much more these days. The computer games but also the fear, parents read the *Daily Mail* horror stories.

TH Which are very rare instances.

IB The local papers like the *Hackney Gazette* are full of it.

TH Even where we are, the mums are frightened. They say: 'You can't be too careful these days.' Although it may be changing: I just came back from a conference of teachers and social workers in Scotland and the theme there was that we have become too 'risk-averse', as the jargon has it.

IB   I can remember hitch-hiking – no one does that now. So, Tom, you mix with a broad church of people, then? Social workers, Women's Institute? A life of ludic pleasure.

TH   And hard graft.

IB   It's hard work being playful all day. Don't you think the *Idler* will be sucked into the corporations and you'll be bought out and take the money and run off to Alex James's organic farm? It's inevitable.

TH   I think it would have happened by now. We have been doing it for 17 years.

RRJ When I get the dole now, they ask me what do I do, and I take up old copies of *The Roughler*, and I say, 'Can I use that computer?' and they say, 'Yeah, type this in,' and I show them my TV station, Roughler TV. Now, why don't they jump up and down and say, 'Look at this bloke, he's actually doing something!' Instead of saying, 'There's a job in this factory.'

TH   I was on the dole when I started the *Idler*, round here, and they did send me on a sort of dolies' business-training course for a week.

IB   You were on the dole and they sent you on a course to produce the *Idler*!

TH   Ha! But it's kind of unrealistic because they are asking these 17-year-old dolies to produce a business plan. There was the Enterprise Allowance Scheme. Can we not, though, find simple ways of working, which is making things and selling them? Women can make things at home.

IB   You want women staying at home?

TH   That's surely better than working at Asda, to have your own small business?

IB   What about the camaraderie and the saucy banter?

TH   I'd rather be at home making jam with a couple of friends than being bossed around by an idiot at Asda.

IB   Women at home … cottage industry! I'm going misty-eyed.

TH   The Women's Institute is coming back among young people. There are art students at places like Goldsmiths who are starting their own Women's Institute branches. It's creative.

IB   You really do see the good in everything.

TH   It is a good thing, though!

IB   Those organisations have always been around. The Women's Institute has been making jam at home for years, but you're saying it's a new trend.

TH No, I'm saying that I'm into the old ways.

IB The old ways!

TH It's the old ways that politicians hate. They don't have a sense of history, Left or Right. They are all Whiggish.

IB Or they make up versions of the old ways – myths.

TH The yeomanry. Old-fashioned Tories. You must have found with *Class War*, it made people realise that they were not alone.

IB Oh yeah. We would express the wish that the Queen Mother would die of cancer. And you would get an enormous postbag with people agreeing.

TH I think the over-60s are more radical than the young ones. How old are you two?

RRJ I'm 58.

IB 62. We know the old ways. How old are you?

TH Me? 41.

IB Ohhh! And he talks of the old ways!

TH Well, why do you think I've brought you together? So I can pay my respects and sit at your feet.

Ian gives me the last four issues of *Class War* and also a pamphlet written by Tom Vague about the radical history of Notting Hill. Ian asks me, teasingly, whether I was in the Bullingdon Club when at Cambridge. No, I say. I was playing in hardcore punk bands and doing fanzines. Finally, we discuss schools.

TH I went to Westminster.

IB School?

TH Yes.

IB Fucking hell. They're all the same, Ray!

Bill Drummond

by Tom Hodgkinson

IDLER 44 · 2011

BILL DRUMMOND HAS BEEN A MAJOR INFLUENCE ON ME
since the late Eighties. All his projects – Echo and the Bunnymen,
the Jams, graffiti campaigns, the KLF, *Chill Out*, *The Manual*,
the K Foundation, burning a million quid and now The 17 – have
showed courage, spirit and a sense of autonomy. Drummond got on
with it.

I went to interview Bill and Jimmy Cauty in 1991 for the *Guardian*.
It was around the time when the ambient house movement was starting, and this intrigued me. The KLF had just released the excellent
Chill Out album. At around the same time, I read their book *The
Manual: How To Have a Number One The Easy Way*. This excellent title
sold itself as a guide to go from being on the dole to having a number
one hit single in the British charts in six months, but really it was about
being creative and doing your own thing. I remember thinking about
how the KLF approached life and wondering: why doesn't everybody
do this? *The Manual*, and the activities of the KLF generally, were
among my inspirations to set up the *Idler* magazine.

Later I went to a Shoreditch pub to see the pair giving a screening
of the film about burning the money. I asked Bill if he would do an interview for the *Idler*. 'No,' he said. 'We're not idlers.' I began to realise
that far from being a fun-loving prankster, Bill was in actual fact a
unsmiling Presbyterian Scot with a strong work ethic. The perceived
louche public school hedonism of the *Idler* was anathema to him.

Bill did eventually become a contributor to the *Idler*, writing the
'Bad Advice' column with Mark Manning. I think he had realised that
we were not just Oxbridge dilettantes and that there was a serious mission behind the magazine. A couple of years ago, we took our families

on a trip to Lundy Island, and spent many hours wandering around the cliffs and moors discussing usury, which, as a Puritan, Bill defended.

★

TH When we were on Lundy Island, we talked about the fact that in the Catholic Church up until about 1500, usury was very heavily disapproved of. The idea was that you were committing the sin of sloth, if you were the usurer, because you weren't doing anything creative. You were just sitting around doing nothing. By virtue of time passing you were making money. And secondly you are not allowed to sell time because it doesn't belong to you, it belongs to God. Also they felt that it exploited the poor. They had a more providential attitude towards life: that misfortune had been placed there by God and it was not for someone else to profit from it. The person who needs the money should be an object of charity. But commercial loans did happen for businesses.

BD And they were okayed by the Catholic Church?

TH I believe so ... you had the Medicis, for example. As in Islam today: Muslims still do mortgages, even though they are supposed to be against usury, or *riba*. Do you think that sort of climate would have stifled enterprise, or encouraged it? In setting up our shop, we've had to borrow money.

BD Everything that's happened in Europe since the Renaissance, couldn't have happened if people couldn't rent money, or weren't allowed to rent out the money they had.

TH What has happened?

BD Well, I'm not going to put a value judgement on it, but the West grew. The West became the dominant culture in the world as free enterprise blossomed.

TH Wasn't it the dominant culture before then? Rome?

BD It was dominant in Europe but no, not compared to the Chinese. You couldn't fund an expedition to the Spice Islands or wherever it might be without these methods. Now, you said you shouldn't rent time, but time is part of growing. The time I spend building a chair, that's what you buy when you buy that chair, that time in my life.

TH Now when we first met many years ago, I asked if you'd like to do an interview for the *Idler*. And you said, 'No, we're not idlers.' Does this mean that you would approve of the dynamic hard-working culture that came after 1500 more than the luxurious, Providence-based medieval version of Christianity?

BD You're taking it for granted that that's what society was like before. I wouldn't know whether it was like that or not. I don't have particular opinions about the past. I'm not a historian, but I don't mind having a strong work ethic. When I think of idling, I think: who would want to do that? It's the fastest route to depression. Life is short enough as it is, it's getting shorter by the day, and there's lots of things I want to do. Now, I'm aware, as I've watched the *Idler* evolve and change, that you as chief idler have had to squeeze things in and slightly change it to make it work. And you're one of the least idle people I've met. Lots of people have pointed this out to you: you celebrate idleness, but really ... as a student or a post-student you might have been an idle person, spending time down the pub and smoking your cigarettes. But that isn't how you operate now. So you've changed the definition of what being an idler is over the past 15 or 20 years.

TH Well, this is what is often thought, but if you look at issue one, I actually say, this is not about slobbing around and giving up, it's about doing your own thing. Idleness and entrepreneurialism are in fact very closely related. Idleness in the workplace is an expression of defiance, and the will towards liberty. If you are working for a big corporation, doing a job that you hate, and which you find boring, which is the reality for a lot of people, then slacking off, skiving, is a way of taking back some power for yourself. But when released from that prison, the guy who was previously the idler in the office – because he couldn't stand to be confined in that way, or told what to do – can be quite dynamic. So it has always been about: what's the alternative to the nine-to-five? Being idle is about taking responsibility.

BD But that's not taking responsibility, that's skiving off. That's somehow thinking you've won something; but you've won nothing. Because you're still a slave. One of the problems I've always had with the rebel, is that the rebel spends most of his time kicking against the thing he's rebelling against, instead of walking around that thing, walking away from it, and getting on with whatever it is he wants to be doing. So: don't skive off. Leave the job. Make your own thing happen. As you've done, Tom.

TH It's the first step, though, to freedom.

BD   It's not the first step to freedom. It's the first step to not taking responsibility for your own life. As soon as you get locked into that thing of blaming somebody else for your own predicament, you are entrapping yourself, enslaving yourself. I know you're not actually in bonded slavery, but as soon as you're an adult, you have to take total responsibility for your life. And take total responsibility for everyone else's life in a sense as well, because we have to live together.

TH   Sartre says that the free man has the burden of the whole world on his shoulders.

BD   Absolutely. We are totally free. Now, it's a contradiction, because since God created the universe, everything has been mapped out. But we have to ignore that, and make the decision: we are totally free. We have to take complete responsibility. Part of that freedom is to come up with a society that works, and a society that works is always evolving, always changing, so the morals that we use to make that society work, change. What we think is okay now, will be seen as immoral in a hundred years' time.

TH   The suspicion of the usurer, though, is still here today: it's called banker-bashing.

BD   I think that's a real weakness of people. In the Eighties it was Margaret Thatcher or the South Africans we hated, and now it's the bankers. That's blaming somebody else.

TH   And we're actually complicit in the situation anyway.

BD   Of course we are! When you blame the banker, you give up something in yourself. We should be thinking: right, the financial system hasn't worked. What we thought was good for the previous 20 years, has changed. It needs to be more regulated. It was good to deregulate the City, but now we have to reign it back. It's harder now: we have a global economy, so it's almost impossible for a national government to do that. But to go back to your word usury. If we take out a loan, and we think we've got some free money, it's our responsibility. If you go out and drink loads, you get drunk. And you might do some bad things when you're drunk. But it's your responsibility.

TH   I noticed that people read my first book and said, 'Well, it's all right for you, being idle. I've got to pay this mortgage.' But I said: 'You took on the mortgage knowing the deal. You wanted to live in a bigger house so you took on a mortgage. You can't later complain about it.'

BD   I've made lots of mistakes and got myself in all sorts of scrapes in the past, and still do. But I know, at every point, I created the situation. And as soon as I think somebody else has created the situation, I'm giving away my own freedom.

TH Do people actually want to to be free, in that case? There's something comfortable about being a semi-slave. If you're in prison, life can be easy. There's no responsibility. Your meals are made. I think that's what you put across in *The Manual*. Yes, we accept our complicity in the situation that we've created, and you can't throw all the blame at the bankers or the headmaster or your parents. But at the same time, you can recognise injustice and protest against it.

BD You do something about it, you don't just protest against it; you don't just go on a march. We can all sit and shout at the TV and read newspapers. The only thing that counts at the end of your life, is what you've done. You may have all sorts of opinions. But if you haven't done anything, none of that counts. And that's what's wrong with pubs. Because alcohol encourages people not to do things.

TH It's true that the pub is the handmaiden of work. It's the consolation prize. It's the reward. But it is a pleasure: six o'clock, pint, complain about the boss. I used to enjoy that. It's a surface pleasure, like fast food, but it is kind of fun. But at the same time, reflection, contemplation, prayer, meditation, reading, walks in the country, a long meal taken over a few hours: these are idle pleasure which it is worth defending.

BD OK. But the point I want to get back to, is that a lot of anti-Semitism is based on what you were talking about at the beginning. Christians may have traditionally blamed the Jews for killing Jesus, but because they weren't allowed to have land, they developed other crafts, such as working with gold, diamonds and money. They could build up their wealth not in land, but in money.

TH But don't you see it as a major problem when people are deceived, encouraged to borrow more than they can afford, go into debt, with the result that they get seriously depressed? They get a debt that they can't afford to pay back, for example with a motor car.

BD Yes, and that's why we need laws, that's why we need rules, that's why the City needs to be regulated. But that doesn't mean to say that me renting you £100 is fundamentally wrong. I'll rent you the money for a week and it will cost you £10, just like if I rent you the chair for a week.

TH There's a company called Wonga which lends money at very high rates of interest. Surely that's wrong?

BD Of course it's wrong. But the fundamental thing of renting money is not wrong. There should be laws that govern how money is rented, in the same way that when you rent property, there are laws. In the same way, there isn't something fundamentally evil in the renting of money. We have to be aware of our weakness as human beings. But we have to be grown up as well.

TH But surely usury is a trick whereby the rich steal from the poor?

BD Almost the very opposite. Wealth, until recently, was measured in land. That's where wealth was. What borrowing money meant was that people without any land could make something happen. If they hadn't been allowed to rent that money, they wouldn't have had the money to buy land. I would have had to bang you over the head with a club and steal the land. This way, I don't have to do that.

TH But actually land ownership was conceived of quite differently in the manorial system, where you had rights over land, and you might be able to use land for your whole life, but you didn't exactly own it in the sense that you could sell it, or build on it and sell it for more, as property developers do today.

BD Obviously the way that you own land has evolved over the centuries. There would have been a time when a tribe owned that land. At a certain point, we were no longer hunter-gatherers, we were farmers, so we had to have fixed land. And when you get two cultures that meet each other for the first time and have different ways of dealing with land... Once the white man hit North America, he had a completely different approach to that of the Native Americans who were hunter-gatherers, the majority of them, and the tribe owned the land.

TH That clash is well portrayed in *Little House on the Prairie*. Actually the Ingalls made some silly decisions: they had fantastic energy and optimism, but they built their house in the wrong place. The Native Americans lived quite lightly, with great knowledge of their environment. The Puritans came in and said, 'We're going to build a road and do our thing, with a huge amount of effort.' Then they got it all wrong and had to build another house.

BD But you're romanticizing the Native Americans as having it right, and the Puritans as having it wrong. There is not one wrong or right. There is an evolution, and I don't mean evolving into something that's better ...

TH Some of the Catholic intellectuals in the Twenties, like Chesterton and Belloc, had the idea of Distributism, the idea being that each family would have its acre of land. There is freedom in land, because you can grow your own food and keep animals. Chesterton said that the problem with capitalism is that there are not enough capitalists. Most people are working for the system. There are not enough small businesspeople. So what they were trying to do was to give freedom through the more equal distribution of land. It was called Peasant Proprietorship. Everyone should have their own allotment or acre of land on which they can grow stuff and have some measure of independence. Is that not a sensible scheme?

BD I don't know about that. What I do know is what they did in the Soviet Union with the dachas was almost exactly the same. They had so much land. Moscow was surrounded by all this unused land. Every family got the same amount. And going back to what you were saying, it is the human condition that some of us have more get-up-and-go than others. Some are entrepreneurial and some are not.

TH Although *The Manual* was specifically about the music business, it could be applied to any area of life.

BD The music business thing to me was just an excuse. My main thing is: don't wait to be asked. Don't wait to be given permission. Don't wait for somebody else to validate you. Get up and go and do it. Which does sound horribly close to some horrible American self-help book. Once I became aware of that whole genre, I thought: is that all that all of that was? Which was a bit of a downer for me personally. But I still stick by it.

TH And that is what punk was supposed to be about.

BD Punk though suffered as much from putting icons up there. I see that as what fascism is. We have our Johnny Rottens, and what's he called, from The Clash ...

TH Joe Strummer.

BD And our Joe Strummers up there on pedestals. I do that, too, I put things up on pedestals.

TH It's natural, isn't it?

BD It's also natural to tear them down.

TH I've noticed that with my own readers. They read my books and like them, and then later they go on to forums and give me some real abuse.

BD They shouldn't give you abuse. They shouldn't be on forums, they should be out doing stuff.

TH   Well, that's why I closed down the *Idler* forum. They seemed to be a load of whingeing procrastinators. The medium itself, the forum, seems to encourage whingeing and procrastinating. It's like Facebook which is a short-term solution to loneliness in the office.

BD   I don't do Facebook. I don't know whether it's a generation thing.

TH   Twitter?

BD   I don't do that, either. I've got too much in my life. Too much going on. What's obvious to state, if I'm having a go at our culture, is that all it's interested in doing – and this happened with music in the 20th century – is turning us into consumers. You don't have to make it any more: we'll have the experts, we'll have the geniuses, we'll have the good-looking ones making it.

TH   That's what rock'n'roll is.

BD   Yeah, and that's my big downer. I know that you with your ukulele, are trying to break that down. And what I do with The 17 is another way of breaking it down.

TH   The problem is though that there are levels of ability. John Lennon is a much better songwriter than I am. He's the master carpenter.

BD   That doesn't matter. I mean, I find it hard to believe, but there may be people out there who are better at doing sex than me! But imagine if, the trick had been done, from now on, you don't have to do sex. All you people, we've got this tiny group who will do the sex for you, and you just watch them, and buy into that. That's what happened with music in the 20th century. It was taken away from everybody.

TH   We all used to sing all day long. And more old-fashioned cultures today still do. Are the television talent shows an expression of people trying to take it back, or are they just an extension of the whole thing?

BD   They're just an extension of the whole thing, because all you have to do is sit there and watch. I guess I'm against anything where somebody else is doing it for you. You go and see a film, and people are stealing cars or taking risks, and all you're doing is sitting in a dark room watching this. And I think: no, no, you get out of that cinema now, and steal a car. That's why I think football hooligans are better than regular football supporters. All a football supporter is doing is paying his money to watch other guys playing football. So he's getting his highs and lows from what other people are doing. The football hooligan is getting his highs and lows out of beating people up. So he's actually doing something.

TH [Shocked liberal silence] Erm … singing does happen in football stadiums.

BD It does.

TH That is a case of a real collective singsong, and that's wonderful in a way.

BD It's fantastic.

TH I can see the attraction: singing in a vast group and watching the amazing skills of the football players. Everyone in the world wants to watch David Beckham on a big screen, even the pygmies of Southern Africa. There is something godlike about these football stars.

BD I still say that it's a weakness of us as a species, and that's why we get the Hitlers and the Stalins. This may just be a typical dad-thing, but I said to my 11-year-old son on Sunday: what makes you feel better? Hitting a six, scoring a goal or having a thing bought for you? Obviously, it's actually hitting a six. It's when you've done something yourself.

TH All children seem to want to do though is to watch television and be bought things. Go to entertainment parks. Be entertained.

BD I'm as bad a parent as anybody else so I will use the television.

TH I did used to love watching snooker and darts on television. That is fun. I think you can be a bit too hard on people, Bill.

BD I'm always harder on myself.

TH Which brings me back to the matter of this edition of the *Idler*. It is the business issue. I don't see a contradiction between idling and starting a business. They're actually closely related. I'm actually quite knackered today as we've been working so hard to set up this shop.

BD More of us should be shopkeepers. I think being a shopkeeper is a very, very good thing to be.

TH A nation of shopkeepers now seems like quite a fantastic thing. We're actually a nation of semi-slaves, which is much worse. I think of those pictures of the Victorian draper standing proudly outside his shop and I feel like that now.

BD It's fantastic. One of the most fundamental requirements of the human condition is for our lives to have meaning. That's what religion does. Running a shop gives your life meaning.

TH Trade: this again is where I would part company with socialism. I quite often get the comment: 'you say you're an anti-capitalist, but you're selling T-shirts on your website!' But I see trade as a great thing. It produces an engagement with another human being. We've only been here ten days, and we've met some wonderful people. Things are happening already, and that's because we've set up a stall in the market. That's what I mean by: what's wrong with capitalism is that there aren't enough capitalists.

BD For whatever reason, we in Britain, and especially the white population, have lost that entrepreneurial spirit.

TH Yes, because you see it in the immigrants.

BD Some races are more entrepreneurial than other races. The Turkish people around where I live are really entrepreneurial. They make things happen. And we seem to have lost that.

TH Why have we lost that, what's happened? Have our rulers deliberately tried to create a situation where you've got quite stupid people coming out of school, not well educated, and not very capable either? They've been prepared for a job, a boring job in the economy. In other words, to be a slave. That's the central purpose of education today.

BD I wouldn't say there was a golden age of education. I know that when I was at secondary school, I was on a conveyor belt. I was supposed to get an apprenticeship at the steelworks. Factory fodder.

TH Actually, William Cobbett said the same in the 1820s.

BD What I think is so much better now about education, is that then, it was more about imparting knowledge. It wasn't teaching people how to think. And now they are taught far more how to think, and question. That does mean you've got to put up with all the attitude.

TH Isn't this the system that's created the lazy white people that you mentioned? Lots of self-assurance, but not much knowledge?

BD Is knowledge what is needed now?

TH The point of grammar is that it does teach you how to think clearly, and to detect when you're being manipulated or bamboozled by advertising for example. Or politicians. Cobbett was against state and private schools, but he wrote an English grammar because he wanted people to be able to understand when they were being hoodwinked.

BD Well, these are hunches. Even though I was really rubbish at English, I'm a total stickler, and I can see that bad emails lead to confusion. But I know that it's more that, I'm the problem.

TH My mum went to the grammar school in the Fifties, and this was her total saviour. She knows her Milton and she would be incapable of putting the apostrophe in the wrong place, because it was drummed into her. Moving back to the business thing, one problem is that if you're told you're vaguely creative, an artist or a writer or a musician, then you shovel the responsibility for your finances onto somebody else. Somehow it's seen as uncool to have a filing system, with invoices paid, invoices unpaid and so on, VAT, bookkeeping. But I notice that before the Industrial Revolution, bookkeeping and accounts were taught as a matter of course to the gentlefolk. So what I'm trying to say is that it's not square to take responsibility for your own finances. But the romantic poet is not meant to concern himself with dirty commerce.

BD We should all take responsibility. My experience in the music business shows that bands – and especially lead singers, they're the worst – create a power base out of not knowing what's going on. They loathe and despise their manager and record company and look down on them, but they're addicted to them, and the manager can exploit this weakness.

TH That could be a win-win situation, couldn't it?

BD That's the trade-off! But yes, everyone should be given responsibility. Maybe everyone should be given £1,000 when they leave school and told: 'That's it. You can either go and blow all that on drugs now, or you can set up your own business.' That sounds like one of Jesus's parables, doesn't it?

TH Is there any point in doing anything, though? My actions don't seem to have any effect on anyone else. Sometimes I think, 'What's the point?'

BD If you think that, you're wrong. Of course they do. Maybe your books won't change the world. But you've still got to keep going. You've got to keep opening that shut door and adding up your columns. What I think is good about what you're doing is that we should be making our culture ourselves. I'm totally against the Arts Council.

TH I did look at grants once. But there are so many strings attached.

BD You have to make work that ticks their boxes. But with your shop, you sell some books, sell some coffees, sell some cakes, sell some tickets. And you're free of that control. The greatest culture of the 20th century hasn't been culture that's been state-sponsored, whether it's The Beatles, or Hollywood.

TH I find that I can't get myself in a lather about these cuts! I try.

BD I love the cuts.

That's because Bill is a responsible man who thinks that life is supposed to be hard. And I have to agree, to an extent: Virgil said that Jove sharpened men's wits by making life hard, and the cuts will sharpen our wits and ultimately make us stronger and less dependent on the state. I have spent 20 years searching for the easy life and now I know: it doesn't exist. Even living on a farm and writing for four hours a day is hard work. As Virgil wrote, *labor omnia vicit*, hard work conquered everything!

Oliver Bernard

by Rebecca Wallersteiner

IDLER 45 · 2012

OLIVER BERNARD, THE ELDEST OF THE THREE TALENTED Bernard brothers, is best known for being one of the leading translators of the poetry of Guillaume Apollinaire and Arthur Rimbaud, from French to English, as part of the Penguin classics collection. It is nearly 50 years since Bernard first translated Rimbaud and a new Anthology, published in January 2012 by Anvil Poetry Press, will contain previously unseen verses originally written in Latin. Bernard arrived in Soho penniless, but handsome, at the tender age of 14 and received much of his secondary education from such worldly teachers as Francis Bacon, Muriel Belcher, John Minton, John Deakin, Robert MacBride, Robert Colquhoun, George Barker and Dylan Thomas. At this time Soho was a melting pot of creative talent and ideas. In the 1940s and 1950s Soho was possibly the most cosmopolitan, vibrant place in England – London's equivalent to Paris's Left Bank – where artists and their models, poets, soldiers, refugees, layabouts and aristocracy gathered to carouse in its drinking holes such as the French, Coach and Horses and the Colony Room. The stars of Fifties literary London concentrated within a few streets to exchange ideas, poach each others lovers' and scrounge a drink, or two.

Unlike his two brothers who never stayed away from Soho for long, Bernard has lived in Norfolk for over 30 years. A volume of autobiography, *Getting Over It*, was published by Peter Owen in 1992. Bernard was educated at various schools, including Bunce Court School, in Kent and Westminster School, London. He trained as a pilot in Canada during the Second World War and joined the Communist Party in the early Forties. After the war ended he taught English in France and Corsica and did assorted manual jobs including working at the East Greenwich Gasworks. After taking a BA at Goldsmiths College Bernard became an advisory teacher of drama and later worked as an advertising copywriter. He has written several volumes of verse and acted as director of Speak a Poem Competition since its beginning. Bernard has been married twice and has two sons and two daughters.

Here he reminisces about his colourful life with journalist Rebecca Wallersteiner, who had a poem published as part of an anthology in childhood – but gave up writing poetry and became a hack.

RW Is it true that you and your friends raced cats in Soho, when it was too wet for the horses to run?

OB Yes. Not just cats. We also used to race babies when it was too wet for horses to race. Three of us had toddlers and we pooled them – they loved racing each other.

RW Did any of your friends from Westminster join you in Soho? It must have been very different to the structured and cloistered life of public school.

OB Yes – there were one or two. I talked and drank with John Raymond the journalist and critic, in the Fifties, in the York Minster, now named the French House, in Dean Street. He had been my contemporary at Westminster. Although he was a bit pompous and liked to talk about slap-up meals he was impossible to dislike. I remember him being rather sensitive and quiet as a junior boy.

RW Do you remember your first visit to Soho?

OB My first sight of Soho was obtained while I was running an errand for my mother in the 1930s. She sent me to buy proper spaghetti or ravioli. People gathered to chat on the pavements outside Parmigiani's on the corner of Frith Street and the Bar Italia – which still exists today. There was a continental feel and I began to return late from those errands. There were still yellow horse-drawn Carlo and Gatti ice carts, traces of straw, nosebags and horse-dung. You almost expected to look up from the dingy, grey streets and glimpse blue continental sky.

RW And of course Soho was a great place to hear jazz. I remember going to Ronnie Scott's to hear George Melly perform three or four times during New Year in the 1990s. George was camping it up as usual – wearing his trademark multi-coloured outfits. When did you get into jazz?

OB I became interested in jazz in the Forties. During these years I bought ten-inch records of Fats Waller, Bessie Smith, Jelly Roll Morton and Billie Holliday. I particularly liked Fats Waller and began to collect him – I thought he was called Fat Swallow for a long time.

RW Do you remember the first time you met Dylan Thomas?

OB I first met Dylan in the Duke of York when he bought me a drink or two and asked rather seriously whether I wrote verse. He was with Caitlin – they often went drinking together.

RW Sir Eduardo Paolozzi told me that the Mandrake, downstairs in Meard Street, was like a vast subterranean cavern – rather like Hades – but without the fire. Was it fun to go there?

OB Oh yes – the Mandrake was so vast and sprawling that you expected to stroll into the Piccadilly Circus underground. It was run by Boris Watson who was rumoured to have been in prison for killing a customer of the Coffee An'. I met the poets Allen Ginsberg and Gregory Corso in the Mandrake – they may have been there with George Barker.

RW It is a shame that most of these atmospheric drinking holes no longer existed in the early 1980s, when I first visited Soho. The Bar Italia, Maison Bertaux, French and Coach and Horses are still flourishing despite having to battle with rising rates. Eduardo Paolozzi once took me to the Colony Room, though he preferred to meet at the Chelsea Arts Club. He used to talk about the Caves which no longer existed in the early Eighties – what was this club like?

OB Like the Mandrake and the Colony Room the Caves de France opened at 3 o'clock, the closing time for pubs after lunch, but it may have closed earlier. Pretty much all of 'Soho' came to the Caves. You would regularly see Nina Hamnett, the two Roberts (Colquhoun and MacBride), David Archer and Paul Potts.

RW What was Soho like during the Second World War?

OB The war closed off the Continent. After Dunkirk the cafés and drinking holes of Dean Street and Old Compton Street were suddenly full of free French and Canadians and some Australians and Poles.

RW What do you think of John Deakin's photo of you? He took it so close up that it makes you look like a strikingly handsome escaped convict.

OB I agree that John Deakin's photo of me is rather good. He told me not to shave and to meet him at the Vogue studio the next morning so that he could photograph me unshaven. He wanted me to look like rough stuff and he succeeded.

RW Did you meet the artists Robert MacBride and Robert Colquhoun when you first discovered Soho? I've always thought their painting underrated. They were unlucky in that the English romantic style of painting rather fell out of fashion after the Second World War – with the rise in popularity of abstract art and American Expressionism.

OB I met the two Roberts a few years later when I was around 20 and they were older. Both were charming – they had a studio off Kensington Church Street which they shared with John Minton. We met at the Windsor Castle pub, near Russell Flint's studio and Soho. They lost the flat after the landlord sold it and it was bought by Tony Hubbard, whose mother was an American millionnairess. MacBride's singing and dancing were famous. He danced rarely, but sang often. He liked to sing Scottish songs and often took the woman's part. He and Colquhoun were inseparable, although they often fought. They were friends with Elizabeth Smart and lived in her house in Essex for a couple of years – looking after her children.

RW Was Tony also an artist?

OB No. In a way as he practised the art of living rather well – he had loads of money – so didn't need to work.

RW What happened to the two Roberts?

OB Well, both drank a lot and died young – it was sad. Neither were asked to contribute any work to the 1952 Festival of Britain, partly because they were both very Scottish and good at being rude about the British. It was a bit of an insult not to be asked as many of their friends, such as Lucian Freud and Eduardo Paolozzi, were included and it was a huge event. Robert Colquhoun died of heart failure aged just 47 and Robert MacBride also died young – he was run over by a car in Dublin a couple of years later.

RW Were you friends with the painter, John Minton? I've had a reproduction of Lucian Freud's painting of Minton on my living room wall for the past 20 years. Minton committed suicide in 1957 – just five years after Lucian painted his portrait.

OB I met Johnny Minton when I was 21 and thought he was rather silly at first as he was always clowning around. When I got to know him better I realised that he was rather shy, serious and intelligent. He was also well-read and hid behind his slapstick persona. Johnny and I often drank together in Soho and he sometimes held parties in the evenings.

RW How did you get on with Lucian Freud, who I used to know quite well? I worked for him for six years buying his champagne, paints and taking his midnight calls. It was wonderful to watch his paintings gradually taking shape – including the portrait of your younger brother Bruce. I remember chatting to Bruce at a couple of parties in the late 1980s.

OB Lucian was part of the crowd that met in the Colony Room Club, presided over by Muriel Belcher. He was a good friend of Bruce, but seemed rather suspicious of me and I was rather suspicious of him. We didn't have many long conversations.

RW Yes, Lucian could be jealous of other good-looking men – perhaps he saw you as competition?

OB Yes – we may have competed for women.

RW Did you get on with Muriel Belcher? Eduardo told me that he was rather scared of her as she could be sarcastic – especially if she didn't like someone.

OB Muriel seemed to like me as I never had to pay a subscription to the Colony Room – she always let me in free. She liked attractive young men, even though she was lesbian by inclination. I also enjoyed going to the Gargoyle – but it was much more expensive.

RW What drew you to translate the poetry of Rimbaud and Apollinaire?

OB Penguin asked me to translate Rimbaud's poetry after I had translated the poetry of Apollinaire for them. Isn't it remarkable that Plymouth Arts Centre was the only place in England to celebrate the centenary of Rimbaud's death?

RW How important is your Catholic faith to you?

OB I go to mass mainly because I like the Carmelite sisters in the monastery two and a half miles away from my home in Kenninghall, a little village in Norfolk, and not because I'm a good Catholic. In fact – I'm sometimes an atheist and always an agnostic. But the sisters are so nice.

RW Was your mother also a Catholic?

OB No, she was a Christian Scientist – they don't believe in medical treatments, you know.

RW Your German accent is good – who taught you?

OB I went to a funny progressive prep school in Kent. The Headmistress was Dr Anna Essinger, a Jewish refugee from Hitler's Germany – although I suspect she might have been a Quaker. It had been known as the Neue Herrlingen Schule. I called her Tante Anna – and learnt some German from the other children at the school, most of whom were refugees from Germany. I can still vividly remember Tante Anna warning me that if I skipped lessons I'd regret it – well I still don't more than 70 years later. I still dream about Tante Anna occasionally although it was all so long ago. I'm glad that I went to that school for a couple of years, became an anti-fascist and went for walks in the woods by myself. My mother decided that I needed to attend a proper school after I had been at this liberal, progressive school for a couple of years. She decided to make an English gentleman out of me and sent me to Westminster School.

RW   And how was Westminster? I've read that it produced some interesting people in your era.

OB   Westminster was one of the more liberal public schools in the 1930s although they still used corporal punishment. Tony Benn and the writer Michael Hamburger were both my contemporaries. Tony was a socialist and pacifist from the age of 15 – we were both in the same Scout Troup. There was some sadism among the boys and masters, but I suppose you find that most people who attended English boys' boarding schools in the 1930s had similar experiences.

RW   Yes, I heard about some bullying among younger boys, while I was at the King's Canterbury – a boys' public school overlooked by the Cathedral. The boys were kind to me. It helped that my brother had been at the junior school since he was seven – Anthony became a teacher. We were in the same house as the writer Patrick Leigh-Fermor and the mystic philosopher Alan Watts – but they were in The Grange much earlier in the last century. Edmund de Waal, who wrote the superb book, *The Hare with Amber Eyes*, was my contemporary. I hated leaving King's. Why did you leave Westminster early?

OB   I left school at 14 as my mother ran out of money and went to Soho. I remember getting pissed in the French aged 15.

RW   Is that when you worked at the Communist Bookshop?

OB   When I was 16 I ran away from home and worked at Central Books for a year – a bookshop in Bloomsbury run by the Communist Party. More than half the people who worked there were Jews from the East End of London. They were kind to me – in fact I have known many Jewish people and nearly all have been kind to me.

RW   Is it true that you learnt to fly during the Second World War?

OB I never saw action in the war owing to my political beliefs. I was known to have been an active member of the British Communist Party and I suppose they thought I was a risk, which was ridiculous – of course. While I was training as a pilot they kept holding me up between one course and the next and this went on for around seven or eight months. I reached the stage of learning to fly the last training plane before you got to fly a Spitfire.

RW Your French is superb – when did you learn to speak it?

OB I lived in Paris and Limoges for some time after the war ended and spent a fortnight doing nothing except reading Proust. When a job teaching at a school in Corsica was offered to me I travelled there. After living in France for some time my spoken French improved dramatically as few people could speak English and I might have starved otherwise. When I got back to Soho I could barely order a cup of tea in English. A man in a pub in Marseilles once mistook me for an escaped prisoner in the late Forties when I was skinny and had grown a beard – he wouldn't believe that I held a British passport. I had hitchhiked to Marseilles – so probably wasn't looking my best.

We attended the launch of Eddie Linden's new poetry book *A Thorn in the Flesh* at the Irish Cultural Centre, Hammersmith. It was very noisy and Oliver asked to leave. The river was very close and I invited Oliver for drinks at The Dove, one of my regular haunts.

RW Do you like the river and find it inspiring?

OB Yes. I prefer the tide to be in to looking at banks of mud.

RW Have you been to The Dove pub overlooking the river at Hammersmith before? The poet James Thomson wrote *Rule Britannia* in this pub and William Morris once lived two doors down. It is also said to have been a haunt of Graham Greene.

OB Never, but I would enjoy visiting it and also seeing where William Morris lived. Have you read any of Morris's writings? He is mainly known for his wallpaper patterns and his writing is overlooked. It is little known that Morris was one of the first British communists and a member of the Social Democratic Federation. He corresponded with both Marx and Engels, as well as writing the wonderful *The Water of the Wondrous Isles*. I have just read this book for the fifth time and still love it.

RW Do you have a favourite pub?

OB One of my favourite pubs is the Bird and Baby in Oxford. Do you
know it?

RW Yes – its real name is the Eagle and Child and it has some interesting literary connections. From around 1933 an Oxford writers' group called
'The Inklings' which included C. S. Lewis and J. R. R. Tolkien used to
meet at lunchtimes in a private room called the Rabbit Room at the
back of the pub. C. S. Lewis presented his proofs for *The Lion, The
Witch and the Wardrobe* to his friends in the Rabbit Room in 1950.
Tolkien drifted away from the meetings by the late 1950s – but Lewis
who had lived around Oxford since 1921 continued to drop into the
Bird and Baby until he died in 1963. What would you like to drink?

OB Half a pint of Guinness please.

IDLE MARKET

IDLER BOOKS

THE UKULELE HANDBOOK (Bloomsbury)
by Gavin Pretor-Pinney and Tom Hodgkinson. Signed copy.   £14.99

THE LOST WORLD OF THE LONDON COFFEEHOUSE
by Matthew Green. (Idler Books). Handmade pamphlet. Signed copy.   £12.99

GYWNNE'S GRAMMAR (Ebury) Signed hardback copy.
Mr Gwynne's essential book giving the principle parts of speech and
basic grammatical elements. With free pencil.   £7.99

BRAVE OLD WORLD (Hamish Hamilton) Signed hardback copy.
Hodgkinson's guide to country living, based on ten years living on a Devon
smallholding. Illustrated by Alice Smith, and typeset by Mr Brett.
Now only £6.50. Less than the paperback would cost on Amazon.   £6.50

A LITTLE BOOK OF SILENCE (Idler Books)
A small blind impressed, letterpress printed notebook of blank pages.
An enlightening gift or a handy pocket sized notebook for quiet moments
of reflection and idle meditation. Ltd.ed. made with fine paper stock.   £5.00

Please call in person at The Idler Academy to browse our great range of titles.

IDLER BACK ISSUES

Nos. 41–45 hardback editions are readily available to purchase
at the Idler Academy or order online via the Idler website.
Various earlier issues available, check shop for details.

STATIONERY

Exercise books for mathematicians, problem-solvers, inventors, artisans,
scribblers, picture makers, writers, note-taking and calligraphers.
The Idler Academy's crest is emblazoned on the cover with
a name plate to personalise your exercise book
Pencils, pens also available.

LIMITED EDITION PRINTS

SILENCE ART PRINTS

The Idler presents a series of 7 limited edition letterpress, blind impression and silk screen prints by Alice Smith, with quotes about silence from various Idler idols, inc. Lao Tzu, Francis Bacon, Samuel Beckett, Thomas Carlyle, John Cage, William S. Burroughs, Edgar Allan Poe £20 ea.

FREEDOM MANIFESTO SILKSCREEN PRINT

Text by Tom Hodgkinson, designed by Christian Brett and printed by Alice Smith. Black text printed on beautiful quality Fabriano Rosaspina white 285gsm stock. 500mm x 355mm (will sit comfortably within an A2 frame) hand stamped and numbered edition £25.00

IDLER CLOTHING

T-shirts are £20 and are available in XL, L and M and in girl's fit L and M. Colours and designs change constantly, including the Snail, Work Kills, Do Less, Smash the System. Hoodies are £45. Please check the Idler website for availability, or visit the shop to see more designs, or send a cheque with your size and we will choose design for you.

FREEDOM MANIFESTO T-SHIRTS

Hand Printed, 100% cotton, high quality white T-shirts available in S, M, L, XL £24.00

NO WORK WEAR APRONS

Apron for all idle bakers, chefs, butchers, carpenters and makers. Hand printed black emblem printed on a strong, fine quality red apron, with a handy double pocket, black anti-tangle ties, and a crease resistant finish. 65% polyester/35% cotton twill. One size £15.00

FREEDOM MANIFESTO MUGS

A nice solid Idler mug with the Idler snail, drawn by Ged Wells, on one side, and Tom Hodgkinson's Freedom Manifesto on the other. £7.95

IDLER'S SEEDS

Various seeds are available from the shop
from £2.95

WRAPPING PAPER

A selection of four hand printed gift wrapping paper sheets. Designed and printed by Alice Smith for the Idler Academy. The designs include a humorous Idler themed Toile pattern in two colours – sky Blue and charcoal Black, and the other design is of vintage objects in a beautiful metallic Bronze ink and also in charcoal Black. If you would like to purchase a quantity of a particular design, please contact the Idler for further details. £12 (4 sheets)

GREETINGS CARDS

Limited edition hand printed by
Alice Smith – various designs with
prices starting from
£3.00

IDLER SUBSCRIPTIONS

UK subscription	£50.00
Europe subscription	£75.00
Rest of the world subscription	£90.00

Go to www.idler.co.uk and order online, or write your order and send with a cheque payable to 'The Idler' and send it to:
The Idler, Mail Order Dept.,
81 Westbourne Park Road, London W2 5QH

You must include post & packing costs as follows:
Issues 1–24: £1.50 per issue.
Issues 25–34: £2.75 per issue.
T-shirts and hoodies: £2.50 per item.
For European Community, add 50%.
For rest of the world, add 100%

A downloadable order form is available from the Idler website
www.idler.co.uk

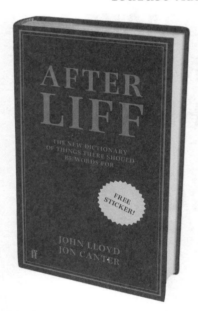